A GUIDE TO
DIGITAL RAILWAY
PHOTOGRAPHY

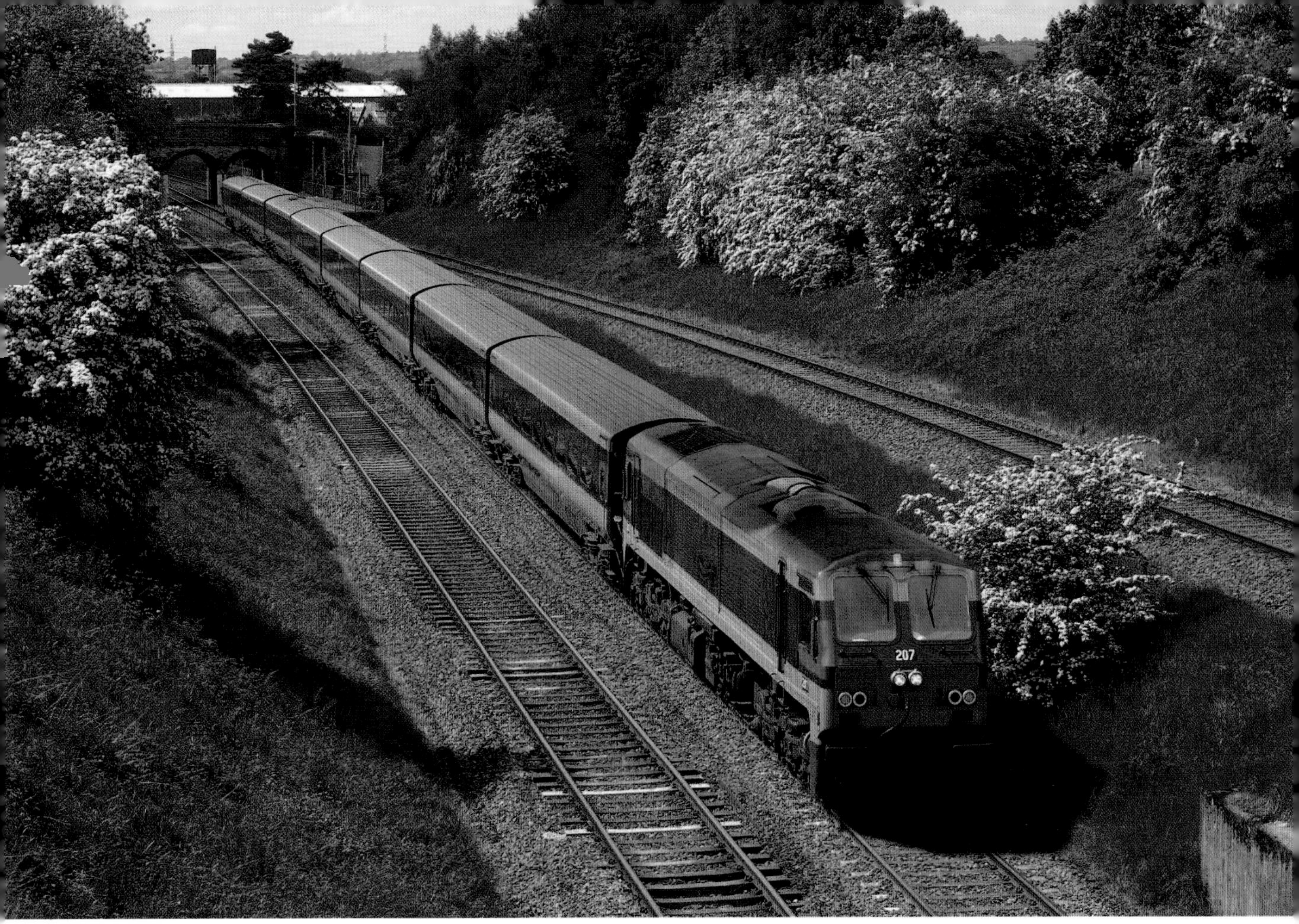

A GUIDE TO
DIGITAL RAILWAY
PHOTOGRAPHY

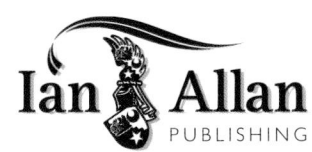

Ian Allan
PUBLISHING

Kim Fullbrook

First published 2008

ISBN 978 0 7110 3341 2

Published by Ian Allan Publishing

an imprint of Ian Allan Publishing Ltd, Hersham, Surrey KT12 4RG.

Printed by Ian Allan Printing Ltd, Hersham, Surrey KT12 4RG.

Code: 0811/B2

Visit the Ian Allan Publishing website at www.ianallanpublishing.com

CONTENTS

Foreword

Like many other enthusiasts I began photographing railways on a 35mm SLR camera loaded with slide film, and after many years using a variety of cameras and slide and print films felt pretty comfortable using film.

In 1996 my colleagues at work started experimenting with a Kodak digital camera. I took my first digital railway picture on it but the quality was poor. The images were fine for use on small web pages but that was their limit. After this unfortunate early experience I vowed to return to digital photography only when the technology had advanced sufficiently for the results to be comparable with those from film.

During 2002 various friends and family members were routinely using digital cameras for general photography and getting good results. When I saw Paul Davis's railway pictures I realised digital technology had reached the point where it had to be considered seriously as an alternative to film. In 2003 Canon introduced the EOS 10D digital SLR camera, which delivered good quality results at a price that was just about affordable. After reading favourable reviews I jumped in and started snapping railway pictures in the digital world. The camera included a free copy of Photoshop Elements 2 for editing pictures but this was where the trouble started. I knew what changes I wanted to make to the pictures but had little idea how to make them. Although various books on Photoshop were available, including some highly recommended books that were supposedly aimed at photographers, they didn't cover the things I wanted to do. After a very frustrating period with a lot of experimentation I managed to figure out some techniques that delivered the results I was looking for with a reasonable amount of effort. Talking with other enthusiasts, I found they were also having difficulty getting started

with photo editing on a computer and I realised that there could be value in a series of magazine articles covering the subject. I approached Colin Marsden, Editor of *Railways Illustrated* magazine, and he agreed to run the 'Digital Photoguide' series of articles which has been running continuously since late 2004. The volume of material covered in the time since then has built up and readers who missed the early articles started to ask for a set of articles to fill in the gaps. This book is based on the material covered in the monthly articles, expanded and brought up to date.

In some ways writing a book is easier than writing monthly articles because the articles are constrained to two A4 pages whereas a book has many more pages and a particular technique can have more pages allocated to it if needed. In a book techniques can reference each other whereas the magazine articles have to stand on their own as far as possible.

I hope you enjoy reading this book and find the information to be useful. If you have any questions or comments please feel free to contact me by email: kim@fullbrook.net

Kim Fullbrook
Burnham, March 2008

Thanks to:

Petra Kagleder for her support throughout

Paul Davis for inspiration

Colin Marsden (Editor of *Railways Illustrated* magazine 2003–6) for initial encouragement and agreeing to run my monthly 'Digital Photoguide' series of articles

Pip Dunn (Editor of *Railways Illustrated* magazine 2006 onwards) for continuing to support my monthly articles

Introduction

The world of photography has undergone a revolution as digital photography has become a viable option to film. Digital quality is continually improving while prices are coming down. With the digital revolution has come the need to learn a set of new skills in order to get the best out of the new medium.

This book is a guide to digital photography written specifically for railway photographers. Illustrated throughout using railway examples, it covers all the techniques needed to successfully capture and process digital photographs. It will be of interest to any railway photographer using a digital camera, whether beginner or experienced. The principles and techniques described can be applied to other transport subjects such as buses, cars, planes and boats, as well as to general landscape photography. The examples are illustrated using images of railway subjects mainly in the UK but the techniques are applicable to railways anywhere in the world. The content covers the technical aspects of photography, both when taking pictures and when processing them on a computer, rather than more subjective areas like composition. Scanning film into digital format is a major subject in its own right and is too large to include in this book. However, although the editing techniques are based around images from a digital camera the same principles can be applied to images scanned from film.

Chapter 1 describes the basic principles of digital photography while Chapter 2 explains the techniques needed to successfully capture railway subjects on a digital camera. For many enthusiasts the methods needed to make improvements to digital images using a computer are a mystery, so Chapter 3 describes simple techniques that any photographer will need to know. Displaying photographs on Internet web sites is a very popular part of the hobby

Nos 67022 and 67021 in top-and-tail formation worked a special Newton Abbot-Exeter shuttle service on 14 August 2008 in connection with the Dawlish carnival. An Exeter-bound working is seen at Langstone Rock near Dawlish.

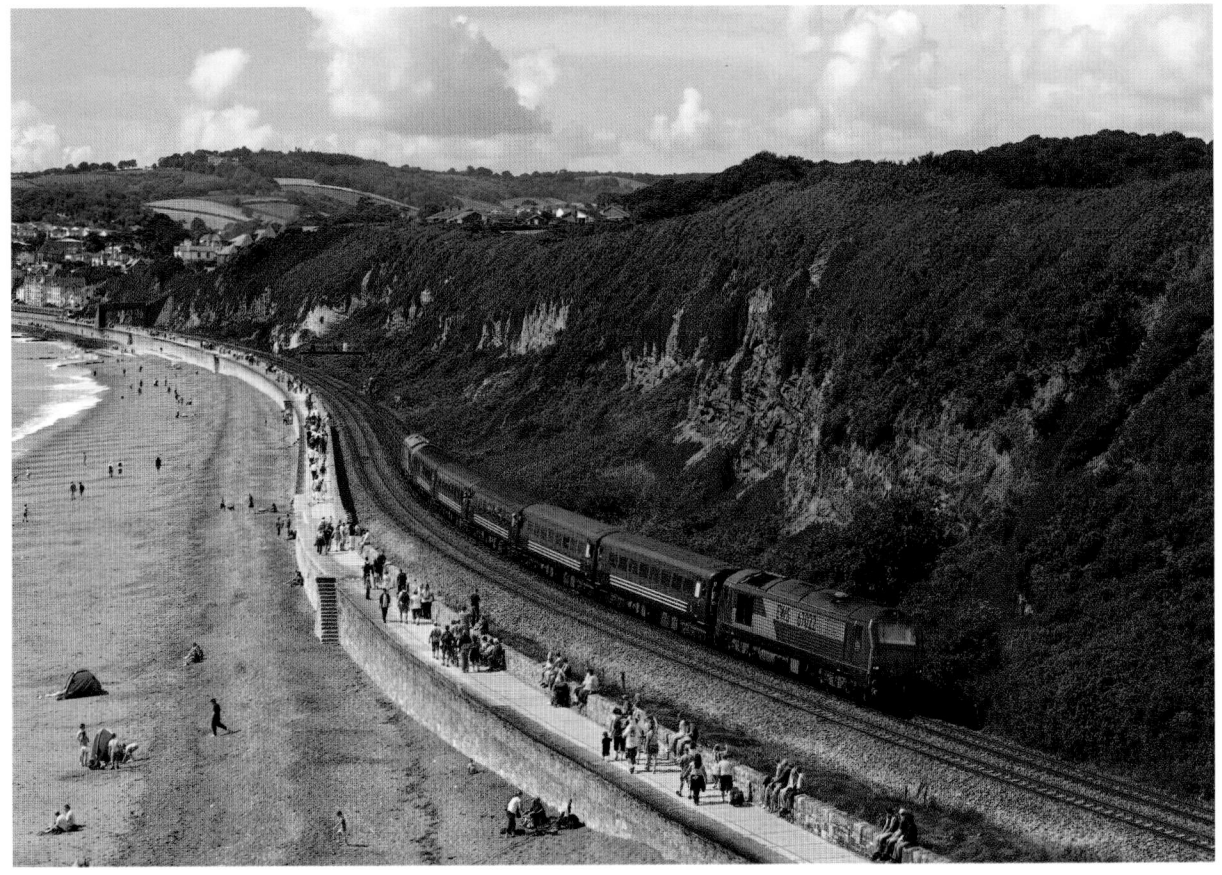

Trademarks

Windows, Windows XP
and Windows Vista
are trademarks of
Microsoft Corporation

Photoshop and
Photoshop Elements
are trademarks of
Adobe Systems

Macintosh
is a trademark of
Apple Computers.

Photomatix is a
trademark of
HDR Software.

and Chapter 4 describes how to prepare pictures for loading on to the Internet. Chapter 5 covers printing and basic editing techniques for improving an image. Chapter 6 describes advanced techniques for those who wish to make more substantial improvements to their pictures. Chapter 7 contains a series of case studies that show a picture before and after making changes. Importantly each case study explains what changes were made, how they were made and why.

Examples are based around Windows Personal Computers (PCs) since these are by far the most popular type of home computer. Screenshots show a Windows XP PC but are generally applicable also to Windows Vista and Macintosh computers. Earlier versions of Windows are not covered as older PCs will not have the processing power necessary to carry out routine photographic tasks. Adobe Photoshop and Photoshop Elements are the most popular photographic editing programs for serious photographers and examples using this software are featured throughout the book. There is no intention of explaining every feature of Photoshop as there are

plenty of reference books already available that do this. Instead this book concentrates on the most common improvements that railway photographers need to make to their photographs and demonstrates how to achieve them in Photoshop and Photoshop Elements.

When processing digital images there are usually many different ways to produce a particular result, each of which are valid. There are only a few cases where there is a 'right' and 'wrong' technique. Readers who are already editing their pictures using a different technique should not think that what they are doing is wrong because it is not described here. Certain simple techniques have many uses and are repeated with variations throughout the book.

Sometimes extra-cost software can be used to quickly produce the same result as slower manual techniques. There is usually a trade-off of speed versus cost. Wherever possible the functions built into Photoshop are described and additional software is only used where the author has found the improvement in speed or quality to be worth the extra cost.

Digital camera technology has made a massive advance during the early years of the 21st century to the point where the quality of the results is better than film. It's not the intention of this book to make an exhaustive comparison of film and digital technology but some of the more significant advantages of digital are listed below:

- ISO sensitivity can be set for each picture
- ISO sensitivity of 400 and higher gives excellent sharpness and colour accuracy
- No problems with film flatness affecting sharpness
- Pictures can be deleted after taking if they are not wanted, freeing up space to take more pictures
- Images are not affected by X-rays so there are no concerns when travelling through airport security
- Copies can be easily made
- Images can easily be sent across the Internet

- Seconds after taking a picture the result can be seen, allowing camera settings and operation to be checked
- No reliance on the post to reach the processors, avoiding delay and risk of loss
- A given number of images can be stored in much less space than negatives or slides

Some of the disadvantages are:

- Digital camera requires batteries
- A computer is needed to process pictures for storage
- More sensitive to over-exposure than film
- Available digital projectors have fairly low resolution
- Dust on the sensor can impact pictures
- Black & white work needs special effort to get tones that are as convincing as black & white film

CHAPTER 1
DIGITAL PHOTOGRAPHY
BASICS

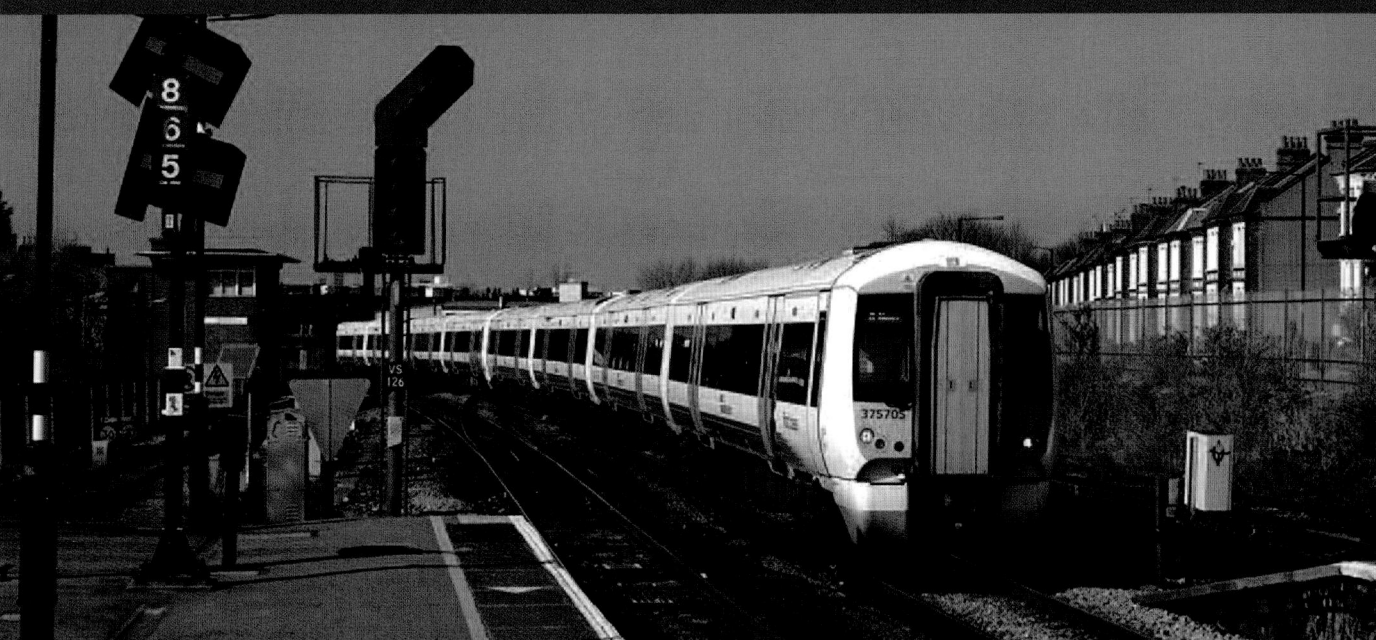

● MEMORY CARDS

Introduction

All digital cameras store their images on a memory card. The technology used in these cards does not need continuous battery power for the memory to be retained and is known as 'non-volatile' or flash memory. There are different types of memory card, referring to their physical size and type of connector. With SLR-type digital cameras the types in common use are called Compact Flash and SD Card. Memory cards are available with different amounts of memory. Memory size of computers and memory cards is measured in a standard computer unit called a byte. Early memory cards contained millions of bytes of memory and the term used is megabytes (may be written as MByte or MB). Current memory cards have a thousand million bytes of memory or more and the term for this is a gigabyte (may be written as GByte or GB). SD Cards with a capacity greater than 2GB are sometimes called SDHC (SD High Capacity) and work internally in a slightly different way to smaller SD Cards. There can be compatibility problems between older cameras and SDHC cards.

The other area where memory cards vary is their speed, which means the speed images can be written to or read from the card. Manufacturers use terms like '10x' or '40x' to rate the speed of their cards meaning that it is 10 or 40 times faster than a reference point whose meaning in the 'real world' has been lost with time. Technically the value of the reference is 150 Kb/sec (150,000 bits per second) so that a 40x card transfers data at a maximum rate of 6 Mb/sec (6 megabits per second). The electronics inside a digital camera limit the transfer speed and a very fast 100x card, for example, cannot transform the speed of an older camera. When digital SLR cameras take pictures the processed images are normally written to memory inside the camera known as a 'buffer' to temporarily store the images before they can be written to the memory card. Provided that the buffer is not filled the write speed to the memory

card is not important. This is an area that is more important for rapid-fire sports photographers than railway photography where bursts during picture-taking are typically fairly small.

A memory card can be plugged into a computer using a device known as a card reader.

Trouble with a Memory Card

Memory cards and card readers can occasionally cause problems. The most common is that the card isn't recognised by the computer. Sometimes a card reader has a problem with a particular card, even a reputable brand, while other cards are fine. The first thing to try is to remove the card from the reader, disconnect the card reader from the computer then re-connect and insert the card. Sometimes the computer may need to be rebooted or even shut down and powered off for a few minutes before restarting. If the card reader still won't recognise the card, check if the camera can display the images. If it can, the problem must be related to the card reader. A repeat of the power off and reboot routine may be needed and ultimately the purchase of a new card reader.

If the camera could not display some or all of the images then the problem is more serious. Memory cards can sometimes fail totally, in which case there is little that can be done. If the card is accessible from the card reader and some or all of the images are visible the file system on the card has probably been corrupted. Specialised Recovery software typically costing from £20-£30 upwards can be used to recover images from corrupted cards. This software is sometimes supplied free with some models of memory card or alternatively is available for download from the Internet from various companies.

To explain in more detail how the recovery process can work requires a little knowledge of the way PC file systems work. A memory card is effectively just another drive on a PC and photo images are just PC files, so the same techniques apply as on a PC. When a file is stored on a PC drive, the file itself is stored in one or more sectors of the drive while summary details of the file are stored in a separate area – the root directory. Normally programs need the root directory to find files on the disk. If the root directory gets damaged some, or all, of the files can appear to be lost. The files themselves may still exist in the various drive sectors. Recovery software uses its knowledge of the structure of PC file systems and digital image files to read the entire memory card and piece together as many images as it can. If the corruption extends to sectors of the drive storing images then those specific images will not be recoverable. Technically memory cards use the standard PC FAT-16 format for cards of 2GBytes or less and FAT-32 for larger ones.

 The most common cause of corruption on a memory card is interrupting the camera while it is in the process of writing images to the card; for example, removing the card from the camera while it is still writing or battery failure. Switching off the camera using the on/off switch is unlikely to cause a problem because cameras generally continue writing to the card after switching off.

When images are deleted from a memory card by reformatting, the root directory is reset so that all the information that was previously in it is lost. The images themselves still exist on the card and all should be recoverable using Recovery software. Images which are months or years old and which haven't been overwritten by newer images may still be on the card.

The author has experienced the card reader itself causing corruption of the contents of the card. In this case all but a couple of the images were recoverable. The only long-term cure was to replace the card reader.

After recovering images from a corrupt memory card, the card should be reformatted in the camera, not in the PC, and it will then be ready to use again. The previous corruption should not normally cause any more problems. In rare cases where corruption continues, Recovery software normally contains a comprehensive reformatting routine which should be used.

● THE COMPUTER

A computer is at the heart of digital photography. The computer manufacturing industry continues to advance at an impressive rate and its products increase in speed while decreasing in price. Cameras are also advancing and the size of images produced by them is also increasing, meaning that more computing power is needed with newer cameras. Digital images are quite demanding to process. For anyone using a recent camera a guideline is that the average home computer is technically obsolete after about five years and will probably struggle with the more intensive aspects of image processing.

Either a PC or Macintosh will be suitable. Linux-based computers have only a limited range of software available and are not a practical choice. Macintoshes are very popular in the publishing industry while PCs are most popular with home users and other areas of industry. The reality is that PCs running Microsoft Windows have around 95% of the market for home computers so this book will concentrate on PCs and include Macintosh information where possible. Microsoft Windows Vista is the latest version of Windows at the time of writing this book, while Windows XP has been around since 2001 and is widely supported and understood throughout the industry. Both are easy to use and stable. It's not feasible to recommend particular brands and models of computer here because they change so often. Anyone needing buying advice is recommended to consult one of the many available computer magazines.

When choosing a computer for digital photography, what are the important areas of the specification? The major items of computer specification are: processor type and speed, memory and disk size. Just as important for photography are the monitor and the types of interfaces used for connecting extra devices.

Avoiding a Computer
Some people hate computers and will do anything to avoid using one. Is it possible to take up digital photography without buying a

computer? The simple answer is 'yes' but life will be difficult and expensive unless the pictures are thrown away after printing.

The most pressing difficulty will be long-term storage of the pictures. When using a digital camera the pictures are written to a memory card. A computer will normally be used to copy the images from the memory card to a DVD or disk drive for long-term storage in order to free up the memory card for re-use. Without a computer the images have to remain on the memory card and new cards purchased on an ongoing basis. As the price of memory cards has dropped this option has become more feasible and it actually costs less now per image to leave an image on a memory card than it does to create a 'conventional' image on a roll of slide or negative film. It remains much more expensive on a per-image basis to store images on a memory card than on, for example, a DVD. Storage options are described in more detail later in this chapter.

Images can be printed without a computer either by taking the images on a memory card to a print maker or by using a camera and printer capable of direct printing. Uploading images on to an Internet web site needs a computer although it is possible to do this without owning a computer by using a friend's machine or an Internet café.

Processor
The heart of a computer is its processor and type and its speed will normally be quoted in the specification. Because manufacturers introduce a new range of processors every two to three years and the available speeds increase with every new model it is not practical to recommend particular processor types or speeds in this book. The best advice is to buy a mid-range model when choosing a new computer because this offers the best value. It's not worth paying a premium price for a small increase in processor speed and any money saved will buy a more worthwhile improvement in other areas.

Memory
Photo processing is much more demanding in its use of memory than any other domestic use of a computer. The computer needs physical memory while it is working on images and as a general rule the more memory the better. If a computer runs out of physical memory it does not 'crash', it uses the disk as well and slows right down because accessing a disk is much slower than accessing memory.

When buying a computer for photo processing it's important to have sufficient memory and this may mean specifying extra memory beyond what is usually installed. In 2008 the norm with Windows Vista is 1 Gigabyte (written as 1Gb) but a high proportion of this space is used by Windows itself. Some models provide 2Gb which is a better choice as more memory is available to applications. While 4 Gigabytes (written as 4Gb) is better still if you plan to do a moderate amount of editing on large images, restrictions within Windows mean that not all of this amount of memory can be used. As memory falls further in price the cost of providing 4Gb of memory will become less of a concern.

Disk Space
Disk space is used for four main purposes:

1 Storing the computer's own software, known as the operating system and applications
2 Storing images as they come from the camera
3 Editing images.
4 Temporary working files created automatically by editing software during the manipulation process.

All computers come with a main disk drive – usually called a hard drive due to the type of technology used. Typical disk size figures for a 2008 machine are 400-500 Gigabytes (Gb). The rate at which disk space is used obviously depends on how much photography and editing you do but as a guide, your author with a 12 Megapixel camera has used about 30Gb in one year for storage of original images and 50Gb for manipulated images. However much disk space is provided initially it is never enough and more disks will be needed at some point. With a new machine it is not worth paying a premium for a slightly larger disk drive as it's better practice to add additional separate drives. So for example, rather than paying an extra £40 for a 500Gb drive in place of a 400Gb drive it's better value to pay £80 for an additional separate 300Gb drive. The subject of image storage is very important and will be covered in depth later in this chapter.

Interfaces

An interface is the technical term for the connection between a computer and another piece of equipment. Older computers have a variety of different types of interfaces for connecting external devices, all of which are slow. In recent years a type of interface known as USB (Universal Serial Bus) has become popular for connecting all sorts of devices – from printers and scanners to disk drives and cameras. There are basically two types of USB – the original, and 'High Speed USB' which is also called USB 2.0. The latter is up to 40 times faster than the original USB and its extra speed can be very beneficial. The first version of USB is now known as USB 1.0 and a later update was made to create USB 1.1. Both of these were made obsolete by the introduction of USB 2.0. If an older computer only has USB it is worth installing a USB 2.0 card to allow connection of compatible devices at this higher speed because the extra speed makes a big difference. USB and USB 2.0 connectors are physically the same so it is not possible to tell the difference simply from their appearance. USB 2.0 devices can be plugged into an 'original' USB computer or an 'original' USB device into a USB 2.0 computer and the connection will work but only at the lower speed of 'original' USB. New PCs have USB 2.0 as well as some Macintoshes. Virtually all digital cameras have a USB interface with recent cameras being USB 2.0. If you need additional USB capability or find the sockets on the PC system box to be inconvenient to reach, it's worth buying a USB hub which typically provides a further four or more sockets.

The cost is fairly low – around £10 to £20. As before, choose one that is USB 2.0. An even faster version of USB called USB 3.0 is expected to appear during 2008.

The Macintosh world has for several years used a different type of interface known as Firewire (also called IEEE-1394) which is almost as fast as USB 2.0 and can be found on a few PCs. Firewire is a good choice of interface for devices that transfer a large quantity of data such as a scanner or disk drive.

CD & DVD

Virtually all PCs and Macintoshes have one or more drives to read CDs and DVDs. It is essential to have a drive capable of creating DVDs containing backup copies of images as explained later in this chapter.

Graphics Card

PC manufacturers make a lot of fuss about providing a powerful graphics card but these are unnecessary for photo editing and are only needed when playing games. A basic graphics card is sufficient for normal PC use including photo editing. When running more than two monitors a specialist graphics card may be needed.

Mouse

It's easy to overlook the basic operation of a mouse when choosing a PC and to be persuaded by unnecessary features like cordless operation and optical sensors. Because so much time is spent interacting with the mouse it is important that the buttons operate positively and the shape is comfortable for your hand. Those who are left handed should consider buying one specially shaped for left-handed people although these can be hard to find. The Microsoft range of mice has high quality construction and the 'Intellimouse' with scroll wheel is robust and comfortable to use for right-handed people. Provided the base and ball are kept free of dirt it should operate smoothly and reliably for a long time. Cordless operation is quite unnecessary and interferes with normal working when the batteries get low.

Card Reader

Some PCs are supplied with a built-in card reader for common types of memory cards. While this is a useful bonus it's not essential as separate card readers are readily available. A separate card reader needs to be USB 2.0 compatible otherwise it will be painfully slow when copying more than a handful of images. Cheap card readers have caused problems for a number of photographers by corrupting the memory card resulting in lost images. Using a card reader from a reputable manufacturer such as Sandisk, Lexar or Kingston is strongly recommended.

Monitor

'Monitor' is the industry term for the computer screen. When working with photo images it is vital to have a monitor which displays a good quality image and is large enough to show a typical picture at a comfortable size. Flat panel screens are now universal on new PCs, having taken over from traditional CRT (cathode ray tube) monitors. Flat panels save desk space while their flatness and excellent clarity make photo editing easier than with a CRT. They also consume less power and produce less heat which can be a useful advantage in the summer months. The range of colours a good flat panel can display is comparable to a CRT.

When buying a new computer consideration should be given to providing as large a monitor as the budget will allow. A large monitor is easier to work with because an image can be made larger and the amount of scrolling needed is reduced. The prices of large monitors – both standard and widescreen – have dropped dramatically in recent years and even a 24in widescreen is surprisingly affordable. You should check out a monitor before buying to be sure that you are happy with the brightness and general clarity as some lower quality models can appear 'fuzzy' in areas of fine detail and may have uneven brightness particularly in the corners. With a flat screen there are two ways of connecting the monitor to the computer – standard analogue (sometimes referred to as VGA) and digital, known as DVI. DVI is less

common, slightly more expensive and requires a compatible graphics card, but will usually give a clearer picture than using the same monitor via a VGA cable.

With the price of standard sized 17in monitors having dropped to £100 or less, those who already own a computer should consider adding a second monitor. This allows, for example, displaying a photo image on one screen with the menus and toolbars out of the way on the other. The two monitors behave like one larger monitor but are much cheaper. With Windows XP PCs and Macintoshes no additional software is required but the graphics hardware must have the capability – which it often does. If the additional monitor is the same type and size as the first it makes the setup and ongoing working slightly easier. It's possible to run three monitors simultaneously for a reasonable cost. This allows the simultaneous use of a web browser, email program or even a PC TV on the third screen.

High definition monitors are starting to appear on the market and are worth considering for the extra detail they can display.

Desktop v Laptop

Is it better to buy a desktop or laptop? Generally speaking a laptop compared with a desktop computer is smaller, more expensive, less powerful, has restricted disk space and has less potential for future expansion. For most users a desktop is sufficient and a laptop is only recommended for photo editing if the PC needs to be carried around or locked away after use for security reasons. For home users an expensive laptop is a waste of money and portability needs are better met using a small, cheap laptop. The price of computing hardware has fallen so much in recent years that those who need portable computing should consider owning both a cheap laptop and a more powerful desktop computer. The major downside of laptops is their relatively small monitor, cramped keyboard and awkward mouse. These limitations can be overcome at home by connecting a larger external monitor into the 'video out' socket and external keyboard & mouse into a USB socket.

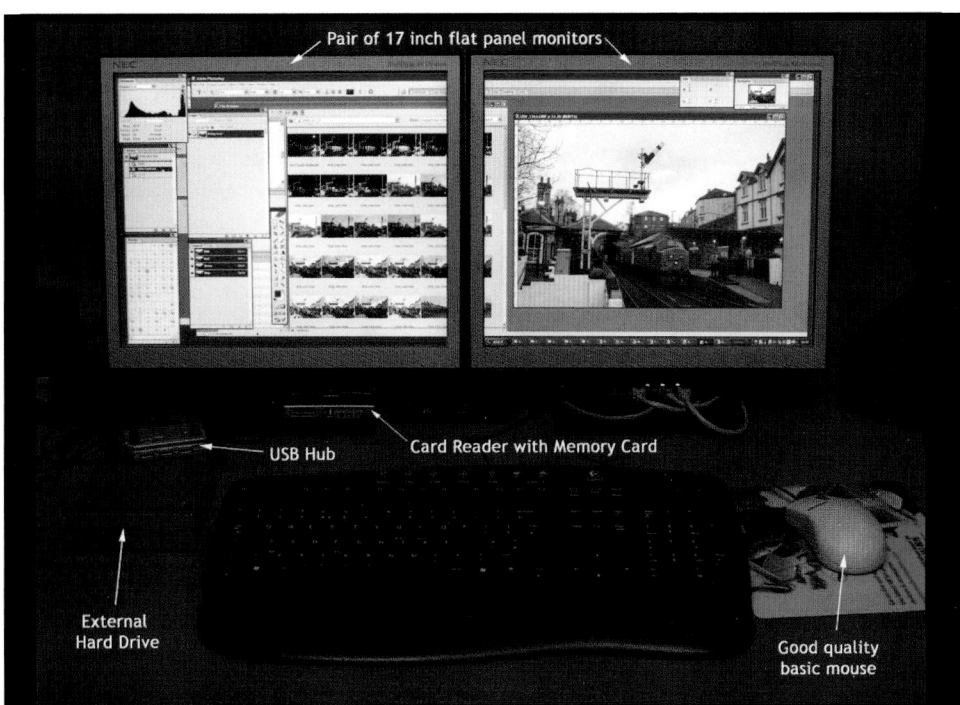

Pair of 17 inch flat panel monitors

USB Hub

Card Reader with Memory Card

External
Hard Drive

Good quality
basic mouse

Figure 1.2.1.
Computer for photo
editing with two
monitors.

Multiple Computers

As an increasing number of people own
several computers it is convenient to share
keyboard, mouse and monitors between
them. By using a device known as a KVM
switch, flicking a simple switch swaps the
keyboard, mouse and monitor from one
computer to the other without having to
mess about unplugging connectors. KVM
stand for Keyboard, Visual display unit and
Mouse and a basic unit is available for £40
or less.

64 bit

The term '64 bit' is not yet widely used with
home computers but will become
increasingly common in future as the price of
memory decreases. It can be thought of in
simple terms as an essential technology for a
computer to be able to fully use more than
4GB of memory. Although '64 bit' versions of
Windows XP and Vista are already available
they have seen only limited popularity
because special versions of applications and
driver software for external devices such as
printers and scanners are needed. 64 bit
technology will only be worth considering
when compatible applications and drivers are
widely available.

Example

Figure 1.2.1 shows the photo editing setup
used by the author. This has two 17in flat
panel LCD monitors to provide plenty of
screen space for editing. The card reader
(containing a memory card), external hard
drive and USB hub are also shown.

Monitor Calibration

If you are serious about getting good quality
results from editing your images it is vital to
calibrate your monitor. Other terms such as
monitor profiling and colour correction are
also used to mean the same thing.
Calibration ensures that the monitor displays
all colours correctly including very bright
areas (highlights) and very dark areas
(shadows). Locomotive underframe areas will
usually show up any problems with shadow
detail, as will night shots. It is still possible to
edit photographs without using a calibrated
monitor but you should consider restricting
changes to small changes only, especially
changes to colour, because of the potential
for making mistakes with colour and
brightness.

If your monitor is not calibrated it is very
likely that you will have problems when
printing and when your edited pictures are

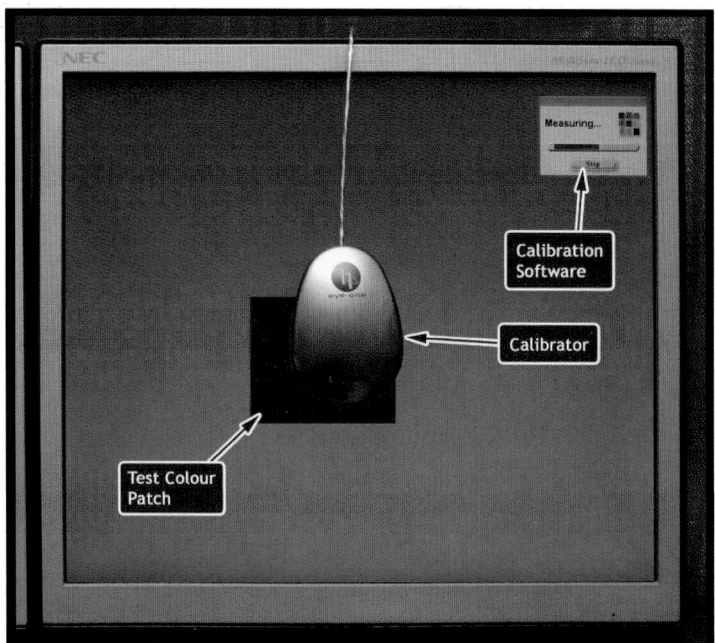

Figure 1.2.2.
Monitor calibration in progress.

displayed on other people's computers. For example your monitor might make a white Eurostar set look very slightly green. When you correct this by adjusting your image to remove green, magenta (pink/mauve) must be added and when the same picture is displayed on a correctly adjusted monitor it will look too pink/mauve. If the shadow areas are not displayed correctly by the monitor the locomotive or rolling stock underframes could easily look too light or too dark and this can't be corrected manually using the controls on the monitor. Much photo manipulation consists of slight corrections to small areas where an accurate view of colour and lightness/darkness is essential, especially when working in shadowed areas.

A monitor is calibrated using a specialist device known as a monitor calibrator which looks similar to a computer mouse. It is connected to the computer via a USB cable and hung in front of the screen. Figure 1.2.2 shows monitor calibration in progress. Special software drives the monitor with various colours and brightnesses while the calibrator reads what the monitor actually displays. By comparing what it reads with what it thinks should be displayed it is able to build up a colour profile which is stored on the computer and from then onwards used by the video display driver and monitor to display colours and brightnesses correctly. Models are available from a variety of manufacturers and typically cost in the region of £50-£200+. Although the cost may appear expensive, particularly when compared to the cost of the monitor itself, in the long run using a calibrator will save a huge amount of time, trouble and wasted materials. They are available from familiar companies such as Jessops as well as specialist suppliers.

To show the benefit of calibration Figure 1.2.3 shows two photos of the same monitor before and after calibration. At a technical level, the picture on the left shows the monitor with the colour profile supplied by the manufacturer and with the colour profile created by a monitor calibrator (right). The standard monitor has a slight blue/green colour cast and poor detail in the shadows: look at the locomotive underframes and fuel tanks. The calibrated monitor has the colour cast corrected and better details in the shadow areas.

Disk Space Fragmentation

After a computer disk has been used for a few months the free space tends to get broken up into small chunks. When a new file is created it will be split up so that it can use the free space. As a file gets broken up into more and more chunks it takes longer to read the file. This process is called fragmentation. It's a good idea to defragment your system every few months. Windows XP and Vista have a built-in defragmentation tool which is easy to use and typically takes an hour or two to run although the time depends on the amount of data on the disk. To run it, use the 'My Computer' program on the Start menu. Place the mouse cursor over the C: drive and press the right mouse button to get a menu and choose the 'Properties' option. A small screen with several tabs at the top will appear. Select 'Tools' and a 'Defragment Now' button will appear. Pressing this gives another menu. Press the 'Analyze' button to get a report on how fragmented the disk is and a recommendation on whether to defragment. Press 'Defragment' to start

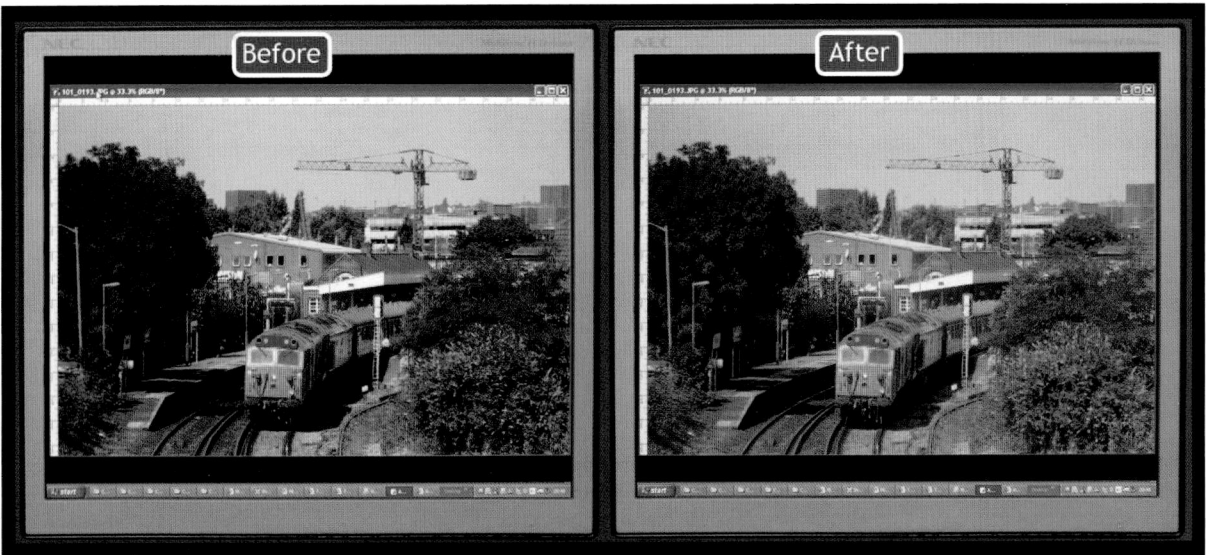

Figure 1.2.3.
**Comparing photos of
monitor before and
after calibration.**

the process. Although the computer can be used when de-fragmentation is running, it is best to close all programs and leave the computer on its own to avoid any interruption to running programs.

Accidental Deletion or Overwriting

Everyone has at some time deleted a file by mistake. Both Windows PC and Macintoshes have a 'recycle bin' where deleted files are placed so you can retrieve them later if you make a mistake. Unfortunately the Recycle Bin can't help if you need to retrieve a file which was overwritten rather than deleted. 'Overwriting' means creating a new version of a file to replace an existing one and normally happens when editing an existing photo or word-processing document and pressing the 'save' option. It's easy to overwrite a file on disk with a newer version of that file containing changes you didn't want to keep.

The answer to this problem is to run an auto-protect utility. This will keep track of files which are overwritten as well as those which are deleted. An example product is Undelete 5 from Diskeeper Corporation.

● STORAGE SYSTEM

After returning home from a photographic trip the images need to be stored. To keep control of your collection of digital images it's vital to have an organised system for storing

them. Once a system is established it should be easier to find images in the collection later on. Decide how you want to organise and store your images. There's no single right answer here. Images could be stored by date, by location, by class of motive power etc, or a combination. There are programs available to automate the transfer of pictures from camera to PC and these have their own image naming and storage systems. There are also programs to help with cataloguing. Choose an option that suits your way of working and stick with it.

The author stores images by date in a simple hierarchy. Each year and month has their own folders, and each day has its own sub-folder. It's a simple and quick system to maintain. The screenshot in Figure 1.3.1 shows how this is organised.

When loading new images on to the computer a new folder is created manually for each day, then the images are copied from the memory card into each daily folder.

Separate Working Area

It's good practice to keep a 'Master' set of images separate from those being worked on. There are two main advantages to this. Firstly it keeps the folder of master images clear of other files that 'clutter' the space, ensuring that you can find something quickly when you need to without being distracted by other files in the same folder. Secondly it reduces the chance of losing 'original' images by accidentally deleting them or by overwriting them with an updated version. If an original is overwritten and you forgot to make a backup copy there's no going back and the original is lost.

A simple way to create the 'Editing' area is to create a set of folders using the same hierarchical system as the master storage area. Another option is to create a folder for the day on which you do the editing. There's no 'correct' way to organise the folders so experiment and choose one that suits your way of working. See the screenshot in Figure 1.3.1 for an example.

● PHOTO EDITING PROGRAM

Choosing a Photo Editing Program

Central to photo manipulation is the use of an editing program that has all the features you need. For many years the market leading program has been Photoshop by Adobe and this is used by industry professionals throughout the world. It is reliable, fast and has practically every function needed either built-in or available as an extra. A major advantage is the ability to add extra functions through the use of 'plug-ins' and 'actions'. These are small programs which are called from inside Photoshop. There are thousands of these available, from many different suppliers and range in price from free to a hundred pounds or more. When using Photoshop to create images you can be sure that most other people will be able to read them. Photoshop's two main downsides are that it is very expensive and difficult to learn.

Adobe has a cut-down version of Photoshop available known as Photoshop Elements. This will do much of what full Photoshop can do at a fraction of the price. Regrettably there are some very useful features absent but in most cases there are alternatives available, albeit restricted or more time-consuming. Some items of photo equipment such as cameras and scanners even include a free copy of Elements.

There are many other photo editing programs available but most are not suitable for serious editing due to having too limited facilities. The two best known are Paintshop Pro and Picture Window Professional. There is also The Gimp which has the advantage of being 'open source' and available to download from the Internet free of charge. Google's Picasa is also free. These programs all have their devotees but unfortunately they either lack some key functions or there are limitations when using those key functions compared to Photoshop.

The techniques described in this book are all based around the use of Photoshop and Photoshop Elements. Instructions for using both programs will be given where possible. Where a particular function is not available in Photoshop Elements an alternative function or workaround will be described wherever possible.

If you've decided to buy full Photoshop there are completely legal ways to buy it at reduced cost. For teachers and those in full time education there is a discounted-price version. Those who already have an old version can buy an upgrade pack to the latest version at a lower price than buying the full package. Sometimes it is possible to buy unused copies of an obsolete version at a heavily discounted price, which can be used

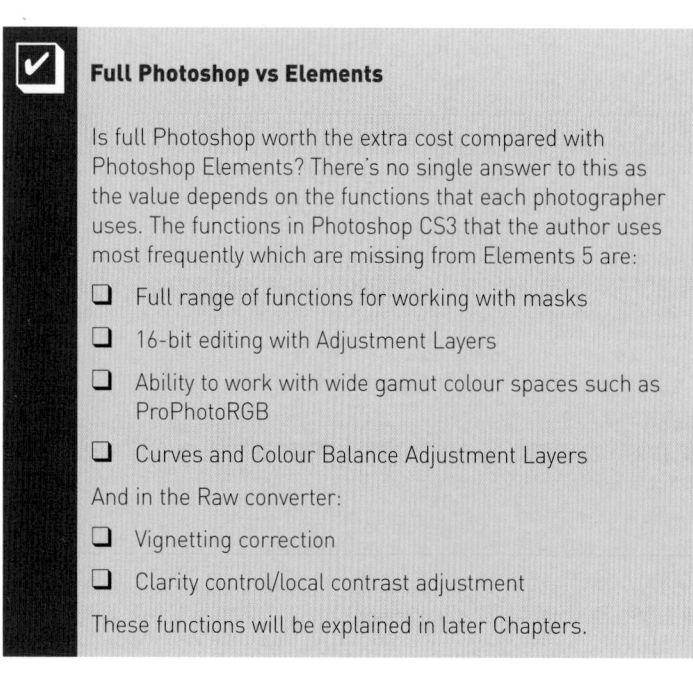

✔ Full Photoshop vs Elements

Is full Photoshop worth the extra cost compared with Photoshop Elements? There's no single answer to this as the value depends on the functions that each photographer uses. The functions in Photoshop CS3 that the author uses most frequently which are missing from Elements 5 are:

❑ Full range of functions for working with masks

❑ 16-bit editing with Adjustment Layers

❑ Ability to work with wide gamut colour spaces such as ProPhotoRGB

❑ Curves and Colour Balance Adjustment Layers

And in the Raw converter:

❑ Vignetting correction

❑ Clarity control/local contrast adjustment

These functions will be explained in later Chapters.

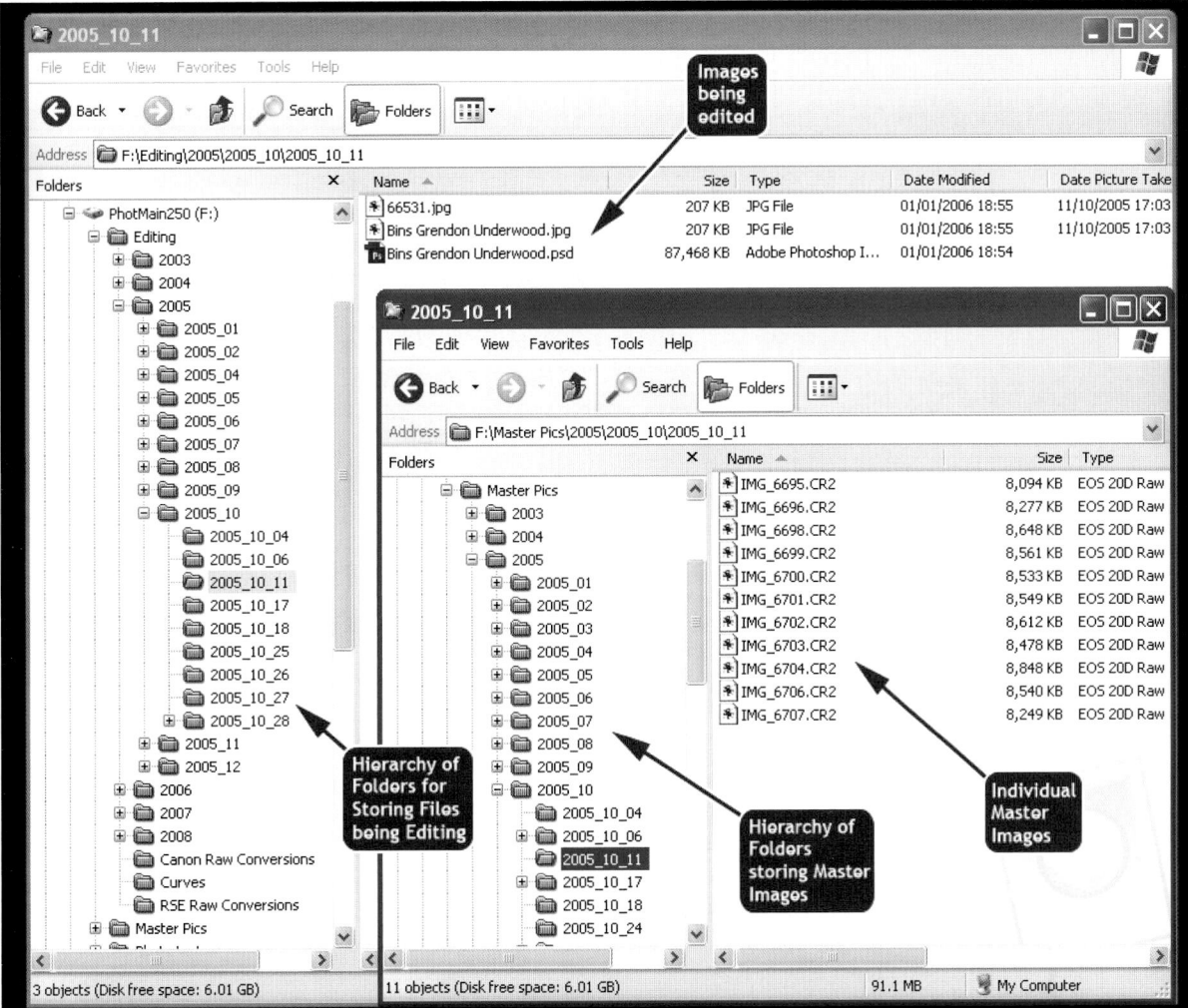

in combination with an upgrade pack to provide the latest version at a lower price than the full version. Never use pirated software.

● MEGAPIXELS, SIZE AND FORMATS

Moving to digital photography from film there is a new vocabulary to learn with terms like megapixels, JPEG, TIFF, compression and 8-bit. What do these terms mean and how do they relate to each other?

Pixels and MegaPixels

Digital images are made up of huge numbers of dots, better known as pixels. The part of the digital camera which creates the image is known as the sensor. Cameras vary in the number of pixels in their sensors and the overall size of the sensor itself. A key point here is that the arrangement of pixels in the image created by the camera is always a rectangular grid. In those cameras where the sensor has a different arrangement such as certain Fuji models, calculations are done by the camera's software to create the standardised rectangular grid. Saying this in another way, whatever the type of sensor in the camera the final image is always a rectangular grid of pixels. The size of the sensor on a digital camera is measured in mega pixels (meaning a million pixels), often abbreviated to MP.

Popular SLR cameras such as the Canon EOS10D and 300D create images which are 3072 pixels wide by 2048 high while the Nikon D70 is very similar at 3008 pixels wide by 2000

Figure 1.3.1.
Screenshot showing hierarchies of folders for storing images.

high. Multiply these pixel figures together and the answer is approximately 6.3 million pixels for the Canon and 6.0 million for the Nikon, which is where the term '6 Megapixels' comes from, also known as 6MP. The '8 Megapixel' Canon EOS 20D, 30D and 350D create a 3504 x 2336 pixel image (8.18 million pixels or 8MP). Recent cameras like the '10 Megapixel' Nikon D80 and Canon 400D offer even more pixels with grid sizes of 3872 x 2592 and 3888 x 2592 respectively, approximately 10 million pixels or 10MP. More pixels allow more detail to be captured.

Image Format Types

There are many different types of image format in use in the world of computer graphics although only a handful of these are popular for photographic images: these are JPEG, 'Raw' and TIFF. Virtually all digital cameras will produce images in JPEG format. All cameras aimed at the photographic enthusiast will produce Raw format images. TIFF format was commonly produced by early digital cameras but is now fairly rare.

JPEG stands for Joint Photographic Experts Group and is pronounced 'jay-peg'. It is the most widely used image format in digital cameras and on web pages as it is a very space-efficient way of storing an image. When a JPEG file is created, a high proportion of the image data is thrown away in order to save storage space.

'Raw' format contains a copy of the unprocessed data from the camera's sensor – hence the term 'Raw'. It needs to be processed and converted into another format before it can be used. Every major camera manufacturer has its own Raw format. Adobe has introduced its DNG (Digital Negative) format and is trying to persuade the industry to adopt it as a standard for Raw images. Many smaller manufacturers have already adopted DNG but the major players (Canon, Nikon, Sony, Fuji) still use their own formats.

TIFF stands for 'tagged image file format'. The important difference between TIFF and JPEG is that when a TIFF file is created, no image data is thrown away.

There are some less commonly used formats that ought to be explained.

Photo editing programs have their own storage formats such as Adobe Photoshop's own 'PSD' and 'PSB' formats. GIF (Graphics Interchange Format) is widely used on web pages but only for non-photographic images such as graphics and logos. Because of patent considerations the PNG (Portable Network Graphics) format was developed to replace GIF but shows no signs of becoming as popular.

The popular formats are now explained in more detail.

JPEG

Without doubt JPEG is the most popular image format created by cameras because it offers an attractive compromise between good quality and not using up too much storage space. A JPEG image can be created with different levels of quality and cameras usually allow the photographer to make their choice of JPEG quality using options with names like 'extra fine', 'fine' and 'medium'. The author's recommendation is to always use the highest quality setting. Using a lower quality setting will compromise quality and this will probably be visible in the pictures. Remember that the process of creating a JPEG 'throws away' some information and any setting other than the highest quality setting may involve throwing away too much. The removal of information can sometimes create unpleasant effects in the picture called 'artifacts' where smooth colour changes become larger 'blocks' of a single colour. The likelihood of these being visible depends on the quality setting, the subject matter and the amount of detail in the picture. The only time there is an advantage to using lower quality settings is when there is a need to fit an increased number of images on a particular memory card. With the price of memory cards and computer storage dropping dramatically in recent years the need to economise on storage space has decreased and it is better to buy a few more memory cards than to use lower quality JPEG settings. If an image is only displayed on a computer screen or web page it will be possible to get away with using lower quality settings without the reduced quality being visible: try experimenting if you really need to fit many images into a small space.

Sharpening is also applied when a JPEG image is created.

Raw

Anyone who wants the highest quality results should consider Raw. The files are larger than JPEG but no image data is thrown away so the result will be more accurate. Some lower end cameras do not support Raw while some cameras have performance limitations with Raw, such as the number of photographs that can be taken in quick succession. The major advantage of Raw is that minimal processing is done to the image in the camera. Once a Raw image is loaded on to the computer it can be processed using a 'Raw converter' to turn the image into a TIFF file or other format for further processing in an editing program. This gives great flexibility and the resulting image will hold more fine detail and have smoother tones than a JPEG image from the camera. The processing of a Raw file can be considered as being analogous to developing a film to produce a negative and, as with film, there are different types of development that can be chosen to suit the shooting conditions. By far the most significant advantage for railway photographers is that Raw can allow detail to be recovered from bright areas of the picture that would have been lost with a JPEG. This is achieved by varying the exposure (also known as brightness) control during the Raw conversion process and the technical term for this is 'highlight recovery'.

Photographs taken at night benefit from using Raw as this allows any colour casts due to artificial light to be removed while also maximising the dynamic range (contrast) of the final image.

Sharpening is not applied to a Raw image by the camera, allowing the choice to be made during the Raw conversion process.

The processing of a Raw image is described in more detail in Chapter 5.

TIFF

Compared to JPEG, the only advantage of TIFF format is that it does not throw away image data. This means that subtle changes in tone are recorded that would often be discarded when a JPEG is created. Whether these differences can be seen in practice depends on the camera, the subject, the lighting conditions and especially, the final size of the prints. Prints of A4 size and larger will demonstrate the advantage of a TIFF but the differences will only be visible when viewed closely. As with JPEG, a TIFF format image will have had sharpening applied during the in-camera processing and probably some changes to colours as well. Because these changes cannot usually be switched off, TIFF offers less flexibility and control than the Raw format and is only recommended if a camera cannot produce Raw images.

8-bit, 16-bit and Storage Space

When a colour image is stored or displayed on a computer each pixel needs to have its colour represented. This is done by a series of numbers using the RGB system ('Red, Green and Blue'). There are two variations (modes) known as 8-bit and 16-bit. In 8-bit mode, the Red, Green and Blue values are each represented by a number between 0 and 255. The name '8-bit' comes about because in binary arithmetic 8 bits (binary digits) are needed to represent a value of 255. In modern computers 8 bits is equivalent to 1 byte. So to represent the colour of one pixel three numbers are needed (one each for Red, Green and Blue), each of which needs one byte of space, which means a total of 3 bytes of storage space for one pixel. Expanding this example, with a 6 megapixel camera the final image will need 6 million x 3 = 18 million bytes of storage space, better known as 18 Megabytes (Mb). This is quite a lot of space for a single image and the graphics industry has done a huge amount of work to reduce the amount of storage space needed per image. The reduction in space is achieved by a process known as compression.

16-bit mode is similar in principle to 8-bit except that a much larger number range (0 to 65535) is used to represent the R, G and B values. The end points of both scales are the same so the only differences are the number of intermediate values and the amount of storage space used – 16-bit requires twice as much storage space as 8-bit. It's easy to think that 16-bit mode is better because colour values can be stored to a greater level of accuracy – for example, 12432 out of 65536 (effectively 48.563 out of 255) instead of 48 out of 255. In practice this extra accuracy only has value during the image manipulation process and a 16-bit image has to be converted to 8-bit for printing or web display. Printers can only print 8-bit images and although computers can display 16-bit images the human eye can't see the difference between a 16-bit image and the same image converted to 8-bit. Today's cameras produce 8-bit JPEG images, with 16-bit images possible only via Raw format.

Although the JPEG standards allow 16-bit images in theory, in practice image editing programs will only create 8-bit images. This is not surprising as the main reason for using a JPEG is to reduce the amount of storage space required and 16-bit will double it. To save a 16-bit image the only realistic options are TIFF or the image editing program's own format.

As a general guide, 8-bit is sufficient for most purposes. Advanced workers may wish to consider working in 16-bit and this area is discussed further in Chapter 6.

Compression
Compression is the process of making an image take up less storage space. There are two types of compression – lossless and lossy. In lossless compression all information is preserved during the compression process. Many computer users will be familiar with 'Zip' or 'PK Zip' files: this is a form of lossless compression where computer files are made smaller for storage purposes and then recreated later by 'unzipping'. If information was lost from a computer file it would probably be a disaster and lossless compression is essential. The same principle is applied to images. As an example of the way it works a plain blue sky where hundreds of consecutive pixels contain the same RGB values could be

compressed by storing the RGB values for one pixel followed by a count of the number of pixels with the same values.

TIFF files can be compressed, or uncompressed, as preferred. There are two popular types of compression in TIFF files, known as LZW and ZIP. The advantage of using compression in a TIFF is that a lot of storage space can be saved. The saving is dependent on the image but typically the compressed image will take up 30-50% of the original space, so the savings are very worthwhile. One disadvantage of using compressed TIFF files is that some imaging programs will only work on uncompressed files, so they need to be converted before use. Another disadvantage is that when moving a compressed file between PC and Mac, sometimes it can't be read on the 'other' machine.

In lossy compression some data is thrown away on the basis that it has less significance to the picture.

The JPEG format achieves huge amounts of compression by 'throwing away' certain types of information. The process of creating a JPEG takes advantage of limitations in the way humans see things – that small colour changes are perceived less accurately than small changes in brightness. Some fine details of colour will simply be 'thrown away' to avoid having to store the information while major brightness or colour changes such as edges of objects will be retained. Typically an image from a 6 megapixel camera, which was earlier shown to take up 18 Mb when uncompressed, can be stored using JPEG format in 3 Mb or less, which is an impressive reduction. When creating a JPEG the amount of compression – and hence the amount of data thrown away – can be finely controlled in a trade-off between file size and image quality. A 'high quality' JPEG will have less compression than a 'Middle Quality' or 'Low quality' image and take up more storage space.

Raw file formats vary between different camera manufacturers and have evolved over time. Most of them are compressed losslessly – that is, in a way that saves storage space but without compromising quality. Canon

(CR2) and the latest Nikon (NEF) Raw have very efficient compression applied. Some Raw formats are uncompressed and take up a significant amount of space. The most notable of these uncompressed formats are early Nikon (NEF) format and Panasonic/Leica format.

Picture Size and Resolution

Perhaps the most confusing area when starting in digital photography is the understanding of the relationship between pixels, image size and resolution.

A digital image consists of pixels arranged in a rectangle as already described – for example 3008 by 2000 on a Nikon D70. Some Canon SLRs produce images which are 180 dpi, Nikon SLRs produce images which are 300 dpi while many compact digital cameras produce images which are 72 dpi. What does this actually mean?

When an image is prepared for display, either on a screen or printed, a decision needs to be made about its size and resolution. The size is measured in inches or centimetres while the number of pixels is fixed by the camera as already described. Resolution means how the pixels are packed together, either in pixels per inch of image (also called Dots per Inch – dpi) or pixels per centimetre. Resolution is usually quoted as pixels per inch (ppi) rather than pixels per centimetre. The higher the resolution, the more pixels and hence more detail can be displayed in a given size of image. The most commonly used resolution figures are those quoted by publishers, who want a minimum of 300 dpi for printing pictures in books and magazines, and when displaying pictures on a computer screen where for historical reasons the figure is 72 dpi.

Take as an example a 6 Megapixel SLR image of 3000 by 2000 pixels. If this is set to a resolution of 300 dpi its size will be 10 by 6.7in (3000 ÷ 300 by 2000 ÷ 300). The image could be stretched to make it bigger without changing the number of pixels. There would then be fewer pixels per inch. At 180 dpi for example it will be 16.7 by 11in and at 72 dpi it will be 41.7 by 27.8in. The

number of pixels hasn't changed. What has changed is how closely the pixels are packed together. On a camera which always produces image at 72 dpi this explains why the image is much larger than the computer screen when trying to display them. The key point is that the image is the same in all three cases and the image is being 'stretched' to fit into the required space by altering the resolution in a process known as resizing.

In the example just described the actual pixels forming the image are not being changed. However it is possible to change both image size and resolution inside an editing program. When this is done pixels must either be added to the image or removed in a process known as 'resampling'. This uses a mathematical process called interpolation which performs sophisticated calculations to ensure the final image looks the same as the original even though the number of pixels making up the image has changed. Examples of different types of resampling are shown in Chapter 5.

Sensor size

Most photographers will be familiar with 'traditional' 35mm film cameras where the size of each frame is 36mm x 24mm. In digital cameras the sensor is usually much smaller, for example 23mm x 15mm in the Canon EOS 10D, 20D & 300D and Nikon D70. This is often called APS-C size because it is close to the 'C' frame size used by the now defunct APS film system. Cameras with full frame digital sensors, ie the same size as a

Figure 1.5.2.
Comparison of full frame sensor and APS-C small sensor.

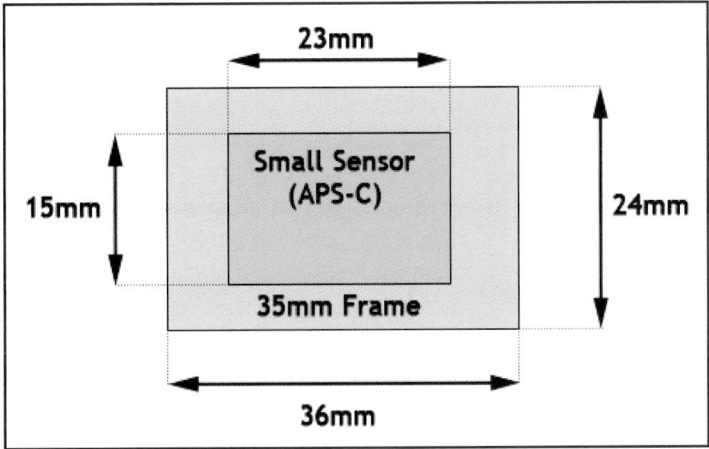

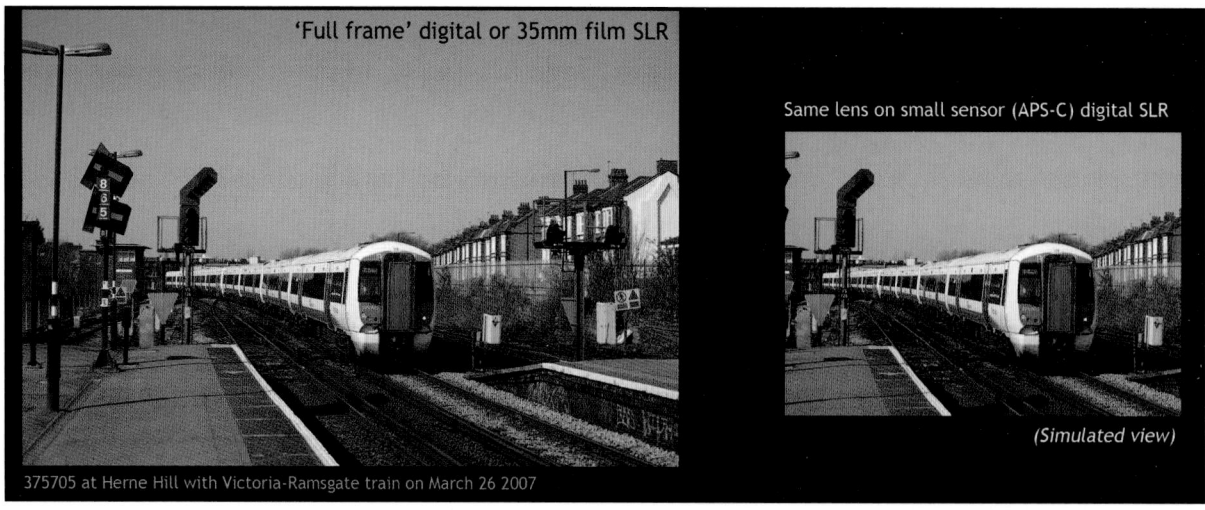

‘Full frame’ digital or 35mm film SLR

Same lens on small sensor (APS-C) digital SLR

(Simulated view)

375705 at Herne Hill with Victoria-Ramsgate train on March 26 2007

Figure 1.5.1.

Comparing the result from the same lens on a full frame camera and a small frame camera.

35mm film frame are available at a higher price. Compact cameras usually have tiny sensors, typically 8mm x 6mm or smaller. Figure 1.5.2 compares a 35mm full frame sensor with an APS-C sensor.

The sensor size has an effect on the lens needed to capture a particular view. The difference between the reduced sensor size and standard 35mm frame is called the multiplication factor and is approximately 1.6 for both the Canon and Nikon cameras mentioned. This means that to get the same coverage area on the small sensor digital SLR as say, a 135mm lens on the 35mm film camera a 135 ÷ 1.6 = 84 mm is needed which in practice means an 85mm lens. In 35mm film SLR photography probably the most popular non-zoom lens is the 'standard' 50mm focal length. If the same lens is tried on a typical digital SLR camera like the Canon EOS 40D or Nikon D200 the view will be more like an 85mm telephoto lens on a film camera. The difference is demonstrated in Figure 1.5.1 where a 50mm lens is used on cameras with a full frame and APS-C sensor to capture the same scene.

To get the same view as a 'standard' 50mm lens on a full frame camera when using an APS-C sensor camera requires a 31mm focal length lens. This would be a wide angle lens on a full frame camera. The nearest fixed lens to 31mm is either a 28mm or 35mm lens. In the same way, a popular standard zoom lens for a 35mm film camera

was 28 to 90mm. The APS-C digital equivalent covering the same angle of view is 18 to 55 mm.

As technology improves digital cameras with full-frame sensors will decrease in price but they will always be more expensive than small sensor cameras due to the extra cost of the larger sensor. It's too early to say whether full frame digital cameras will defeat small sensor cameras in the market place and eliminate the need to consider multiplication factor but currently it looks like the quality and price of the small sensor camera are sufficient to ensure its continued popularity.

In 2008 the digital camera market has reached the point where there are full frame and small frame sensor cameras using the same number of pixels – 12 Megapixels. Although the number of pixels is a major influence on image quality it is too early to say whether just the sensor size makes a significant difference to the overall quality.

● LONG TERM STORAGE

There's little point in going to a great amount of trouble building a collection of photographs, only to lose them all after a computer problem. Photographers must take precautions to avoid a disastrous loss. This section describes the options for long term storage and how to ensure your photo collection is safe.

Disaster

After a shooting session, some photographers copy their images from the memory card on to their computer and do nothing more. This is a foolish practice. The main disk drive on a computer, also known as a hard drive, is a complex, high precision mechanical device and is amazingly reliable given its low cost and the amount of data stored in such a small space. The reality is that a high proportion of hard drives will fail after a life of less than five years and the data on them will be lost. Some will fail after just a few days or months of use. The data can sometimes be recovered by specialist companies but this will cost hundreds of pounds and is not guaranteed to succeed. The best strategy by far is to keep copies of your images so that even if the computer fails your photo collection is safe. Commonly used terms for keeping copies are 'backups' and 'archiving'. When deciding on a backup strategy a few of the disaster scenarios to consider that could potentially result in loss or damage to your photo collection are shown in the separate panel.

Storage Options

Options for storing extra copies are as follows: 1) Extra disk drive(s) inside computer; 2) External hard drive(s); 3) CD; 4) DVD; 5) Memory card; 6) USB drive; 7) Internet-based Online storage. They are pictured in Figure 1.6.1. Each option will be described in more detail

Internal Drives

All computers are sold with a hard drive for storage. It holds the Windows (or Macintosh) operating system, extra programs like Office software, games and can also be used for storing images. The majority of desktop computers are designed so that extra 'internal' devices can be installed. Typically one hard drive and a combined CD/DVD drive are factory-installed, and there is space, mounting points and cables for two more drives. Internal hard drives are readily available from nationwide suppliers such as PC World and Maplin.

Installing an extra disk (or two) is a simple

and cost-effective storage option. Because the drives are directly connected to the motherboard of the PC the performance is excellent and images can be read or copied very quickly. The author has fitted an E: and F: drive to his PC in addition to the standard C: drive, with all images stored on the F: drive and an additional copy on the E: drive. After a shooting session the images are transferred from the camera's memory card to the F: drive and then another copy made on the E: drive. This ensures that if the F: drive fails, the E: drive has a readily accessible copy of all the images, and similarly if the E: drive fails there is a copy on the F: drive. Obviously all the images will be lost if the computer is stolen or damaged and other storage options must be used as well. Using a different drive for photo editing (that is, a drive which is not the C: drive) is faster than editing on the C: drive because the photo editing will have dedicated use of the disk drive. If editing is done on the C: drive the editing program will have to compete with other (internal) programs on the computer for use of the disk drive and this slows down the editing.

External Drives

Disk drives in their own case known as 'external' drives are readily available. These have their own power supply and connect to the PC via a USB cable. Their performance is okay for occasional copying but they are not recommended for extended use due to the speed limitations of the USB connection and

---

Potential scenarios that could cause loss of photos

- ❏ Hard drive stops working
- ❏ Computer stolen in a burglary
- ❏ Images deleted due to user error
- ❏ CD or DVD degrades over time
- ❏ Virus wipes hard drive
- ❏ Power surge damages the computer hardware
- ❏ Failure of the disk drive controller damages all disk drives
- ❏ Flooding of computer, due to burst pipe
- ❏ Flooding of house after high rainfall

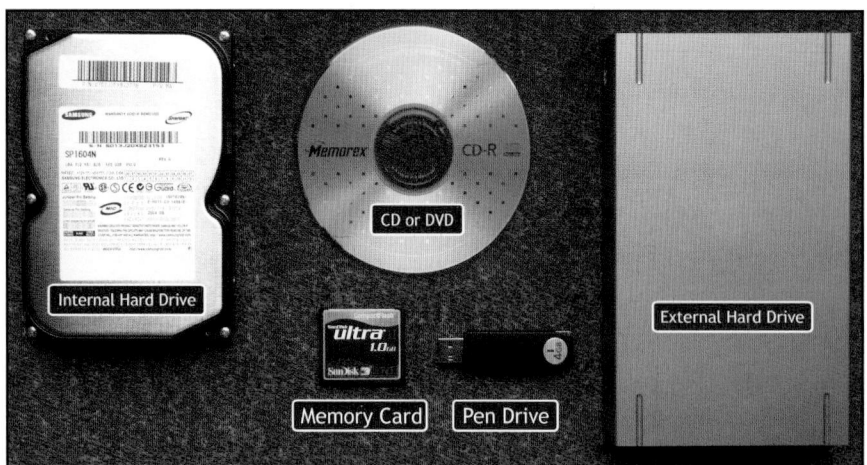

Figure 1.6.1.
Screenshot showing hierarchies of folders for storing images.

be in place. Cabled networks use a technology known as Ethernet with a device known as a switch to connect the computers together. There are three different speeds in common use: 10 Megabits per second, usually written as 10 Mb/s, 100 Mb/s and 1000 Mb/s which is also written as 1 Gigabit per second or 1 Gb/s. For the network drive to have a reasonable transfer speed the Ethernet speed must be 100 Mb/s or preferably 1 Gb/s. Only PCs from around 2006 onwards have Gigabit capability installed so it may be necessary to add a new network card plus a new switch for connecting the devices together. Equipment with Gigabit Ethernet functionality will always work with slower speed equipment at the slower speed.

the weak power supplies. USB 2.0 drives work well and drives using the 'Firewire' interface system (also known as IEE1394) are available. Prices are continually falling, specifications improving and there are frequent special offers. They actually consist of an 'internal' drive in a small case and the more technically-capable can swap drives around between the inside of their PC and the external case.

The recommended way to use this option is to copy images to the external drive, then disconnect it and store in a safe place in a different room in your home, ideally in a locked cabinet. This reduces the risk of it being stolen at the same time as the PC and a burst pipe is less likely to affect both rooms. Every week or two, update the drive with the images taken since the previous update. This should be a simple and fast operation.

It is worth buying several external drives and keeping them in different places. Storing one at a friend or relative's house provides protection against a disaster like a major fire and ensures your images will be safe. This is known in the IT industry as an 'off site backup'.

Network Storage

A variation of the external drive connects to the computer via its network connection and is known as a network drive or network storage. It allows the drive to be shared between several PCs and/or Macs on a network. A cabled or wireless network must

CD and DVD

Many people find this area confusing – surely a CD is for music and a DVD for films? The answer is that a CD or DVD is just a storage device as far as a computer is concerned, and it doesn't care what sort of information is stored. The only practical difference between CD and DVD is the amount of data each can store.

There are two categories of CD and DVD – those that can only be used once (known as write-once), and those that can be re-used (known as read/write). A CD that can only be used once has the acronym CD-R while a read/write CD is CD-RW. Only CD-R should be used for long term backups because a CD-R backup is cheaper, faster to create and theoretically more stable than a CD-RW disk. Using a CD-RW is pointless when there is no intention of re-using it. Technology has overtaken the CD and it is more economic and efficient to use a single DVD than a handful of CDs.

There are many different types of DVD: DVD-R, DVD+R, DVD+RW, DVD-RW, DVD-RAM, HD DVD and Blu-Ray to name just a few. For backups it's only worth bothering with write-once disks like DVD-R and DVD+R.

Most DVD formats use a single layer for storing information although there are dual-layer disks available that have a higher storage capacity. Older DVD drives can be fussy about what types of disk they work with, so be aware that there could be compatibility problems with older PCs or DVD software. Newer DVD drives tend to be multi-format and able to cope with most types of disk. With a PC from 2005 or earlier it is probably worth upgrading the DVD drive to a fast multi-format device. These are available for £40 or less and are very easy to fit. Simply remove the old one and slot in the new one. There should be no need for any re-configuration as the hardware is usually compatible and any software changes will be made automatically.

A single-layer DVD can store about six times more information than a CD and a dual layer more than ten times: 4.7 GB for the single layer DVD, 8.5 GB for the dual layer DVD and 0.7 GB (700 MB) for a CD. Blank disks of most types are widely available and are inexpensive.

To put images on a CD or DVD is simplest with special software as this allows images to be easily selected for backup and shows how much space is available on the disk. The best known of these is called Nero and available cheaply on eBay. Older versions of Nero will not work with recent DVD drives. There is free software called AVS Disk Creator available from www.avsmedia.com which does a reasonable job.

A little known feature of a CD or DVD is that new images can be added to it many times until it is full. This means that, for example, a batch of images can be copied to a CD or DVD, then a week later another batch copied and so on until full. When writing to a CD or DVD, a process usually known as 'burning', there is an option called 'finalise' which prevents further material being written in future. Provided that the CD or DVD is not finalised images can be added until it is full. This allows maximum use of the available space.

There have been various scare stories in the press about CDs and DVDs degrading over time. Because this phenomenon will take time to show up, it is hard to know whether it is likely to be a serious problem in the future or not. The author's oldest CDs are more than five years old and show no degradation. One precaution against degradation is to always use a CD/DVD from a major 'brand name' manufacturer rather than a cheap 'no name' product. Another precaution is to use other types of backup as well as CD/DVD.

Memory Cards

The price of memory cards has fallen so much that it's possible to store copies of an

Figure 1.6.2.
Screenshot showing the various drives on a typical PC.

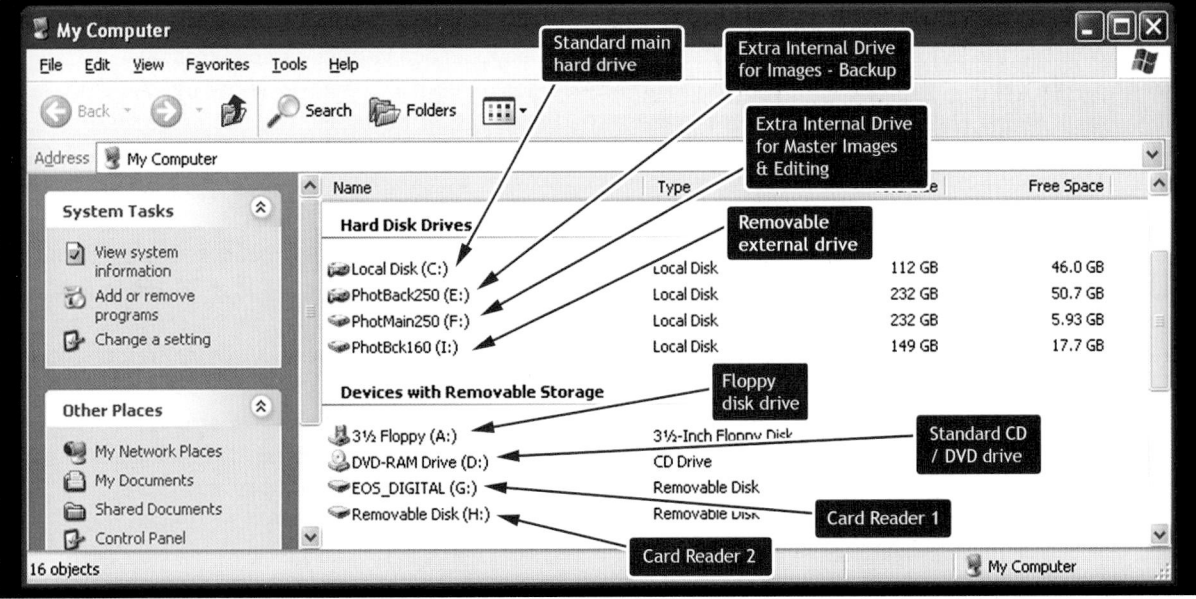

27

image collection in a box full of memory cards without spending a ridiculous amount of money. Instead of re-using each memory card in the camera it is instead used only once and a new memory card taken on the next trip, rather like a user of a film camera starting a new roll of film when the previous one is full. Although this is a technically feasible option, the economics mean that it is expensive. It has the advantage of being space efficient and would be a good short-term choice if you were planning to take a large number of pictures on a long holiday. As memory cards prices continue downwards this option will become more viable from a financial perspective. One disadvantage is that memory cards can fail, although generally they are very reliable. Another disadvantage is that trying to find a particular image in a large set of memory cards requires good labelling and indexing.

USB Drive

A USB drive is the name given to what is effectively a memory card with a built-in USB plug that can be plugged directly into a computer. Generally these are slightly cheaper than memory cards. As with the memory card option just considered, this option is technically feasible but too expensive to be realistic.

Online Storage

A relatively new option is to use online storage operated by a specialist company that is accessed via the Internet. The best known of these services in the UK is 'Digital Vault' from BT. The way it works is by copying images over the Internet from your computer to their system. You are charged for the amount of space used, either per month or per year. The major advantage of this system is that the images are stored away from your home and therefore totally immune from being affected by whatever happens to your PC – for example theft or flood. The downside, apart from the ongoing cost, is that you have to trust the company not to lose your

images and to remain in business. If they go bust there is the risk that you could lose the images although since the images are a copy their loss is only disastrous if all your images and other copies are lost at the same time. There are some practical limitations. Firstly you must have a broadband connection because the amount of data being transferred is high. Secondly, many broadband companies have monthly limits on the amount of data you can transfer so copying, for example, images from just a handful of 1 GB memory cards to the storage company might breach your limit. This option will undoubtedly become more popular in future as the cost decreases.

What format?

What format should be used for image storage? There have been concerns raised that if a camera manufacturer goes out of business or produces new models that are incompatible with their old ones, it might not be possible to decode a Raw image in say, 50 year's time. Should everything be converted to TIFF or JPEG before storing? The author's recommendation is to leave all images in the same format as produced by the camera. Don't alter them due to the risk of corrupting the contents. Unless you are using a very obscure camera it is unlikely that the image format will become totally obsolete in our lifetimes. There will always be a market for companies to produce converters so that old image formats can be accessed.

Comparison

Because the cost of computer equipment and consumables is continually changing it is not realistic for this book to quote costs for the different options. Readers may be interested to know that at the time of writing, creating DVD copies was by far the cheapest option. Any backup strategy should include most of the options described – for example, extra internal disk drives, external disk drives and DVD copies. This ensures a problem with one format will not cause a disastrous loss.

Anyone using a digital camera to take railway photographs needs to learn the basic techniques. This section explains all the important areas when taking a photograph using a digital camera. For anyone already familiar with a film camera the techniques for composition, framing and focusing are the same, but exposure is different and there are new areas to learn including the histogram and how to deal with dust on the sensor.

CHAPTER 2
TAKING THE
PICTURE

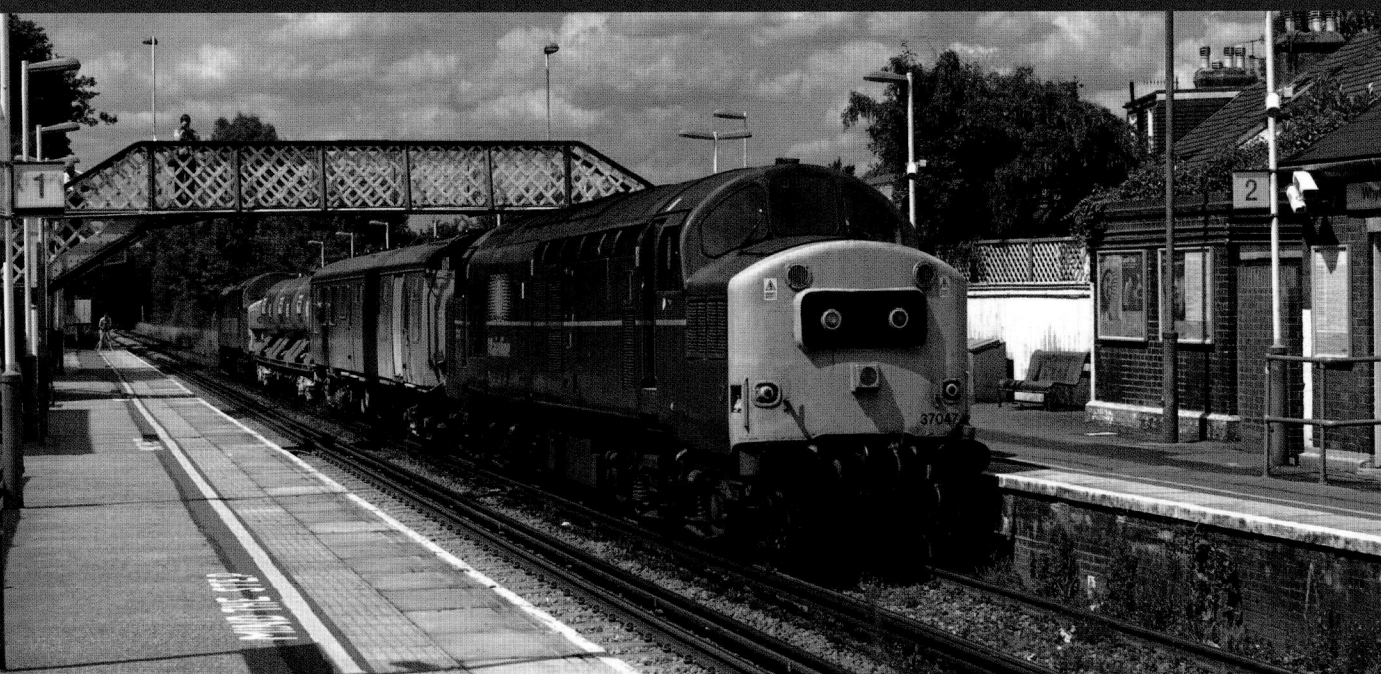

● BEFORE SHOOTING

Memory Cards

Before starting a shooting session the memory cards need to be prepared for use, whether new cards or previously used. The first step is to check that any old images have been copied to the computer and backup copies made as described in Chapter 1. Then the card is prepared using the appropriate menu function on the camera to 'format' the memory card. The act of formatting the card resets the file system on the card to make it appear empty and creates the necessary folders to hold the images. The camera should always be used to reformat the card rather than a computer because there can sometimes be problems due to minor incompatibilities between memory cards, card readers and cameras. For example if the computer is used to reformat the card the camera might be unable to write to the card. Theoretically everything is compatible, but unfortunately in practice there can be occasionally be problems, more often with cheap memory cards and card readers. It's worth noting that if a memory card has been reformatted by mistake before copying the previous images off the card, the 'lost' images can usually be recovered using specialist memory card recovery software provided the old images have not been overwritten with new ones. This is because the formatting process does not delete the images themselves, just the pointers to them.

● EXPOSURE

Metering Systems – Automatic and Manual

Digital cameras have a built-in light meter that measures the amount of light entering the camera and chooses appropriate settings for taking the picture, known as the exposure settings. Most commonly the settings are chosen automatically while cameras oriented towards photography enthusiasts have manual controls as well. When taking photographs – whether digital or using film – the photographer decides whether to set the exposure manually or have the camera choose it automatically. What is the best choice?

Experienced photographers will already have a favourite strategy for film cameras but this will need to be changed when using a digital camera. The advantage of manual exposure is that, barring unforeseen breakdowns, the results are predictable. Once the photographer is used to interpreting the exposure meter and setting the controls manually, mistakes are less likely than with automatic exposure. Photographers are all too familiar with the sunny day phenomenon when the sun disappears behind a small cloud at the wrong time and, with a film camera, having to adjust the exposure slightly. With digital these adjustments are undesirable when the background or sky stays bright. Better quality is possible by

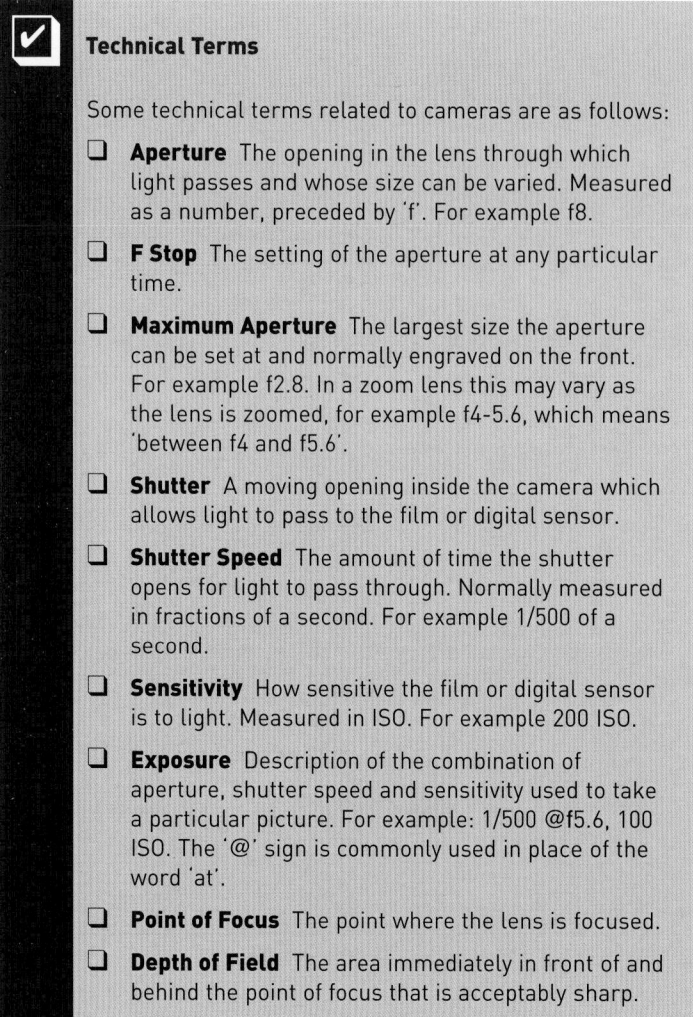

Technical Terms

Some technical terms related to cameras are as follows:

- ❑ **Aperture** The opening in the lens through which light passes and whose size can be varied. Measured as a number, preceded by 'f'. For example f8.

- ❑ **F Stop** The setting of the aperture at any particular time.

- ❑ **Maximum Aperture** The largest size the aperture can be set at and normally engraved on the front. For example f2.8. In a zoom lens this may vary as the lens is zoomed, for example f4-5.6, which means 'between f4 and f5.6'.

- ❑ **Shutter** A moving opening inside the camera which allows light to pass to the film or digital sensor.

- ❑ **Shutter Speed** The amount of time the shutter opens for light to pass through. Normally measured in fractions of a second. For example 1/500 of a second.

- ❑ **Sensitivity** How sensitive the film or digital sensor is to light. Measured in ISO. For example 200 ISO.

- ❑ **Exposure** Description of the combination of aperture, shutter speed and sensitivity used to take a particular picture. For example: 1/500 @f5.6, 100 ISO. The '@' sign is commonly used in place of the word 'at'.

- ❑ **Point of Focus** The point where the lens is focused.

- ❑ **Depth of Field** The area immediately in front of and behind the point of focus that is acceptably sharp.

leaving the subject dark and lightening it later on the computer because the darker settings ensure the background does not 'burn out'. An example of this is described in Chapter 5. On the other hand, those photographers who prefer not to do photo manipulation later will need to adjust the exposure in a case like this so that the foreground is bright, although at the expense of the background being over-exposed.

Exposure Characteristics
Experienced film users know that each film has its own exposure characteristics. Negative films have good exposure latitude which means the exposure can be varied within a reasonable range while still giving a good result. They are quite happy being over-exposed. Slide films need to be exposed carefully and prefer being slightly under-exposed to over-exposed.

Digital sensors have their own exposure characteristics and do not like over-exposure at all. When this happens the image disappears from the affected area, becoming 'burned out'. A blank white area is left containing little or no detail. The transition to 'burn out' is more abrupt than with over-exposed slide film. With railway photography over-exposure can be a particular problem. Skies are normally very bright and can be easily over-exposed, and the same applies to the modern rolling stock liveries that have light coloured paint schemes such as the Eurostar, South Eastern and Chiltern liveries.

As electronic technology advances it may be the case that the sensor characteristics in future cameras will be improved so that over-exposure causes fewer problems. With today's cameras a choice needs be made when taking a picture whether to: i) accept over-exposure, or ii) take all reasonable steps to avoid it, or iii) take alternative action. Too much under-exposure is not a good idea, however, as this will itself cause a loss in quality.

Histogram
When compared with a film camera, the most important 'new' feature to learn on a digital camera is the histogram and it is vital to understand what it shows. Although most digital cameras have a small panel on the back for displaying pictures after they are taken, only a rough judge of exposure should be made by looking at the image itself on the display. For more accuracy the histogram should be examined. When you are not sure of the right exposure setting, normal practice should be to take a photograph of the scene just before the train comes, check the histogram, adjust the camera settings as necessary and then delete the image. With manual exposure the photographer can be fairly confident that the exposure will be correct when the train comes providing that the light does not change.

Before describing the histogram, a recap of some points from Chapter 1. In a digital image the colours of a pixel are represented by numeric values for Red, Green and Blue because this is the RGB system. For each colour, zero represents the darkest value while 255 is the brightest (note for purists – this is with an 8-bit image). A simple histogram combines the values for the three colours into a single brightness value and plots the value 0 to 255 along the base (x scale) with the number of pixels having that value along the vertical scale (y scale). The more pixels having a particular value, the higher the plot. The left side shows the dark pixels and the right side the brighter pixels. The range along the base of the plot is sometimes known as the Levels. Images contain a range of brightness values and the challenge for the photographer is to capture this range properly without compressing it too much or losing values at one end.

Figure 2.2.1 shows a Class 37 locomotive with a weedkiller train taken on a Canon EOS 10D camera. Figure 2.2.2 shows the corresponding display on the back of the camera with information about exposure, time and date etc, plus a small version of the picture itself. The important part for judging exposure is the small histogram. Observant photographers will

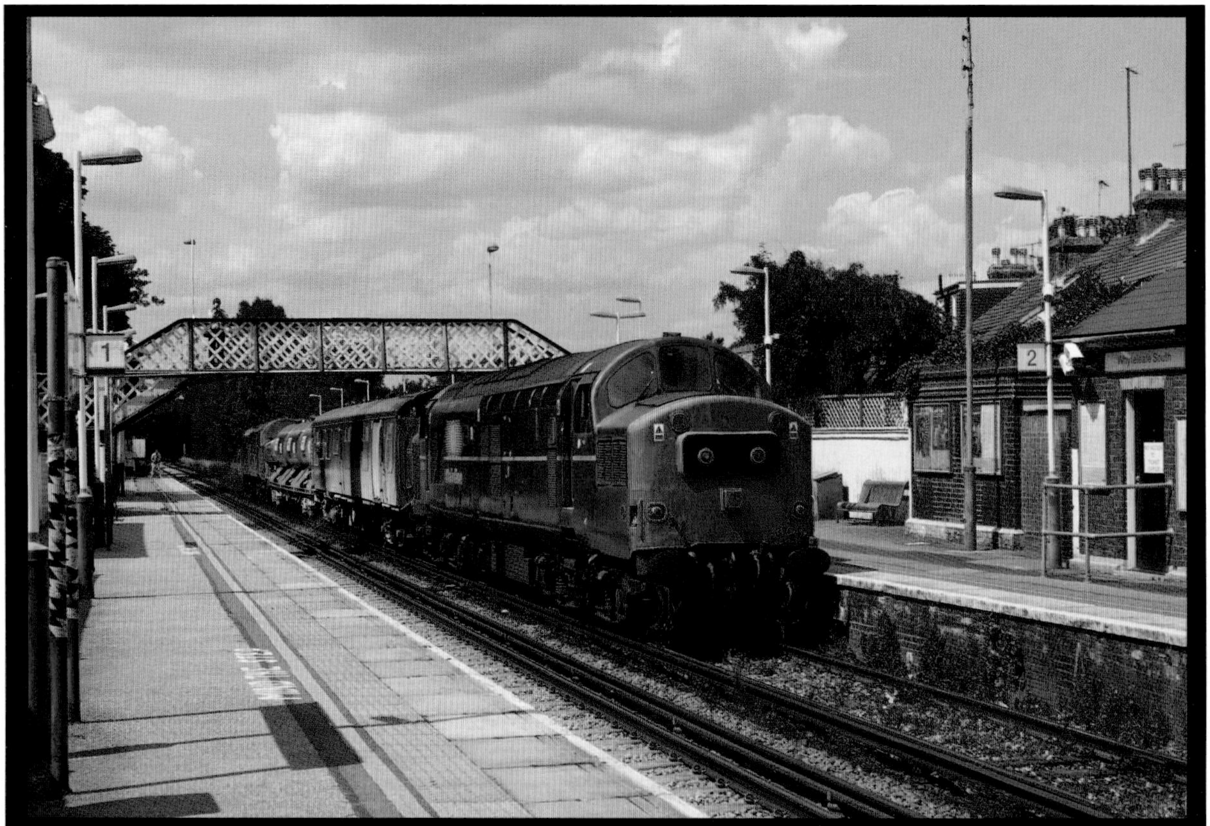

37047 at Whyteleafe South with weedkiller. July 6 2004

Figure 2.2.1.
Whole picture of No 37047 on a weedkiller at Whyteleafe South.

Figure 2.2.2.
View of the rear of the camera for the picture of No 37047.

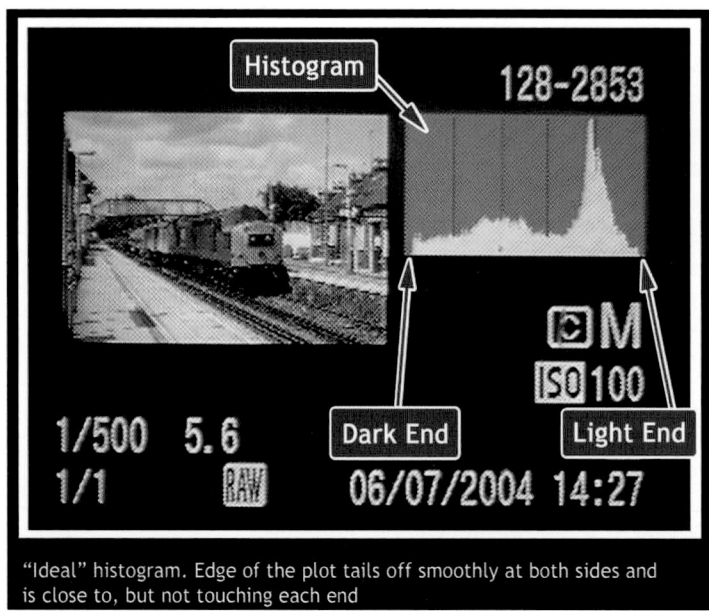

Histogram
128-2853

□ M
ISO 100

1/500 5.6
1/1   RAW

Dark End   Light End

06/07/2004 14:27

"Ideal" histogram. Edge of the plot tails off smoothly at both sides and is close to, but not touching each end

note that the sunny day exposure was 1/500 f5.6 on a 100 ISO setting, which is the same exposure that would be used in full sun with Fuji Provia 100F slide film, for example.

Interpretation

How should the histogram be interpreted? As background, the human eye is sensitive to contrast and when looking at an image likes to see a wide range of brightness values. If there isn't a wide enough range the image will have a dull appearance. A 'good' image contains pixels with a full range of brightness values from minimum to maximum (that is, from 0 to 255) and as a result the histogram should extend all the way from the left side to the right side. When taking a picture the histogram should have no fully bright or fully dark pixels because this indicates that when the picture was taken there were some even brighter or darker pixels which could not be captured properly. In such a case, image information has been lost and the histogram is said to be 'clipped'. Generally speaking, clipping is undesirable in anything larger than small areas because the lost detail will look ugly. The normal intention when taking a picture is to obtain a histogram which tails off gracefully on both sides. To achieve a full range of contrast in the final image, the range of brightness will be expanded during the processing phase on the computer. The histogram in Figure 2.2.2 is near-perfect. The overall shape is fairly smooth with a peak about 80% of the way across resulting from the bright sky and platform tones. The left and right ends of the plot are smooth and hit the base of the histogram, not the sides, meaning that there has been no 'clipping'.

Full Picture

The full size picture in Figure 2.2.1 shows how an image with a 'good' histogram produces a full range of tones from very bright to very dark although it has had a small brightness adjustment. When the image is edited on a computer minor clipping becomes visible in tiny areas. There is clipping of bright areas on the CCTV cameras beside the Platform 2 sign to the right of the locomotive, while parts of the dark areas of the underframe are also clipped. Both these are to be expected and because the clipped areas are small the loss of detail does not spoil enjoyment of the picture.

Histogram vs Metering

The exposure meter inside a camera will suggest a combination of shutter speed and aperture when pointed at an object. With a film camera the photographer can choose whether to use the meter or ignore it and rely on their eye for setting the exposure. How should the meter be used in a digital camera when the histogram is also available? This is an area where personal preference plays a large part and there is no single 'right' answer. As a general guide, the meter is used to establish the brightness of a scene and an initial exposure setting. If the photographer feels from experience that there is something difficult about a particular scene, taking a test picture allows the histogram to be examined. If necessary the exposure settings can be changed and another test taken. The ultimate reference is the histogram rather than the meter.

Effect of exposure in image quality

The effect of different exposures on image quality is demonstrated by a set of pictures of a Class 180 unit (Figure 2.2.3). They also show the need to allow for white liveries when judging exposure.

Exposure Comparison – Unchanged Images

The first set of photographs in Figure 2.2.3 shows the same subject. All pictures are taken from unmanipulated JPEG format images so that they can be compared fairly and the only difference between each one is the exposure setting. The actual camera histogram for each picture has been taken from photographs of the display on the back of the camera.

The conditions were standard summer 'full sun' so with an ISO setting of 100 the expected exposure is 1/250 @ f8, as in Picture 1 at top left. The histogram has a good gap on the left side but is showing slight signs of clipping on the right side, indicating minor overexposure somewhere. Picture 2 was exposed at 'one stop under' and its dark appearance demonstrates the under-exposure. The histogram is 'bunched' towards the left side – although not 'clipped' – with a narrower width than for Picture 1 and a fair sized gap on the right side. This demonstrates lower contrast than the other pictures, also known as reduced dynamic range. Picture 3 was taken at 'one stop over-exposed': the histogram is heavily bunched over to the right side and is severely clipped. There is a fair sized gap on the left side. Again the dynamic range is reduced but the more significant problem is the loss of detail in the highlights. This is severe and it would take several hours of 'transplant' and corrective work to fix this picture on the computer. Picture 4 – with half a stop less exposure than Picture 1 - shows a smooth histogram with small gaps on the left & right sides and no clipping. This is as good as you'll get. It's

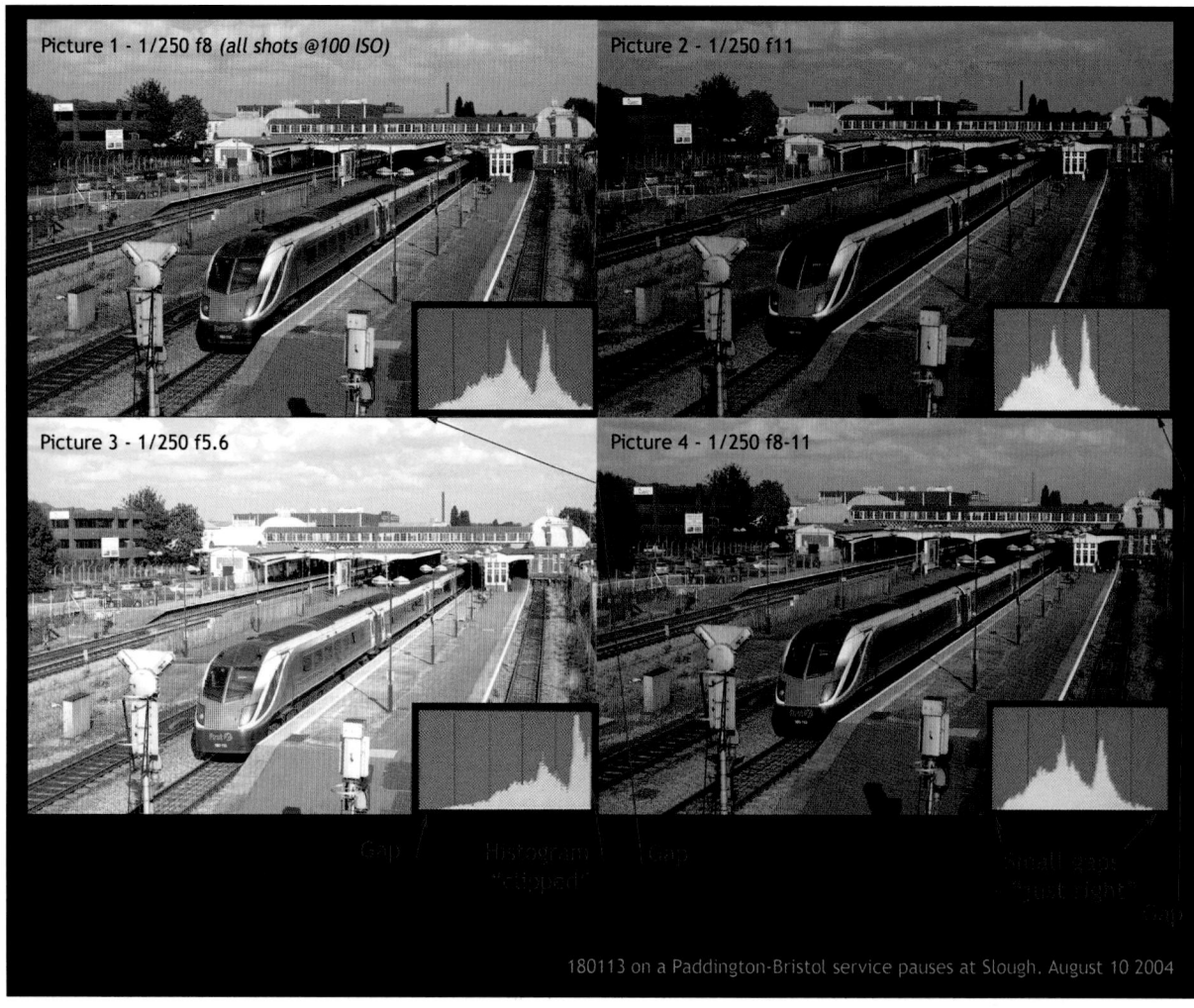

Picture 1 - 1/250 f8 *(all shots @100 ISO)*

Picture 2 - 1/250 f11

Picture 3 - 1/250 f5.6

Picture 4 - 1/250 f8-11

180113 on a Paddington-Bristol service pauses at Slough. August 10 2004

Figure 2.2.3.
Comparing different exposures for the same scene (Inset shows shows photo of the camera's histogram).

pleasing to the eye, has good dynamic range (contrast) and, being a shade dark, will look even better after slight lightening during later processing.

The lesson to learn from these pictures is that there is a benefit to slight underexposure when very bright areas are present because detail in the highlights is preserved.

Over-exposure Warning

Because of the detrimental effect of over-exposure on image quality, many camera manufacturers include an over-exposure warning on their informational display. This causes over-exposed areas to flash. On the Canon EOS these over-exposed areas flash alternately white then black. In Figure 2.2.4 a photograph of the camera's display panel for Picture 3 shows that the problems in this picture are sufficiently bad that they show up

clearly. Several parts of the picture are flashing: not just the sky but also the windscreen pillar on the Class 180 and the rear of the signals.

It is worth noting that some of these areas are also actually burned-out on Picture 1 as well, but the clipping can't be clearly seen on the histogram. On careful examination the cut-off histogram on the right side of Picture 1 is a clue to the existence of the problem even though the picture itself looks fine. The white parts of the livery are so bright that they have 'burned out' and detail has been lost. Trains with white liveries are easily over-exposed accidentally on sunny days because the white parts are so bright. The problem is also visible in typical summer 'puffy' clouds where the white parts can be very bright when viewed at certain angles. The solution for avoiding clipping comprises three parts:

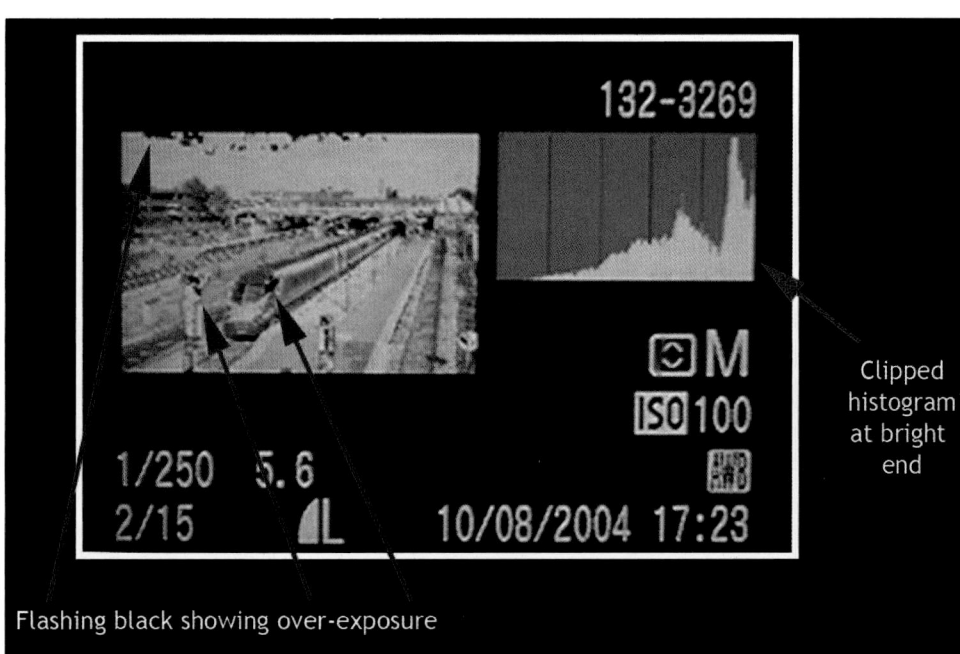

Flashing black showing over-exposure

Figure 2.2.4.
View of the rear of the camera for the over-exposed image (camera display for picture 3 in figure 2.2.3.).

Clipped histogram at bright end

Figure 2.2.5.
Adjusted versions of three of the earlier pictures.

i) always checking the histogram; ii) looking out for the flashing over-exposure warning on the camera display (where available), particularly in clouds; iii) make a mental note to remember that if the train has a white livery and the sun is bright, under-expose by half a stop compared to normal. So, for example, use 1/500 f5.6-8 @ 100 ISO instead of 1/500 f5.6. Camera sensitivities and individual lenses may behave slightly differently so it's worth experimenting.

Exposure Comparison – Manipulated Images

Can errors in exposure be fixed during later processing? Small errors usually can be. With larger errors it depends on the format used to take the shot. JPEG format images generally can't easily be fixed whereas Raw format images can be. This topic is covered more fully in Chapter 5 'The Raw Advantage'.

To demonstrate this, in Figure 2.2.5 small sections of three of the same images used in the previous picture have been adjusted. Each section has had the brightness and contrast individually adjusted to try to produce a picture that looks right to the eye.

The main point to show here is the adverse effect of over-exposure on image quality. On Pictures 1 and 3, note how the

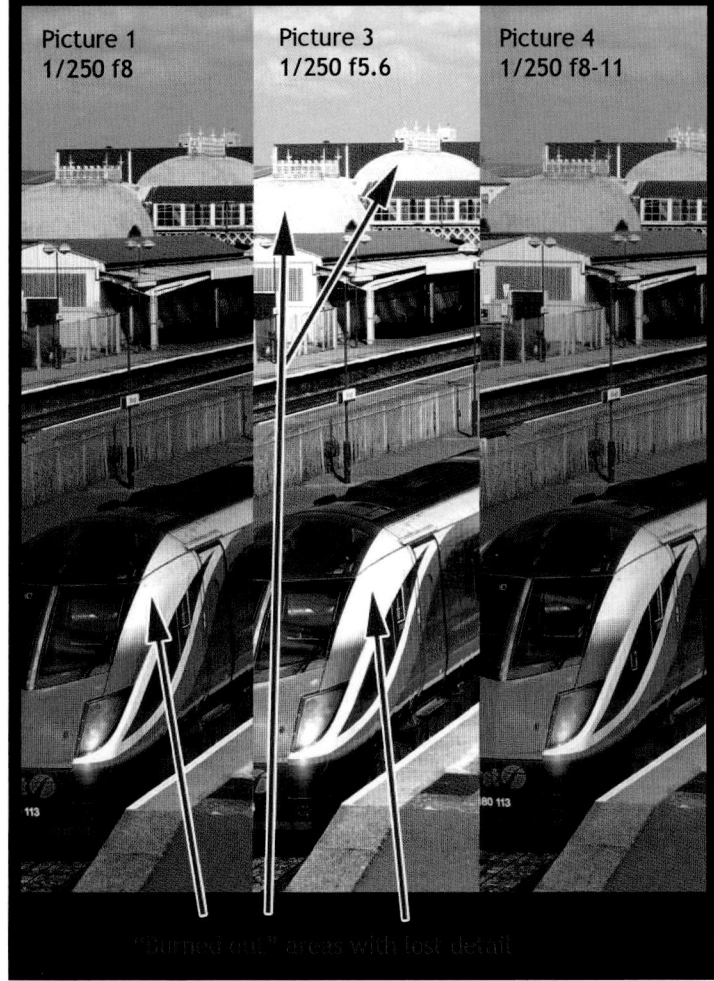

Picture 1
1/250 f8

Picture 3
1/250 f5.6

Picture 4
1/250 f8-11

fine textures in the white cab side pillar have disappeared when compared with Picture 4. This demonstrates what 'burning out' really means – the detail has been burned away by the over-exposure. More noticeable is the roof of the background building in Picture B where all the tile details have vanished compared with Pictures A and C. The yellow front of the Class 180 is no longer the right colour in Picture B and requires more elaborate treatment to correct. Ironically the blue sky is a pleasing colour in Picture B but the clouds have lost detail in the same way as the building roof already mentioned. The best result comes from the slightly underexposed image.

Severe Lighting Conditions

There are some conditions where underexposing to prevent 'burning out' will cause some parts of the picture to be so dark that they could lose quality. This happens most often when taking a shot looking towards the sun – also known as a 'back lit' shot. Much of the sky in the background will be very bright. The way out in many situations is to take two pictures, one at a suitable exposure for the darker areas and the other perhaps 1½ to 3 stops darker to capture the bright parts without over-exposure. The pictures will be re-assembled and blended together on the computer. This is an advanced and effective technique, which will be described later, in Chapter 6. When taking the picture of the sky, try to use a similar angle to the original shot while also avoiding any wires or poles so that there is only sky in the frame.

Minimum Recommended Shutter Speeds for common focal length lenses to avoid camera shake

Lens focal length (mm)	24	28	50	100	135	200	300
Minimum recommended shutter speed (seconds)	1/30	1/30	1/60	1/125	1/125	1/250	1/500

The above table should be used as a guide. With practice each photographer will develop their own preferences.

Warning.

The examples have shown the harmful effect of over-exposure on image quality but the reader should not over-compensate by thinking that an excess of under-exposure is a good thing because it isn't. Severe under-exposure leads to muddy tones, a build-up of noise and loss of shadow detail which is almost as hard to correct as burned out highlights. The best advice is to work hard at achieving good exposure technique. Using the histogram is a simple aid while also remembering that slight under-exposure will reduce burnout in bright areas and is easily corrected by adjustment.

● SHUTTER SPEEDS

What shutter speed should be chosen for shooting a moving train? The simple answer is that 'it depends'. The starting point is the combination of how fast the train is likely to be going, the direction it is moving in the picture and how much speed blur is considered acceptable on the final image. Most viewers prefer not to see any speed blur so the decision involves choosing a shutter speed which will reduce the blur as far as is feasible.

A good starting point for a typical front three-quarter photograph with a train moving at about 50mph is a shutter speed of 1/500th of a second. A mainline train like a Pendolino running fairly fast at 90mph would need a shutter speed of 1/1000sec, while an HST running at 125mph might need something even faster like 1/1500sec if the camera has this setting. The more 'side-on' the angle of view, or the larger the train is in the viewfinder, the more important it is to use a high shutter speed. If a train is viewed fairly head on with a telephoto lens a lower shutter speed can be used such as 1/250sec. Figure 2.3.1 shows some typical pictures and the shutter speed used. There is no such thing as a 'correct shutter speed' and the examples should be used as a guide.

Another factor to be taken into account when choosing a shutter speed is the likelihood of camera shake. This happens

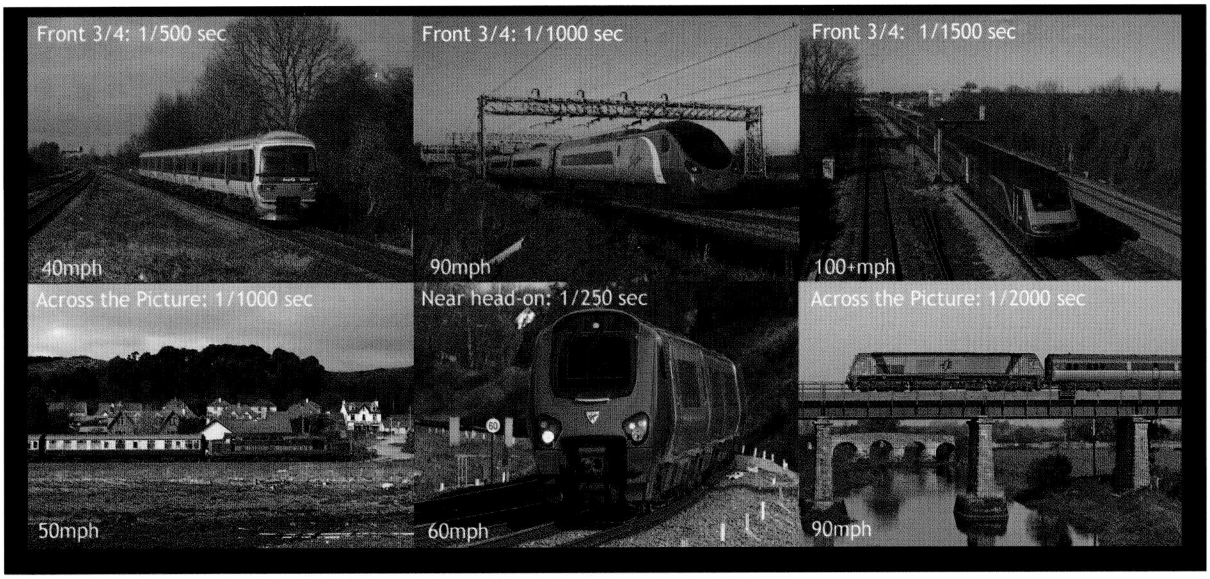

Front 3/4: 1/500 sec — 40mph

Front 3/4: 1/1000 sec — 90mph

Front 3/4: 1/1500 sec — 100+mph

Across the Picture: 1/1000 sec — 50mph

Near head-on: 1/250 sec — 60mph

Across the Picture: 1/2000 sec — 90mph

Figure 2.3.1.
Guideline minimum shutter speeds for different situations to avoid speed blur.

when the camera is moved accidentally during the picture taking. The slower the shutter speed, the more likely it is that camera shake will be visible. A commonly used guideline is that the slowest shutter speed when hand holding a camera is the nearest speed to 1 over the focal length of the lens in millimetres. So if using a 50mm lens, for example, the slowest recommended shutter speed is 1/50sec. The nearest shutter speed on a camera is 1/60sec. In windy conditions this rule needs to be modified and the lowest recommended speed might be much higher, for example 1/500sec. The table below shows a selection of common lenses and the minimum recommended shutter speed to avoid camera shake. These recommendations apply to any type of camera and depend only on the focal length of the lens. Photographers should use a sturdy tripod to avoid getting a blurred picture when slow shutter speeds are used. Some cameras and lenses are fitted with an 'image stabiliser' which compensates for a certain amount of camera movement and allows a lower shutter speed to be used.

● LENS APERTURE SETTING

The amount of light a lens allows to fall on the image is indicated using a value known as the 'f stop'.

Technically the 'f stop' indicates the size of the opening in the lens, better known as the 'aperture'. Traditionally lenses have f stop values which follow the sequence, from widest to smallest: 1.0, 1.4, 2, 2.8, 4, 5.6, 8, 11, 16. Intermediate values such as f3.5 or f4.5 are known as half stops. The smaller the 'f stop' value the wider the opening and the greater the amount of light that passes through the lens. For example, more light passes through the lens when it is set to f4 than f8. The advantage of using a higher numbered 'f stop' setting (also known, perhaps confusingly, as a smaller aperture) is that more of the subject matter will be in focus. In practice f5.6 will give good depth of field for most railway pictures. It is rarely necessary to use f8 or f11 purely for depth of field reasons except with long telephoto lenses.

● SENSITIVITY

Digital cameras allow the user to choose the sensitivity of the sensor within a range of values. Sensitivity is indicated using 'ISO' values, and the higher the number the greater the sensitivity. The disadvantage of choosing a higher value of sensitivity is that the image will feature increasing amounts of 'noise'. This is a coloured speckled pattern and looks similar to film grain. There is a significant difference in noise performance between 'compact' cameras and 'SLR' cameras that feature interchangeable lenses. 'Compact' cameras generally are typically restricted to an ISO range of 80 to 400 and have high amounts of noise visible at the highest setting. 'SLR' cameras have excellent noise performance at settings of 100 or 200 and are capable of being set to values up to 3200 ISO or higher depending on the model. Although there will usually be a lot of noise visible at the highest settings, intermediate values like 800 ISO are still very usable.

A major advantage of digital cameras is that the sensitivity can be varied for each picture taken. Compare this with a film camera where the sensitivity is fixed by the film manufacturer. A popular film like Fuji Sensia 100 has a sensitivity of 100 ISO and to change the sensitivity a different film must be loaded. Films offering higher sensitivity deliver results with more grain, less sharpness and weaker colours.

As a general rule, for the best image quality in daylight photography the lowest sensitivity setting which allows the required shutter speed and aperture combination should be chosen, starting from 200 ISO. With modern SLR cameras there is no need to use a lower sensitivity than 200 ISO in railway photography as the difference in noise performance between 100 and 200 ISO is insignificant. The exception is digital cameras introduced before about 2003 where the difference in noise between 100 and 200 ISO is more noticeable.

● FOCUSING TECHNIQUES

The majority of cameras sold – both digital and film - since the late 1980s have automatic focusing. Sometimes the automatic settings do not give the best results and other techniques should be used. This section will describe focusing techniques applicable to typical autofocus SLR-type cameras as used by most railway photographers and applies to both digital and film models.

Operation

How does autofocusing work? In most SLR cameras there is a set of autofocus sensors inside the camera behind the mirror. As light enters the camera through the lens, most of it is reflected by the mirror and passes up to the viewing screen where the photographer can view the subject. A small amount of light passes through special areas on the mirror to reach the autofocus sensors. When the shutter release is pressed lightly a motor inside the camera or lens moves the relevant parts of the lens until the autofocus sensors signal that the subject is in focus. In automatic mode the camera has to make its own decision on which part of the subject is in focus, and this may not always be what the photographer wants.

Accuracy

Some photographers have seen the autofocus accuracy of their cameras decline over time. This is typically due to dust and dirt building up on the mirror and obstructing the optical path to the autofocus sensors. Cleaning the mirror restores focusing performance. Proper optical-grade materials and gentle movements should be used when cleaning the mirror as the silvered coating is soft and easily damaged. Keeping the mirror clean is particularly important with a digital camera as dust can be blown on to the imaging sensor when the shutter opens. Dust particles on the sensor cause dark marks on pictures that are particularly visible in skies.

Depth of Field

The amount of a picture that is in focus depends on three things: the focal length of the lens, the distance between camera and point of focus, and the aperture setting used to take the picture. The aperture is the size of the opening in the lens through which light passes to the film or digital sensor and is normally given a number like f4, f5.6, f8 etc. The higher the number the less light passes through and more of the picture is in focus. A setting of f8, for example, will give more in focus than f4. Using an aperture setting of f16 or higher is not a good idea because of a phenomenon called diffraction which decreases sharpness. Increasing the aperture number is known as 'stopping down', leading to the commonly used phrase that stopping down will improve depth of field.

As the point of focus gets further away the depth of field increases so a photo of a distant 'train in the landscape' will have more in focus than a closer shot with the same lens.

The shorter the focal length of the lens being used, the greater the depth of field. This explains why photos taken with a standard or wide angle lens have more of the picture in focus than photos taken with a telephoto lens. More care needs to be taken when focusing telephoto lenses to get the subject sufficiently sharp than with standard lenses. It's worth noting that compact non-SLR digital cameras have very short focal length lenses and high depth of field.

With 35mm film cameras and 'full frame' digital models, as a general rule particular care needs to be taken when focusing lenses of around 100mm focal length upwards, apertures of f4 and lower, or when the train is closer than about three coach lengths.

Focus Lock

Most cameras have a focus lock where the focus setting is temporarily locked while pressure is maintained on the shutter release. This is suitable only for periods of a few seconds. Typical use involves locking the focus on a particular object, then quickly re-aiming the camera and pressing the release fully to take the picture.

Manual Focus

Autofocusing can normally be turned off via a switch on the camera or lens. Some cameras provide an indicator in the viewfinder or beeping sound to tell when good focus has been achieved during manual focusing. Otherwise the eye needs to examine the image on the viewing screen as the focusing is altered manually. With modern cameras this can be difficult as the viewfinders lack optical focus aids such as the split-image rangefinder commonly used on older manual-focus SLRs. The viewfinders are often small and are usually quite dark when zoom lenses are used.

Push-button Focus

Automatic focusing on today's cameras is really a combination of two separate

functions: i) push-button control where pressing a button causes the camera to start focusing; ii) combining the focus control with the shutter release. By pushing the shutter

release button slightly the lens focuses, and pushing it further fires the shutter. Some cameras, notably the Canon mid-range and professional EOS models allow the focus control to be moved away from the shutter

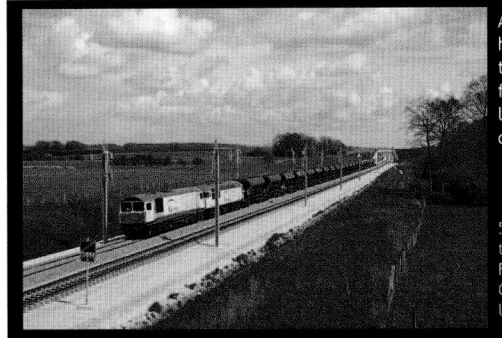

Figure 2.6.1.
Example showing where autofocus will work well.

Autofocus works well here. The subject is in the middle distance and fairly central while the lens is a 'normal' angle of view.

58046 and 56038 work on the LGV-Est in eastern France. April 27 2005. Canon EOS 20D, 35mm lens, 1/500 sec @f5.6-8.

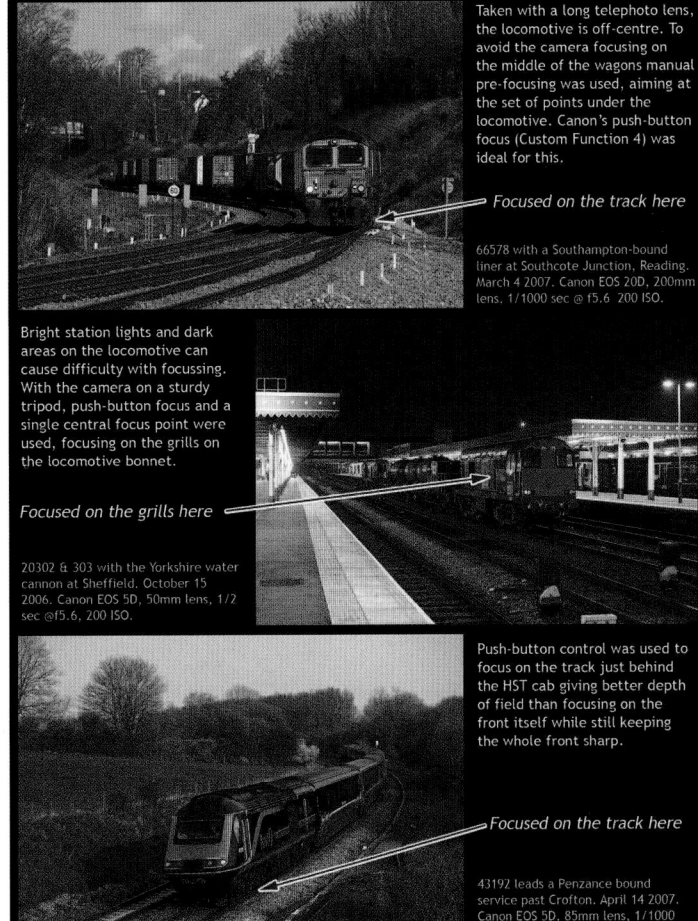

Taken with a long telephoto lens, the locomotive is off-centre. To avoid the camera focusing on the middle of the wagons manual pre-focusing was used, aiming at the set of points under the locomotive. Canon's push-button focus (Custom Function 4) was ideal for this.

Focused on the track here

66578 with a Southampton-bound liner at Southcote Junction, Reading. March 4 2007. Canon EOS 20D, 200mm lens. 1/1000 sec @ f5.6 200 ISO.

Bright station lights and dark areas on the locomotive can cause difficulty with focussing. With the camera on a sturdy tripod, push-button focus and a single central focus point were used, focusing on the grills on the locomotive bonnet.

Focused on the grills here

20302 & 303 with the Yorkshire water cannon at Sheffield. October 15 2006. Canon EOS 5D, 50mm lens, 1/2 sec @f5.6, 200 ISO.

Push-button control was used to focus on the track just behind the HST cab giving better depth of field than focusing on the front itself while still keeping the whole front sharp.

Focused on the track here

43192 leads a Penzance bound service past Crofton. April 14 2007. Canon EOS 5D, 85mm lens, 1/1000 sec @ f4-5.6, 200 ISO.

Figure 2.6.2.
Examples showing where to focus manually.

release on to a different button so that one button focuses the lens while another fires the shutter. Canon calls the feature Custom Function 4. It will be described here as push-button focus.

Pre-focusing

Pre-focusing is a technique that works well in many situations. It's not necessary to have the train in the picture as focusing on the track is sufficient. When the train approaches, the photographer focuses the lens on the point in the track where it is planned to 'stop' the train. The camera is then aimed towards the train and the shutter release pressed to take the picture a few seconds later when the train is in the right position. Focus can be achieved through any of the methods previously described.

Focus Problems

Common problems when using autofocus are:

i the camera can't find a point of focus and the focus mechanism rotates backwards and forwards. This behaviour is known as 'hunting'.
ii the lens focuses in the wrong place causing the main subject to be out of focus.

Each of these will be discussed.

Hunting

Hunting for focus is particularly frustrating as many cameras prevent the shutter being fired until good focus is achieved so hunting means no shot, not even one that is out of focus. There are several possible causes. Focus sensors need areas of reasonably high contrast and preferably vertical or horizontal lines to achieve focus. If pointed at a dark or smooth area the sensors may have trouble locking on to the subject. The camera should be pointed to an area close to the main subject that has mid-brightness with obvious lines in it. When focus has been locked, the camera is aimed in the desired direction and the shutter release pressed fully to take the picture.

Headlights cause hunting, particularly in a head-on view with a telephoto lens. Pre-focusing on the track as previously described avoids this. If a sequence of pictures of a moving train is wanted the focus will usually need to be changed between shots. Pointing the camera at the train and relying on the camera focusing automatically between shots may fail because of the headlight. A technique that works but needs practice is to repeat the pre-focusing technique for each shot in the sequence. Focus on the track, re-aim the camera and take a shot, focus the camera on the track further forward, re-aim the camera and fire again, and so on. Push-button focus is ideal for this technique. Manual focusing using the viewfinder image requires skilful hand-eye co-ordination.

Photography at night has its own focusing challenges. Bright lights confuse the focusing sensors and dark areas can be too dark for the sensor to work. With the camera on a tripod the best option is to point it at an object away from bright lights that has distinct lines on it, then focus the lens. With auto-focus switched off, the camera is aimed for the desired composition, the tripod head locked to prevent vibration and the shutter released using either the self-timer or a remote release.

Wrong Place

Taking a photo with the focus set to the wrong place is annoying because usually the mistake is only discovered when it is too late to be able to do anything about it. How does the camera decide on the right place to focus? Although camera manufacturers compete to build a camera with the greatest number of focusing points, in practice all cameras decide to focus on the centre of the picture to a greater or lesser degree. When photographing a scene where the main point of interest is off-centre the camera will probably focus somewhere in the middle if left to make its own decision. Similarly when the camera is pointed upwards and the picture contains a lot of sky, it may try to focus on the sky. Some cameras allow manual selection of a particular focus point and in this case an off-centre focus point could be chosen. The disadvantage is the need to keep fiddling with the camera. The photographer has to remember to change the focus point setting for each shot and in a rushed situation it's easy to forget. Manual control of focus using only the centre focusing spot is an easily remembered way to guarantee a sharp result. Figure 2.6.1 shows a situation where autofocus should easily cope and deliver a picture with excellent focus and depth-of-field.

Where to Focus

When photographing a train in a typical ¾ front view, where is the best place to focus? Some may be surprised to hear that in most cases it's not the front of the train. Focusing a little further back – typically behind the cab doors on a locomotive or on the first window of a multiple unit – provides better depth of field. The front of the train will be sharp and more of its body towards the rear. The exceptions are when using a telephoto lens, such as a 135mm focal length lens on a 35mm film or full frame digital camera, or a wide aperture such as f4 on a shorter lens, when the depth of field is sufficiently small that there is little margin for error and it's best to focus on the front. Figure 2.6.2 shows different types of view and where to focus for best sharpness and depth-of-field.

● SUN ANGLES

Railway photography is particularly popular on sunny days and the angle of the sun has a huge impact on the appearance of the pictures. Photographers should always consider the position of the sun relative to the subject of their pictures and adjust their techniques accordingly. Typical of the problems caused by not allowing for the sun angle are a white or miscoloured sky when blue was expected and ugly deep shadows.

To demonstrate the effect of the sun angle on the appearance of a picture, the author took a series of test shots in both JPEG and Raw format of Freightliner's Bardon-liveried No 66623 at Rugby on a sunny afternoon. The shots are not intended as examples of interesting composition because the purpose was only to compare pictures of all four 'corners' of the locomotive in the same sunny conditions.

Dynamic Range

There is an important point here, which is essential to understanding the effect of sun angle on the colour of the sky. The background is that the settings on any camera have to be adjusted to let in the 'right' amount of light to take a satisfactory picture. The technical term for this is setting the exposure. But what is the 'right' exposure setting? The technical term for the range of brightness in a picture is 'dynamic range'. Today's digital cameras have a restricted dynamic range and on a bright sunny day they can't cope with the full range of brightness in the picture. This means they can't deliver good detail and colour everywhere. With manual exposure the photographer has to choose which part of the picture the camera will be set for and with automatic exposure, the camera makes the choice for the photographer based on where they point the camera.

Test Photos of No 66623

The test photos in Figure 2.7.1 demonstrate the effect of camera exposure settings on the appearance of different areas of the picture. Views of the four corners of the locomotive were taken and numbered View 1 to 4. For each corner two pictures were taken – one with the camera set for sunny conditions and the other with it set for the shadows. Manual exposure was used to be sure that the pictures can be compared fairly. All views are JPEG images as taken, without any manipulation.

In View 1 both the locomotive side and end are in the sun. The 'sun settings' picture looks superb, with realistic, pleasing colours and good detail. Note how the sky is an attractive shade of blue. The 'shadow settings' picture is too bright everywhere, with washed out colours and a pale sky.

In View 2 the side of the locomotive is in the sun while the end is in shadow. In the 'sun settings' picture the side of the locomotive has a realistic colour but the cab end is dark and the detail, particularly around the

Figure 2.7.1
Pictures of the same locomotive from different angles and using different camera settings.

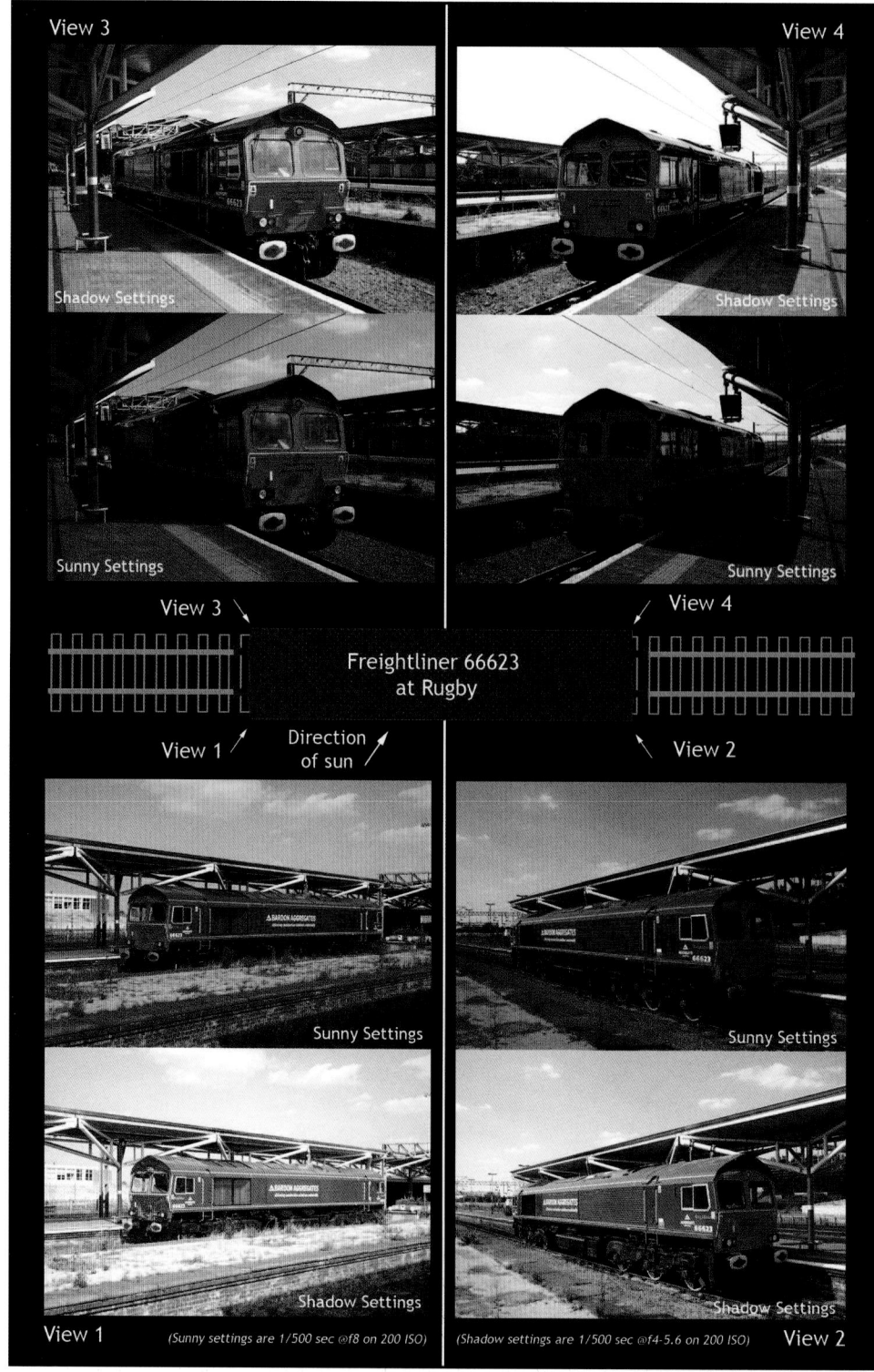

buffers, struggles to show through. In the 'shadow settings' picture the cab end looks good with plenty of detail but the side of the locomotive is slightly too bright and the sky is washed out.

In View 3 the side of the locomotive is in shadow while the end is in sun. In the 'sun settings' picture the side of the locomotive is too dark and shows little detail while the cab end looks good. The sky is bright but has some colour. In the 'shadow settings' picture the side of the locomotive is about right while the cab end and sky are washed out.

In View 4 both the side of the locomotive and the cab end are in shadow and the camera is pointing towards the sun. In the 'sun settings' picture both the side of the locomotive and the cab end are dark with little detail showing. The sky has some blue colour but is still a little washed out. In the 'shadow settings' picture the side and cab end of the locomotive look reasonably good with plenty of detail but much of the rest of the picture is too bright including the sky, which is almost completely white. Both pictures have harsh, unappealing colours.

The amount of detail visible on the locomotive and the colour of the sky depend on both the camera settings used and the angle of the sun compared to the locomotive. When 'sun settings' are used on the camera, the sunny areas of the locomotive look colourful and the sky has varying degrees of blue colour but the shadowed areas are dark. When 'shadow settings' are used, the shadowed areas of the locomotive look good with plenty of detail but most of the rest of the picture is too bright. When the sky is too bright for the camera to cope it loses its blue colour and turns white. On some occasions compromise 'half way' camera settings may work, but equally these may give inadequate results for both bright and shadow areas.

Amount of Shadow

How do you photograph a train so that its colours look realistic with plenty of detail visible while avoiding a washed out sky? The only simple solution for avoiding problems with shadows is to check the angle of the sun and never take pictures on the shadow side of a train. Shadows could be caused either by the angle of the sun or the train being in a dark area, such as in a deep cutting or behind a tall building. On a cloudy day shadows are usually much less of a concern.

When taking a picture at a particular location the photographer has no control over the amount of shadow on the train, since this is fixed by the position of the train,

the environment around the railway and the angle of the sun. On a sunny day the photographer therefore has to choose a location which suits the position of the sun. Most railway lines follow a series of curves as they cross the country and as a result the angle between the train and the sun changes. By choosing a location where the sun angle is suitable, any shadow on the side of the train can be eliminated. For example taking a picture in the style of View 1 rather than View 3 will give a more pleasing appearance to the side of the train. Of course it's also important to stand in the right spot and at a bridge, the photographer must choose which side to stand on. Whether the side of the train is in shadow or not will be just as important as the background. Most experienced photographers will plan their day based on the time of the expected trains and the sun angle at that time. When the sun angle is wrong at a given location they will move to somewhere with a better sun angle.

The second choice is what time of day to take the picture of the train. For a specific working there is probably no flexibility on the time, but for a stationary train it may be better to return to the spot in several hours' time when the sun has moved further round into a better position. In some cases it may be best to abandon the location and return on a different day at an earlier time.

Unwritten Rule

Some photographers get upset when told there are rules on how to take pictures. For most readers of this book, railway photography is a leisure pursuit and they are free to shoot as they wish without following a set of rules. Nevertheless there is an unwritten rule within the hobby that applies particularly to photographs submitted to books and magazines: photographs on sunny days should be taken on the sunny side of the train.

In practice this means pictures in the style of View 1 or 2 are preferred. An image like View 1 may be referred to as 'sun on the nose' for obvious reasons while View 2 is 'back lit' as the sun is lighting the rear of the train. Although a 'sun on the nose' image may be more colourful and is preferred by certain

Figure 2.7.2.
Two similar views of
BNSF intermodal
trains taken with
different sun angles.

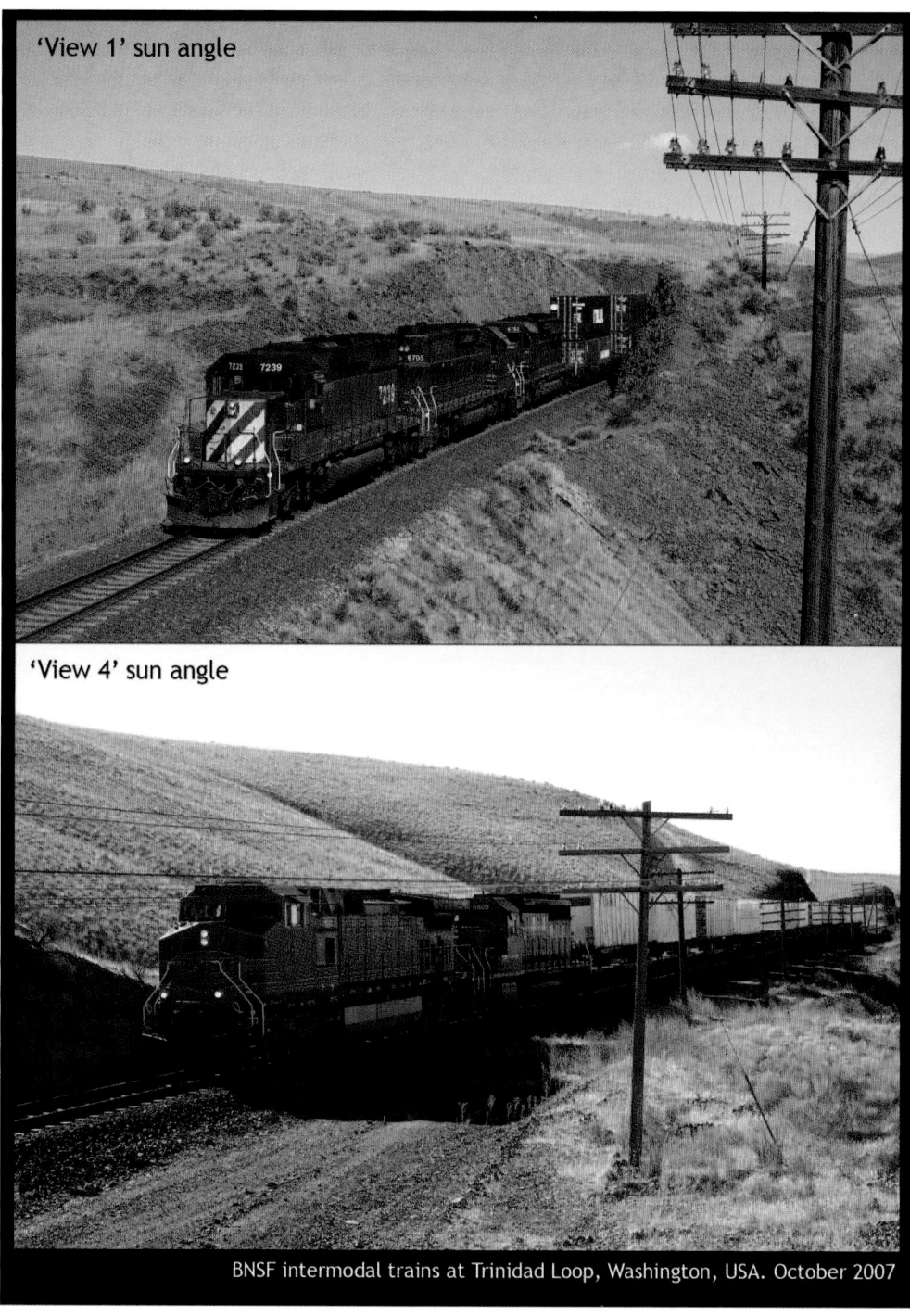

'View 1' sun angle

'View 4' sun angle

BNSF intermodal trains at Trinidad Loop, Washington, USA. October 2007

groups of photographer, a backlit image can have a stronger visual impact. Both types are normally accepted for publication. While a photographer is free to take a picture in the style of View 3 or 4, a shot with large amounts of shadow down the side of the train is likely to be rejected when submitted for publication. See Figure 2.7.2 which compares two similar

pictures of American intermodal trains and see which you prefer – a 'View 1' type picture with the sun behind the photographer or a 'View 4' picture where the camera is pointing towards the sun.

Pictures on cloudy days are sometimes used in magazines to illustrate a newsworthy working but are less likely to be used in features when alternative sunny views are available. Black & white photographs have the advantage that shots taken on cloudy days are readily accepted providing there is sufficient contrast in the image.

On a personal web site the photographer is free to publish railway pictures featuring whatever sun angle they wish, but when submitting pictures to other web sites which select their pictures the same 'unwritten rule' applies. Web sites containing pictures that take the sun angle into account are usually more attractive to the eye and consequently attract more viewers.

Optimum Sun Angle

For a View 1-type 'sun on the nose' shot the best results are obtained when the sun angle is in a certain range for flat-fronted motive power like Class 47 or 66 locomotives. For units with sloping fronts like HSTs and Eurostars, a wider range of angles will produce good results. Personal preference will play a part with some photographers preferring a narrower range of angles. See the chart in Figure 2.7.3 which shows the best range of angles for a typical flat-fronted train.

Shadow Side Photography

There are times when a photographer has to take a picture on the shadow side. In these circumstances there are a number of different recommendations and suitable techniques, both when taking the picture and when processing the results on a computer. Getting good results is difficult and shadow side photography is not recommended for the novice. The techniques are described in Chapter 6.

● DUST

One of the downsides of digital photography compared with using film is the effect of dust. If a dust particle lands on the film it will affect one frame and then move with the film as it is wound on, leaving a clean frame for the next photograph. When dust lands on the digital sensor inside the camera it tends to stay in place and affects many pictures. Although some recent cameras have been fitted with

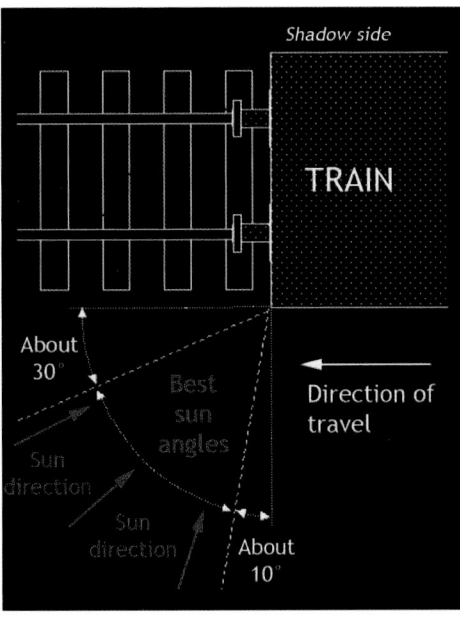

Figure 2.7.3.
Demonstration of the best sun angles for photographing a flat-fronted train.

'anti dust' sensors that vibrate in an attempt to shake off dust particles it's too early to say whether these systems are effective against dust in the long term. It's inevitable that all digital photographers will encounter dust marks at some time and it's important to know how to deal with them.

Marks

How do you know if you have dust on your camera's sensor? The tell-tale sign is small dark marks in the sky although the strength of the effect varies. It's not a matter of how much you have used the camera as new cameras often arrive from the factory with dust already in place. It is sometimes said, perhaps cruelly, that if you have had your camera for a while and haven't been affected by dust, then you haven't looked hard enough. Cameras with removable lenses are more likely to be affected as the dust can enter when the lens is removed but fixed lens cameras can still suffer from the problem.

The strength of the marking effect varies with camera settings or, strictly speaking, with the lens aperture. When using a small aperture setting like f8 or f11 the dark spots will be more clearly visible than with a setting like f4 or f5.6 and explains why the strength of the effect varies between images. At small aperture settings the light through the lens

Figure 2.8.1.
A sensor stick on its own and wrapped with an optical tissue ready for cleaning a sensor.

arrives at the sensor in a more tightly focused beam and the dust particle is outlined more strongly. To make an analogy, when a lamp casts the shadow of an object on to a wall the object will be more clearly defined with a spot lamp than when using a bare light bulb.

Avoiding Dust

SLR-type digital cameras with removable lenses are more likely to get dust in the sensor area because dust can get in through the lens mount when the lens is removed. It's advisable to reduce the amount of time that the lens mount is open. If storing the camera without a lens, a body cap should be fitted. Keep the inside of the camera clean including the surface of the mirror. The back of all lenses should be kept clean as they will be close to the sensor when the shutter is open. When changing lenses 'in the field' avoid removing the lens in an environment which is obviously dusty. When lens changes are needed in dusty conditions go to a spot which is shielded from the wind and use the camera bag as a 'safe area' for lens changing.

Some photographers avoid changing lenses at all and keep a particular zoom lens permanently attached. The author's experience in the UK is that even with a moderate number of lens changes when out on a trip, provided reasonable precautions are taken dust is rarely a problem. Once the sensor is dust-free, a period of three to six months is sufficient before even another light cleaning is necessary.

Cleaning

When you get dust on the sensor what can be done? Many camera repairers offer a sensor cleaning service but this can be expensive and the camera must either be taken to them or sent in the post. Either option means being without the camera or having to make a special journey.

It is possible to clean the sensor yourself but like any Do It Yourself operation carries the risk of making a mistake and damaging the camera. The author of this book and its publisher cannot be held responsible for any damage caused to cameras during sensor

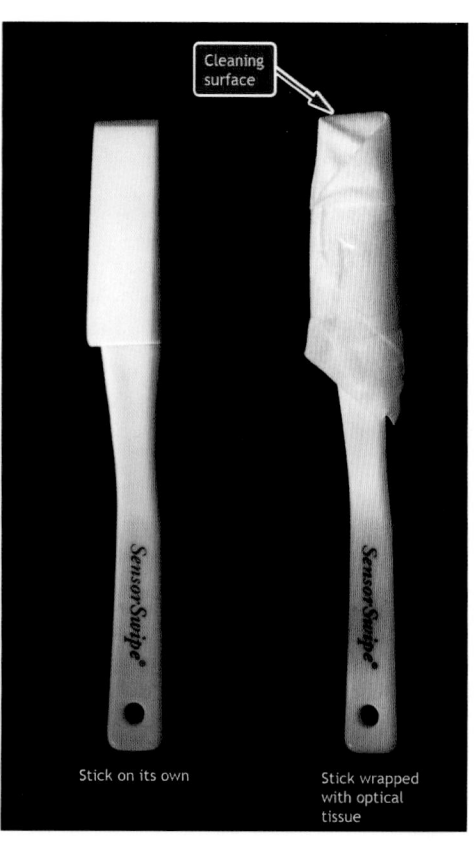

Cleaning surface

Stick on its own

Stick wrapped with optical tissue

cleaning. There are some things that really must not be done such as blowing the dust away using breath. Particles of saliva can land on the sensor and cause a serious mess. Any technique that involves blowing the dust away, even with a 'blower brush', really only moves the problem temporarily before the dust returns later. It is best to remove the dust completely. Using ordinary tissue, lens tissues and cotton buds is also a bad idea because they carry their own loose fibres and dirt and will probably apply as much mess as they remove. Proper optical cleaning tissues and cleaning fluid applied using a specialised sensor cleaning stick are the best solution in the author's opinion. With care and practice it is possible to achieve a fairly clean sensor. The sensor stick is needed so that it can reach through the narrow opening and reach the sensor with a flat surface at the end to wipe the surface of the sensor and remove dust and dirt. Figure 2.8.1 shows a sensor stick on its own and with an optical tissue fixed to it. Sticks are available in a width to suit a full frame sensor or a small sensor. The smaller size is easier to use in the confined space of a camera's sensor area. Figure 2.8.2 shows a cross-section through a sensor stick with the angled cleaning surfaces at the tip covered with an optical tissue.

To find how severe the dust marks are on the sensor the simplest way is set the lens to f11 or f16 and take a photograph of the sky on a cloudy day. When looking at the resulting picture on the computer there probably will be small dark areas caused by the dust. Sometimes it can be hard to see the dust marks. It is easier to see them on the screen when zooming in, increasing the contrast and darkening the picture.

Before any cleaning operation the optical tissue has to be fixed to the stick. Figure 2.8.3 shows the steps involved in doing this but note that to avoid picking up dust on the tissue the tissue should be held in the air when this is done. The tissue is folded in half over the top of the stick. The sides are then folded over at an angle so that the area around the tip is kept clear. The difficult part is keeping the tissue tightly stretched during this operation. Lastly the folds are wrapped around the stick and adhesive tape applied around the stick to keep the tissue in place. A single drop of cleaning fluid is applied to the tissue so that it is moist when wiping the sensor, encouraging any dust to stick to it. Cleaning fluid should never be applied directly to the sensor due to the potential for

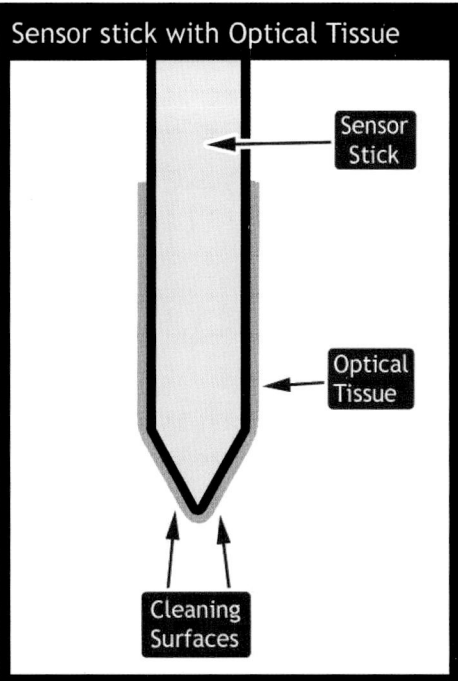

Figure 2.8.2.
Diagram showing section through tip of sensor stick wrapped in an optical tissue.

damage if too much is applied. The shutter must be opened and cameras usually have a special setting to hold the shutter open while cleaning takes place. Potentially the shutter can be damaged if it closes and hits a sensor stick.

The motion for cleaning depends on the size of sensor and stick. If the width of the stick covers the whole sensor a simple wipe at an angle from one end to the other should be enough as shown in Figure 2.8.4.

Figure 2.8.3.
The stages involved in wrapping an optical tissue around a sensor stick.

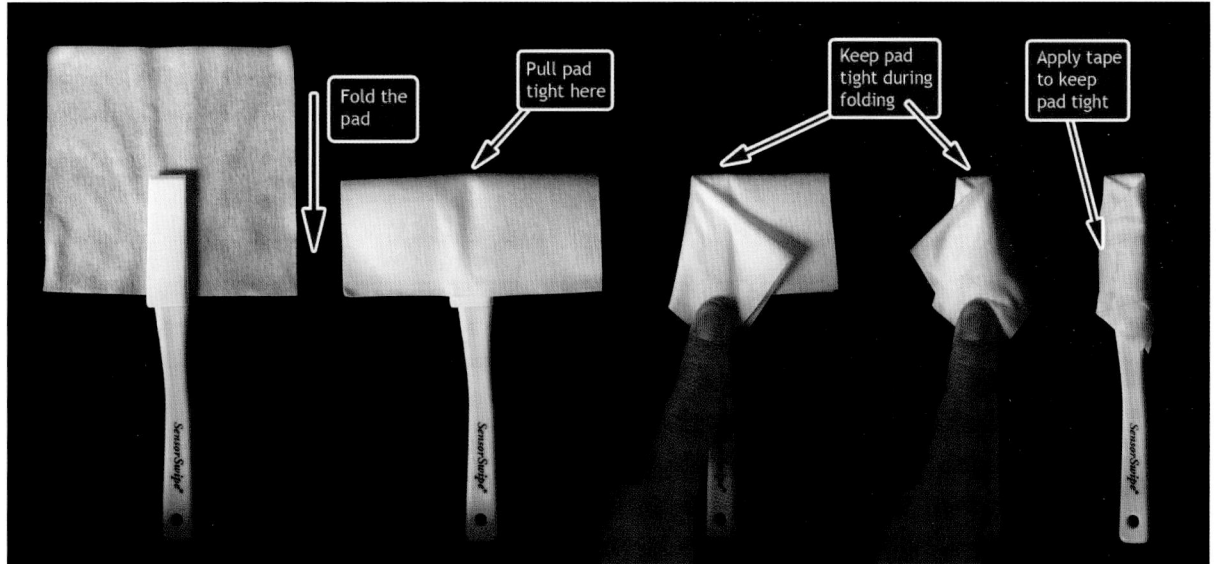

Cleaning a Small Sensor

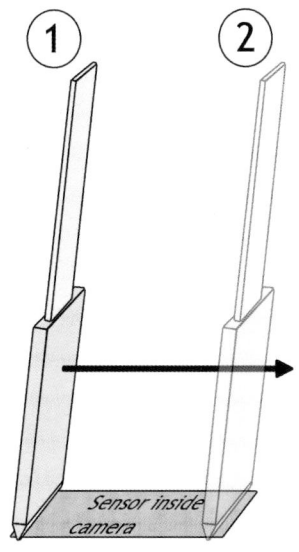

Cleaning a Full-Frame Sensor

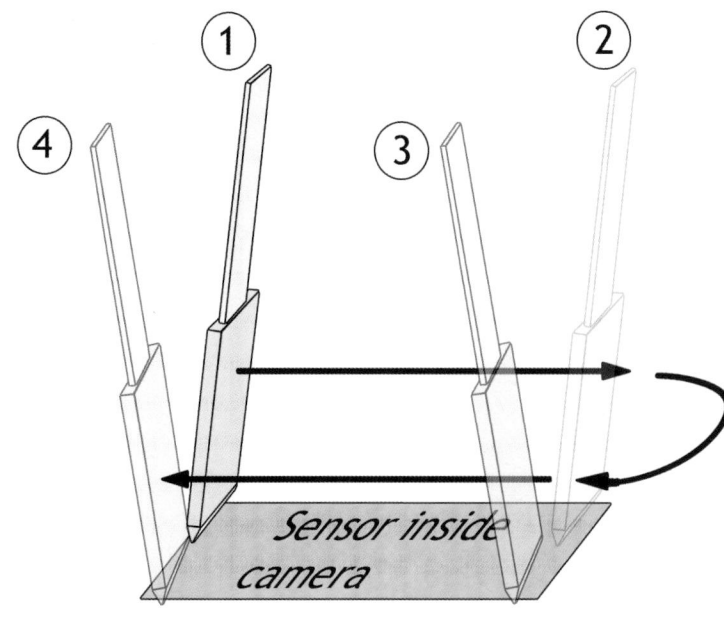

Figure 2.8.4.
Diagram showing how to move a sensor stick when cleaning a small sensor camera.

Figure 2.8.5.
Diagram showing how to move a sensor stick when cleaning a full frame sensor camera.

Sometimes dust remains and a wipe is needed in the other direction – using the other side of the stick tip to avoid spreading the dirt that was wiped up in the first cleaning movement. With a full frame sensor and stick for a small sensor the stick should be drawn across at a slight angle, rotated and then drawn across in the other direction using the same side of the stick tip as shown in Figure 2.8.5. Once the movement is complete the sensor should be checked for dirt by taking a picture as previously described. If further cleaning is needed, the other side of the stick tip can be used. For further cleaning do not re-use the stick just used as this could spread any dirt now on the tissue. Remove the dirty tissue and apply a new one.

photographers ought to know how to make. They are intended for those situations where an image doesn't need much work done on it or the photographer is not interested in making more complex adjustments. The format of the picture could be JPEG or a Raw image after conversion. Some of the subjects described in this chapter are covered in more depth in later chapters of this book.

CHAPTER 3
GETTING STARTED
SIMPLE IMPROVEMENTS

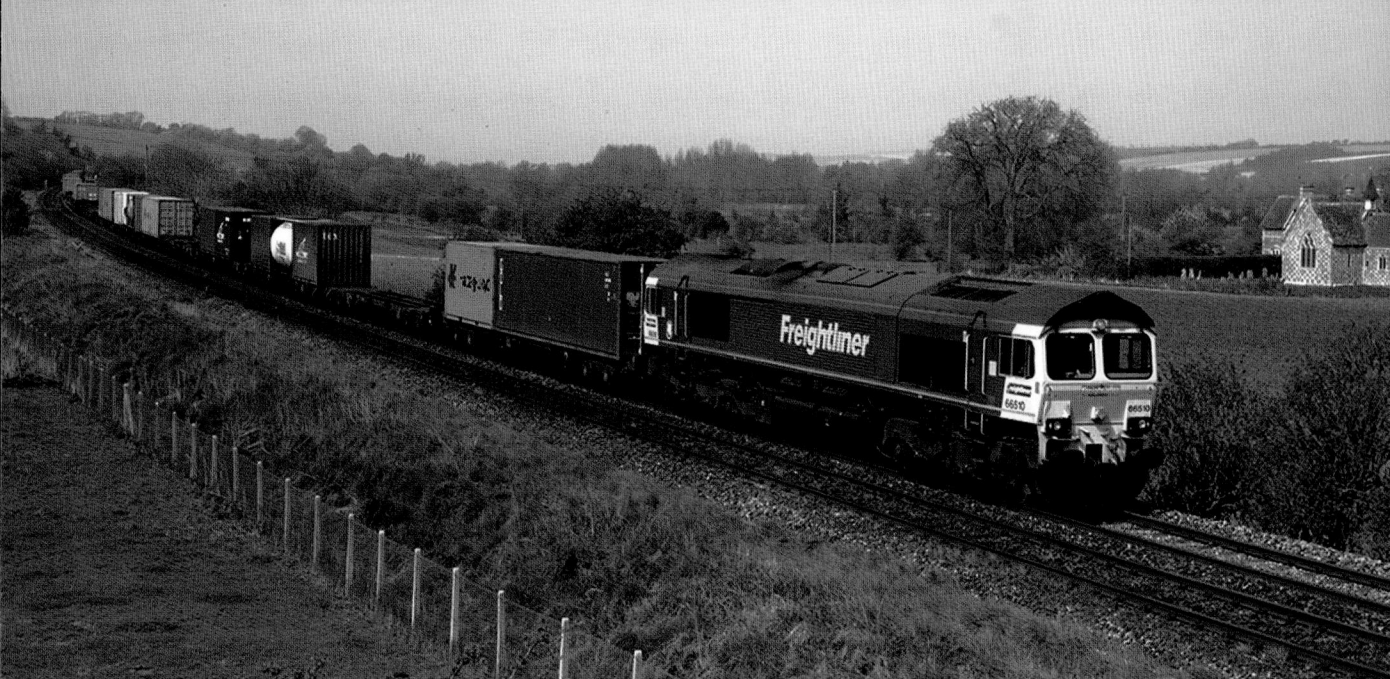

● PREPARATION

It's important to always work on a copy of the original image. If this isn't done it is possible to update the original image and lose its original state. Put a copy of the original image in a folder used only for editing, well away from any folders used for storing 'master' images. Then the improvement process can be started.

● REPAIRING DUST SPOTS

Dust spots on an image can usually be repaired fairly easy. Typically they are visible in a plain area of sky and barely noticeable anywhere else. The principle used to cover them is to copy a small area of pixels from one area to another using the Cloning Tool. Figure 3.2.1 shows dust spots in the sky where 'good' sky will be used to cover the 'dusty' sky. An important principle is to avoid changing the existing image. Instead the cloned sky will be added to a new Layer that sits on top of the existing image and covers the dust spot. If a mistake is made or

there is some other reason for changing the existing cloning later this practice allows the change to be made without having to re-start work from scratch or fix bad repairs on the original image.

Sometimes it can be hard to see the dust marks. Figure 3.2.2 shows one way which involves zooming in, increasing the contrast and darkening the picture. The simplest way on a 'cloud-only test' is to use Photoshop's Auto Levels feature. With normal images the best way is to create a new Brightness/Contrast Adjustment Layer as shown in the example. The contrast change is not wanted for future editing so the 'Undo' function should be used to reverse the change. In the example there are two dust spots. Spot 1 is in a plain piece of sky and is easy to fix. Spot 2 needs a modified technique. Although there is a third spot showing in the enlarged picture with increased contrast, it doesn't show in the standard picture and so can be left untouched.

As the first step in removing the first dust spot, select the Cloning Tool. Then choose a soft brush which is approximately the same

Figure 3.2.1.
Preparing to cover a dust spot using the Cloning Tool.

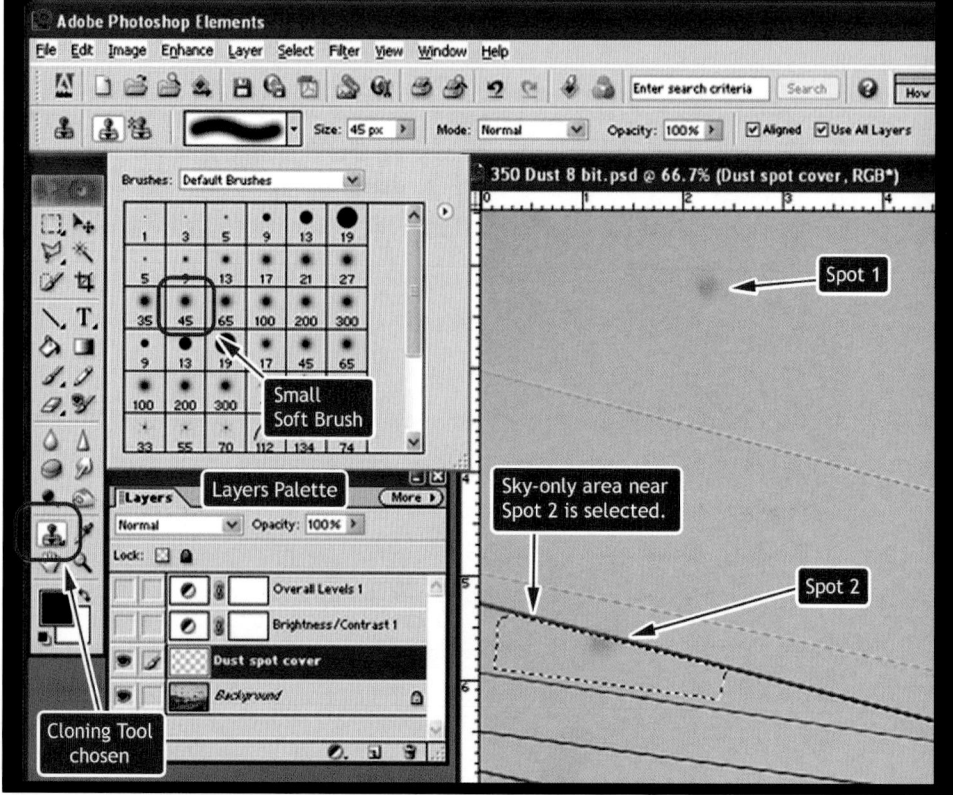

size as the dust spot: 45 pixels in this case. Figure 3.2.1 shows this brush selected in the palette of preset brushes. Using a soft brush is important because the soft edge ensures that the copied material blends seamlessly into what is already there. To tell the Cloning brush where to copy material from, hold the [Alt] key and click the left mouse button while pointing the mouse pointer at the desired spot. This should be near the dust spot but not too close. Create a new Layer using the 'New... → Layer...' menu command and give it a name like 'Dust Spot Cover'. Check in the Layers Palette that this new layer is the active layer (highlighted in blue) and above the main image. To actually copy the material, position the cloning brush over the dust spot and click the left mouse button. The new material should cover the dust spot. If it's not completely covered, move the mouse with the left mouse button held down to copy more material until it is covered.

The second dust spot is a little more complex to fix because it is adjacent to a power wire. Normal use of the cloning brush, as with Spot 1, would cover the wire with sky, which is not wanted. The solution is to select a small area around the dust spot which includes the dust spot but not the wire. When a selection is active new material can only be added to the selected area and not to anywhere else. Put another way, use of the selection ensures the dust spot is covered but not the wire. Figure 3.2.1 shows the selection active before the dust spot is covered. Use the Polygonal Lasso Tool with a feather of 0 to create the selection so that it has a hard edge and the dust spot does not show against the wire. The rest of the cloning process is the same as for the first dust spot.

A word of warning when using the cloning tool. If there are any Adjustment Layers in the image, de-activate them before doing any cloning by clicking on the 'eye' in the visibility box for the layer in the Layers Palette, otherwise the new cloned areas will not match the colour of what is already there. The example shows the Adjustment Layers de-activated. Also, be sure that the 'Aligned' and 'use all Layers' boxes on the toolbar are ticked.

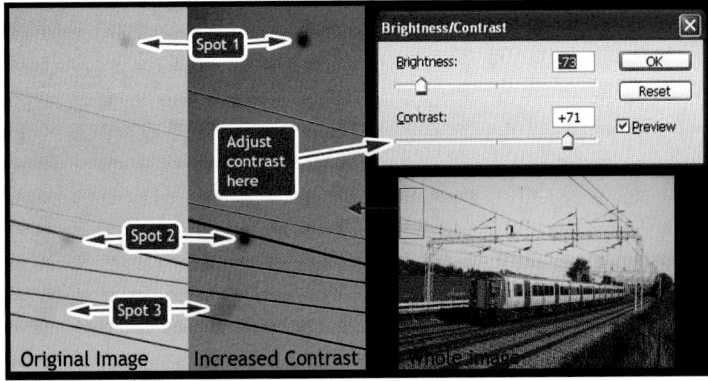

At this point it is a good idea to save the work using Photoshop's own '.PSD' file format so that you can come back to it in future and won't lose it if the computer crashes.

Figure 3.2.2.
How to clearly show dust spots before removing them.

Other Work

You can now proceed with other editing work. Before printing or processing for a web page it will be necessary to get rid of the layers using the 'Layer → Flatten Image' menu option.

● SIMPLE COLOUR & CONTRAST ADJUSTMENTS

Most images can be improved by increasing the contrast. In some images just a simple adjustment is needed whereas in others the amount of work required is more wide-ranging.

Improving Contrast – the Simple Approach

Perhaps confusingly, the name of the operation in Photoshop for increasing contrast is a Levels Adjustment. For those who do not want to make many edits to a picture the simple way of improving the contrast is to use one of Photoshop's built-in functions. These are: 'Auto Levels', 'Auto Contrast', and 'Auto Colour Correction' and can be found on the Enhance menu in Photoshop Elements or the 'Image → Adjustments' menu in full Photoshop. Each of these three has a slightly different effect. With any image it is worth experimenting

Figure 3.3.1.
Comparing different automatic adjustments.

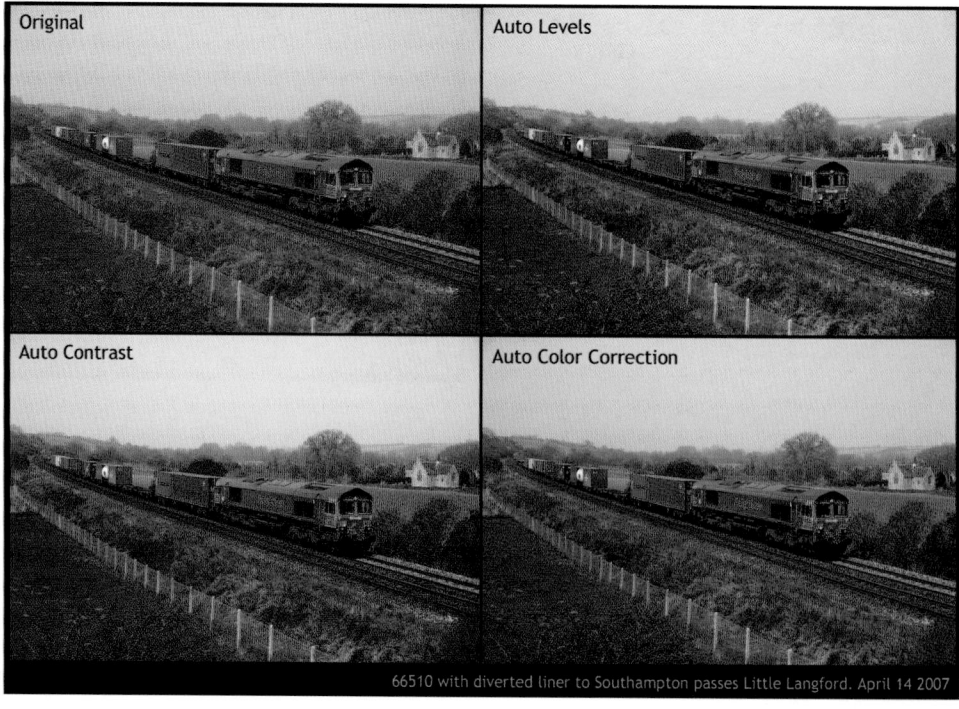

66510 with diverted liner to Southampton passes Little Langford. April 14 2007

Figure 3.3.2.
A second example comparing different automatic adjustments.

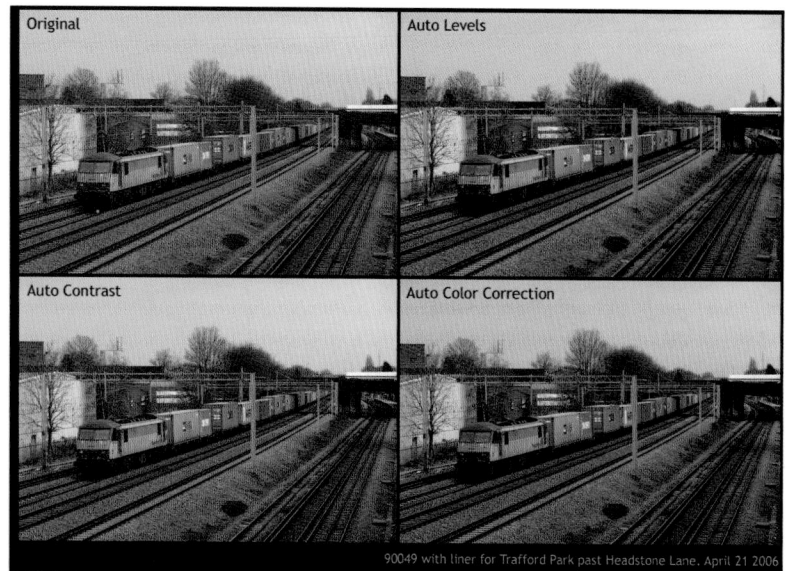

90049 with liner for Trafford Park past Headstone Lane. April 21 2006

with each function in turn, then using the 'Undo' function to return the image to its original state.

Figure 3.3.1 shows a Class 66 hauled liner train in the Wylye valley near Salisbury and the intention is to show the different effect of Photoshop's built-in automatic adjustment functions. The same original JPEG image was used for each of the four versions. The weather is hazy sun and the original image has rich flat colours that need

improvement by increasing the contrast slightly. 'Auto Levels' has given an image with a more blue colour balance and the sky is particularly blue, to the point where it is unrealistic. 'Auto contrast' has the same basic colour balance as the original and with more contrast. 'Auto Color correction' has created an image with a colder colour balance and less colour saturation.

Figure 3.3.2 also shows a liner, this time Class 90 hauled near Watford. The weather features high cloud causing the sun to be soft with an overall cool colour balance. The original JPEG image has good colours but overall is slightly flat. Auto Levels gives a pleasant blue sky and heavy shadows. Auto Contrast has increased the contrast everywhere while lightening the sky. Auto Color Correction is somewhere between the two.

Which is the best choice in the two examples? The author's experience is that 'Auto Levels' is the most likely to produce a pleasing result, but it is not effective every time. In these examples there is no single 'best' adjustment and all the alternatives have their strengths. Personal preference will be

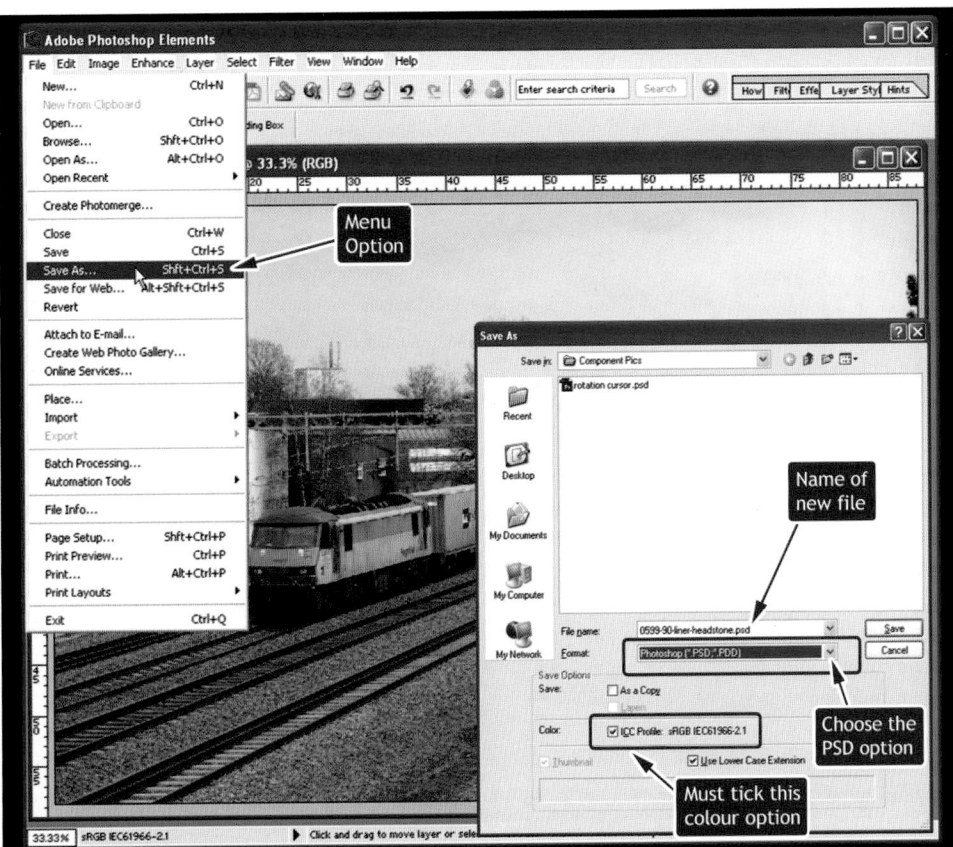

Figure 3.4.1.
Saving an image in Photoshop's PSD format.

the decider. The two lessons are: i) that it is always worth experimenting with the different options and doing an 'Undo' if the result is not to your liking; ii) making your own adjustments offers much more control.

● SAVING

Editing photos is usually with a goal in mind, either printing, display on the web or submission for publication. After improving contrast and cropping you have the choice of ploughing straight on or saving what you've done so far. Saving is a good idea because it means that if you have a problem later you can get back to this point rather than having to go all the way back to the start. Using Photoshop's own PSD format allows the picture content to be saved without throwing information away, particularly the various layers if dust has been covered by cloning. JPEG is not a good format for saving because it involves throwing away a lot of subtle information. Saving before cropping allows you to produce a version with a different crop

if needed in future. If the save was done after cropping, it would be necessary to go back to the start if the new crop needed to include a part of the image that had been cropped off first time round.

To start the Save, use the 'File → Save As...' menu option and a screen will appear giving various options. These are shown in Figure 3.4.1 with the important choices ringed in red. PSD format is chosen in the 'Format' box by clicking on the small downward arrowhead. Below this is a small tick box labelled 'ICC Profile' which should always be ticked. This area is explained in detail in Chapter 5. The name of the new file is put in the 'file name' box. Finally the 'Save' button is pressed to save the file.

● CROPPING

Many pictures benefit from cropping in order to improve the composition or correct mistakes. Photoshop contains an excellent 'Crop Tool', which simplifies the task by allowing the framing to be checked before

Figure 3.5.1.
Using the Crop Tool to
crop an image.

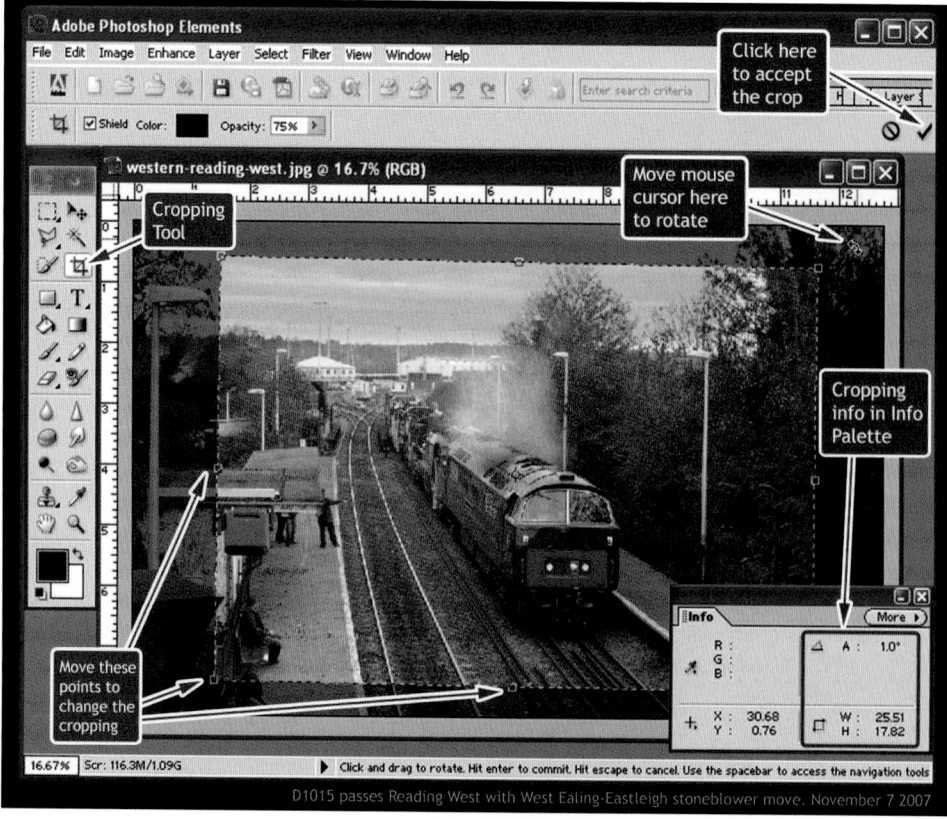

completing the crop. A 'wonky' image caused by having held the camera at an angle can easily be corrected. An alternative but less flexible method is to use the Rectangular Selection tool to select the area of the picture to be kept, followed by the 'Crop' command on the 'Select' menu. The Crop Tool is, as usual, available in the Tools Palette. Once you've chosen the Crop Tool, choose the basic framing by placing the mouse pointer on the picture in one corner, pressing and holding the left mouse button, then dragging the mouse to the opposite corner with the left mouse button still held down. The framing can be modified by clicking and dragging the side bars and rotated by clicking and dragging one of the corners. If the Info Palette is open it will show the size of the crop in various units. Displaying the crop in pixels can be very useful if you want to trim an image to an exact size to fit on a web page. Once you're happy with the crop, click the 'tick' which is at the top of the screen in most versions of Photoshop and Elements or at the bottom of the screen in recent versions of Elements. If you don't like it, click the 'cross'

or press the [Escape] key and all will be cancelled.

Figure 3.5.1 shows an image being cropped in Photoshop Elements 2.0 and includes the Info Palette in the lower right corner.

● SUMMARY – SEQUENCE

In summary, simple improvements are recommended to be done in a particular sequence:

● Put a copy of the image to be edited into the editing area
● Fix any dust spots
● Optionally adjust the colour and contrast
● Save to PSD format
● If you have more than one layer in the image, flatten the image to remove the layers
● Crop

Either:
Print the image or process for a web page as described in Chapter 4

Displaying pictures on Internet web sites is a popular part of the railway hobby. This chapter describes how to prepare an image for web display and shows examples. Those photographers who want to do the minimum amount necessary to put their pictures on the web without doing any editing should follow the techniques described here, while those who wish to edit their pictures can follow the techniques described in later sections of this book and return here for web preparation.

Web Images – the key points
When creating images for display on the web, everyone wants their web page to be popular with viewers, so it is good practice to:

● Crop any unnecessary material out of the picture and concentrate on the subject

● During cropping straighten the image if the camera was tilted when the shot was taken

● Ensure the image looks good with appropriate colour, brightness, contrast and sharpness

● Minimise the download time for the person viewing your web page

CHAPTER 4
PICTURES FOR
WEBSITES

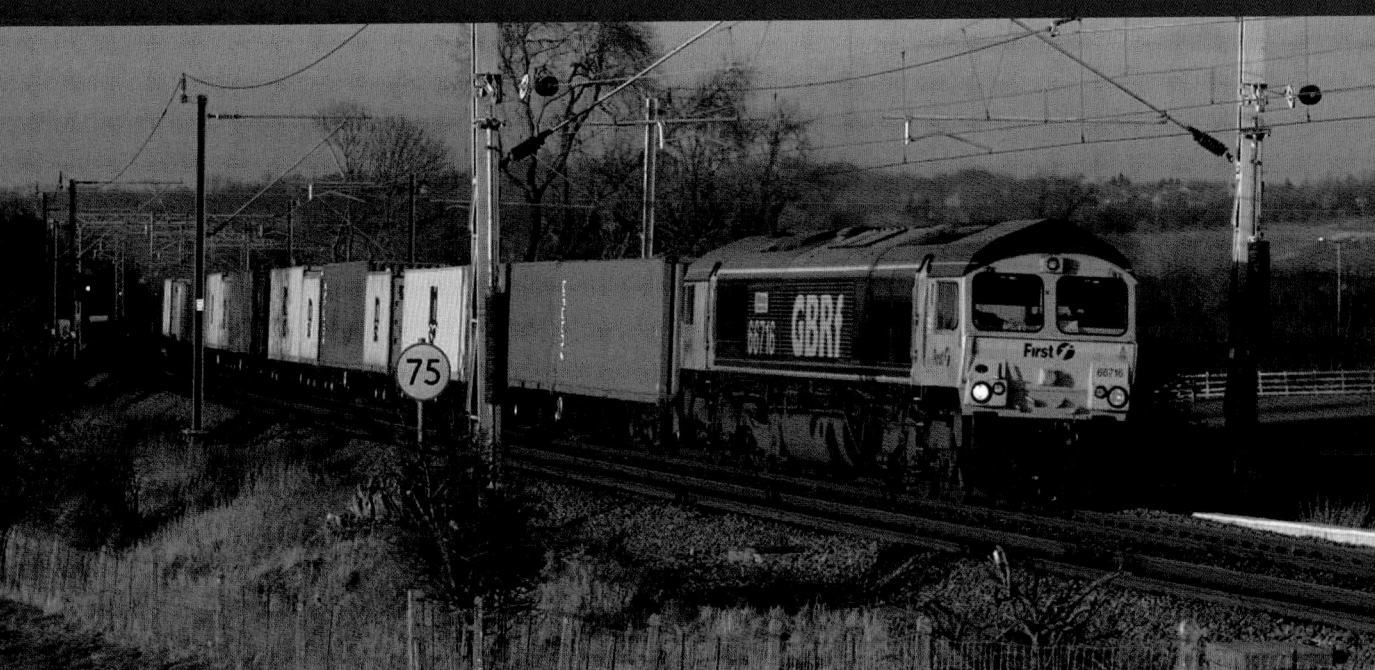

● CONSISTENT COLOUR

One of the areas least understood by photographers is how to ensure the colour of a web image will appear as intended when viewed on someone else's computer screen. This is one of the few areas in digital photography where there is a 'right' and 'wrong' method. Of course the way colours are displayed on someone else's computer is outside your control but at least the image can be created correctly.

Good practice involves calibrating your computer screen so that the colours look right and this is described in Chapter 1. If your screen is not calibrated there is the potential risk of making the colours look wrong when manipulating your pictures. To avoid this risk it's a good idea to avoid making anything more than small changes to the colour balance of an image during the editing process.

PCs and Macs are designed with a powerful capability in the software to ensure that colours are reproduced properly when images are created, viewed and updated. The general term for this is Colour Management. Working in a colour-managed system involves keeping to two simple rules: firstly that editing images involves working in a particular colour space, and secondly that all images created should have an embedded colour profile.

Colour Space

Photographers who wish to do the minimum amount of editing should set up Photoshop to use the best colour space for this approach, which is known technically as 'sRGB'. The setup is done only once and the necessary screen is accessed via the 'Edit → Color Settings...' menu option. Older versions of Photoshop Elements hide technical terms like 'sRGB' and use the

Figure 4.1.1.
Setting the colour settings in Photoshop Elements 2.0 and 5.0.

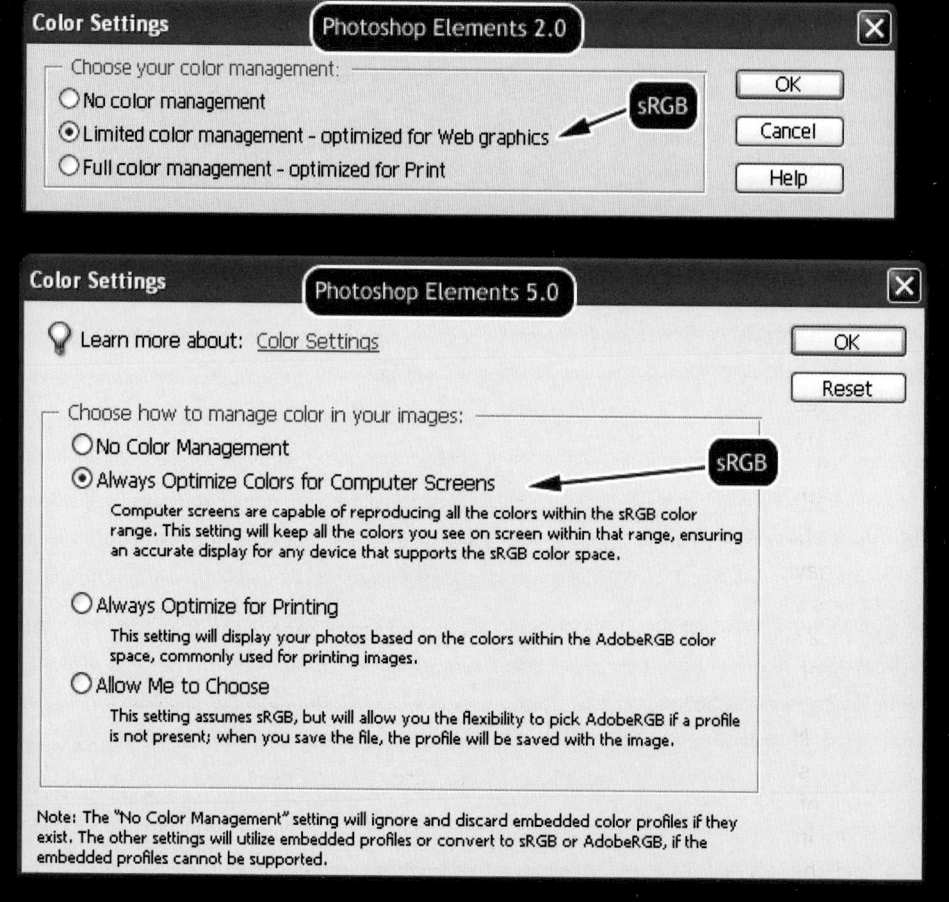

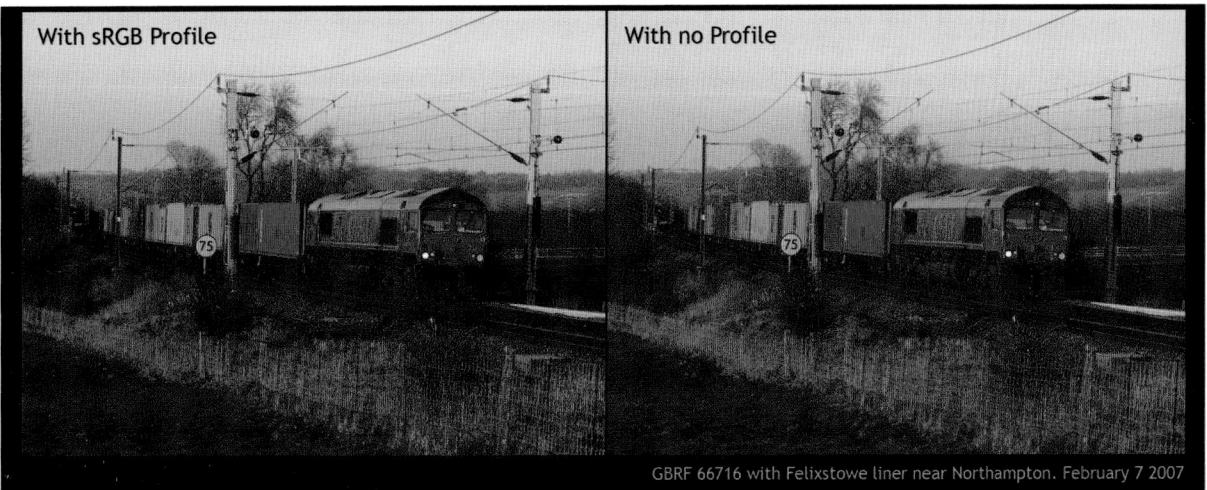

With sRGB Profile

With no Profile

GBRF 66716 with Felixstowe liner near Northampton. February 7 2007

label 'Limited color management'. Figure 4.1.1 shows how to set the right values in Photoshop Elements versions 2.0 and 5.0. Using just the sRGB colour space avoids the need to convert images between different colour spaces. Photographers who wish to get more deeply involved in editing and printing should follow the slightly different strategy described in Chapter 5, which uses another colour space.

Embedded Colour Profile

Images created for use on the web should always have an embedded colour profile of type 'sRGB'. There are other types of colour profile suitable for different circumstances and this area is explained in detail in Chapter 5. If an image doesn't have a sRGB colour profile some colours will appear weaker than they should when the image is viewed in a web browser such as Microsoft Internet Explorer, Apple Safari or Mozilla Firefox. If some other type of colour profile such as Adobe RGB is used the behaviour will be the same as if no profile was used.

Figure 4.1.2 shows the difference between two versions of the same image where the only difference is embedding a sRGB colour profile (or not). Note how the image on the left containing an sRGB colour profile captures the warmth of the late afternoon winter sunshine. The image on the right has lost the warmth and the colours are weaker. Some colours are affected more than others and

this image was chosen because the difference between the 'with profile' and 'without' versions are particularly noticeable.

● IMAGE ADJUSTMENTS

When preparing an image for the web the brightness and contrast often need to be adjusted. There are no particular tricks involved and the relevant techniques are described in Chapters 3 and 5 of this book. The brightness and contrast of an image should be adjusted so that it looks good on your monitor when viewed at the same size as it will appear on the web page. Any cropping and straightening is done using the Crop Tool as described in Chapter 3.

● MINIMISING DOWNLOAD TIME

When accessing a web page, no-one likes to wait a long time for the page to load and so image size should be kept small. Although more than half of the UK's computer users now have fast broadband connections the remainder are still using dialup modems: for them, images will take much longer to load (about 10 to 20 times longer than for those users with broadband connections).

There are several areas that influence the download time for an image: its dimensions, resolution and JPEG quality as described in the following sections.

Figure 4.1.2.
The effect on picture appearance caused by a missing sRGB colour profile.

Dimensions

Although new desktop computers have reasonable size screens – 17 inch or larger – there are many computer users with small screens – 15 inch or less – either because they have a small laptop or an older computer from the days when small screens were common. The web page should be designed so that it is easily read by someone with a small screen without having to do an excessive amount of scrolling. The height, width and position of each image needs to fit into the page layout. Although a web browser will resize an image automatically to fit the available space it's best to make an image the right size for its location in the first place.

Resolution and resizing

Computer screens are limited in the amount of detail they can display – much less than a print. If a JPEG format image is copied straight out of a camera on to a computer it will be too large to be displayed unchanged and any display program must reduce the size of the image to fit on the screen before it can display it. There is no point in loading an image with more detail than can be displayed on the screen as it just wastes download time and the web browser will have to do extra processing work when it resizes the image to fit the space. Generally speaking, all images must be resized before loading on to a web site although some photo web sites will do the resizing automatically. This automatic resizing may look worthwhile but in practice it has a couple of major disadvantages. Firstly a much larger image has to be loaded on to the web site before the resizing can take place and this takes much more time to load than a small image. Secondly it is not possible to apply sharpening after the resizing so the appearance of the image will be slightly softer.

What are the guidelines for resizing? To explain resizing the term 'resolution' needs to be introduced. The resolution of an image is a measure of the amount of detail it contains and is measured in pixels per inch (ppi). When preparing an image for display on the web it is normal practice to set the resolution to 72 pixels per inch (72 ppi). This is a figure that was agreed by the computer industry years ago and is the accepted value for displaying images on a screen. Strictly speaking it is not

Figure 4.3.1.
How to resize an image.

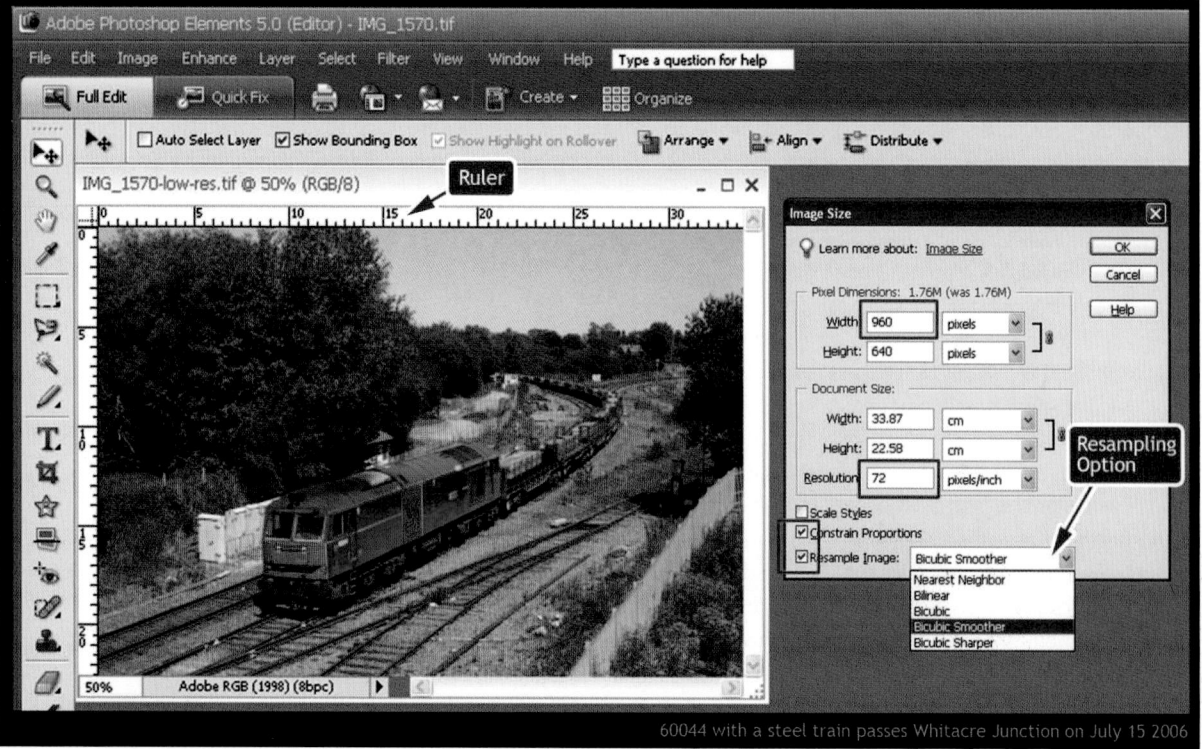

60044 with a steel train passes Whitacre Junction on July 15 2006

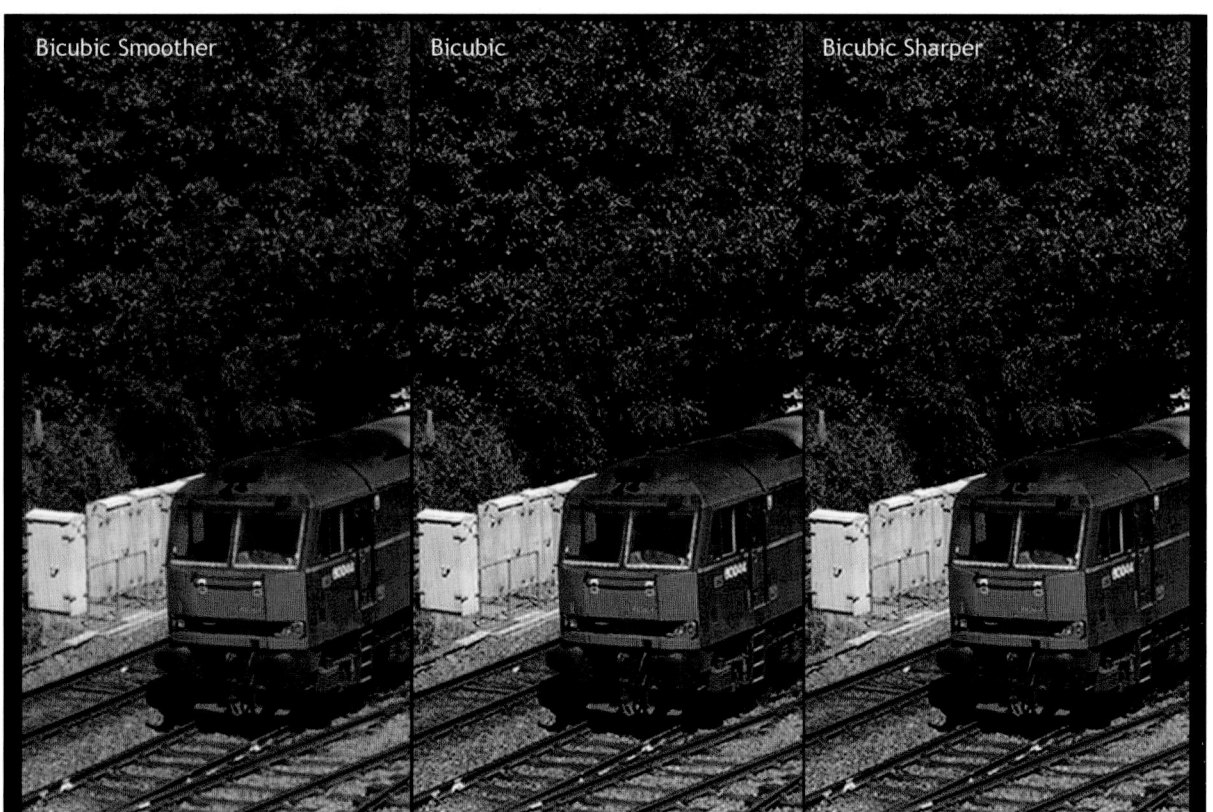

Bicubic Smoother   Bicubic   Bicubic Sharper

necessary to set the resolution to 72 ppi because the resolution setting is ignored by web browsers but when the value is set the rulers optionally displayed by Photoshop will show the dimensions of the image in inches (or centimetres) and serve as a guide to its size on the web page.

The important point here is that by resizing an image straight out of a camera to 72 ppi and fixing its dimensions to, for example 8in wide by 6in high, detail will be removed from the image and it will be much smaller, which speeds up the downloading process.

Figure 4.3.1 demonstrates an image of a Class 60 on a steel train being resized for the web. Values that need to be entered have been ringed in red. In this case the size of the image has been specified as 960 pixels wide rather than a dimension in inches. With the 72 ppi value for the resolution having been set, the rulers give a rough indication of the final size in inches of the image on a screen.

Experienced web site designers resize images to dimensions in pixels, not inches or cm because the design of a web site often standardises on a particular image size. For example 800 pixels wide in a 'Gallery' section. Recommended maximum sizes (approximate) are 1000 pixels wide for a 'landscape' format image and 800 pixels high for a 'portrait' format image. This ensures images will fit on to most screens without needing too much scrolling or resizing.

Resampling

When an image is resized a process called resampling takes place. Different mathematical options can be chosen for the resizing and the available options vary according to the version of Photoshop. All versions have Nearest Neighbour and Bilinear which are basic and not recommended. All versions also have Bicubic which is versatile and works fairly well. Recent versions of Elements and full Photoshop have additional options – Bicubic Smoother and Bicubic Sharper. The differences between the variations of Bicubic are small but visible. Figure 4.3.2 compares them with enlarged sections of the same original image. Bicubic Sharper, as its name

Figure 4.3.2.
Comparing image appearance after applying different resampling options to the same original image.

Figure 4.5.1.

Demonstrating how a lower quality JPEG setting impacts image appearance.

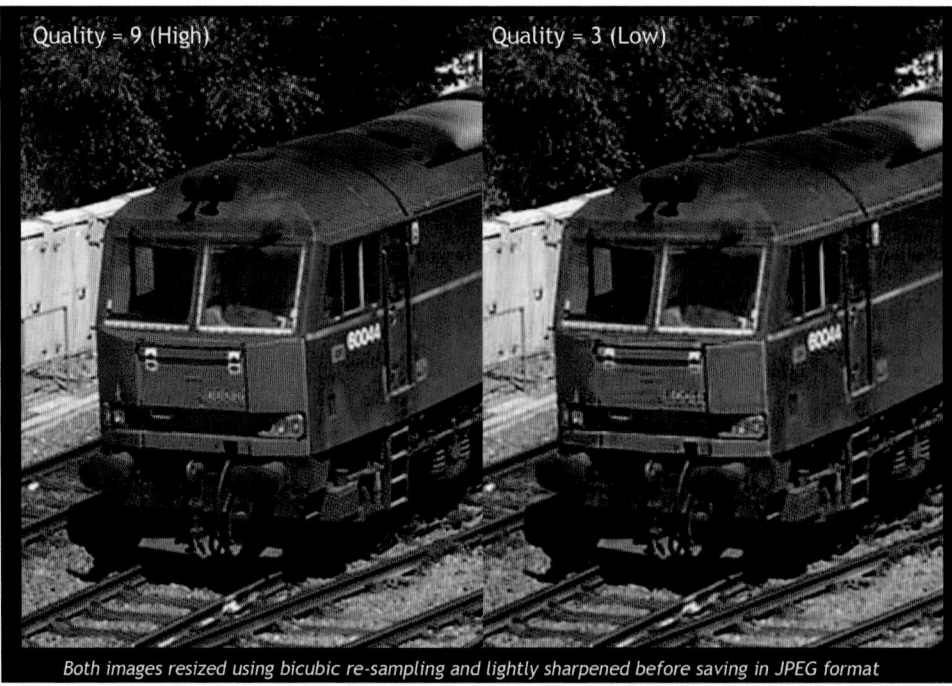

Quality = 9 (High)   Quality = 3 (Low)

Both images resized using bicubic re-sampling and lightly sharpened before saving in JPEG format

suggests, produces a result that appears sharper than the others but has the downside that fine areas of detail such as the trees in this image look slightly over-sharpened. Bicubic Smoother looks a little soft but light sharpening cleans it up nicely. Bicubic also sharpens nicely. There is no 'right' answer for which one is best - personal preference will play a major part. The key message is that the resampling options do produce noticeably different results and photographers should compare them to decide which they prefer.

● SHARPENING

All digital images need sharpening. JPEG format images created by the camera are sharpened during the creation process. When a Raw format image is created in the camera no sharpening is applied. The sharpening takes place during the Raw conversion stage on a computer when the Raw format image is processed.

A simple strategy is to apply a medium amount of sharpening either during the in-camera JPEG creation process or during the Raw conversion stage so that the image looks reasonably sharp when displayed on the screen at the intended final size. Over-sharpening should be avoided.

After an image has been resized it needs sharpening. This is a knock-on effect of removing detail and means that every image is being sharpened twice – a medium amount when it is created and then a light touch after resizing. The image should be sharpened so that it looks fine to your eyes when viewed at full size as intended on the web page. Another way to describe the size is viewing at 100%, or to view 'Actual Pixels'. If in any doubt as to how much sharpening to apply, it is best to under-sharpen rather than overdo it.

There are many tools available to do the sharpening and a simple way is to use the confusingly-named 'Unsharp Mask' function built into Photoshop. After choosing this menu option a small screen will appear that contains three controls: Amount, Radius and Threshold. The amount of sharpening needed after resizing depends on the initial sharpness of the image, its size, the resizing option used and personal preference. Try using the following values as a starting point and experiment with different amounts to develop your favourite settings: Amount 35%; Radius 1.0; Threshold 4.

More comprehensive information on sharpening is given in Chapter 5.

● JPEG Quality

JPEG format should always be used for image display on the web since this is the global standard and is efficient in its use of storage space. When creating a JPEG format image its quality level can be varied. By choosing a lower 'quality' the file size can be reduced but with the penalty of introducing unpleasant distortion in the picture known as JPEG artifacts. The higher the desired image quality the larger the file size and hence the longer the download time. With a smaller image size a slightly lower quality setting can be chosen than with a large image because the compromises and quality degradation will be less visible in a small image. Low JPEG quality settings should be avoided.

To demonstrate the visual damage caused by a low quality JPEG setting Figure 4.5.1 shows enlarged versions of the same image converted to JPEG format in high quality (9) and low quality (3) forms. On the low quality image the locomotive numbers are harder to read. A bigger problem is strange coloured shapes in various places in the blue body area behind the cab door caused by the JPEG compression.

● CREATING THE JPEG-FORMAT IMAGE

To create the final JPEG file there are two different options. The first uses the 'File → Save As...' option in Photoshop while the second uses the 'Save for Web...' option to perform the resizing and JPEG creation in one operation. The 'Save for Web' option is not recommended for best quality results because it does not permit any sharpening after resizing.

Figure 4.6.1.
Saving an image in JPEG format.

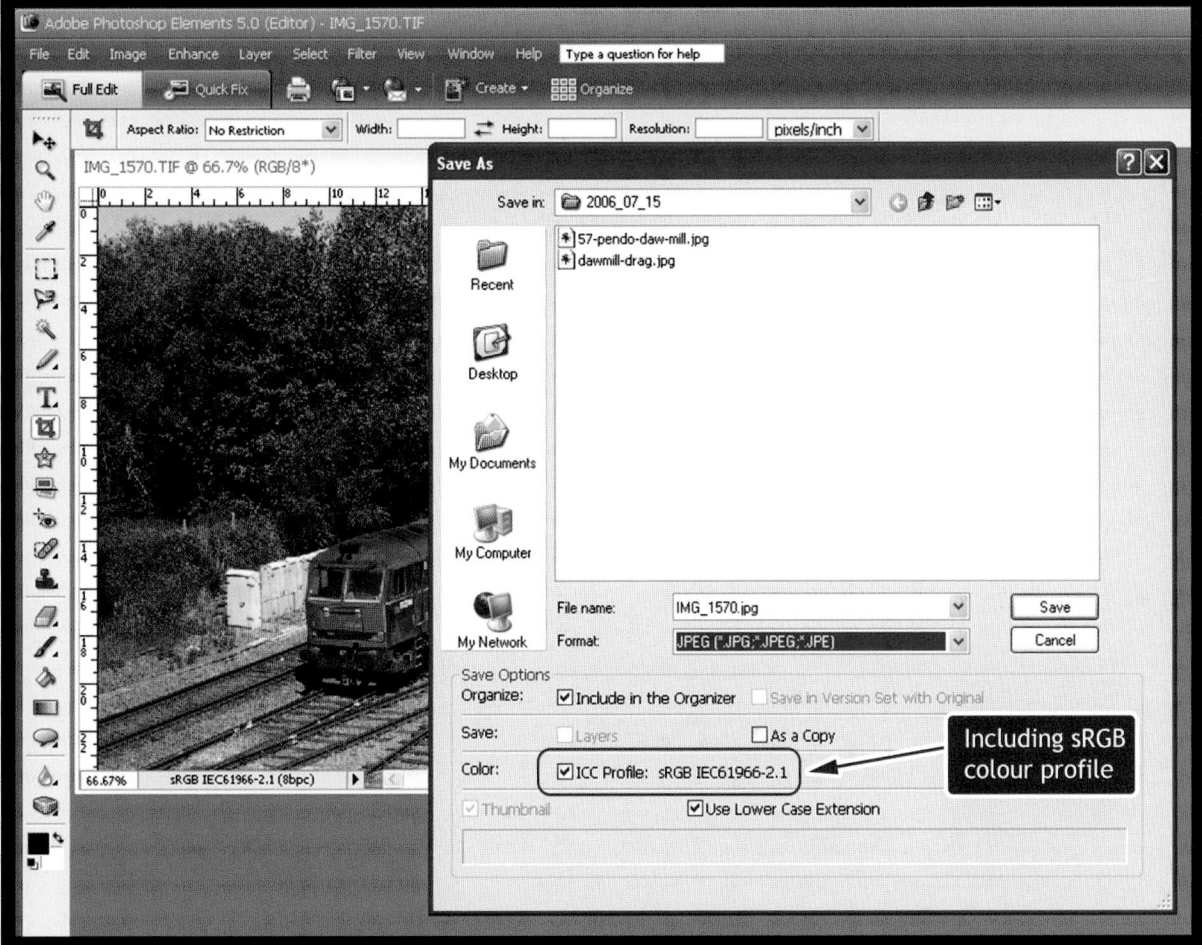

When using the 'File → Save As...' menu option in both full Photoshop and Elements an important point is to be sure that the 'ICC Profile' box is ticked so that an sRGB profile is included with the image as described earlier in this chapter. Failing to tick this box is a common mistake and the result is that the image has weak colours when displayed in a web browser. Figure 4.6.1 shows this option with the 'ICC Profile' box ringed in red and ticked.

● PHOTO WEB SITES

There are many web sites on the Internet that allow free display of photo collections. Instead of charging a fee, advertising appears on the web pages, which can be off-putting, while some sites provide an optional paid-for service that does not have advertising.

It's not practical to describe the photo web sites themselves (for example fotopic.net or flickr.com) as web site details change frequently.

Most internet providers offer web space as an inclusive part of a broadband or dialup Internet package. Photographers can create their own web sites and load them into the web space for no additional cost. While there is more work and technical skill involved in creating a web site from scratch, with modern web site packages it is reasonably straightforward and has the benefit of much more flexibility than when using a commercial photo site.

small improvements. The sum of several small improvements usually adds up to more of an improvement than you might expect. Consequently it's easy to spend a lot of time adjusting a picture and judgement needs to be exercised on when to stop improving. By far the most common improvement is increasing the contrast. This and a handful of other simple techniques will deliver most of the improvements you need. All the essential techniques are described in this Chapter.

CHAPTER 5
ESSENTIAL
TECHNIQUES

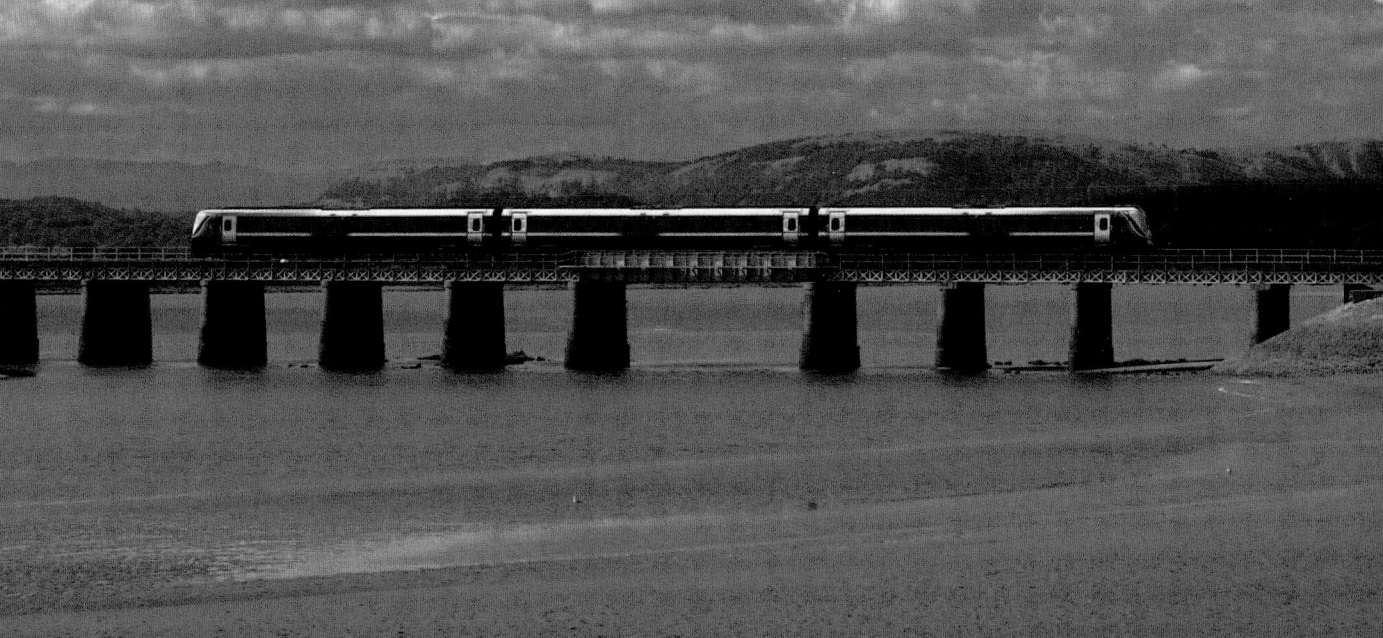

● EDITING PRINCIPLES

Before describing editing techniques, a few words about the key editing principle used throughout this book. Information in images will not be changed or deleted until the final stages of the editing process. At first sight this sounds to be a contradiction. How can you edit an image if you don't change any information in it? And why is this principle important?

First, answering the question 'Why?' By following this principle you can be sure of getting the best possible quality. Just as important is the potential time saving: provided work is saved at the right point, if you need to make changes to an image in future it is possible to pick up where you left off previously and to make further changes without compromising quality or having to restart the editing process from scratch. Most of the creative part of the editing process involves selecting areas of the image and adjusting brightness, contrast and colour. This is achieved by using a feature of Photoshop called Adjustment Layers: when these are used, information is only added, never changed or removed from the original image. The settings used for any adjustment are saved and can be varied at any point until the final image is created by removing the layers in a process known as 'Flattening'.

Of course a picture has to be cropped, thereby removing information – and the sharpening process does alter information. So these stages are done last after flattening. In the early stages of the editing process the use of adjustment layers ensures that information is only ever added and the original image is never changed.

Working on a Copy

It's important to always work on a copy of the original image. If this isn't done it is possible to update the original image and lose its original state. Technically this is known as overwriting. Potentially the image could be ruined. For example, suppose that you crop a signal out of a picture and save it in a way that overwrites the original. Then later you change your mind and decide that you want the signal

in the picture after all. Unfortunately this will not be possible because the original was overwritten and the 'with signal' version of the shot has been lost forever. One other way around this problem is to always take copies of images as soon as they are loaded on to the computer in a process known as backups or archiving as described in Chapter 1. Every photographer should be rigorous about making backup copies to avoid losing pictures.

A simple way to enforce this is to have separate areas on your PC for storage of 'Master' images and for editing. When working on an image the first step is to put a copy of it in the editing area.

Editing Sequence

The general sequence for editing images is shown below:

- Put a copy of the master image into the editing area.
- If working on a Raw format image convert the Raw image into a format that can be edited
- Open the image in Photoshop
- Repair any image faults such as dust, unwanted birds and pieces of litter
- Optionally save the image in Photoshop PSD format
- Adjust the contrast and brightness using Adjustment Layers
- If necessary adjust the colour balance
- Save the image again in Photoshop's.PSD format
- Crop the image and straighten if necessary
- If creating a web image, resize to suit the dimensions of the web page and change the resolution to 72ppi
- Sharpen to suit use on the web or printing as appropriate
- If intended for the web save in JPEG format
- If intended for printing, save in TIFF format

Extra steps may be needed when using some of the specialised techniques described later in this chapter but the editing sequence will always be broadly the same. Saving part way through the editing process provides protection against problems later on. For example the computer might crash or very occasionally the photo editor might lock up. A power cut might interrupt working. Saving ensures that only a small amount of work is lost after a crash rather than losing all of it. The photo editing software's own format will normally be using for saving, which for Photoshop means a format called PSD.

● CONSISTENT COLOUR – COLOUR MANAGEMENT

The main reason for doing any image editing is to ensure that your images look their best, whether printed or displayed on a web site. For the final image to look good requires careful adjustments to enhance the colour, brightness, contrast and sharpness of the original image. Whenever colour is displayed, printed or manipulated there is the potential for unwanted changes to occur. The subject called Colour Management was invented to ensure consistency of colour right through the entire process of taking, processing, viewing and printing colour images. For Colour Management to work correctly the settings at each major stage in the editing process must be right and consequently an understanding of the basics of colour management is essential when working with digital images. If the settings are wrong somewhere, unforeseen difficulties can occur and it can be hard to track down the cause.

Colour Management, Colour Spaces and Colour Profiles

By using colour management in every stage of the editing process unwanted colour shifts can be avoided. Images are intended to be viewed, manipulated or printed in a particular colour space and they have a colour profile embedded in them which corresponds to the colour space. The term colour profile is also known as an 'ICC profile'. There are a handful of widely used colour spaces, each intended for different uses.

The most commonly used colour space is known as 'sRGB' and most photographers use this without realising it. The sRGB colour space was designed for viewing images on a computer screen and its main advantage is that it is widely used. Web browsers such as Internet Explorer or Mozilla Firefox will display the colours of an image correctly when it contains an sRGB profile. The disadvantage of sRGB is that it was not intended for printing images and there are certain colours it cannot display. To overcome the limitations of sRGB, Adobe invented the 'Adobe RGB (1998)' colour space, which can contain a wider range of colours and is widely used for photo editing and printing. (It will be abbreviated to 'Adobe RGB' from here onwards). Because there are certain colours that even Adobe RGB can't display, colour spaces with a wider capability were invented, the two best known being Wide Gamut RGB and ProPhoto RGB. Both these colour spaces are intended to display the widest possible range of colours, and are so wide that some of their colours cannot be displayed on a screen or printed.

When shooting in JPEG or Tiff format, digital cameras will normally embed an sRGB colour profile in the image. Some SLRs can optionally be set to create images with an embedded 'Adobe RGB' colour profile. When shooting in Raw format the colour settings on the camera are irrelevant because the desired colour space is chosen during the Raw conversion stage.

As a general principle, recommended practice when manipulating an image is to start in the right colour space and stay with it until doing any conversions at the latest possible stage. Full Photoshop has a function to convert an image to any other colour space when necessary. Photoshop Elements is more limited and versions earlier than 4.0 do not allow any colour space conversions. Newer versions only allow conversion between sRGB and AdobeRGB.

What Colour Space should I use?

Choosing the best colour space depends on several factors – whether shooting JPEG or Raw, what you wish to do with your finished pictures, how much effort you want to put into photo editing and whether you have full

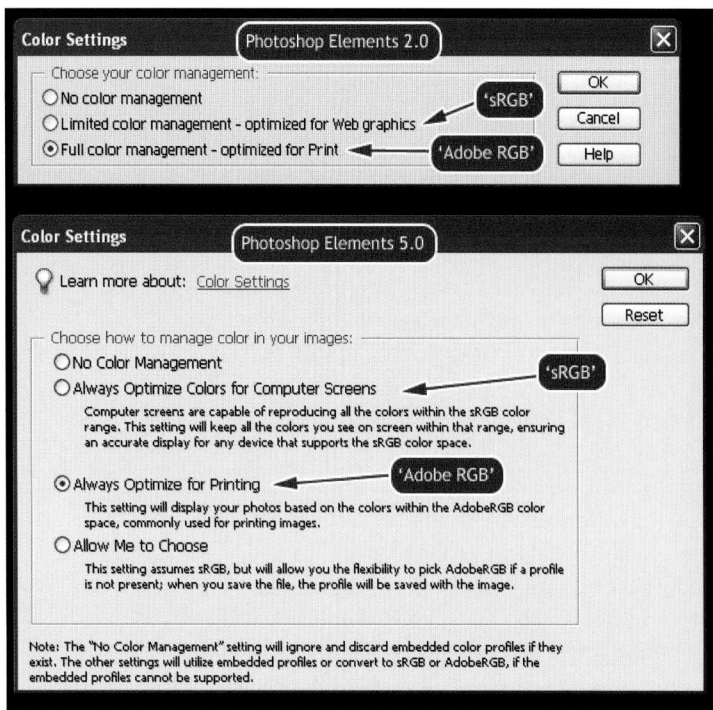

Figure 5.2.1.
Recommended colour setup for Photoshop Elements.

Photoshop or Photoshop Elements as your editing program.

Those who want to keep things simple should use sRGB colour space. This applies to those who shoot in JPEG format and to those who shoot in Raw format and are content with simple photo editing. This option will be very suitable for creating photos for web display and fairly suitable for printing.

Those who strive for good quality results and want to edit their pictures should chose Adobe RGB colour space. By shooting in Raw format the colour space can be chosen during the Raw conversion process. Adobe RGB colour space is used for general photo manipulation and colour printing and, when creating images for display on the web, images are converted to sRGB during the final stage of processing. Because older versions of Photoshop Elements cannot do a colour space conversion, users are recommended to upgrade to Version 5.0 or newer. For those who have an older version of Photoshop Elements it is possible to work around the limitation with web images by generating an image in sRGB colour space during the Raw conversion process, then editing throughout in sRGB colour space before saving for the web.

A disadvantage of using Adobe RGB is that only 'publishing' type programs such as Photoshop can interpret an Adobe RGB colour profile. Viewing programs like web browsers, Irfanview and the Windows Picture Viewer can only interpret sRGB colour profiles and ignore every other type. This can cause trouble when viewing an image with an Adobe RGB colour profile in a web browser. It will have weak colours because it is treated in the same way as if it had no colour profile.

Railway photography involves capturing images of trains and recording their colours accurately. Modern liveries have a much wider range of colours than were used in the past and this leads to a difficulty because some colours used cannot be recorded by the sRGB and Adobe RGB colour spaces and need wider colour spaces like Wide Gamut RGB or ProPhoto RGB. This is recommended only for experienced workers and is covered in Chapters 6 and 7.

Setting up Photoshop's Colour Management

Photoshop needs to be set up with your choice of colour space. This is something that is normally only done once, after installing the software and before using it the first time. To access the setup screen in both full Photoshop and Elements, choose the 'Edit → Color Settings...' menu option. In full Photoshop set the desired colour space such as 'sRGB' or 'Adobe RGB (1998)' according to the recommendation in the previous section. Older versions of Photoshop Elements try to avoid using technical language and use terms like 'Limited Color Management' when they mean 'sRGB' and 'Full color management' when they mean 'Adobe RGB'. The best setting for most Elements users is 'Limited Color Management' (actually sRGB colour space).

Those with full Photoshop are recommended to set other options as shown so that it will warn if there is a mismatch between the type of colour profile in an image and your preferred colour space, or if the colour profile is missing. The benefit of this is avoiding propagating mistakes.

The recommended settings for both full Photoshop and Photoshop Elements are shown in Figure 5.2.1 and 5.2.2.

● PREPARING THE PHOTOSHOP WORKSPACE

Before doing any editing work in Photoshop it is worth spending a small amount of time preparing the editing environment. Colour settings are the most important settings because these ensure consistent colour and were described in the previous section.

Palettes

There are many small displays known as 'Palettes' which show useful information that is not available elsewhere. They also provide buttons for accessing useful functions. In most cases the information shown in a particular palette is not available elsewhere from other menus. When closed down, Photoshop remembers the position of all the palettes for the next editing session.

Each photographer will develop their own preferences and it is worth trying out all the Palettes. They are opened via the 'Window' menu by clicking on the relevant option. The author has found the most useful palettes to be: Tools, Layers, History, Info, Brushes, Histogram and in full Photoshop only, Channels. These are now described.

Tools Palette

The Tools Palette is the most important of all the palettes because it is where the current working tool is chosen. It is difficult to work in Photoshop without this palette being visible.

Layers

The Layers Palette is the next most important palette because layers are fundamental to editing. It shows all the layers in their top-to-bottom sequence.

History / Undo History

This palette lists all editing steps in sequence and a new line is entered every time an editing step is made on an image. If

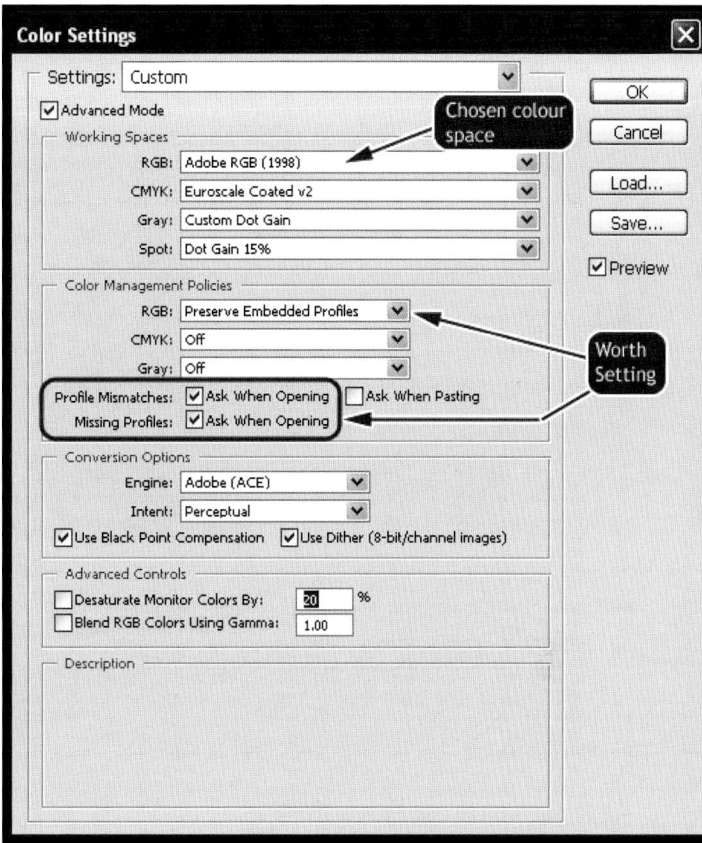

you make a mistake or change your mind during editing it is easy to reverse (undo) any changes by clicking on the relevant line(s) in the palette. The steps are only saved during the current editing session and the History for a particular image is cleared when the image is closed. Having this palette open is essential for being able to accurately step backwards through changes. Saving the History steps can use a lot of memory and lead to Photoshop slowing down during a long editing session. Ways around this are to close the image and re-open it or to clear the history, provided that the steps are no longer wanted.

Info

The Info palette displays information about the pixel underneath the mouse pointer at any time. It can be customised to display one of several different sets of information. The most useful show the Red, Green and Blue values for the pixel, plus its brightness value (K). Another area of the display will show the size of the current crop or selection, which

Figure 5.2.2.
Recommended colour setup for full Photoshop.

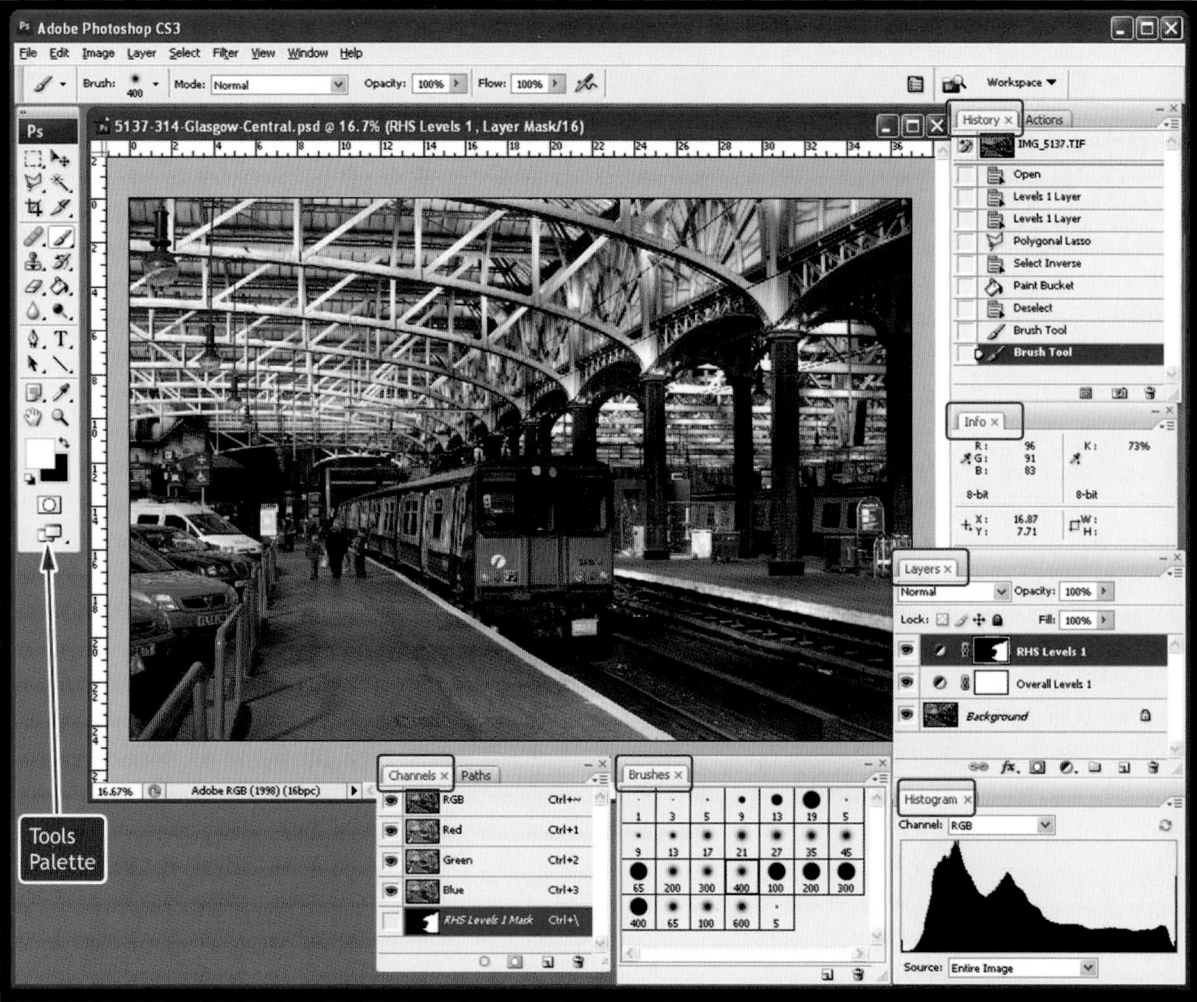

Figure 5.3.1. **Setting up the workspace in Photoshop CS3 ready for an editing session.**

can be useful when trying to create a crop of a particular size.

Histogram

As its name suggest this palette displays the histogram for an image and is useful for checking that the range of contrast is as wide as it needs to be. A practical limitation is that the display is often out-of-date and needs to be refreshed by clicking on it. Older versions of Photoshop Elements do not have this palette.

Brushes

Much work in Photoshop involves editing masks by painting on a mask using an appropriate brush. Masks are described later in this Chapter. A quick way to choose the right brush is to have a small set with different sizes and hardness saved. Full

Photoshop has a Brush Palette that can be permanently displayed while in Elements brushes are managed by the Preset Manager, which can only be displayed temporarily.

Channels (full Photoshop only)

The most useful feature of the Channels Palette is the ability to make a mask visible by clicking on it in the palette.

Example

Figure 5.3.1 shows a typical image editing session in Photoshop CS3 with all the useful palettes open and their names ringed in red. The palettes in Photoshop Elements are similar. It's easy to see that the screen is cluttered with palettes leaving only a small amount of space for the image itself. The benefit of using a much larger monitor or a multiple monitor setup is that these palettes can be put in their own area away from the main picture to leave a clear space for editing the image.

● IMPROVING THE CONTRAST

By far the most common improvement in image editing is to increase the contrast and the majority of images will benefit from even a small increase. Contrast is increased using the 'Levels' adjustment function, which is not obvious given that a 'Brightness / Contrast' adjustment function is also available. Understanding the principles of the histogram, described in Chapter 2, is important for understanding this subject.

Figure 5.4.1 shows a Class 86 hauled liner train near Northampton. The original photograph was taken on a sunny evening when the light had gone soft due to typical summer haze. As a result the image is lacking in contrast. There are no obvious faults with the image which need to be repaired first. Although Raw format was used for the original image the principles and technique used here apply equally to Raw or JPEG format.

What we're trying to achieve

When improving the contrast the intention is to adjust the image so that its histogram is as wide as possible but not so wide that information gets lost or colours distorted. For best appearance and general clarity an image should contain brightness values (Levels) all the way from 0 to 255, that is, from full black to full white. The histogram should extend from one side to the other but should have only a small number of pixels at the extreme left and right ends. In the original image the flat appearance meant the brightness values only went part way across – from approximately 14 to 230 in this case. The range can be widened by adjusting the Levels with a 'Levels Adjustment Layer'. This is done in either Photoshop or Photoshop Elements by opening the image and then choosing the menu option: 'Layer → New Adjustment Layer → Levels...'. A small screen gives the opportunity to change the name of the new layer from 'Levels 1' and it is probably best to rename it 'Overall Levels' to reflect the intended result which is to adjust the Levels across the whole image. After clicking 'OK' a small screen will appear containing a histogram, which gives the opportunity to make adjustments. This is shown in Figure 5.4.2.

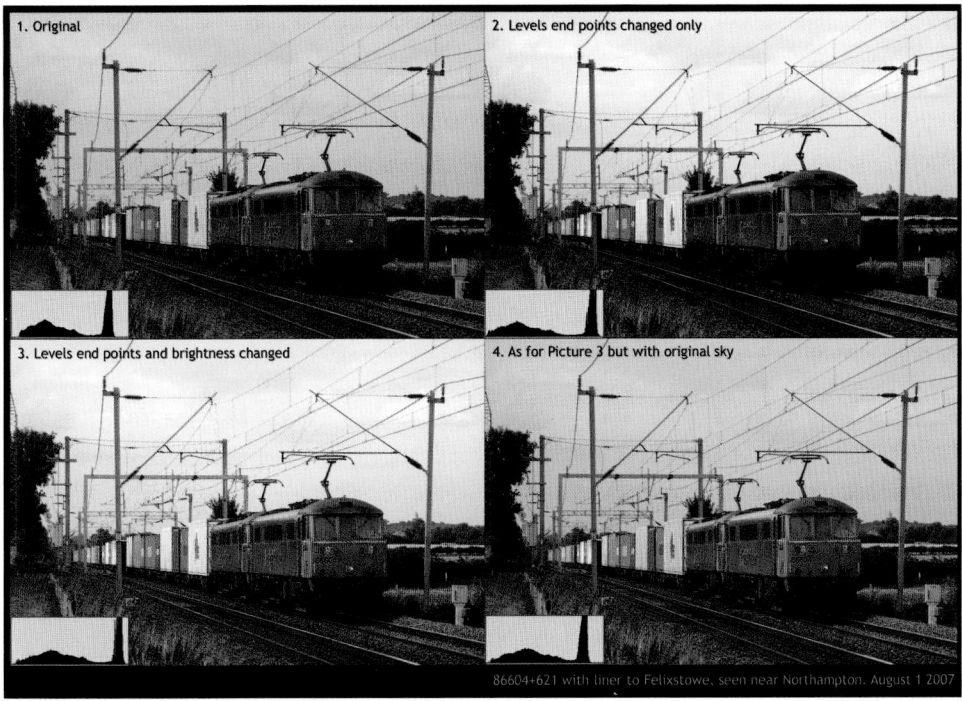

Figure 5.4.1. **Different stages during Levels Adjustment and showing the histogram.**

1. Original
2. Levels end points changed only
3. Levels end points and brightness changed
4. As for Picture 3 but with original sky

86604+621 with liner to Felixstowe, seen near Northampton. August 1 2007

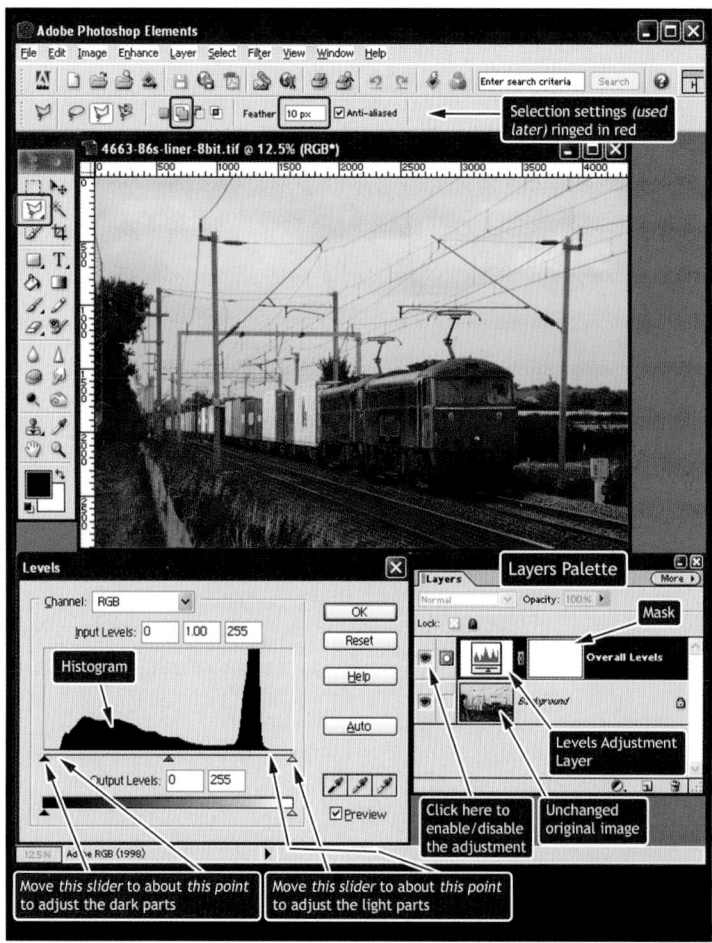

Figure 5.4.2.
Preparing to make the first Levels Adjustment.

Adjusting the Levels

The Levels are adjusted using the two small triangular sliders at the sides – shown in Figure 5.4.2 by the red arrows. The left triangle is moved to the right to darken the picture and stopped at the point shown so that the triangle meets the edge of the histogram. If the 'Preview' box has a tick mark showing, the effect of the change on the image will be visible. Similarly on the right side the triangle is moved to the left to the point where the edge of the histogram meets

Quick Zoom

Often it's useful when editing to enlarge the picture to check some details (ie Zoom In) and then zoom out again to get an overall view. Both Photoshop and Elements have useful keyboard shortcuts to make this zooming process quick. Press the [Ctrl] and [+] keys together to zoom in, and the [Ctrl] and [-] keys together to zoom out.

the base. What is being done here, in effect, is to stretch the histogram to meet the left and right sides; Photoshop adjusts the levels appropriately. Sometimes the image will now appear too light or too dark: in this case it is slightly too dark. By moving the middle triangle the brightness can be adjusted and is moved until the appearance looks right to the eye. When happy with the appearance of the image click 'OK'.

Checking the Results

The human eye quickly adapts to a change in appearance and so it's worthwhile doing a 'before' and 'after' comparison to check that the adjustment does actually improve the image. A benefit of using Adjustment Layers is that this comparison is quick and easy. To disable the adjustment, go to the Layers palette and click on the 'eye' symbol as shown. When the eye disappears, the 'Levels' adjustment is disabled. Click again to enable the change. If you don't like the appearance you can easily change it by altering the settings on the Adjustment Layer. To do this, double-click the 'graph' icon on the Adjustment Layer named in this case 'Overall Levels' in the Layers Palette. The 'Levels' screen will be opened again and allows changes to the settings by moving the triangles.

Having reached this point the work should be saved in the Editing area by using the 'Save As' option on the 'File' menu to avoid overwriting the file containing the original image. Save the file in Photoshop's own 'PSD' format because this will ensure all the layers are saved to allow changes later.

Why use so much effort?

Having completed this first stage it's easy to wonder why it's worth bothering with the effort involved in Adjustment Layers. Why not just edit the image directly by using basic enhancements? The answer is straightforward – it's due to following the editing principle described at the beginning of this chapter. The principle allows the image to be updated as many times as desired both now and in the future without compromising image quality.

During an image editing session it is a good idea to take short breaks away from the computer to give your eyes a rest because the eyes can compensate for a particular adjustment and it is easy to make an editing change which is too large. Often after returning from a break you'll find you need to slightly re-do something. Using Adjustment Layers ensures that any change is easy to make and that you never lose information from the image or compromise quality.

Considering the Sky

Quality conscious photographers should always pay close attention to the sky and ensure it captures the atmosphere at the time of shooting with realistic colours and brightness. Looking at this image after adjusting the Levels, the sky is too light and lacks tone. It's not a major problem and can be improved fairly easily in one of several different ways. In this case the original unadjusted sky captures the look of a hazy summer sky and the simplest approach is to cancel the Levels Adjustment in the sky area only so that it has the appearance of the original sky.

Mask

A piece of useful background information is that when an Adjustment Layer is created, a 'mask' is automatically created with it. A mask is potentially very useful because it allows the changes due to the Adjustment Layer to be applied to some parts of the picture and not others. This is ideal for correcting the appearance of the sky as described in the previous paragraph.

How does a mask work? It's easiest to explain this using an analogy. Many readers will be railway modellers or have built models in the past. Suppose you were building a model of a Class 47 locomotive in retro rail blue livery and wanted to use a spray gun to apply the paint in a nice thin, even covering. You could spray the whole body in rail blue first, then spray just the ends with 'warning panel' yellow. How would you ensure that the yellow paint went just on the ends, not the sides, and had a smooth

border edge around the cab area? The answer is that you would use masking tape or similar to cover up the rail blue areas where you didn't want the yellow paint, and leave uncovered just the ends where the yellow paint should go. In this example the tape acts as a mask. After running the spray gun to apply the paint you would have yellow paint on the ends and tape, with untouched blue paint underneath the tape (mask). The analogy with Photoshop is very close: you create a mask in black on the Mask part of the layer to cover up the areas where you don't want an adjustment to apply. Where the mask is blank/white the adjustment will take effect. A slight difference with the modelmaking analogy is that a Photoshop mask allows a gradual transition from 'no effect' to 'full effect' so if the mask is 20% white for instance (so mask has a shade of grey) the adjustment will be 20% effective.

To correct the sky by restoring its original appearance as described earlier requires the Levels Adjustment to be cancelled in the sky area only. The principle to be used is to select the area which is going to be masked and the selection is complete it will be filled in with black 'paint'.

So that the boundary between adjusted and non-adjusted areas is not obvious the boundary will be extended to the trees and parts of the train. Black paint will be applied to the mask belonging to the Levels Adjustment area in the sky area. This could be done simply by using the Brush Tool but would be time consuming and a simpler way is to use a Selection because it is easy to control the position of a selection.

Introduction to Selecting

When making these changes the aim is to create an improvement that is undetectable by the viewer. Or put another way, what isn't wanted is an improvement that stands out from the rest of the picture and the overall appearance is worse than before. The way areas are selected for change is key to this because the boundaries between changed and untouched areas should be invisible.

When creating a selection a 'hard' edge might be needed for a clear distinction

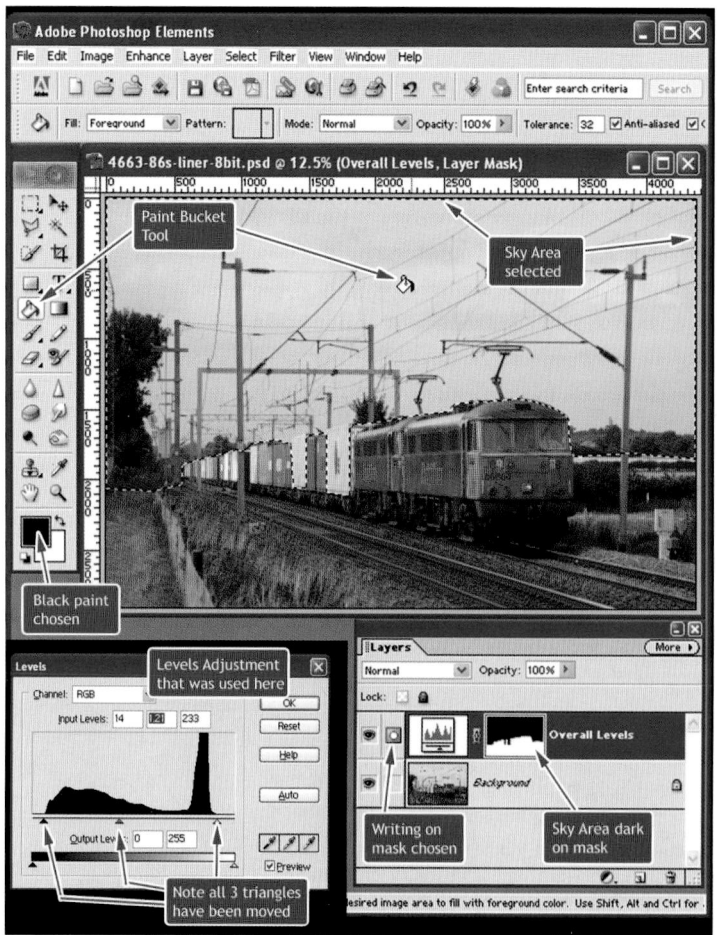

Figure 5.4.3.
Cancelling the Levels Adjustment in the sky by painting the mask.

Selection Tools

Photoshop has various different selection tools that could potentially be use to create the desired selection. There is no single 'right' answer when creating selections as the choice involves personal preference and a trade-off of speed against accuracy. The use of Selection Tools is sufficiently important that it will be covered again later in this chapter. With this image the selection can be created with a few straight lines, so the Polygonal Lasso Tool is a suitable choice.

Selection tools are chosen from the Tools Palette. There are several selection tools sharing the same position on the Palette. By positioning the mouse pointer over the selection tools (ringed in red in Figure 5.4.2) and clicking the right mouse button, a small menu will pop up to allow the preferred tool to be chosen by clicking on it with the left mouse button. Each tool has its own icon.

Sky Selection

The soft edge to the selection in this example is achieved by setting the 'feather' value to about 10 pixels. The selection settings are shown at the top of the Levels adjustment screenshot in Figure 5.4.2. Selecting the sky involves clicking the left mouse button to create a series of points below the horizon, along the trees and grass and the locomotive roofs. The white containers in the train would benefit from slight darkening so the selection follows their edge to include them. If a mistake is made, pressing the [Delete] key deletes the most recent point. To include the whole sky, the mouse is clicked with the pointer outside the picture area. Once the selection has gone all the way round the sky area, it needs to be completed by joining its beginning and end. This is done by double-clicking the left mouse button or pressing the [Enter] key. If the selection unexpectedly disappears, pressing the [Escape] key makes it appear again. The selected area will be surrounded with a moving black and white dashed border which is sometimes known as the 'marching ants'.

between where the selection begins and ends. Normally this will be used where there is a distinct edge between two areas – for example between the locomotive roof and sky. Alternatively a soft edge can be used so that the selected area gradually blends into the area around it. In Photoshop a soft edge is known as 'feathered', just like the edge of a bird feather with its gradual edge. A selection can be composed entirely of hard edges, or feathered edges, or any combination of these. To create a combination, the 'hard' and 'feathered' edged selections must be created separately.

In a hard edge the mask changes directly from black to white whereas with a soft edge it passes gradually from black to white through shades of grey.

In this image, because the change is fairly small a single soft-edged selection should be sufficient.

Sky Levels

With the selection created the black paint can be applied to the mask. This is done in one step using the Paint Bucket Tool. Black paint needs to be chosen in the square at the base of the Tools Palette: In Photoshop-speak the Foreground Colour needs to be set to Black. If the front square is not already set to Black, the Foreground and Background colours may need to be swapped over by clicking on the tiny curved arrows. Possibly a full Foreground/Background colour reset may be needed to reset them to Black and White, which is done by clicking on the tiny black and white icon at the bottom left. If the colours are the wrong way round, clicking on the tiny curved arrows will swap them over. This is shown in Figure 5.4.3.

The mask on the Levels Adjustment Layer must be selected by clicking on the miniature mask in the Layers Palette. When this is done the background to the layer turns blue (indicating it is the current layer). In older versions of Photoshop and Elements a small symbol appears (white circle in a grey box) while in newer versions the miniature image of the mask is ringed in white. Lastly the mouse pointer, which has changed to a tiny paint bucket, is positioned in the sky and the left mouse button clicked. Provided all the settings have been made correctly the selected area will fill with black paint. The sky will darken and the miniature image of the mask in the Layers Palette will be updated to show the revised mask.

Figure 5.4.3 shows all the major items involved in cancelling the Levels Adjustment in the sky:

- The selection containing the sky and white containers while excluding the locomotives
- Layers Palette with the Levels Adjustment Layer selected and showing a miniature version of the mask
- Tools Palette showing Paint Bucket Tool and black paint chosen

It also shows the Levels Adjustment that was applied to the image finally. The tiny triangles under the histogram plot have all been moved to achieve the right contrast & brightness.

Checking the Mask

With the mask created it is always worth checking that the edge of the Levels Adjustment is not visible due to unwanted light or dark lines. By looking at different areas of the picture and enabling and disabling the Levels Adjustment using the tiny 'eye' symbol in the Layers Palette the adjustment can be checked by comparing the image 'before' and 'after' the adjustment. It is straightforward to edit the mask by painting on it using the Brush Tool and either black paint to make the mask larger or white paint to delete it. With full Photoshop the mask can be displayed by clicking on the 'eye' symbol for the mask in the Channels Palette as shown in Figure 5.4.4.

Displaying the mask in Photoshop Elements is more difficult because the mask-manipulation functions are limited with no exact equivalent of the mask display function in full Photoshop. The nearest equivalent is to use a coloured layer to shine through the layer and display the area where the mask does not apply. To do this, select the Levels Adjustment Layer in the Layers Palette. Then create a new colour fill layer using the 'Layer

Figure 5.4.4.
Displaying the mask on the sky when using full Photoshop.

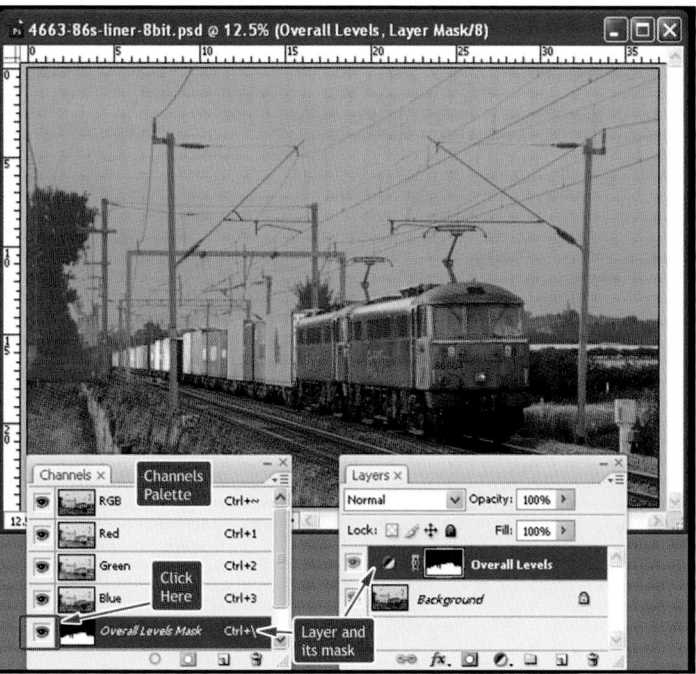

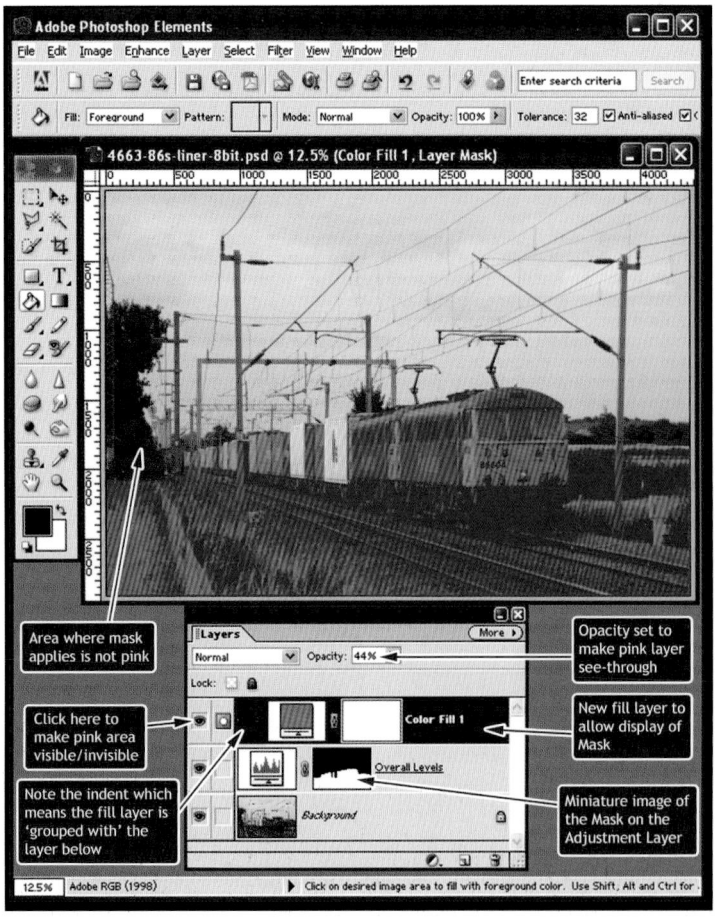

Figure 5.4.5.
Displaying the mask on the sky when using Photoshop Elements.

crashes later, only a small amount of work will be lost, not all of it.

Summary and Comparison

The comparison image in Figure 5.4.1 summarises the work that has been done on the image. It shows four versions of the same original image, each with their corresponding Photoshop histogram:

1 The original image. There are gaps between the left and right sides of the histogram and the edges of the display. This is a sign that the contrast can be improved.
2 The result after moving just the left and right triangles, corresponding to just a change in contrast. The sides of the histogram now meet the edges of the display.
3 The result after moving the middle triangle, after adjusting the brightness to lighten the image. The left and right sides of the histogram are unchanged. The lightening of the image has caused the 'hump' on the centre left of the image to move slightly to the right.
4 The final result after darkening the sky. In the histogram the very large 'hump' on the right due to the sky has moved back to the same position as in the original image, which is expected given that the sky is the same in both images.

→ New Fill Layer... → Solid Color...' menu option. A small screen appears which allows the new layer to be named. There is a small tick box called 'Group with Previous' which should be ticked so that the colour layer only affects the layer immediately below it. Choose a bright colour. By making the coloured layer partially see-through by changing the opacity settings it is easier to see where the mask does or doesn't apply. Everything is controlled by settings in the Layers Palette as shown in Figure 5.4.5. If using this method to display a mask, be sure to make the coloured layer invisible at later stages of the editing process when flattening the image otherwise the result will have an unwanted colour cast.

Save

After doing a lot of work like this, the work should be saved again in Photoshop (.PSD) format and overwriting the previously saved version. This ensures that if the computer

In summary the work that was done was to apply a Levels Adjustment Layer to the whole image making the sky too bright, then on seeing the effect, limiting the adjustment to the train and foreground by cancelling the adjustment with a mask. A selection was created to include the sky and a little of the ground area. The same thing could have been done in a slightly different way by deciding when first viewing the image to apply the Levels Adjustment to just the train and foreground, creating the selection and then creating the Levels Adjustment layer – in that order. A mask would have been created automatically that limited the levels adjustment to just the area of the selection.

● WIDE-RANGING IMPROVEMENT – THE ZONE APPROACH

Some photographs need significant adjustments to improve them. Every photographer has experienced the sun disappearing behind a cloud just before an important train arrives and getting a disappointing image where the train looks dull. How can the appearance be improved? As in the previous section, contrast is improved by using a Levels Adjustment but the cloudy day picture presents a more difficult challenge because different parts of the picture will require different amounts of adjustment.

The 'Zone Approach' involves dividing up a picture into zones and applying an individual Levels Adjustment to each zone. It is particularly effective for pictures taken in cloudy conditions and the resulting image can be surprisingly good. Arguably it is the most powerful improvement technique and can be used to improve any picture. However, the amount of work and skill needed to apply the full approach means that it can only realistically be used for a limited number of images. Nevertheless knowledge of how to apply the full approach is valuable because by using the same principles in a stripped-down form many more images can be treated, including those taken when the sun was shining.

Because of the difficulty and amount of effort involved the technique is not recommended for total beginners.

Example image

The example in Figure 5.5.1 features an image of No 87002 on a passenger train near Northampton. The sun disappeared less than 30sec before the train arrived and the result as shot is substandard with a bright sky and everything else dull. After manipulation using the Zone Approach the result, as shown, is perfectly acceptable. Raw format was used for the original image. Some of the adjustments used here are quite strong and a JPEG original format image would be less suitable as a basis for editing, giving harsh colours and rough details in places.

What needs to be done

The image of No 87002 as shot is dull all over except in the sky. It needs the contrast increased on the train and land area and the sky darkened. The simple approach of making a single adjustment which applies to the whole picture will not be sufficient here because although much of the picture is dark, the sky is bright. By dividing the image up into different zones, each zone can be given its own set of adjustments. Although it takes more work, the 'Zone Approach' delivers much better results because the different zones benefit from different amounts of correction.

Exposure

Before even considering adjustment on a computer, the first factor to take into account in this situation is the exposure when originally taking the picture. This needs to be set appropriately, otherwise it may not be

Figure 5.5.1.
Before and after applying the 'Zone Approach' to an image.

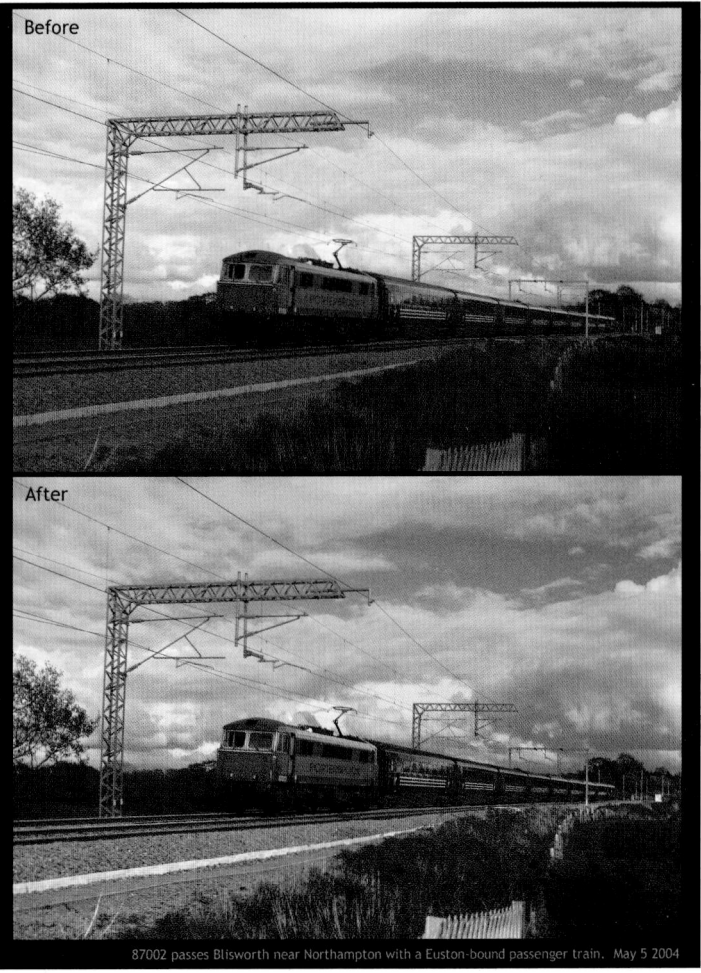

Before

After

87002 passes Blisworth near Northampton with a Euston-bound passenger train. May 5 2004

Figure 5.5.2.
The image after dividing up into individual zones.

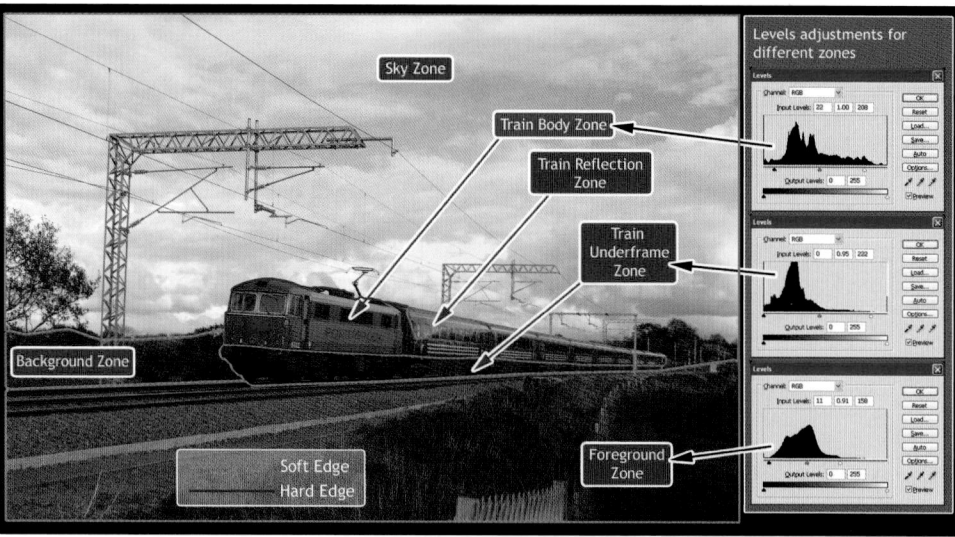

possible to produce a good result at all. The exposure should be set so that the key parts of the picture are not too dark, while avoiding any bright areas of the picture 'burning out' where the sun is still shining. The exposure of No 87002 was taken using the equivalent of standard 'UK full sun' setting – 1/500 sec @ f5.6 at 100 ISO – even though the light level on the train had fallen. Because the train was moving very fast the actual settings were 1/1500 sec @ f3.5 at 100 ISO with manual exposure and Raw format.

Editing Principle

The usual editing principle will apply with no data in the original image being changed until the very last stage. For each 'zone' in the picture one or more Adjustment Layers will be used to apply the contrast increase together with a mask to restrict the adjustment to that zone only. A Levels Adjustment Layer is a better way of adjusting contrast than a 'Brightness/Contrast Adjustment Layer' because it gives finer control over the changes and avoids 'burn out' of bright areas or 'clogging' of dark areas. In most zones this is the only adjustment needed.

Zones and Zone Boundaries

Dividing the image into zones involves two important sets of decisions: where to put the zone boundaries and whether the boundaries to the zone have a 'hard' or 'soft' edge.

How do you decide where the zones should be? The key is choosing areas of similar brightness and character. The first zone to consider is the train because it is usually the focal point of the picture and therefore needs careful treatment. The train body and underframe will usually be separate zones because their colouring and brightness are so different. Depending on the picture the body of the train might be split up into two zones: locomotive and coaches/wagons. In some cases the locomotive front and side may also be separate zones. The track could be in another zone, either combined with the foreground or separate. The sky area will usually be in its own zone and normally benefits from slight darkening to improve the range of tones.

The zones chosen for this image are shown in Figure 5.5.2. The train body and underframe form two separate zones (Train Body Zone and Train Underframe Zone). There is also a special case because of the annoying reflection on the upper body of the first coach. This can be dealt with by special darkening, so the 'reflection' area forms its own zone (Train Reflection Zone). The dark, murky foreground becomes another zone (Foreground Zone). The left background could be combined with the foreground zone but in this case was left separate because of the electrification mast passing through the zone. This allows the brightness of the whole zone to be adjusted while ensuring that the piece of the mast in the zone matches the rest of the mast (Background Zone). Lastly the sky forms a zone (Sky Zone), making a total of six zones.

When there are more than a handful of zones it is best to ensure that zones do not overlap, otherwise it's too easy to get confused and apply unintended corrections.

The other decision when creating a zone is whether it should have a 'hard' or 'soft' edge. A 'hard' edge has a sharp boundary between the zone and the rest of the picture, meaning that the adjustment will be clearly visible unless the edge of the zone coincides with a line in the image. Putting this another way, a 'hard edge' between different adjustment zones is suitable for following an obvious line in the picture so that the adjustment can be hidden. In the No 87002 picture the 'hard' edges are shown in green and have been used where the body of the locomotive meets the sky and left background. A 'soft' edge is appropriate when the change due to the adjustment will gradually blend into the surrounding area. Having decided on the 'hard' edges the remainder are 'soft'. Figure 5.5.2 shows all the zones with hard edges in green and soft edges in pink.

Creating the Zones

Each zone has one or more Adjustment Layers which apply only to that zone. If a Selection is active when the Adjustment Layer is created a suitable mask will automatically be created. The first stage, therefore, is creating the selection with hard or soft edges as required. A zone with a mix of 'hard' and 'soft' edges is built in stages, with one type of edge can be created at a time. A large zone may have to be assembled from several smaller selections. This is a time-consuming process. The selections need to be created carefully to avoid obvious boundaries between adjusted areas, although they can be created later.

Creating a 'Hard' Edge

A 'Hard' edged selection is used when following an obvious edge, so the best selection tool to use here is the 'Magnetic

Lasso' as this is intended to follow edges. It shares a single position on the Tools Palette with the Polygonal Lasso tool. To pick the right tool, first click using the right mouse button with the pointer on this position. There are several tools available, each with its own icon. By pausing the mouse pointer over each icon in turn it will display its name. The desired tool is chosen by clicking with the left mouse button. The 'hard' edge is achieved by setting the 'feather' value to 0.

Before starting work, zoom in on the picture so that it is easier to see the edge being followed. To start the selection, click somewhere on the edge of the locomotive body. As the mouse pointer is moved, the line of the selection will follow the edge and periodically an 'anchor' point will automatically be created. This is shown in Figure 5.5.3.

If an anchor point is in the wrong place, pressing the [Delete] key will remove the most recent point, while pressing the [Escape] key will completely cancel the selection. To complete the selection, double-click the left mouse button or press the [Enter] key. If the selection disappears after double-clicking, press the [Escape] key and it

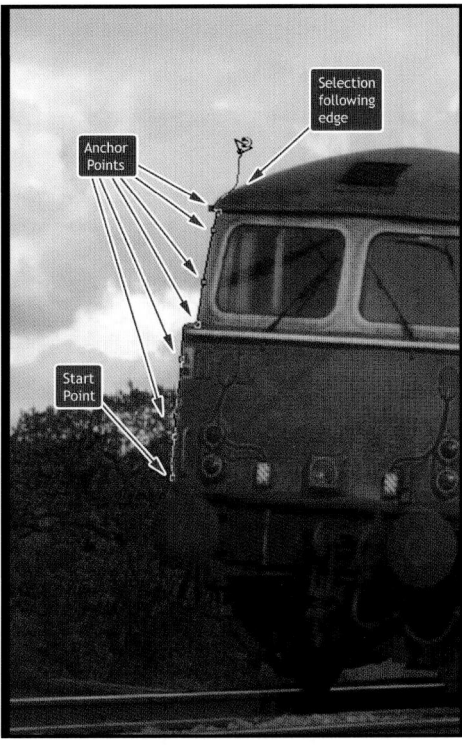

Figure 5.5.3.
Using the Magnetic Lasso Tool.

will re-appear. There will be times when the selection does not follow the right path. To deal with this, either create an anchor point manually by clicking the left mouse button or if it happens too often it may be necessary to alter the settings for the Tool: by increasing the 'contrast' value the line will only follow more strongly defined edges. Typical values for the 'contrast' are between 3% and 10%. In extreme cases it may be necessary to abandon the Magnetic Lasso Tool in favour of the Polygonal Lasso tool.

Soft Edge

The Polygonal Lasso Tool will be used to create the 'soft edge'. It is selected via the Tools Palette as described earlier. For the soft edge the 'feather' value should be set to a non-zero number. The number represents the number of pixels over which the edge will 'fade'. A typical 'feather' value will be between about 5 and 8 but as always it is worth experimenting to choose your own favourite setting.

Zoom in so that you can see the zone to a reasonable level of detail – such as 25% to 50%. If the whole zone does not fit on the screen at once the display will automatically scroll. Another option is to create the selection as the sum of several smaller selections. To create the selection, click the

left mouse button to create the start point. As the mouse pointer is moved towards the next position a straight line will be created. Move the mouse pointer so that the line follows the desired path and then click the left mouse button to create the next anchor point and fix the edge of the selection. By moving the mouse and clicking to create more points the selection will soon be formed. This is a fast and straightforward technique that gives good results when used in the right places. It's usually a good idea to make the line coincide with a line in the image such as the bottom or top edge of the coach body or the edge of a line of trees. As with the magnetic lasso, use the [Delete] key to erase the most recent point, [Escape] to cancel and double-click or press the [Enter] key to complete the selection.

Zone with Hard and Soft Edges

A zone can have both hard and soft edges. To create a selection with both types of edge requires two or more stages of work. In the example image the 'Train Body' zone has a hard edge on the locomotive cab and roof and a soft edge elsewhere. An enlargement showing this zone being created is shown in Figure 5.5.4. Two stages are required – one for the hard edge and one for the soft edge.

The first stage creates the Hard Edge using the Magnetic Lasso Tool as described in the earlier section. The key point here is that the hard edge is only wanted on the left side and top of the locomotive, not on the right side or bottom. Therefore the selection is brought across the locomotive body diagonally from top right to bottom left and its jagged dotted line can be seen in the image.

The second stage creates the soft edge using the Polygonal Lasso Tool. Before starting, the 'Add to Selection' option must be chosen on the menu bar at the top of the screen as shown. As the name suggests, this option ensures that the new selection is added to any existing selection. A very common mistake is having the wrong setting here. For example if the 'New Selection' option is chosen, when the second selection is started the first one will be cancelled. The second selection is created by starting at the

Figure 5.5.4.
Creating the selection for the Train Body zone.

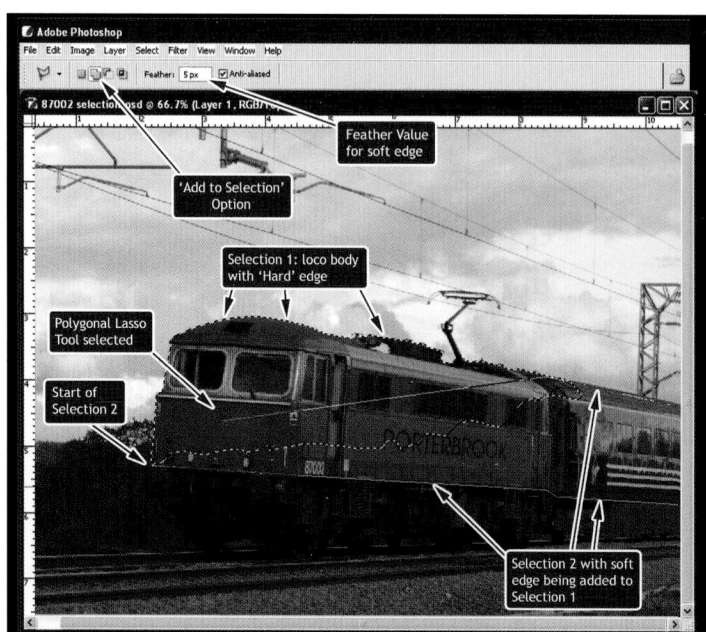

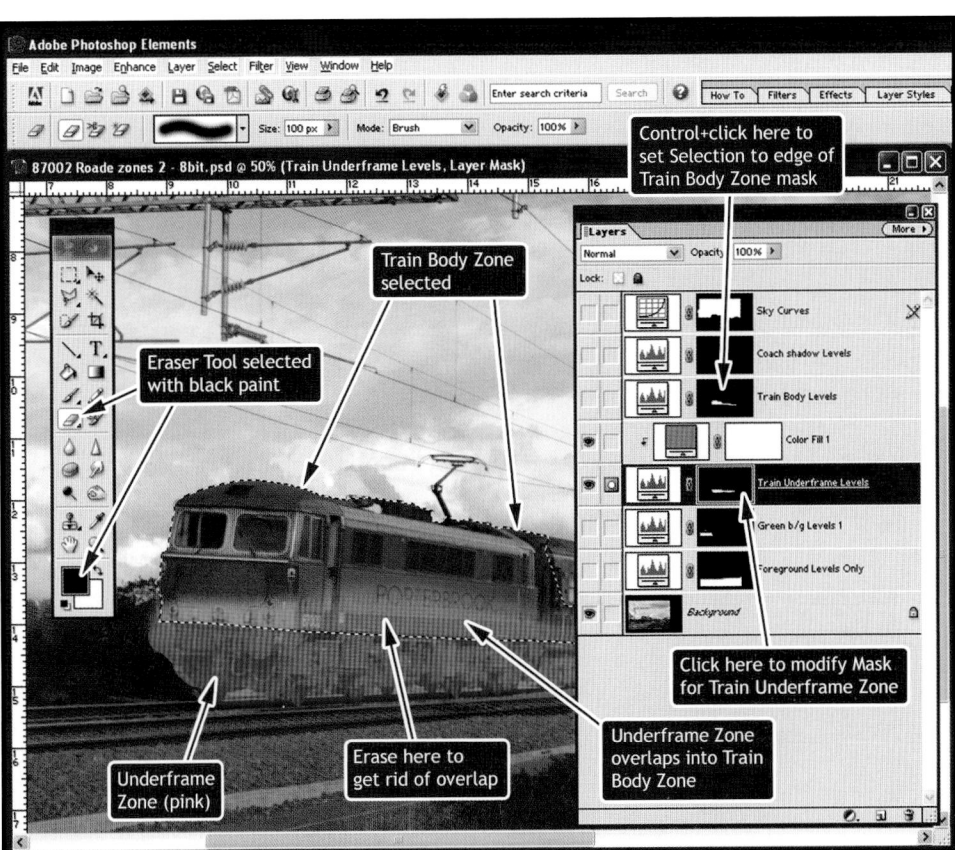

Figure 5.5.5.
Cleaning up the
overlap between zones
when using Photoshop
Elements.

bottom left of the locomotive front, then following the bottom of the locomotive body and coach bodies to the end of the train on the right side, then brought back along the tops of the coaches before crossing the locomotive body diagonally from top right to bottom left. In Figure 5.5.4 the selection is almost complete with the mouse pointer in the middle of the yellow loco front. It is vital that the new 'soft edge' selection overlaps the existing 'hard edge' selection so that the whole of the locomotive is included. Double clicking the left mouse button completes the 'soft edge' selection. The action of completing the selection also adds it to the existing 'hard edge' selection to complete the 'Train Body' selection.

Boundaries Between Zones

In the full Zone Approach there will usually be places where different zones meet. When this happens it's important to ensure that the boundaries of the zones match each other so that adjustments don't overlap or leave a gap. If there is an overlap, the parts of the image inside the overlap will be adjusted twice. A gap means that area will not be adjusted at all. Either of these situations will probably cause an unsightly line where the adjustment is obvious. The best way to deal with this is to check the zones and tidy up the overlap as you go along.

Dealing with Overlapping Zones

Where two zones overlap, the boundary needs to be changed to remove the overlap. The process to do this depends on whether you have full Photoshop or Photoshop Elements and is more complex with Elements due to its limited range of features.

This example has used Photoshop Elements 2.0 and Figure 5.5.5 shows the Underframe Zone overlapping into the Train Body Zone. Although not essential, it makes the task slightly easier if the masked area is visible. It's not possible to display a mask in Photoshop Elements and the nearest equivalent is the ability to make the unmasked area visible by using a coloured layer. A Colour Fill Layer (pink in this case) is created immediately above the Train Underframe Levels adjustment layer. The 'Group with Previous Layer' option must be chosen during layer creation otherwise the whole image will turn pink. When viewed in the Layers Palette the Colour Fill layer will be indented slightly to the right, confirming the use of 'Group with Previous'. If the 'Group with Previous' option was not used (so the whole image is pink) it can be fixed by selecting the Colour Fill Layer in the Layers Palette and choosing the 'Layer → Group with Previous' menu option.

The edge of the Train Body mask is now made visible by pressing the [Ctrl] key while simultaneously clicking on the miniature mask in the Layers Palette using the left mouse button. This sets the current selection to the edge of the Train Body mask and is displayed using a moving dotted line. A selection is very useful in a case like this because when using a paintbrush or eraser its action is restricted to the area inside the selection so that it has no effect elsewhere. The material inside the selection is removed either by using the Eraser Tool with black paint or the Brush Tool with white paint. The necessary actions and settings are shown in Figure 5.5.5.

In full Photoshop the mask is displayed by clicking on its 'eye' visibility symbol in the Channels Palette. Then a similar method to that just described can be used or an alternative simpler process as

follows: by clicking with the right mouse button on the mask of the Train Body Zone adjustment layer in the Layers Palette, a menu appears. The option 'Subtract Layer Mask from Selection' does what its name suggests and removes the overlap. The Adjustment Layer is created next and will use the active selection to create the mask exactly in the right place.

In either full Photoshop or Elements, repeat the process with any other zones that may overlap.

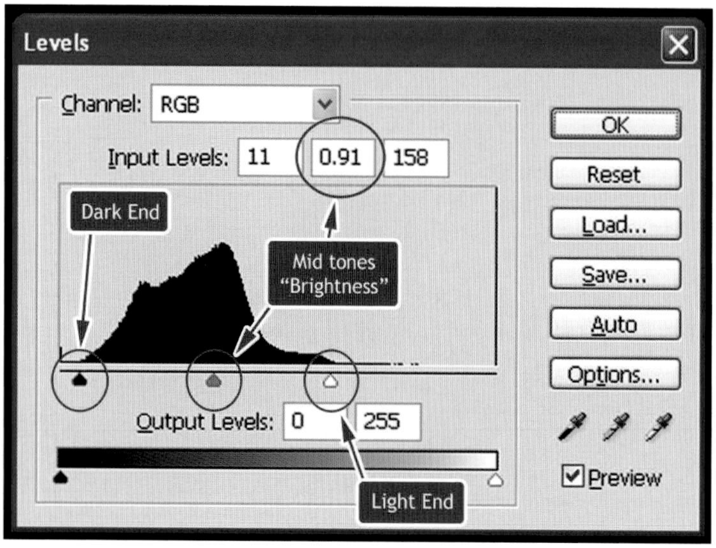

Levels Adjustment

When creating the Levels Adjustment Layer for each zone, a selection must already be in place as described in the previous section. The 'Layer → New Adjustment Layer → Levels Adjustment' menu option is used to create the new layer as usual.

An example Levels Adjustment for the 'Foreground Zone' is shown in Figure 5.5.6. The contrast is increased by moving the small black and white triangles underneath the 'graph' towards the middle. The black sliding triangle at the left side is moved inwards to the point where it meets the end of the 'graph'. This makes the image darker and is labelled 'Dark End' on the example. Similarly the white sliding triangle at the right side is moved inwards. This makes the image lighter and is labelled 'Light End' on the example. Check the appearance of the colours in the image to ensure they remain realistic because sometimes they can turn slightly garish, in which case it's necessary to 'back off' and move the sliding triangle outwards a little. If the picture overall is too light or too dark, this can be dealt with by moving the middle (grey) slider to the right to darken, or to the left to lighten. This is labelled 'Mid tones brightness' in the example. When this slider is not touched, the middle of the three 'Input Levels' boxes will have a value of 1.0. Click on 'OK' to create the Layer and save the changes.

Changing the levels in this way on an image can have a dramatic effect, especially on track, trees and grass so avoid adjusting to the point that the image looks unrealistic. As always it's worth experimenting. Use of

Figure 5.5.6.
Levels adjustment screen for the Foreground Zone.

Adjustment Layers has the major advantage that changes can be made to the settings without harming the underlying image. If you don't like any of the changes you can click the 'Cancel' button or delete the Adjustment Layer altogether.

Figure 5.5.2 shows the individual Levels Adjustments for three of the zones. Compare the shape of the graphs and the position of the small triangles in each one. The adjustments and graphs for each zone are very different and demonstrate why a single adjustment for the whole picture can't give the best result.

In most images the Levels Adjustment for each zone will be sufficient. There may be some images where additional changes are necessary such as correcting a colour cast, in which case further Adjustment Layers would be created. To make these changes effective only in a single zone, the layer should be created immediately above the Levels Adjustment for that zone in the Layers Palette and the 'Group with Previous' option chosen (known as 'Create Clipping Mask' in full Photoshop).

Sky Zone
The contrast in the sky doesn't need increasing but it does benefit from slight darkening. This can be done using a Levels Adjustment Layer by moving the middle grey triangle. There are other techniques described later in this book that could be used instead and a Curves Adjustment Layer was used on this picture.

Manual Changes to Masks
Sometimes manual changes to masks are needed and can be made using the Brush Tool with either black or white paint.

Finishing the Image
The image should be saved in Photoshop's .PSD format as this allows you to go back to the image if changes are needed in future and pick up where you left off. If you don't need to do any more editing the next major stage in editing is to flatten the image to remove the layers using the 'Layer → Flatten Image' menu option. The last

stages involve cropping and preparing for printing or web display as described in Chapters 3 and 4.

Summary
This set of techniques is very powerful and can be used to improve most images, especially those taken in dull weather. In summary, the process to follow is:

- Identify the various zones, beginning with the train itself
- Decide whether the edges of each zone are 'hard', 'soft' or a combination
- Build each zone in turn by creating the selection following the edges of the zone
- Edit the boundaries of the zone to prevent missed areas or overlap with other zones
- In each zone create the Levels Adjustment Layer and alter the Levels to increase the contrast
- Adjust the sky
- Check the edited picture for any unsightly boundaries between zones and tidy up where necessary
- Save in Photoshop's PSD format
- Flatten, sharpen, crop, resize etc ready for web viewing or printing.

● THE RAW ADVANTAGE

Introduction
Raw format offers numerous advantages over the popular JPEG format and will be explained in detail in this section. A brief introduction to Raw format was given in Chapter 1.

What is Raw?
Raw format means literally Raw, as in 'not cooked' or more accurately 'not processed': after the shutter has finished exposing the digital sensor to light received through the lens, the pixel data from the camera's sensor is copied to the memory card with minimal processing. (Strictly speaking there is a small amount of processing as a Raw file usually contains a tiny embedded 'thumbnail' image in JPEG format which allows the image to be viewed quickly). To create an image from a

Raw file requires special Raw conversion software, which is run on a PC or Macintosh computer after the shooting session to create a JPEG, Tiff or other format image.

Why Shoot Raw?

To answer the question 'why shoot in Raw format' it's probably easiest to start by explaining the benefits of shooting in the most popular format – JPEG. When shooting in JPEG format the camera creates an image which requires no further processing before it can be viewed. It has also been compressed to maximise the number of images that can be fitted on to the memory card. For anyone who needs a final image quickly, doesn't want to spend time doing any processing on a computer, or need to fit as many images as possible on to a memory card, JPEG format is an excellent choice.

The amount of processing done by the camera when creating a JPEG image is considerable. There are a lot of decisions to be made and in general most cameras make a very good job of this. With Raw format you make your own decisions when processing the image on a computer. You do not have to accept the choices made by the camera manufacturer and can also override the 'processing' settings chosen on the camera at the time of taking the picture. Processing can be tailored to take account of particular features of the image and certain processing steps can be done later using specialised software on the computer rather than having to accept more generalised processing done by the camera. Most of the decisions made during JPEG creation cannot be 'undone' because data is 'thrown away' or irrevocably altered. Although doing your own Raw processing takes time and trouble, with experience and suitable software you should be able to get a better quality image from Raw than JPEG.

Because JPEG processing has been refined to a high standard by camera manufacturers the advantage of Raw processing is unlikely to be seen in normal sized images created for the web because fine detail and subtle tones are hard to see on a computer screen unless the image is enlarged considerably. In printed images differences will generally only be seen when prints are A5 size (8in x 6in) or larger.

In 2007 cameras started to appear on the market which allowed a Raw format image to be processed by the camera at any time after shooting to produce a JPEG format image. The only real advantage of this option is that Raw conversion can be done without needing a computer.

The difference between Raw and JPEG is, in summary, all about decisions. With JPEG you are forced to accept the image processing decisions made by the camera based on your shooting settings and the camera manufacturer's choices. With Raw you are free to make your own decisions whenever you process your images so that you can (hopefully) produce better images. With Raw you can take advantage of future developments in computer-based image processing whereas with JPEG you are stuck with the processing done by the camera when the picture was taken.

Raw plus JPEG

Many cameras allow both a JPEG and Raw image to be created when taking a single photograph. This can be seen as providing a good compromise: you have a JPEG image available to use immediately and if you need to do more serious processing on a computer later you can use the Raw format image. The only downside of this approach is slightly increased processing time on the camera and increased storage space required on the memory card, computer disks and backups.

In-camera Processing

The areas where the camera has to make decisions are: brightness, contrast, colour 'character', colour saturation, colour bit depth, amount of compression, white balance, noise reduction, sharpening and colour space. These areas will be explained in turn.

BRIGHTNESS AND CONTRAST The brightest areas of the picture (highlights) and darkest areas (shadows) are important to the overall appearance. With JPEG format the camera will choose how to set these and provide good 'average' settings of brightness. Most cameras allow you to adjust on the camera your preferred level of contrast before taking pictures. With Raw you make your own choice on how to set the highlights and shadows. In many images you can make useful improvements, especially in the highlights where you can restore detail from a Raw file that would be lost from the equivalent JPEG. Put another way, you can avoid unwanted 'burn out' in the highlights. This feature is very valuable when dealing with white liveries on sunny days and skies. Similarly, skies and clouds on sunny days will often benefit from highlight recovery. A JPEG format image is often too bright and loses surface detail from the bright areas that cannot be recovered, whereas you can recover the detail from a Raw image provided any over-exposure was not excessive. Similarly in the dark (shadow) areas the amount of detail visible can be increased instead of leaving it buried in the shadows, which is particularly useful for locomotive and rolling stock underframes. If you make a mistake setting the exposure when taking the picture you can usually salvage a reasonable result from a Raw file when the JPEG equivalent is only fit for the bin. Overall this area is where the railway photographer will see the most obvious benefit from shooting in Raw.

COLOUR 'CHARACTER' AND SATURATION Cameras have settings to allow the colour to be varied on JPEG images. When processing Raw images these settings are used as a starting point and can be over-ridden. Because of the flexibility available for colour control in Raw processing software it's easier to get the colour settings 'right' than shooting in JPEG and manipulating afterwards.

COLOUR BIT DEPTH This area was described in Chapter 1. Digital cameras produce JPEG images in 8-bit format which are fine for display, printing or limited editing. 16-bit format images are worthwhile when you need to do extensive editing, in which case the final image will retain smooth colours and tones where an 8-bit image might degrade. The

only way to generate 16-bit images from digital cameras is by processing Raw images: the Raw conversion software will give the choice of '8-bit' or '16-bit' output. 16-bit images can be viewed as having 'more accurate' colours than 8-bit but the extra accuracy is unnecessary for printing, display and simple editing. (For purists: most cameras only create images to 12 or 14-bit accuracy and the result is 'padded' to 16 bits).

COMPRESSION When a JPEG file is created, certain image data is 'thrown away' to reduce the amount of storage space used in a process known as compression. The processes which create a JPEG rely on the image capabilities of the human eye which is very sensitive to brightness changes and sharply defined edges but fairly insensitive to small changes in brightness or colour. A JPEG therefore has a pretty good rendition of sharply defined detail – such as window edges or a locomotive grille – but may lose subtle changes in tone or colours elsewhere in the picture. For example, fine patterns in grass, station platform surfaces or plain coach and locomotive body sides will be simplified and as a result they will have less visible fine detail and texture.

JPEG compression is very effective and typically a JPEG image will use about a third to a half of the space of the equivalent Raw image. Different JPEG compression levels can be chosen (generally cameras use the term 'JPEG Quality') to trade off quality against storage space used. In comparison, although most Raw images are compressed, this is done in a way that loses no image data.

COLOUR SPACE As described at the beginning of this chapter, an image displays its colours correctly in one particular colour space and should contain a corresponding colour profile. JPEG images are most commonly created in the 'sRGB' colour space and some cameras allow the use of 'Adobe RGB'. The 'sRGB' colour space has a fairly restricted range of colours which means there are some colours that cannot be stored in an 'sRGB' JPEG and the camera has to choose the nearest equivalent. Although images can be converted later in Photoshop to a wider colour space this does not help if a particular shade of colour was lost at the time of taking because it is difficult to manipulate colours convincingly to compensate for a few lost shades. Raw format has the major advantage that all colours recorded by the sensor are available for processing. The colour space is chosen during Raw processing where a range will be available to chose – the standard sRGB and Adobe RGB as well as alternative wider colour spaces for use in specialised circumstances.

SHARPENING All digital images need sharpening. A JPEG image is sharpened during processing and the amount is determined by the camera manufacturer or user-defined setting.

WHITE BALANCE Different lighting conditions affect the colour balance of the image. White balance involves adjusting the colours so a white object appears white in the image. Another way of describing this is getting rid of a colour cast. Normally the white balance is set automatically by the camera. It is easier to change the white balance in a raw image than a JPEG.

NOISE REDUCTION Noise is the digital equivalent of film grain and is a speckled pattern commonly seen when using higher

ISO settings such as 400 and above. Fine speckled patterns can sometimes be seen in dark areas such as locomotive underframes even when using lower ISO settings such as 100 or 200 and the amount is increased if the image is underexposed. Noise reduction software is generally very effective at eliminating these patterns but has the unfortunate side-effect of removing fine detail. In the worst cases images after noise reduction have good detail in areas such as windows and grilles but a flat mushy representation of grassy fields and track ballast. Raw conversion software provides the choice of either using the built-in noise reduction features or turning off the noise reduction, leaving the noise in place and processing it later using specialist noise-reduction software. This area is described in Chapter 6.

Raw vs JPEG

Figure 5.6.1 shows two comparison images of a subject which is a severe test for any camera. A white-liveried Class 375 unit stands in a bright station (Hastings) on a sunny day with dark shadowy areas behind. The original picture was taken on a Canon EOS 20D camera with both JPEG and Raw images created simultaneously. The Raw image was created using the 'Raw Shooter Essentials' Raw converter and adjusted to ensure detail was retained in the white areas of the unit front while keeping detail in the shadow areas under the station canopy. The original JPEG was too bright in the light areas and too dark in the shadowy areas so it was adjusted slightly in Photoshop in an attempt to allow a fair comparison. The original JPEG is shown small size and unaltered for brightness at the top of the comparison. The unit fronts are cropped from A4 full size images.

The brightness differences between (adjusted) JPEG and Raw are fairly small and subtle but the Raw image manages to have slightly better contrast while also having better shadow detail. Sharpness in the details is also better. Look at the area around the unit's coupler to compare shadow detail. Also of note is the detail in the stones forming the

Figure 5.6.1.
Comparing Raw and JPEG versions of the same scene.

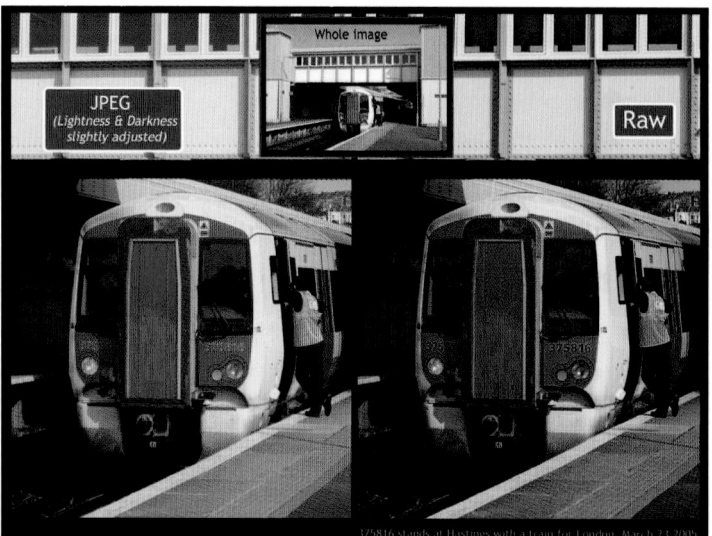

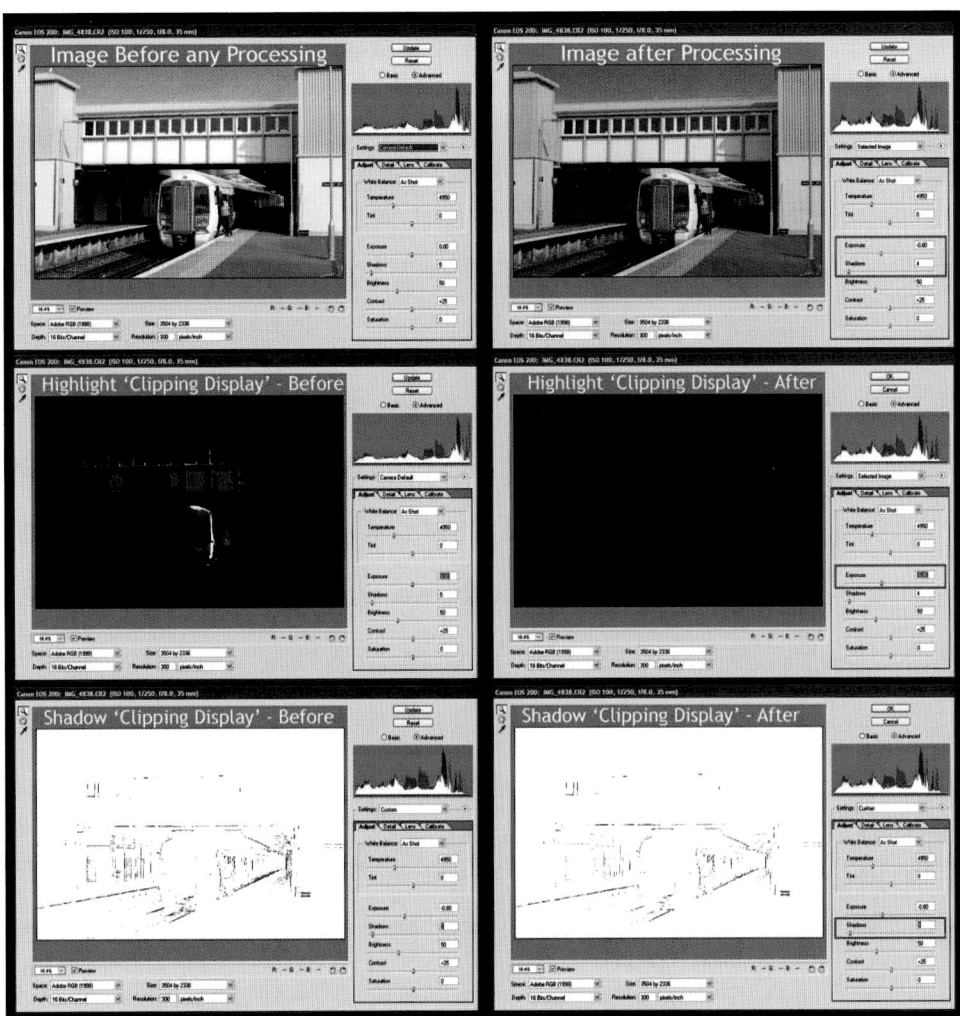

Figure 5.6.2.
Stages during Raw conversion using Photoshop CS.

edge of the platform. The JPEG image has rendered them as a fairly uniform mush while the Raw image retains all the detail. Compare the sharpness of any part of the unit cab between the two images.

Processing a Raw Image using Adobe software

Most camera manufacturers produce their own Raw conversion software and it is always worth trying the software that matches your camera. The quality of the results is usually very good but typically the software will lack features compared with Raw conversion products from independent software companies. 'Adobe Camera Raw' software (ACR) is the most popular independent Raw conversion software and is available for both PC and Macintosh. Photoshop Elements 3.0 (and newer versions), Photoshop CS (and

newer versions) and Lightroom (all versions) all include ACR. Its main advantages are a large range of features and being able to process Raw images from the majority of available cameras. When a new camera model is introduced, existing users of ACR cannot process Raw files from it until Adobe has updated ACR. Users must download a new version of ACR from the Adobe web site and replace their old version. The example in Figure 5.6.2 shows ACR in Photoshop CS. ACR in other version of Photoshop will operate with similar principles but have slightly different controls. The Case Studies in Chapter 7 show an example of Raw conversion with Photoshop Elements 5.0.

Target Result

Before describing how to make a Raw conversion it's worth recapping on the general intention when following the Raw conversion process. A converted Raw image should have a full range of tones from maximum brightness to maximum darkness, with any major colour casts corrected and with initial sharpening applied. Photographers can decide if they want to further enhance the converted image in Photoshop using any of the techniques described in this book. With many images further work is not needed and it is sufficient to resize, crop and save in the desired output format – for web or printing.

Initial Settings

Before converting an image in ACR the first step is to fix some settings for the output image. The most important of these are:

- Colour space. This area was described in detail at the beginning of this Chapter. Broadly, when producing an image only for use on the web choose sRGB.
If the intention is to print the image choose 'Adobe RGB (1998)'. In some circumstances – explained later – those with full Photoshop may need to consider 'ProPhoto RGB'.
- Bit Depth. The options here are either 8-bit or 16-bit. Photoshop Elements users should chose 8-bit as it cannot edit 16-bit images. Users of full Photoshop can choose either option. As a guideline, when making simple manipulations 8-bit will be sufficient. When doing a moderate amount of manipulation 16-bit should be chosen. See Chapter 1 for more information.
  Resolution is a less important setting because it can be easily changed later. '300 pixels/inch' is a good starting point corresponding to the usual setting for making prints.

White Balance

The first adjustment is setting the white balance. This can be thought of as getting rid of any unwanted colour cast. Normally the Raw conversion software will use as a starting point the white balance set on the camera when the picture was taken. For daylight pictures this will usually be fine and if any change is needed it will be small. With

night shots there is often a major change required. It's much easier to change the colouring in the Raw converter than to do so later during editing and has the advantage that a full range of tones will be maintained. To set the white balance, choose the 'white balance tool' (the 'eyedropper' symbol near the top left), then click somewhere in the picture that ought to have a white or grey appearance. This will cause the colour of the image to change. It is worth experimenting by clicking on different objects in the picture as the colour change will vary. Sometimes the desired colour can't be achieved by simply clicking on an object and it is necessary to adjust the Colour Temperature control.

Brightness and Clipping

The next step in Raw conversion involves adjusting brightness. Although the eye is able to judge general brightness the most important aspect is to avoid 'clipping'. Clipping means that there are areas of pure white in the bright areas (highlights) or pure black in the dark areas (shadows). Clipped areas rarely cause a problem when they are very small and contribute to an overall bright contrasty appearance. When they are larger they distract attention and are ugly. The ACR software has two 'Clipping Displays' to show which parts of the picture are clipped, one for highlights and the other for shadows. Control of clipping is vital in photo editing and a common mistake among photographers is ignoring it. The subject of clipping will be mentioned throughout this book.

First Adjustment – Highlight clipping

The 'Exposure' control sets the overall brightness of the image. The intention is to set the image as bright as possible without significant white clipping appearing in the highlights. The way of activating the highlight clipping display depends on the version of ACR. On newer versions there is a small push button by the histogram. A more fiddly method that works on all versions involves positioning the mouse pointer on the 'Exposure' slider while simultaneously pressing the left mouse button and holding the [Alt] key ([Option] key on a Mac). In some images such as the Class 375 unit here, clipping is already visible so the exposure level needs to be reduced to get rid of it. This is shown in the Figure 5.6.2. Changing the 'Exposure' setting has a different effect to the 'Brightness' control and the difference will be explained later.

All colour images are made up of three colours – Red, Green and Blue – also known as channels. Any of these can clip. The highlight clipping display is black wherever there is no clipping. In this image there is noticeable clipping in the red channel, which is shown where the display is red. There are small amounts of green and blue channel clipping and the display turns yellow where both red and green are clipped. The most serious situation is where the display is white because all three channels are clipped, such as in the area around the unit cab. The way to deal with this is to decrease the 'Exposure' setting. In many cases the clipping can be eliminated and worthwhile detail recovered. This process is called 'Highlight Recovery' and is a powerful advantage of using Raw format over JPEG. It can often be used to 'rescue' an over-exposed image that would have been material for the bin if shot in JPEG format.

Normal practice is to alter the 'Exposure' control until clipping in important areas like the train body has disappeared. Clipping is expected in certain very bright areas like headlights or station lights and will normally be kept. As the Exposure control is reduced the image will get darker. If the value showing on the Exposure control is less than about - 1.0 the image will be quite dark and has reached the stage where other methods need to be used to deal with the clipping, as described in some of the Case Studies in Chapter 7.

Sometimes clipping can't be fixed by altering the exposure control and the damage needs to be repaired. One technique for doing this is patching and is described under the heading of 'Burnout' in Chapter 6.

Second Adjustment – Shadow clipping

With the highlights corrected, attention now turns to the shadows. First action is to check the Shadow Clipping Display by placing the

mouse pointer on the 'Shadows' slider and pressing both the left mouse button and the [Alt] key ([Option] key on a Mac). Newer versions of ACR have a small button beside the histogram instead. Images need a certain amount of 100% black to achieve a full range of tones so the aim is to retain a few tiny black points while preventing formation of larger areas. This aspect can always be improved after Raw conversion by using a Levels adjustment to darken more of the shadows so at the Raw conversion stage it is better to have too few clipped dark areas than too many. The Clipping Display is white where there is no clipping. Clipped channels are shown individually, or black where all three are clipped. In this image a small reduction was made to lighten the shadows and a small change in the Clipping Display can be seen.

Brightness

ACR has a third control which affects overall brightness, called perhaps confusingly 'Brightness'. Although at first sight similar to the 'Exposure' control it has the key difference that it lightens or darkens the image without affecting the extreme highlights or shadows. So having set the highlight and shadow clipping points in the previous two adjustments, the brightness control is adjusted so that the image looks 'right' to the eye. In practice making any large changes to the brightness control can cause clipping so the Clipping Displays should be checked again and adjusted as necessary. The final test is what looks right to the eye.

Other Adjustments

Most of the time it is not necessary to use the other adjustment controls. Occasionally it may be necessary to increase the colour saturation but the author's advice is to use this control sparingly. A picture with high colour saturation looks unnatural and although acceptable in some branches of photography the general intention in railway photography is to create a result that looks realistic without obvious manipulation work having been done. Often an image will benefit from a small Levels adjustment in Photoshop after Raw conversion and the process of

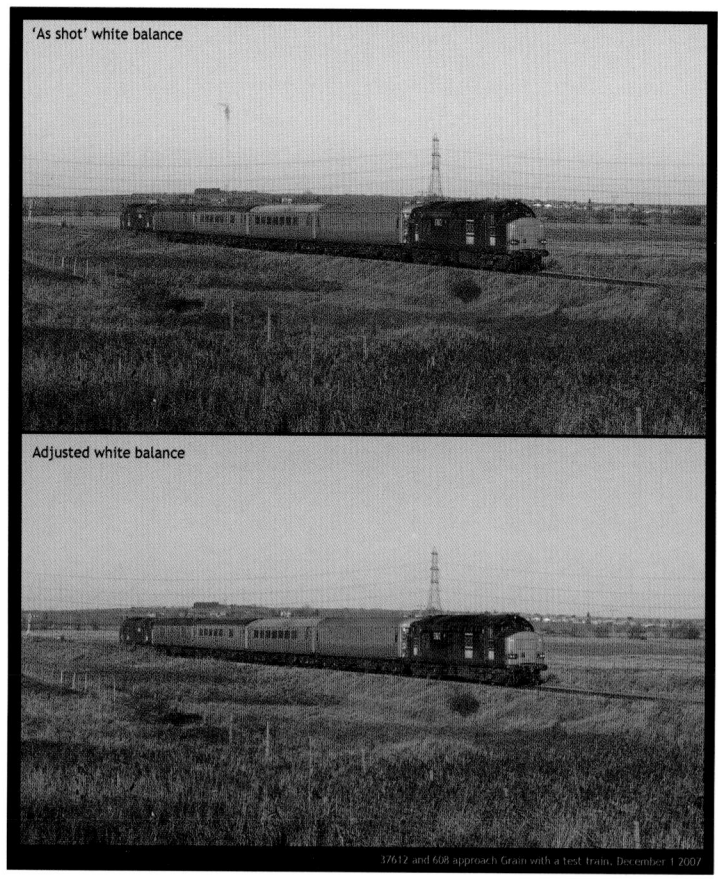

'As shot' white balance

Adjusted white balance

37612 and 608 approach Grain with a test train, December 1 2007

Figure 5.7.1.
Two versions of the same original image with different white balances.

adjusting the shadows will make the colours slightly richer. For this reason it is better at the Raw conversion stage to have colours which are slightly too weak than too rich.

The standard level of sharpening (25, on the Detail tab) is usually sufficient. If an image has sharpness problems it is better to address them with special techniques as described later in this chapter.

Before and After

Figure 5.6.2 shows the ACR software with the 'Before' image that has no adjustments applied and the 'After Image' which has finished the Raw conversion stage. The 'Before' and 'After' Highlight and Shadow Clipping Displays are also shown. The Class 375 image has had: i) the overall exposure reduced to eliminate highlight clipping and generally darken the image; ii) Shadow setting decreased slightly to brighten the dark areas. A JPEG image created in the camera will normally have the same brightness and contrast as the corresponding

'Before' Raw image so the improvement gained by using Raw format and appropriate adjustments can be clearly seen.

● COLOUR CORRECTION

Pictures sometimes need a small colour adjustment to look realistic. This area is a potential minefield because on the one hand a small adjustment can make the image look better, but on the other hand if you need to make frequent colour corrections it could be a sign that your equipment is not properly set up.

When the colour balance needs adjusting there are several ways to make it. For a colour adjustment to the whole picture the recommended technique is to use the white balance adjustment at the Raw conversion stage because it is simple to do and the Raw conversion software keeps the overall appearance fairly realistic. Also, those who use Photoshop Elements have restricted options available for adjusting the colours.

Figure 5.7.1 shows a situation where some photographers might wish to adjust the overall colour balance. A pair of DRS Class 37 locomotives operating a Serco test train on the Isle of Grain are approaching their destination at about 0900 on a December morning. The sun is very low in the sky and gives a strong golden glow to the scene, which is clearly visible in the upper image. This shows the view using the 'as shot' white balance setting from the camera without any changes. The lower image uses the same Raw conversion settings except for the white balance, which was set using the method described earlier in this chapter. The image was enlarged in the Raw converter so that the white locomotive numbers were clearly visible, then the 'eye dropper' white balance tool was clicked on one of the numbers to tell the software that this area should be white. The software then changed the colour balance to remove the yellow glow, which is the same thing as adding more blue and made the overall colour balance rather 'cold'. Comparing the two images there is no 'correct' version and the choice of which one is more pleasing depends on personal preference.

A more extreme example of changing the colour balance is in night photography under certain lighting conditions as described later in this chapter.

What happens if you are part way through the editing process in Photoshop and decide that you want to change the white balance in the Raw conversion software? At this point the Raw conversion will already have been done and the image is inside Photoshop. Does this mean having to scrap all the work done so far and starting again? It's fairly simple to re-do the raw conversion and then replace the original image. The only downside is that any covering of dust spots will have to be re-done because the colour will no longer match. The principle for the replacement relies on the use of Adjustment Layers for contrast and brightness changes with the original image lowest in the stack of layers. The new image is put into the stack just above the original image using 'drag & drop' and the original image is then deleted. The example in Figure 5.7.2 of a Class 67 locomotive hauling tanks through Whifflet station demonstrates this. The edited image and the new image are both opened in Photoshop Elements 5.0 as shown in the upper screenshot. There are four layers in total in the edited image as shown in the Layers Palette – the image itself (labelled 'Background') and three adjustment layers with various masks. The Background image was created by raw conversion and will be replaced with an updated version. The Background layer is selected by clicking on it in the Layers Palette to ensure the new layer is added just above it. Then the replacement image is made the current image by clicking on it and its one layer (Background) appears in the Layers Palette. Next it is moved by placing the mouse pointer on the Background layer in the Layers Palette and clicking with the left mouse button while also holding the [Shift] key, then dragging the mouse pointer across the screen until it is above the edited image. This is shown in the lower example

where the mouse pointer has a tiny 'hand' symbol with a miniature rectangular outline of the layer. The mouse button is released to complete the copying. It is important to hold down the [Shift] key as this makes the new image line up with the images already there. The newly updated 'Layers Palette – after replacement' is shown in the lower example image. Note how the new image has appeared in the Layers Palette labelled as 'Layer 1' immediately above the original. The original image (Background) can now be deleted by using the 'Layer → Delete Layer' menu option or by clicking and dragging it to the trash can symbol in the Layers Palette.

What technique should be used for changing the colour balance when editing a JPEG image? Or perhaps the colour in only a part of the image needs to be changed. In full Photoshop the choice is easy – use a Color

Figure 5.7.2.
Replacing the original image in the layer stack with a new Raw conversion.

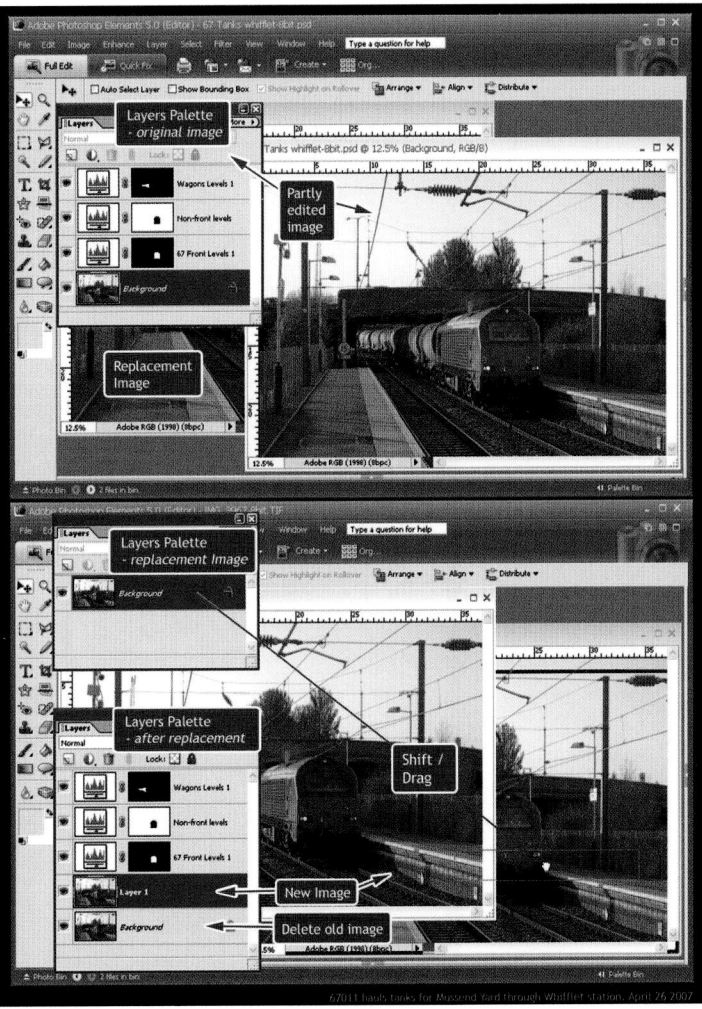

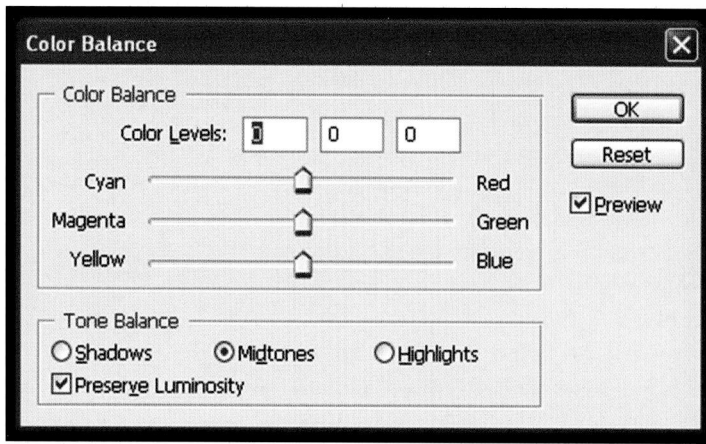

Figure 5.7.3.
Changing the colour balance in full Photoshop using a 'Color Balance Adjustment Layer'.

effect on all colours or, put another way, it alters all three channels together. If it is set to alter one channel only the colour balance is changed. The example in Figure 5.7.4 shows a colour change being made to just the locomotive in the previous example of the Class 67 at Whifflet. The locomotive body is slightly too red so it is selected using the Polygonal Lasso Tool as described earlier in this chapter. With the selection active a new Levels Adjustment Layer is created. When the name screen appears its name is changed to 'Red Colour Balance' to show what it is meant to do. The Levels screen itself is shown. The Drop Down box for 'Channel' is changed from RGB to Red so that only the red channel is changed. Then the middle triangle (ringed in red) under the graph is moved to the right to make the selected area less red. A couple of points to note are: i) the mask visible on the layer in the Layers Palette restricts the colour change to just the selected area; ii) the selection is shown active at the same time as the Levels Adjustment is made, but this is just for demonstration purposes and in practice the edge of the selection disappears at this stage. When satisfied with the changed colour, press 'OK'. Save the result containing all the Layers in Photoshop's PSD format.

Balance Adjustment Layer as shown in Figure 5.7.3. There are three slider controls with a fairly obvious function, for example moving the Red Slider towards 'Red' makes the image more red. Generally the Midtones option should be chosen as this affects colours in the middle of the range and avoids changing the brightest and darkest areas. Ticking the 'Preserve Luminosity' box is worthwhile to leave the overall brightness of the image unchanged.

In Photoshop Elements a colour adjustment can be made but is more complicated because the 'Color Balance Adjustment Layer' is missing. Instead a Levels Adjustment Layer is used. A Levels Adjustment Layer normally has the same

Figure 5.7.4.
Changing the colour balance in Photoshop Elements using a Levels Adjustment Layer.

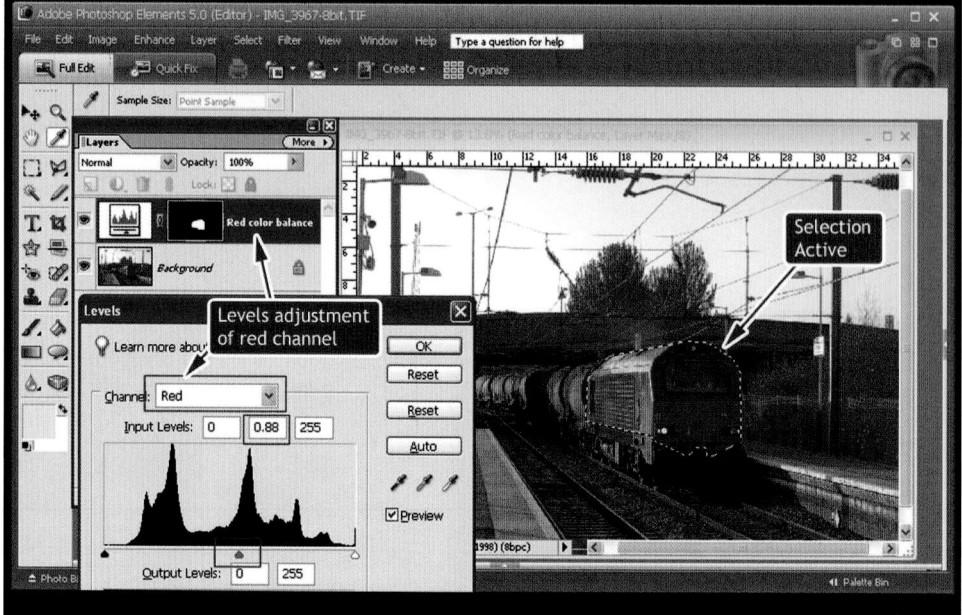

● SHARPENING

For newcomers to digital photography, sharpening is often a mis-understood technique. Why should an image need to be sharpened? Surely applying sharpening is a form of cheating? The reality is that all digital images need to be sharpened. This is because the majority of digital cameras deliberately blur the image during the capture process to avoid problems with strange patterns or colours when photographing fine regular patterns. In railway photography this would apply to, for example, photographing a locomotive grille or a chain link fence. By blurring the image before capture and sharpening it afterwards these problems are minimized. The blurring is done by a special layer in front of the digital sensor called an anti-aliasing filter. Digital cameras without an anti-aliasing filter are available for specialised applications such as astronomy.

Strictly speaking, images after sharpening are not sharper than before as the amount of detail in the picture is unchanged. The human eye is sensitive to contrast between different areas, particularly at edges, so what 'sharpening' does is to increase the contrast between adjacent pixels so that the picture appears to be sharper. When applying sharpening it's important to get the right balance: an image will look sub-standard if either too little or too much sharpening is applied. Sharpening techniques can often be used to 'rescue' the appearance of an image that wasn't sufficiently sharp initially but in reality this is just a way of fooling the human brain. Success depends on the degree of 'unsharpness' at the start and the amount of noise present. Sharpening cannot rescue images with gross mistakes but it can improve a less-than-perfect image to 'acceptable'. Really noisy images can be improved but the final result may not look as intended because the sharpening process can't tell the difference between noise and fine detail.

Raw vs JPEG

The major advantage of shooting in Raw format is that it allows the photographer to make their own choices about areas such as sharpening during processing on the computer after the image has been captured. A JPEG image has sharpening done inside the camera during processing before the image is saved to the memory card. Sharpening is a destructive process and with JPEG the results of in-camera sharpening are permanent and can't be reversed. When a JPEG image has a sharpness problem, the results after trying to fix it will be less good than if fixing the same problem on a Raw format image.

Amount of Sharpening

Personal taste will vary as to what is the appropriate amount of sharpening. A general word of advice is that if you are not sure how much sharpening to apply, it is better to under-sharpen than over-sharpen. A characteristic of over-sharpening is 'halos' in certain areas and a general over-processed look, which cannot be fixed later. All digital cameras sharpen images as part of the in-camera processing when they create JPEG and Tiff format images. The amount of sharpening varies by camera model and often there are settings in the setup menus to vary it, such as Low, Medium and High. Because additional sharpening can always be applied later a guideline for the camera stage is to use the Low or Medium sharpness setting. When shooting in Raw format, no sharpening is applied by the camera and maximum control is available during later processing on the computer. This is one of the advantages of using Raw format.

When sharpening for printing, very slight over-sharpening is preferable and a guideline is to choose an amount which looks right to the eye on the screen and then increase it by another 20-30%. Alternatively, display the image at about two-thirds of the final print size and then sharpen so that on the screen it looks 'right' to the eye.

Two-Step Approach

There is no 'right' or 'wrong' approach to sharpening. For most images the author recommends a two-step approach. Step One involves sharpening the image during the

Raw conversion process so that it looks sharp on the screen. Some photographers refer to this as 'capture' sharpening. Step Two involves a small amount of sharpening as one of the last steps in image processing. The amount will vary according to the size of the final image and whether preparing for web display, inkjet printing or publishing. This is known as 'output' sharpening.

Three-Step Approach

A small number of images need an additional sharpening step after Capture Sharpening, often known as 'creative' sharpening, leading to a 'three-step' approach. Any sharpness problems will be tackled during this extra step.

Output Sharpening

If the image is to be used on the web it needs to be resized to reduce its resolution. Mild sharpening is needed to compensate for the removal of data from the image. This area is described in more detail in Chapter 4. When printing, slight over-sharpening is preferred, as described earlier.

Sharpening in Photoshop

Photoshop has various sharpening functions named 'Sharpen', 'Sharpen Edges' and 'Sharpen More' but the downside of these are the lack of control: they either sharpen too little or too much. The most useful sharpening function has the confusing name of 'Unsharp Mask' – sometimes called USM – which allows a range of control. The name comes from the way the function actually works and originates from an advanced and difficult technique used in a traditional darkroom. Most commonly sharpening is applied to the whole picture and Photoshop assumes this is the case unless a specific area has been selected. To apply sharpening the 'Filter → Sharpen → Unsharp Mask' menu option is used. A control box will then be displayed. Sliders for three settings appear as explained below:

1 Amount: how much sharpening is to be applied to the image. Increasing the value increases the amount of sharpening, or more accurately, increases the contrast. Dark areas become darker and light areas lighter.

2 Radius: the size of the area around each pixel that will be affected by the sharpening. The value should be increased as the resolution of the image is increased. For web images a radius of around 0.5 is a good starting point. For higher resolution images to be printed a radius in the range 1.2 to 3.0 is recommended.

3 Threshold: determines how different in brightness adjacent pixels have to be before they are considered to be a light-dark transition which is sharpened. The lower the value of the Threshold setting, the greater the number of pixels that will be sharpened throughout the image, so with a value of 0 everything is affected. As the threshold value is increased the sharpening will be less detailed. A value of 3 to 4 is a good starting point.

Figure 5.8.1.
Different levels of sharpening applied with USM to the same unsharpened Raw image.

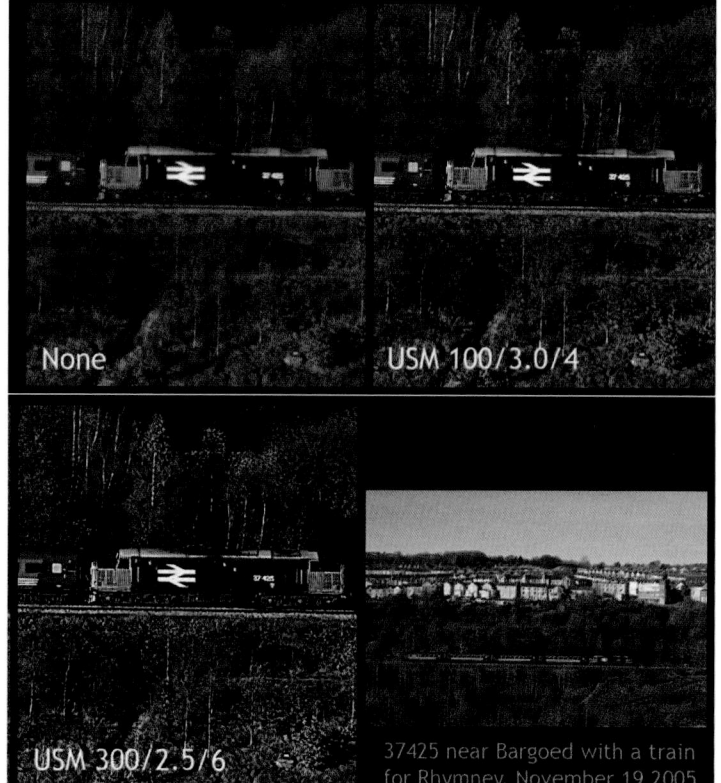

None

USM 100/3.0/4

USM 300/2.5/6

37425 near Bargoed with a train for Rhymney. November 19 2005

The amount of sharpening an image needs during editing depends on how much sharpening was applied at the Capture stage when it was created, either as a JPEG created by the camera or when a Raw format image was processed. Care needs to be taken with images taken at high ISO sensitivities because the amount of noise will be greater than those taken at a low ISO and there is a danger of sharpening the noise as well as the subject.

Appropriate general purpose settings are: Amount 80% to 100%; Radius 3.0, Threshold 4. It is worth experimenting with different values of the 'Amount' to see how the image looks.

Where an image has been resized to low resolution for web display a light application of sharpening is worthwhile to restore the sharpness that has been lost during the resizing process. Appropriate USM settings for a 'Light touch' are: Amount 35% / Radius 1.0 / Threshold 4

When printing an image the amount of sharpening required is greater than when viewing the same image on a screen. A guide is to give between 50% extra and double the amount. USM settings to start with are: Amount 120% to 150%; Radius 3.0, Threshold 4

Figure 5.8.1 shows small sections from the same image with different amounts of sharpening. The original was taken in Raw format and no sharpening was applied at the Raw conversion stage. Note that the first picture is fuzzy in appearance due to the blurring effect of the camera's anti-aliasing filter. A light amount of sharpening using USM in the second picture looks fine. The third image has been deliberately over-sharpened to demonstrate the destructive effect of sharpening.

● SHARPNESS PROBLEM

The train is approaching, the light is right and you're ready with your camera. You press the shutter release then look at the mini image on the review screen on the back of the camera. It seems fine, then you zoom in to make a final check. Oh dear, it's not sharp. Is it ruined?

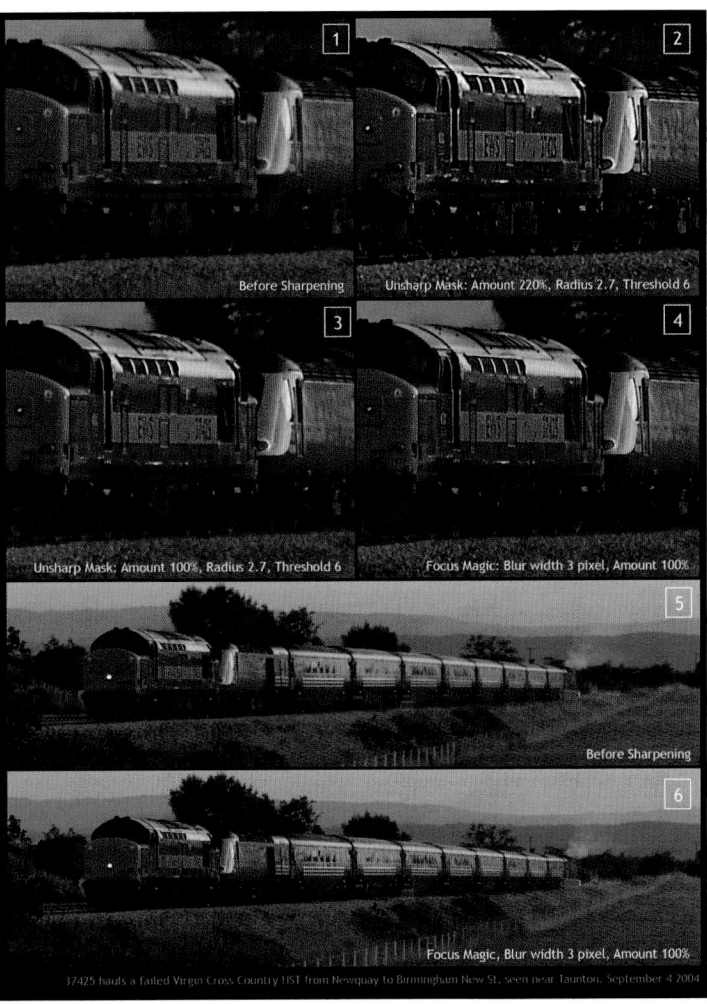

Example

In the example shown in Figure 5.9.1 the original image is not sharp because the camera was not focused correctly. A small printed image, say 6in by 4in, would look okay. A larger print or examination on a screen using the '100%' zoom setting in Photoshop will clearly show that it is blurred even when initial sharpening has been applied at the Raw conversion stage. There are two main alternative techniques for dealing with this. The first is using the standard 'Unsharp Mask' tool built into Photoshop (abbreviated to USM). The second is to use one of a number of specialised tools intended for dealing with out-of-focus images. These two options will be demonstrated.

At this stage it must be pointed out that these techniques have limits. A slightly sub-standard image can usually be turned into

Figure 5.9.1.
Comparing sections of the original image with different methods for sharpening.

something that is adequate either for display on the web or printing up to A4 size and viewed at arm's length. The techniques will not be able to turn a no-hope image into a highly detailed masterpiece.

Capture Sharpening

The Raw image is first processed in the Raw converter and a 'normal' amount of sharpening applied. It is then opened in Photoshop for Levels and other adjustments to be applied in the usual way.

Option 1 – USM

The sharpening tool built into Photoshop has a confusing name – USM (Unsharp Mask). The name comes from the way it works, which is to take an image and compare it with a blurred version of the same image (hence the term 'unsharp' mask). It modifies the image slightly to increase the contrast in the 'difference' area and fools the human eye into judging the image as sharper than the original. The downside of this approach is that it is quite crude and can have unwanted side-effects, particularly when the degree of sharpening is too high, causing images to look over-processed and unnatural. Two different settings were used here, the first shown in Picture 3 with a typical set of values: Threshold 6, Radius 2.7 and Amount 100%. The second used a much stronger amount of 220%, shown in Picture 2.

Option 2 – Plug-in

The author has used a specialised sharpening tool called Focus Magic which is available from www.focusmagic.com as a standalone program and Photoshop plug-in. A free trial is available. The tool allows the sharpening to be matched to the degree of blur in pixels and the strength of the sharpening effect can be varied. Picture 4 shows the results from a setting of 3 pixels and 100% strength. The difference between this picture and Picture 3 (100% USM) is fairly small but significant to the experienced eye. The halos are minimal, edges slightly sharper and surfaces such as the side of the HST have some texture instead of being blurry. These small differences all contribute to a noticeable improvement in the final result and the benefits of using the specialised software are more obvious when viewing an A4-size print.

Comparison

Picture 3 looks sharper than the original, whereas Picture 2 looks over-processed and unnatural with a 'crunchy' appearance. One of the giveaway signs of over-use of USM is a white halo-like border on edges such as in Picture 2. Look at the roof area above the locomotive centre window. Where the blue sky meets the roof there is a small white border between the two, which has been created by the USM application. Similar effects can often be seen in the sports section of daily newspapers. Picture 3, where the amount of USM has been kept to a more reasonable level, has a much smaller white border while in Picture 4 Focus Magic has created a minimal border.

Pictures 5 and 6 show a section of the overall picture 'before' and 'after' use of the Focus Magic sharpening tool. The difference between the two is noticeable in a high-resolution inkjet print. The 'after' version looks very acceptable in an A5-sized print and surprisingly good at A4-size. Without the use of the sharpening tool the picture would have been suitable only for a tiny print.

Web Sharpening

Focus Magic does an excellent job of sharpening images for the web and is both simple to use and fast to run. To use it, provided that the image looks sharp after normal preparation, resize and then apply sharpening using a setting of 1 pixel and 25% or 50% strength.

● NIGHT PHOTOGRAPHY

Night photography is a popular branch of the hobby, especially during winter months. Good results need plenty of care when taking the picture as well as when processing the results on the computer afterwards. In some circumstances it's possible to take pictures of moving trains at night using the techniques described in Chapter 6. Traditional night photography involves stationary trains and a typical example is shown here of a water cannon train at Worksop station.

Taking the shot

With traditional night photography a tripod needs to be used to hold the camera still because of the length of the exposure. When choosing a tripod it is best to pick one with legs long enough that the camera is at the right height for the composition without having to raise the centre column because this provides more rigidity. A tripod made from carbon fibre is worth considering because although more expensive than metal it is lighter, very rigid and both cooler to touch in the summer and less cold in the winter. A ball head on the tripod is much quicker to set up than the 'pan and tilt' type head used by video photographers and a 'quick release' plate is strongly recommended so that the camera can be removed from the tripod quickly and easily. It can be difficult to find a good quality tripod in the shops as the ones sold by high street retailers are generally low priced models with flimsy construction. Suitable models can be found at suppliers in large cities that focus on the professional photographic market.

A remote shutter release should always be used rather then pressing the camera's own shutter release button to avoid shaking the camera and causing a blurred picture. The camera's self timer (where fitted) is an alternative that also avoids shaking the camera but has the drawback of a delay before taking the shot that can burn up valuable time. While it's a good idea to protect the lens with a filter during general use, any filter is better removed for night shooting to eliminate a potential source of flare and reflections. Some photographers using zoom lenses have noticed more flare and 'ghost' reflections than expected. This is due to the number of elements inside the lens and a simple fixed length lens with fewer elements will usually give sharper, clearer results.

Exposure

With night photography judging the exposure is always difficult and normal practice is to

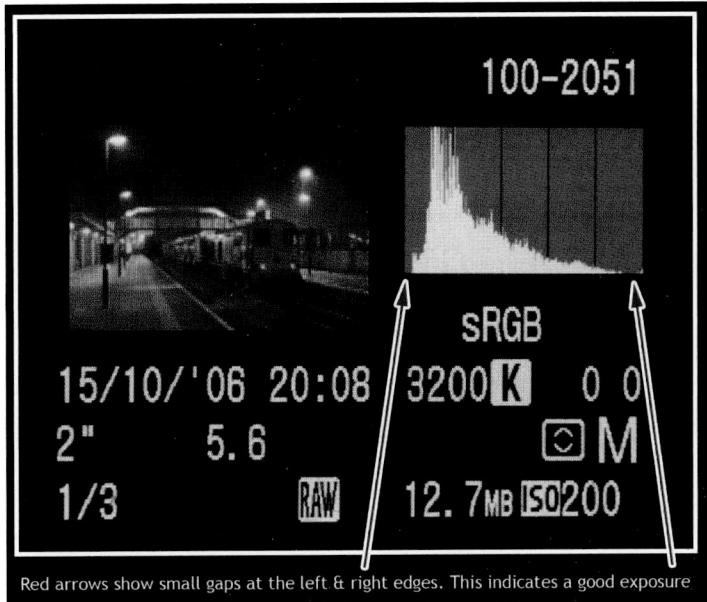

Red arrows show small gaps at the left & right edges. This indicates a good exposure

take a series of pictures at slightly different settings in a process known as 'bracketing'. Digital cameras provide a small version of the image on the rear display showing the overall brightness plus a graph-like display known as the histogram as shown in Figure 5.10.1. The histogram was described in Chapter 2 and the same principles apply to night photography. A well-exposed image will have a similar histogram to the one shown here where the line of the 'graph' does not cross the left or right sides but instead crosses the bottom of the graph at both sides. There should always be a gap between the point where the graph crosses the bottom edge and the sides. This is shown by the red arrows on the example. There will usually be one or more small 'blobs' near the bottom right corner of the histogram that are caused by very bright areas such as lamps and can be ignored provided they are small. If they are large this means the image is probably over-exposed, so it is best to adjust the camera to use a faster shutter speed and try again. A test picture should always be taken, even if the train has not yet arrived, so that the histogram can be checked and the settings adjusted as necessary. The histogram should be checked again during the actual shoot. Digital SLRs usually give excellent low noise results when set at 200 ISO. In older cameras 100 ISO will give results with less noise and it

Figure 5.10.1.
View of the rear of the camera including histogram after taking a night shot.

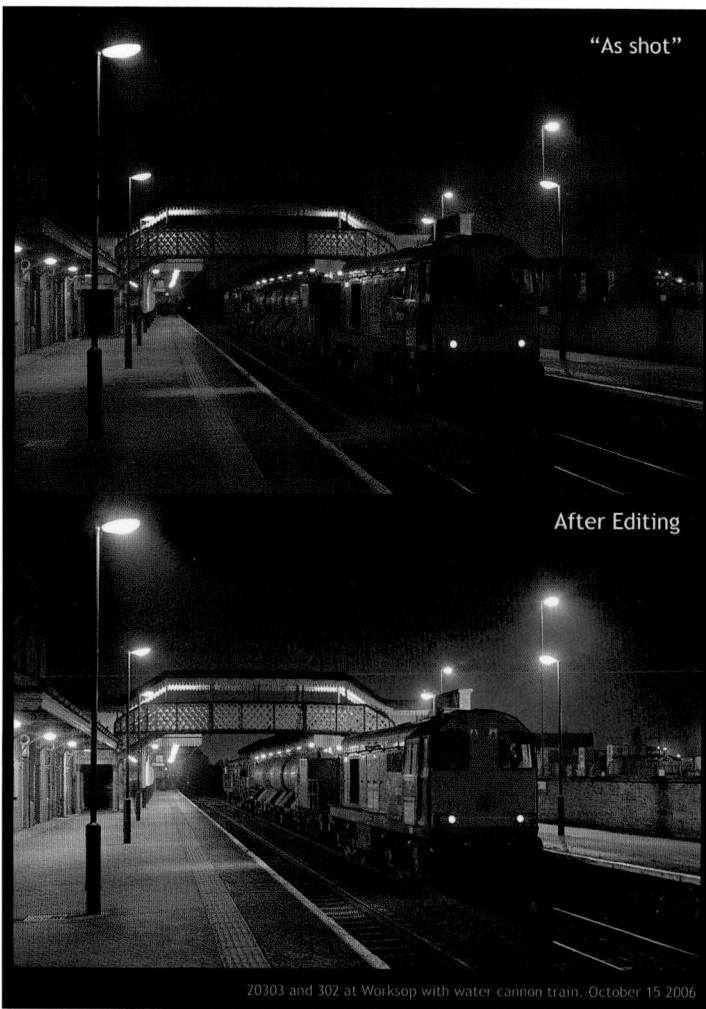

"As shot"

After Editing

20303 and 302 at Worksop with water cannon train. October 15 2006

Figure 5.10.2.
Night photograph before and after editing.

Colour Cast

The most obvious area where a night photograph can be improved is the colour balance. The human eye adapts well to its surroundings and many people do not realise that most station lights introduce a strong colour cast of some kind. The lights at Worksop, for example, give a strong orange cast. This can be corrected using a technique known as 'setting the white balance'. The extent to which any colour cast is removed is a subject of controversy and debate among railway enthusiasts. Some feel that the cast is ugly and should be removed while others feel that the subject should be left as it was recorded. The example here does not attempt to say which is the 'right' approach and simply shows how to remove a colour cast for those that wish to do so. Two versions of the same original image before and after editing are shown in Figure 5.10.2.

Raw format is strongly recommended for night photographs as it gives higher quality and much more flexibility than JPEG when processing the image on a computer. Raw conversion software is used to create an image file that can be edited in Photoshop or similar editing program. There are many different Raw converter software programs available, provided by camera manufacturers and independent software companies. The first step in processing a Raw image in the converter software is to set the white balance. Normally this is done by clicking on a part of the image that should be white. The software then changes all the colours accordingly. The colour balance can be changed by clicking elsewhere. The Raw conversion process is described in more detail earlier in this chapter.

Brightness

When processing the image the usual considerations apply. The image should contain a full range of tones and without clipped large areas – full brightness or full darkness. Chapter 6 describes an advanced technique to improve the appearance of lights in a night picture.

is worth experimenting with different ISO settings. Many lenses give optimal sharpness at an aperture of f5.6 while a few lenses may be better at f8. Manual exposure and focusing are recommended so that the camera settings don't change unexpectedly. A typical exposure in the example that looked good was 2sec at f5.6 on 200 ISO. Despite taking care some pictures still end up with camera shake or inaccurate focus so it is always a good idea to take several sets of images. Part way through the shoot, move the tripod slightly or try a different lens, then re-focus the camera and take another set of pictures at similar exposure settings. This gives a range of different exposures and compositions so that there is the opportunity to pick the best one when viewed at home on the computer. Focusing techniques are described in Chapter 2.

● DARKENING THE SKY

It's common for landscape pictures to need improvement by darkening the sky. There are many ways in which this can be done and several techniques are included in this book. The technique described in this section uses a Curves Adjustment Layer and is quick to implement.

Principle

The principle relies on the fact that in the majority of images the sky is noticeably brighter than the ground where it meets the sky, or brighter than any poles and wires. To darken just the sky needs a set of instructions that says 'In the sky and its immediate surroundings, darken everything with sky brightness and leave everything with ground brightness unchanged'. This is achieved using a powerful Photoshop function known as Curves. Those using Photoshop Elements rather than full Photoshop will need to use a variation of the same technique due to limitations in Elements' functionality. Obviously any light coloured wires or electrification poles in the sky will potentially be impacted by any darkening. Either they are darkened as well or excluded from the darkening process, noting that the work necessary to exclude them can be quite involved. The sky will be darkened by creating a Curves Adjustment Layer that progressively darkens everything with sky brightness but leaves untouched everything with land brightness. By including a mask the effect is restricted to the sky and the immediately adjacent area in order to avoid unwanted darkening of light area elsewhere in the picture.

Background – Brightness and Levels

The example shows a Class 175 unit crossing Arnside Viaduct in typical summer conditions. The sky is very bright with a pale colour and needs to be darkened to emphasise the clouds.

A little background information first. Photoshop provides a tool – known as the Eyedropper Tool – which can measure the brightness of any part of an image. The brightness is displayed on the Information Palette (actually called 'Info Palette') as a % value where 0% is maximum brightness (minimum darkness) and 100% is maximum darkness. By using this tool the brightness can be checked in the sky and adjacent areas to be sure that the principle is feasible. The brightness values for various points in the Arnside picture are shown in Figure 5.11.2.

Levels

The first adjustment to the picture is, as usual, a Levels Adjustment to improve the overall contrast. To recap, one of the main principles of editing is that a pleasing photograph has a full range of contrast. It should contain brightness values of 0% and 100% and everything in between. When the sky is darkened using a Levels Adjustment, any areas of maximum brightness (0%) are left unchanged while other light areas are progressively darkened.

Selection

All of the sky and a little of the land near the horizon should be selected using the Polygonal Lasso Tool. Selection techniques were described in detail earlier in this chapter. A graduated (feathered) edge on the

Figure 5.11.1.
Strips from the same original image with different amounts of sky darkening.

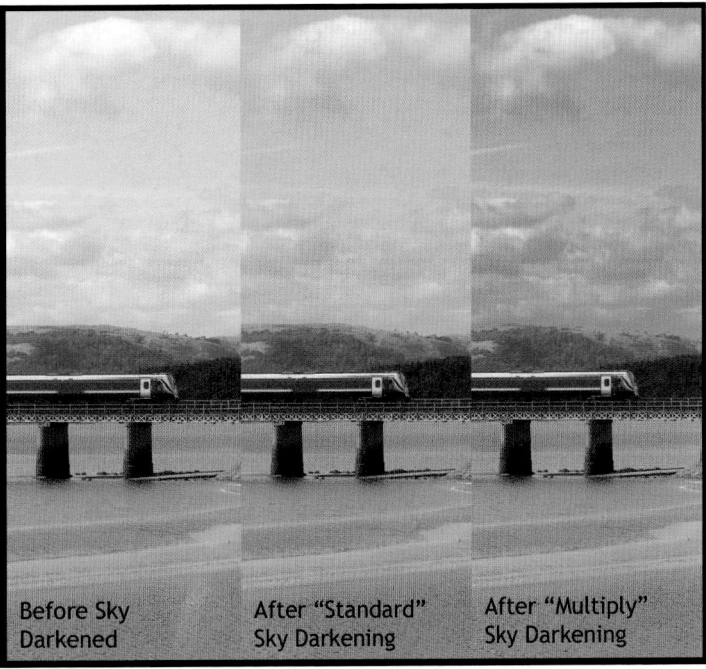

Before Sky Darkened

After "Standard" Sky Darkening

After "Multiply" Sky Darkening

Figure 5.11.2.
Creating a curve to darken the sky using full Photoshop.

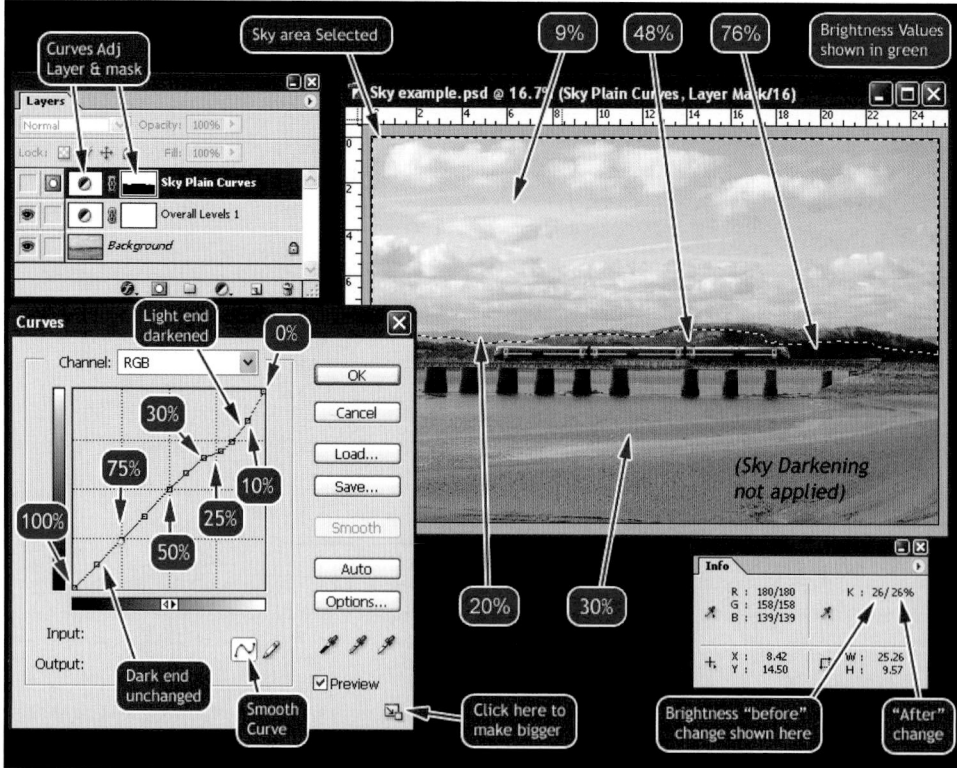

land part of the selection ensures that any unwanted changes in brightness are gradual. If there are any very bright areas in the land they are excluded from the selection. The selection is intended to be quick and easy to create.

Curves – full Photoshop.

For those with full Photoshop, the Curves Adjustment Layer is created using the 'Layer → New Adjustment Layer → Curves…' menu option. This will display a screen with a graph-like display where the curve can be adjusted. Initially the line of the curve is actually a straight line from bottom left to top right. It is necessary to click on the curve to create points to fix it in position. As the points are moved around, the line will try to create a smooth curve wherever possible, hence the name 'curves'. Points are created by clicking on the curve and can then be moved around by clicking & dragging with the mouse. To check the brightness of areas in the main picture, clicking on the picture displays its brightness value on the curve. In this way it is easy to be sure that the curve is in the right place.

Because a selection was active when the

Adjustment Layer was created, a Mask will be added automatically. The mask ensures that the changes are only applied to the selected area, that is to the sky and a little of the horizon. Figure 5.11.2 shows the selection of the sky and land, the curve itself and various examples of brightness.

The point of about 30% brightness has not been moved, and the curve is a straight line between here and 100% brightness (lower left). The curve therefore has no effect on any areas of the picture with between 30% and 100% brightness. Similarly the 0% brightness point in the top right is unchanged to ensure the areas of maximum brightness stay bright and contrast is maintained. The curve dips downwards in the area around 10 to 20% in order to achieve the darkening effect in the region of 'sky brightness'. The key to success here is keeping the curve smooth and avoid it running horizontally or vertically. The effect on the image can be seen as the curve is changed provided that the 'Preview' box is ticked. Abrupt movements in the curve will cause unrealistic coloured effects.

By clicking on the 'OK' button the Adjustment Layer will be created. The curve can be changed at any time by double clicking on the Adjustment Layer in the Layers Palette to open the same adjustment screen. The 'before' and 'after' images are shown in Figure 5.11.1.

It's worth commenting that this technique is suitable for many images, especially those with objects in the sky like trees and poles. The only occasion where it may have difficulty is where there are light coloured poles because the darkening effect may be unwanted.

Curves – Photoshop Elements

Photoshop Elements is somewhat 'stripped down' in functionality and although the 'curves' function is included inside the software there is no built-in menu option to be able to get to it. Fortunately an enterprising photographer from Australia, Paul Shipley, has created some software to gain access to Curves within Elements and made it freely available. By doing an Internet search for 'Paul Shipley Photoshop' it is possible to find his web site and download the necessary software together with full installation instructions.

With this software loaded a Curves Adjustment Layer can be created in exactly the same way as already described for full Photoshop. There is, however, a major downside to the Curves function added in this way – once created it cannot be changed. It is only possible to delete the existing curves layer and create a new one. It is necessary to keep a record of the curve previously created (either on paper or as a screenshot) so that you know what you did previously. To take a screenshot on a Windows XP PC of just the Curves adjustment screen, click on it, then press the [Alt] and [Print Screen] keys at the same time, then use the 'Paste' function to copy the screenshot into the desired program such as Word or Photoshop. This is rather limiting if

you frequently need to update the curve and is one of the incentives to purchase full Photoshop.

Advanced Option – 'Multiply Curve'

The method just described may not deliver a strong enough darkening effect for some images and a more powerful option called the 'multiply curve' may be appropriate. To explain how this works needs a description of how layers interact with each other by the use of the 'Blending Mode' setting. In most cases 'Normal' blending mode is used with an Adjustment Layer. The resulting brightness is calculated using a simple transformation of the brightness value of a pixel in the layers below it. 'Multiply' blending mode has a stronger effect because it calculates the adjusted brightness by multiplying the brightness value of an existing pixel by the value of the curve. By using a suitable curve with 'Multiply' blending mode much stronger

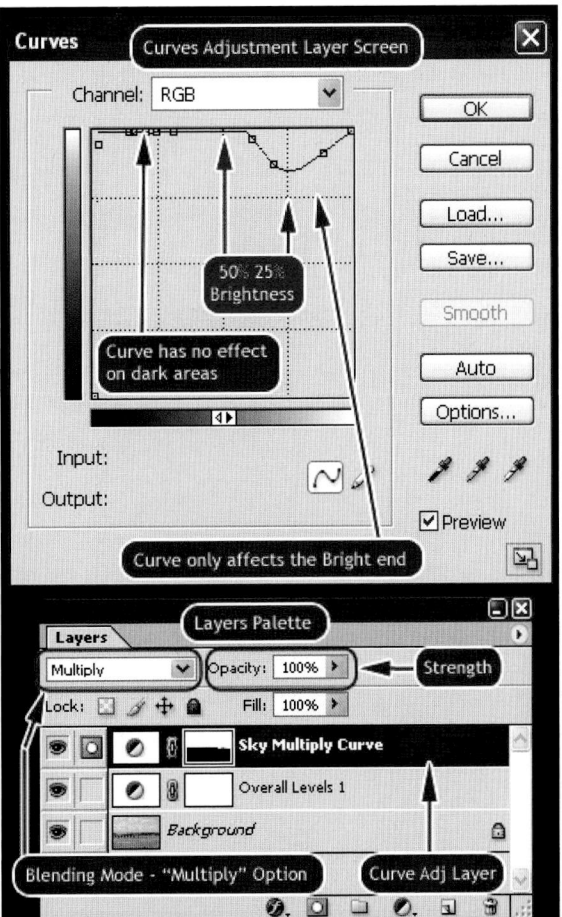

Figure 5.11.3.
The settings involved in creating a 'Multiply' curve.

darkening can be achieved. The 'Multiply' curve looks quite different to a 'Normal' curve: where darkening is not wanted the 'curve' hugs the top of the chart, then dips downwards where an effect is wanted. The 'Multiply' option must be set by first selecting the layer in the Layers Palette and then changing the drop down box to 'Multiply' – this option is known as the 'blending mode'. This option is shown in Figure 5.11.3. A couple of tips: i) use lots of points to 'anchor' the curve at the top of the chart; ii) keep the curve smooth in the 'darkening' area. The effect can be weakened either by changing the path of the curve or decreasing the 'Opacity' setting from its usual 100%. With this option care must be taken to avoid unrealistic effects in the sky resulting from a badly shaped curve. Figure 5.11.4 shows the same original image 'before' and 'after' applying a 'Multiply' curve.

Figure 5.11.4.
Before and after darkening the sky using a 'Multiply' curve.

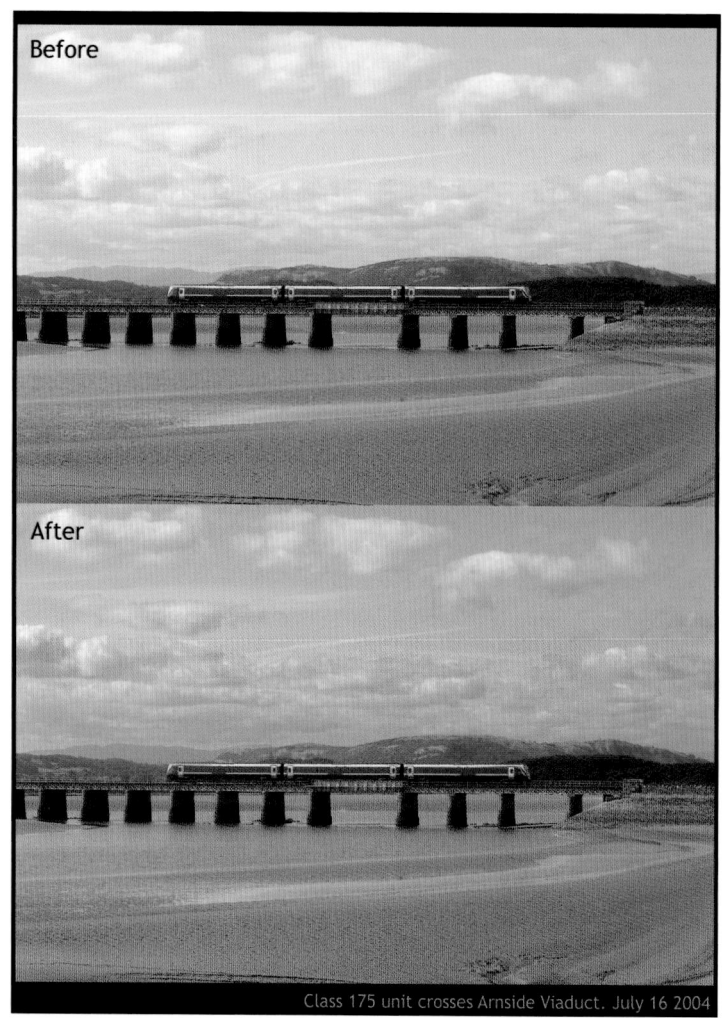

Before

After

Class 175 unit crosses Arnside Viaduct. July 16 2004

● 'THE SUN DIPPED'

Every photographer has experienced that agonising moment. The sun is shining brightly and just as the train approaches the sun goes behind a cloud. A disappointing photograph results, with a dark foreground and beautiful sunny background. A technique to deal with this situation will now be described. To set expectations, it must be said that a pleasant result can be created in most cases, even when the sun is partly behind a thick cloud, but the deep shadows and rich tones produced by true 'full sun' conditions cannot be recreated. Thin cloud can, however, usually be dealt with very effectively.

Example

The example in Figure 5.12.1 features a rare working – a pair of DRS Class 37 locomotives powering a Serco test train into London Bridge. As the train approached, the foreground started to darken and when the front of the train reached the point where the author planned to press the shutter release, the front locomotive and most of the first coach were in shadow under a cloud while the rest of the picture was bathed in glorious summer afternoon sunshine.

Taking

The first part of dealing with a situation like this is the strategy used when taking the picture. The clouded area – the foreground in this example – must stay dark while the rest of the area is 'normal'. What must be avoided at all costs is for the camera to automatically adjust to the dark area and make the overall picture brighter because this usually leads to the sunny area being so bright that some areas experience 'burnout'. Digital cameras are particularly susceptible to over-exposure and once detail is lost from an area it is usually difficult (and often impossible) to fix it properly. The best strategy when taking a picture in these conditions is to use manual exposure settings so that the camera behaves in a predictable way. Automatic settings may compensate too much for a dark area and make the bright areas too bright. The recommended strategy when the light dips in a small area is to either leave the manual settings unchanged, or to make only a small change. Obviously on a fully cloudy day, appropriate settings for the lighting conditions should be used including compensation for any dark areas.

Raw

The second part of the solution is processing the Raw image on the computer. The Exposure control is set so that the sunny parts of the image look normal. This causes the dark parts to look relatively dark but they are dealt with later.

Adjustment

The last part of the solution consists of adjusting the image on the computer. What needs to be done sounds simple – lighten the dark areas in a way that gradually blends seamlessly into the sunny area of the picture. In practice there is more to it than this. If the image is only lightened it will look flat, ugly and unrealistic so the lightening process has to include increasing the contrast. Both operations are done using a single Levels adjustment.

The gradual blending of the manipulated areas into the sunny areas will be achieved using a soft brush with very light brush strokes operating on masks. Photoshop Elements has been used in the example to make the changes but the operation is virtually the same in full Photoshop. Do not be tempted to use Photoshop's built-in 'Shadow' option as it lacks the fine control that is needed.

The trick here is to temporarily apply a slightly stronger Levels adjustment than is needed to the whole picture. The next step is to disable it, followed by gradually re-applying it to the 'clouded' area using soft, light brush strokes.

Levels

To make the Levels Adjustment a new Levels Adjustment Layer is created using the 'Layer → New Adjustment Layer → Levels...' menu option, giving it a name like 'Cloudy area Levels'. Then the contrast is adjusted by

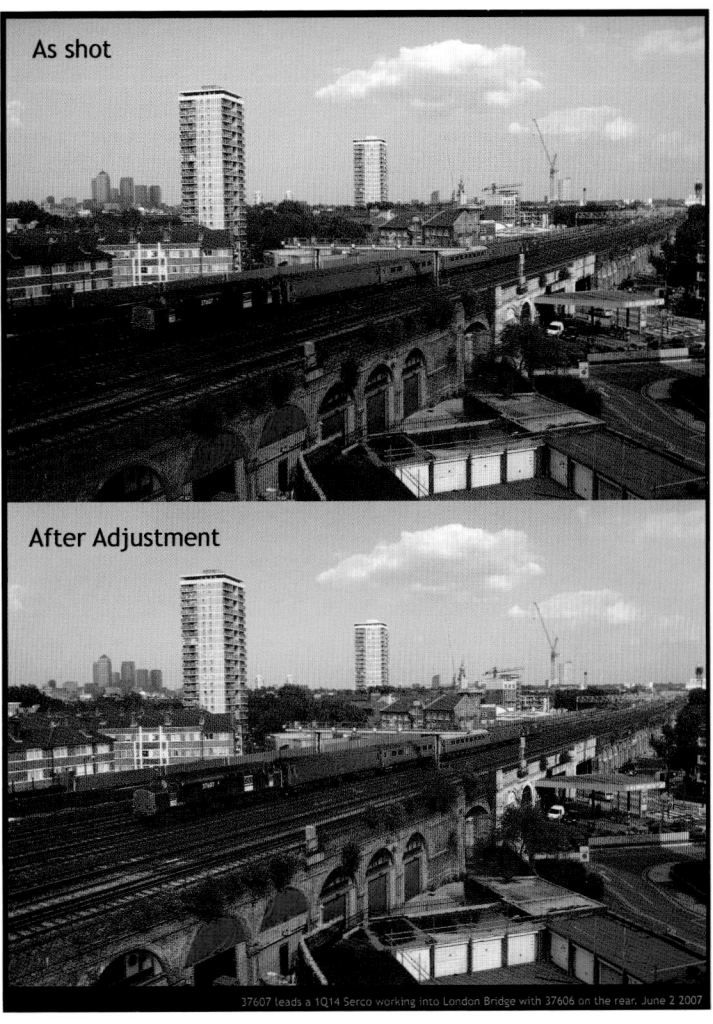

Figure 5.12.1.
Before and after improving the image.

moving the black and white triangles. This is shown in Figure 5.12.2. Begin by moving the white triangle on the right side towards the left. As this is done the picture will lighten – provided the 'Preview' option is ticked. Ignore the sunny area and concentrate on the 'clouded' area only. Stop when the brightest parts of the cloudy area start to look unrealistically bright. Then work on the dark areas: move the dark triangle on the left side in towards the middle. This will cause the shadows to deepen. Stop when detail starts to disappear in the darkest areas. At this point the brightness might need to be adjusted so that the dark areas look about right. To do this, move the middle triangle left or right until the brightness in this area looks okay. Ignore the sunny areas of the picture which will look much too bright. The example shows this. When happy with the appearance, click

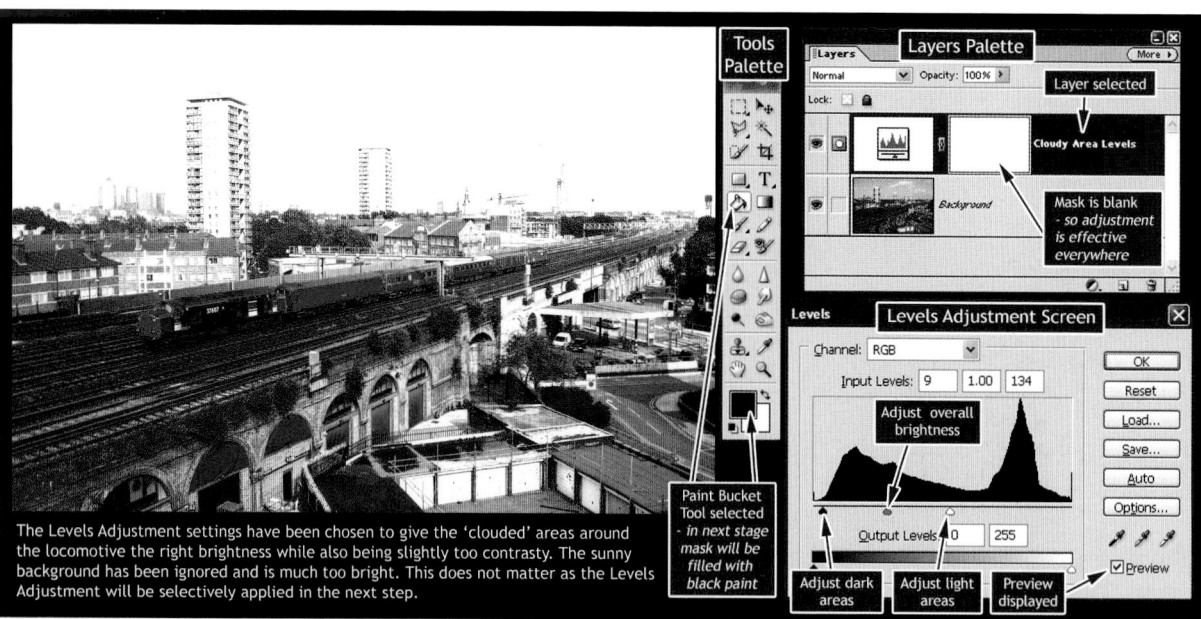

The Levels Adjustment settings have been chosen to give the 'clouded' areas around the locomotive the right brightness while also being slightly too contrasty. The sunny background has been ignored and is much too bright. This does not matter as the Levels Adjustment will be selectively applied in the next step.

Figure 5.12.2.
Adjusting the brightness & contrast in the shadowed area.

'OK' to save the Levels Adjustment Layer. To change it later, double click the left mouse button after selecting this layer in the Layers Palette and the same adjustment screen will appear.

Disable

At this point the image looks too bright because the adjustment applies to the whole picture. It needs to be disabled using the mask facility before being re-applied selectively. The mask is shown in the Layers Palette and at this point will be all white. By making it black the adjustment will be disabled. To make it black, it is necessary to fill it with black paint using the Paint Bucket tool. Three things need to be done first: i) select the Paint Bucket Tool by clicking on it in the Tools Palette; ii) ensure that black is showing as the current foreground colour in the Tools Palette; iii) that the adjustment layer is selected in the Layers Palette – it will have a blue colour to confirm it is selected. If black is not selected, click on the tiny squares that have been labelled on the example as 'Brush colour reset'. If white is showing as the current Foreground colour, swap to black by clicking on the tiny curved arrows. To fill the mask with black paint, check that the three settings described above are correct, then click anywhere on the picture. The black paint on the mask will cause the levels

adjustment to disappear and the image will revert to the way it looked originally. If this operation doesn't work it will be because one or more of the three settings described above is wrong. Check the miniature image of the mask in the Layers Palette to see if black paint was applied to it, or not.

Re-applying

The creative work can now start – gradually applying the lightening. This is done by deleting the mask in small areas. As these holes appear in the mask, the Levels Adjustment 'shines through' and the image is lightened. There are two different ways to do the deleting. The first is using the Eraser Tool with black paint, while the second is using the Brush Tool with white paint. For Photoshop Elements users the Brush Tool has the advantage that a preset set of brushes is available. Whichever tool is used, a large soft brush with a size of between 400 and 1000 pixels and 0% hardness is a good starting point, although the size might need to be changed to suit the picture. The critical part of the operation is to set the Opacity value to about 15% to ensure the erasing only has a very mild effect. Click the mouse button while the brush is above the clouded areas, and move it around. This will partially delete the mask and gradually apply the Levels effect. Repeat this lots of times in the clouded area,

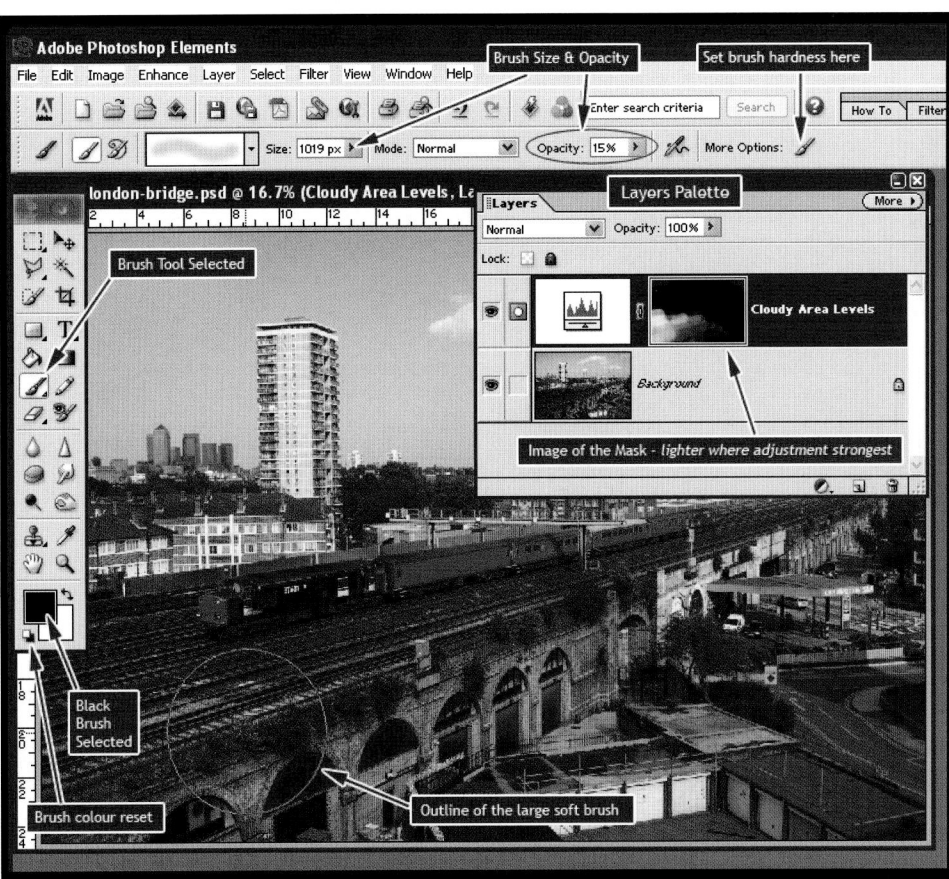

Figure 5.12.3.
Gradually lightening
the shadowed area by
editing the mask.

trying not to work in the same area each time. By this means a gradual edge to the adjustment can be created so that there is a seamless transition into the sunny area. There are two ways to reverse any changes: i) use the 'Undo' option; ii) paint on the mask using the Brush Tool with black paint. There will be some areas where a sharper edge to the transition is needed – use a smaller brush or greater hardness value or both. Figure 5.12.3 shows all these settings.

The wide angle lens used to take the example picture caused very slight darkening of the sky in the top corners of the picture – known as vignetting. This was lightened using the same technique – using a very large soft brush with low opacity to put white paint in the corners of the mask.

Finishing

To finish the edit, the image is saved in Photoshop's own .PSD format so that changes can be made later if desired. Adjustments can be made to other areas of the image in the usual way and the image saved again after completing these. The final step involves flattening the image to collapse the layers, cropping and resizing as necessary, then sharpening before either printing it or saving as a JPEG for web use.

● UNWANTED OBJECTS

When taking a photograph there may be objects in the picture that spoil the composition or distract the viewer. Editing the photograph on a computer allows them to be removed quickly and easily. This section describes a couple of simple removal techniques.

Ethical Questions

The ethics of changing the appearance of a scene after taking a picture can be questioned. Professional photo journalists know that changing images is seen within the news-gathering industry as an 'offence' that could lead them to lose their job. There is a

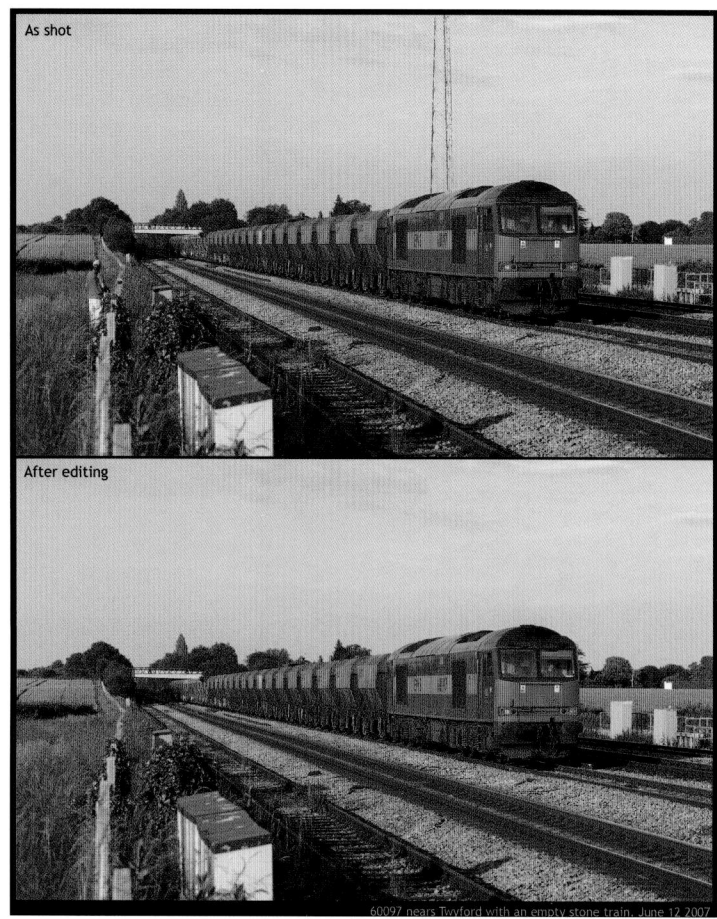

As shot

After editing

60097 nears Twyford with an empty stone train. June 12 2007

Figure 5.13.1.

Comparing an image 'as shot' with an edited version that has removed the mast and photographer in the background.

line to be drawn between what they can reasonably change and changes that are unacceptable. On the other hand an amateur photographer is free to change their own images as they wish, although there might be difficulties if they submit an altered image for publication. The techniques that can be used are described here without any attempt to discuss what is ethically appropriate so that photographers can see what is possible.

Example

Figure 5.13.1 shows a Class 60 locomotive in evening light near Twyford on the Great Western main line heading west with a late-running train of empty hopper wagons. It is normally a morning working and the shot cannot be repeated. Unfortunately the author was caught slightly out of position when the train appeared and as a result the photograph is compromised with an ugly radio mast and a figure in the middle distance. Both these unwanted objects will be removed.

Covering

The sky around the radio mast is fairly plain so it will be straightforward to cover the mast with pieces of sky copied from the area around it. This technique is called cloning and is performed in Photoshop and Photoshop Elements using the 'Clone Stamp Tool'.

Covering up the background figure is less straightforward because of the detail in the area behind him. Although the cloning tool could be used to cover up the area of plain grass, achieving a seamless repair in the detailed areas would be more difficult, particularly in the shadowed corner of the field. It would be possible to cover the whole area with plain grass copied from elsewhere in the image but this would probably look unrealistic. The best method in this situation is to recognise when taking the picture that work will be needed later and take an additional photograph from the same viewpoint when the unwanted object has moved. A small 'patch' can be copied out of the second image to cover up the object in the first image.

Successful Cloning

Generally speaking, use of the Clone Stamp Tool is most successful when covering small areas and when copying irregular patterns or plain colours. If a larger area, distinctive object or stronger pattern is involved it is usually more successful to copy a small patch from another area using the select-copy-paste technique described later. When cloning it is a good idea to use frequent short mouse movements so that any mistakes can be undone easily. By comparison if a lot of cloning was done in one step, undoing that step might remove cloning that was wanted as well as the cloning that was not. Most images require manipulation (such as a Levels Adjustment to increase the contrast)) and the best practice is to finish the cloning and related repairs before making the manipulations. This applies especially to Adjustment Layers in order to avoid unexpected problems with colour mis-matches.

Editing Principle

Maintaining the overall editing principle described at the beginning of this chapter that content of the original image will not be changed, the only action will be to add new material. This ensures that it is easy to compare the updates with the original unchanged version and it is simple to start again if necessary. Following this principle, cloned material or patches will be put in a new layer rather than overwriting the original image.

Select-Copy-Paste

In the Class 60 example image the most awkward area for cloning is where the radio mast meets the locomotive roof because of the difficulty of copying sky right up to, but not over the edge. To get a seamless join, the easiest technique is to first select a large area of sky (including the mast) immediately above the roof. When the Clone Stamp Tool is used inside this selected area it will only copy material inside the selected area, leaving the area outside the selection untouched. This gives a clean edge to the cloned sky and prevents writing cloned sky on top of the roof.

Figure 5.13.2 shows the sky selected above the locomotive body in the area of the mast. To create the selection, the Magnetic Lasso Tool with a feather of 1 pixel is used to follow the roof while also creating a selection that has a very slight fade to its edge. The fade ensures that when new sky is copied, the join with the locomotive roof does not look unnatural.

To work on the mast, the Clone Stamp Tool is chosen in the Tools Palette. A soft brush is chosen which is slightly narrower than the width of the mast: 100 pixels in this case. Using a soft brush is important because the soft edge ensures that the copied material blends seamlessly into what is already there. To tell the Clone Stamp Tool where to copy material from, the [Alt] key is held while clicking the left mouse button and pointing the mouse pointer at the desired spot. This should be from the area beside the mast but not too close otherwise the mast itself might be copied. A new Layer is created using the 'New... → Layer...' menu command and given a name like 'Cover Layer'. It is worth checking in the Layers Palette that this

new layer is the active layer (highlighted in blue) and positioned above the main image in the set of layers. If it's not the active layer the new material will be copied in the wrong place. To actually copy the material, the cloning brush is positioned over the mast and the left mouse button pressed. The new material should cover part of the mast. The mouse is moved with the left mouse button held down to copy more material until the width of the mast is covered. There are small clouds high in the sky so the area from which material is copied should be chosen carefully to ensure a match between new cloud and what is already there. A smaller brush is used for copying the cloud so that the gaps are filled in a natural way.

Patching

The author took a second photograph when the train had passed and the figure in the distance had moved slightly. To cover up the figure a small piece was copied from the second photograph and pasted in. After doing this the crouching figure will be covered using cloned grass. Raw format and the same manual exposure settings were used when taking both pictures. It is important to use the same exposure and Raw converter settings for both pictures so that the colours and brightness match exactly.

Figure 5.13.2.
Selecting part of the sky to provide a working area for cloning.

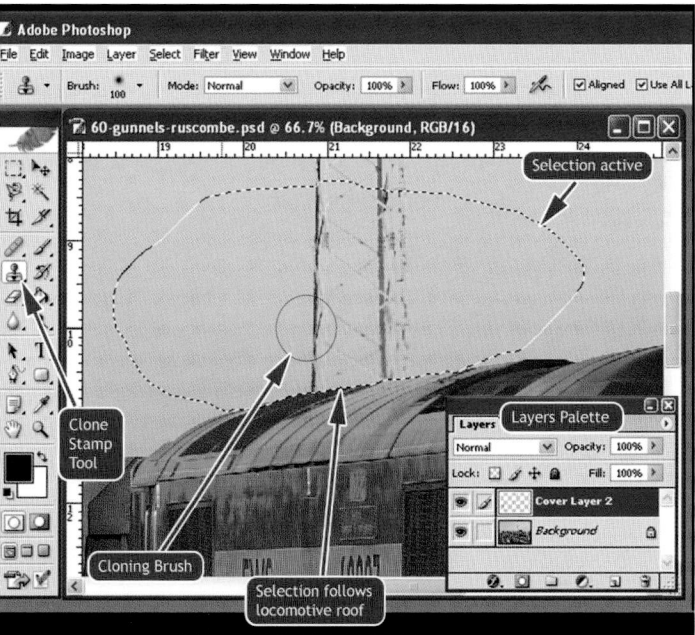

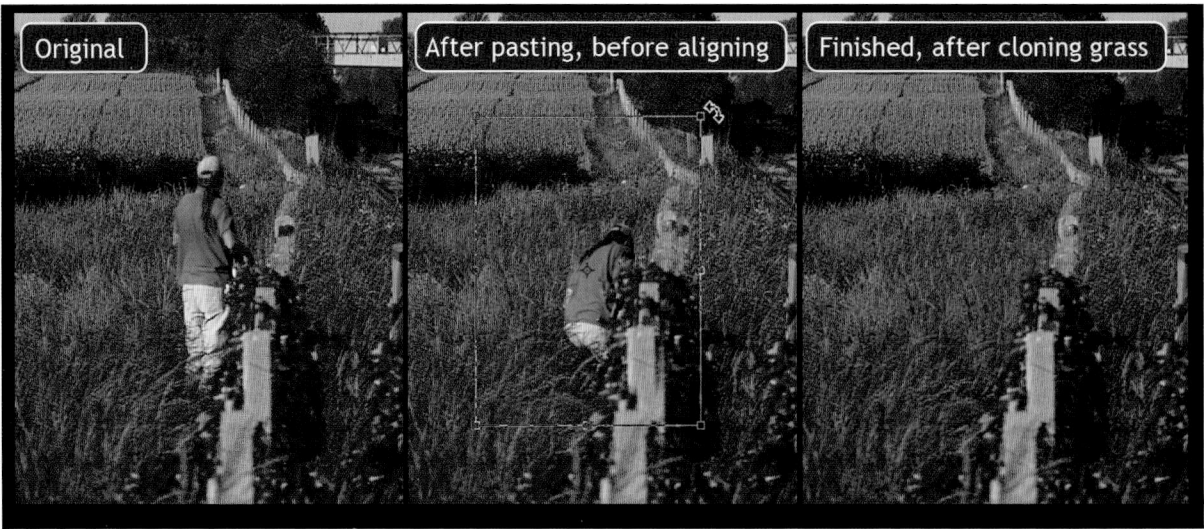

Figure 5.13.3.
Covering the figure using a combination of patching and cloning.

To select the area for copying, the Polygonal Lasso tool is used with a feather of about four pixels so that the edge of the new piece is gradual rather than abrupt. Clicking the left mouse button adds an anchor point. If any points are in the wrong position, pressing the [Delete] key deletes the most recently added point before trying again. A rough rectangle is drawn around the piece of the field and double-clicking the left mouse button or pressing [Enter→] completes the selection. In the Layers Palette the current layer should be the one that contains the original image (unless the name has already been changed it will be the Background layer). The 'Copy' option on the 'Edit' menu is then used to copy the patch to the clipboard.

Choosing 'Paste' from the 'Edit' menu automatically copies the piece of field into its own new layer which is above the original image when viewed in the Layers Palette. It's a good idea to rename this new layer to something like 'Field Piece'. This is done by double-clicking the left mouse button while placing the mouse pointer over the layer name in the Layers Palette and then typing in the new name. Next, the new material is moved close to its final position to make it easier to decide how to blend it into its new position. To do the move, the 'Move Tool' in the Tools Palette is chosen. The new field piece (which may not be clearly visible as it will probably be directly on top of the area it

was copied from) is then dragged nearer to its new position. A 'drag' operation involves holding down the left mouse button while the pointer is above the object, then moving the object with the mouse button still held down, then releasing the mouse button when the object is in its desired position. There is no need to select anything during the 'Move' operation as the whole object is selected automatically when the Move Tool is chosen. Enlarging the view on the computer screen makes it easier to position the patch exactly. In this example the new piece of field needed to be rotated very slightly in order to match the original. Movement and rotation of a small object is achieved in full Photoshop using the 'Free Transform' option on the 'Edit' menu. In Elements choose 'Image → Transform → Free Transform'. When choosing this option a border appears as shown in Figure 5.13.3. Holding the mouse pointer slightly outside the corner causes the pointer shape to change to a set of curved arrows (also shown) which allow the piece to be rotated by dragging. 'Free Transform' allows the object to be moved in the same way as the 'Move Tool' so the new piece can be placed in exactly the right position to cover the figure and match the material already in place. To complete the transform the 'Tick' mark at the top of the screen is clicked.

A tip – with either of these tools pressing the arrow keys can be used to 'nudge' the object in any direction – up, down or sideways. This is a convenient way of positioning the replacement object. When zooming in closely, the amount the object moves is less so fine positioning is possible. If the new patch is too large, material can be deleted from it using a soft brush to make the change invisible. Advanced workers are recommended to remove the material using a mask rather than permanently deleting it, as this allows an easy 'undelete' if necessary.

Next Steps

The usual contrast adjustments follow, followed by saving in Photoshop's own PSD format. Then flattening the image to remove the layers, cropping, resizing as necessary and saving in the preferred format for the web or printing.

● SHADOWED TRAIN FRONT

When photographing a backlit train (where the sun is on the same side of the train as the photographer but the camera is pointing towards the sun) the front will be shadowed. The appearance of the front is usually improved by lightening it slightly. The lightening process needs to increase the contrast slightly at the same time because the result looks more realistic than with a brightness adjustment on its own. The difficult part is judging how far to go

because a front end that is too light looks unnatural and worse than the original.

The principle is to use a Levels Adjustment on just the front to lighten it and increase the contrast in a single adjustment. A mask on the Levels Adjustment restricts the lightening to just the front. The operation is the same in both full Photoshop and Photoshop Elements. The left side of Figure 5.14.1 shows an MGR train at Coatbridge in low autumn sun where the angle of the sun has caused the locomotive front to be fairly dark. The right side shows the same image after adjusting the locomotive front.

The first stage of the lightening process is to create a selection around the area to be adjusted. It is best to zoom in to somewhere between 50% and 100% so that the area appears quite large on the screen and the selection can be created accurately. A simple and quick way of making the selection is to use the Polygonal Lasso tool and follow the edge of the cab. A feather of one or two pixels gives a graduated edge to the selection so that after making the change the join between adjusted and unchanged areas is not visible. The mouse button is double clicked to complete the selection or alternatively the [Enter] key is pressed. With the selection active a new Levels Adjustment Layer is created using the 'Layer →→ New Adjustment Layer →→ Levels...' menu option. A screen containing a graph-like chart called the histogram appears. Because a selection was already active the effect of the

Figure 5.14.1.
Lightening a backlit locomotive front.

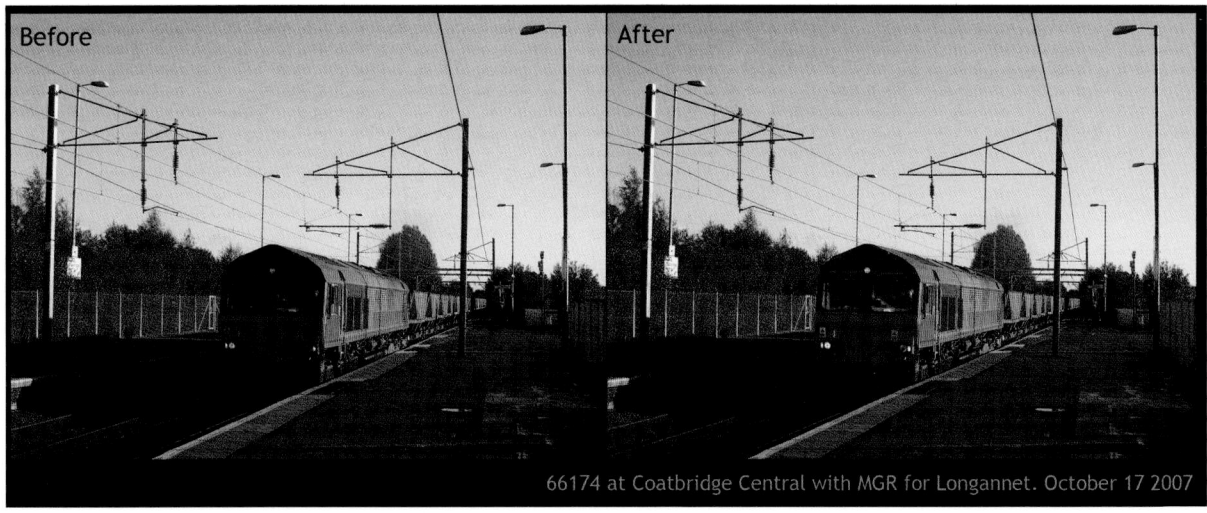

Before

After

66174 at Coatbridge Central with MGR for Longannet. October 17 2007

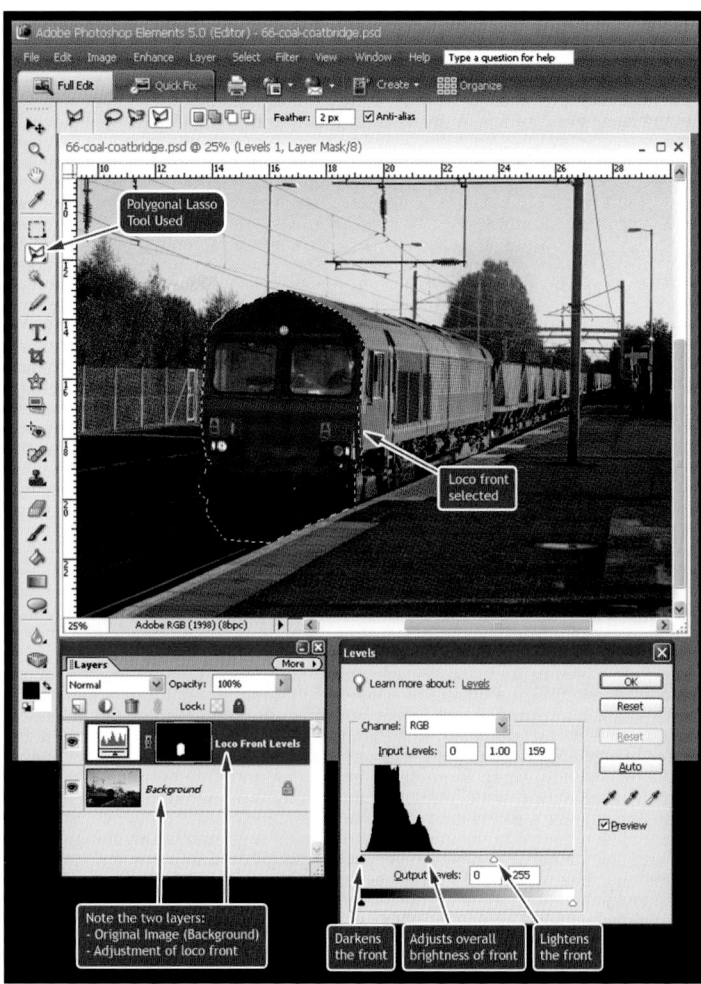

white triangle on the right is moved inwards to lighten the locomotive front while also increasing the contrast. Similarly the black triangle on the left is moved inwards to darken the locomotive front while also increasing the contrast. Once the level of contrast looks about right the middle triangle is moved left or right to change the overall brightness as appropriate. The amount of contrast must not be too high otherwise it looks false, and similarly the lightening must not be too strong. Figure 5.14.3 compares the same locomotive front with different amounts of lightening. The difference is only the position of the right triangle as ringed in red. Sometimes the edge of the mask may not quite be in the right place causing fine light or dark lines. This is fixed by minor adjustment of the mask and is achieved by painting on the mask using the Brush Tool with black paint or white paint as described earlier in this chapter. To get the alignment right it is usually necessary to zoom in to 100% to clearly see the line. Figure 5.14.4 shows the locomotive front with fine lines caused by misalignment before and after correction. The fault is fairly minor and some photographers will not feel the need to fix it.

When happy with the appearance the resulting image should be saved in Photoshop's own PSD format to preserve the layers so that, if needed, it's possible to go back and make further changes to the

Figure 5.14.2.
The detail of adjusting the levels to do the lightening.

Figure 5.14.3.
Comparing different amounts of lightening of the same area.

Levels Adjustment is restricted to just the train front end by a mask that is automatically created. This is shown in Figure 5.14.2. The

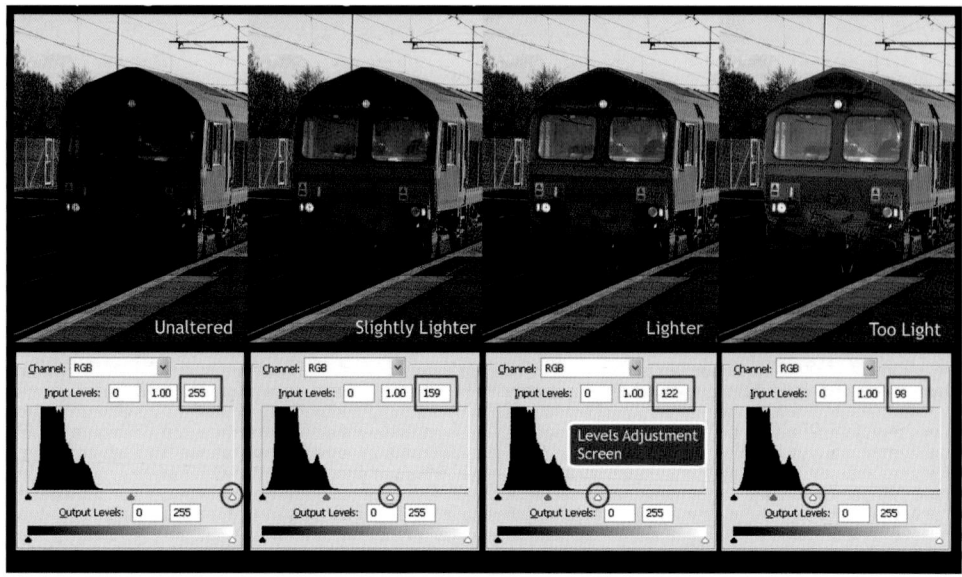

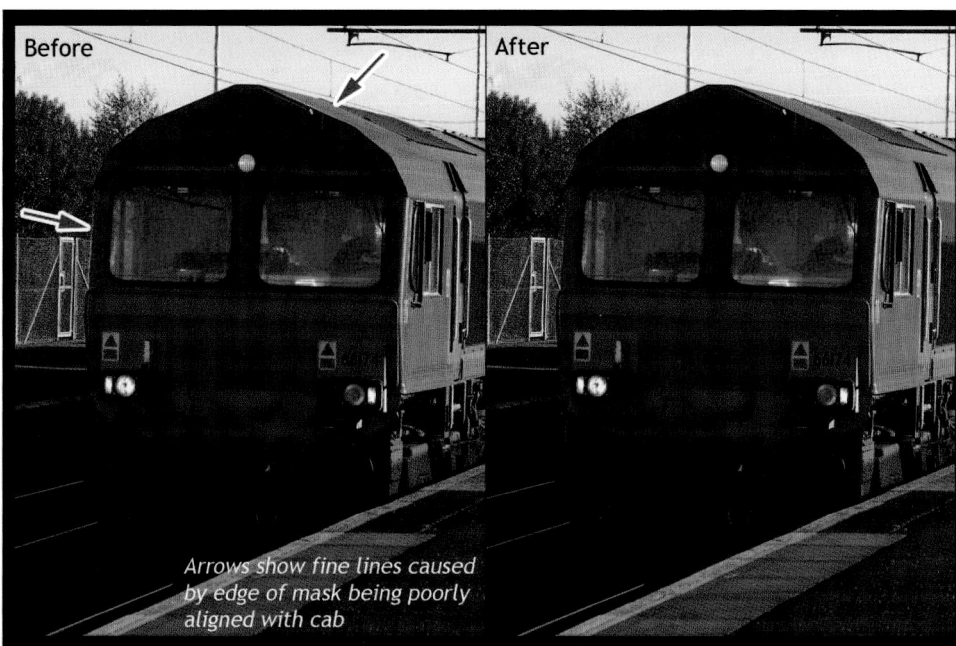

Before

After

Arrows show fine lines caused
by edge of mask being poorly
aligned with cab

Figure 5.14.4.
A small error in the
mask before and after
correction.

settings in future without having to start from scratch. The 'File → Save As... menu option is used to save the file, and includes choosing the PSD file type. After saving the work it's a good idea to take a break and return to the image an hour or more later on with 'fresh' eyes to check that the results look right. On some pictures the difference in brightness between body area and underframe means that the two areas are best treated separately with their own adjustments.

● PRINTING

Computer-based printing technology has made huge advances in recent years, to the point where excellent quality prints can be made at home. What equipment and techniques are needed to make a good quality long-lasting print?

Printer

Printers using two main types of print technology are widely available: inkjet and laser. Inkjets are inexpensive and are the favourite option for home printing but with the downside of high running costs. True photo-quality inkjet printers are much more expensive than standard multi-purpose models. Colour laser printers are

available for lower prices than ever before and are extremely versatile, especially for printing business documents and web pages. Unfortunately the affordable laser models do not produce true photographic prints and compare unfavourably with inkjet colour printers. High end laser printers used by professional print bureaux produce surprisingly good results but the inkjet has them soundly beaten for value-for-money when the cost of the printer is taken into account.

Inkjet options – types of ink

There are two main types of inkjet printer, based around the technology used by their inks – dye and pigment. The most established of these is dye and has the advantages of a wide choice of printers and papers and the ability to print on both matt and glossy paper. Colour fidelity in the latest printers is excellent. The big disadvantage of dye ink is longevity. Some dye inks fade after only a few months, especially when subjected to direct sunlight. Although most prints last longer than this, particularly when stored in the dark, the fade resistance is still very much hit and miss, depending on the brand of ink and the combination of ink and paper used. All the major manufacturers – Epson, Canon and HP – produce dye-based printers, and good photo-quality results can be obtained from their products.

Pigment inks have the advantage of very much better resistance to fading. With older printers the main disadvantages of pigment inks were the difficulty of getting realistic colours and an inability to print on glossy papers. Recent printers and inks have completely overcome these problems and excellent results are achievable. Epson, HP and Canon all produce pigment-based printers.

Ink cartridges sold by printer manufacturers are expensive and it is tempting to use cheaper alternatives. In many cases these substitute inks will give poor colour fidelity and are even more prone to fading, so are best avoided. That said, some products from specialist ink companies give good results, but this is an area of risk – it is best to use ink from the printer manufacturer for colour work, at least until you have enough experience to tell the difference between a printed image that has

Figure 5.15.1.
Examples of printer problems.

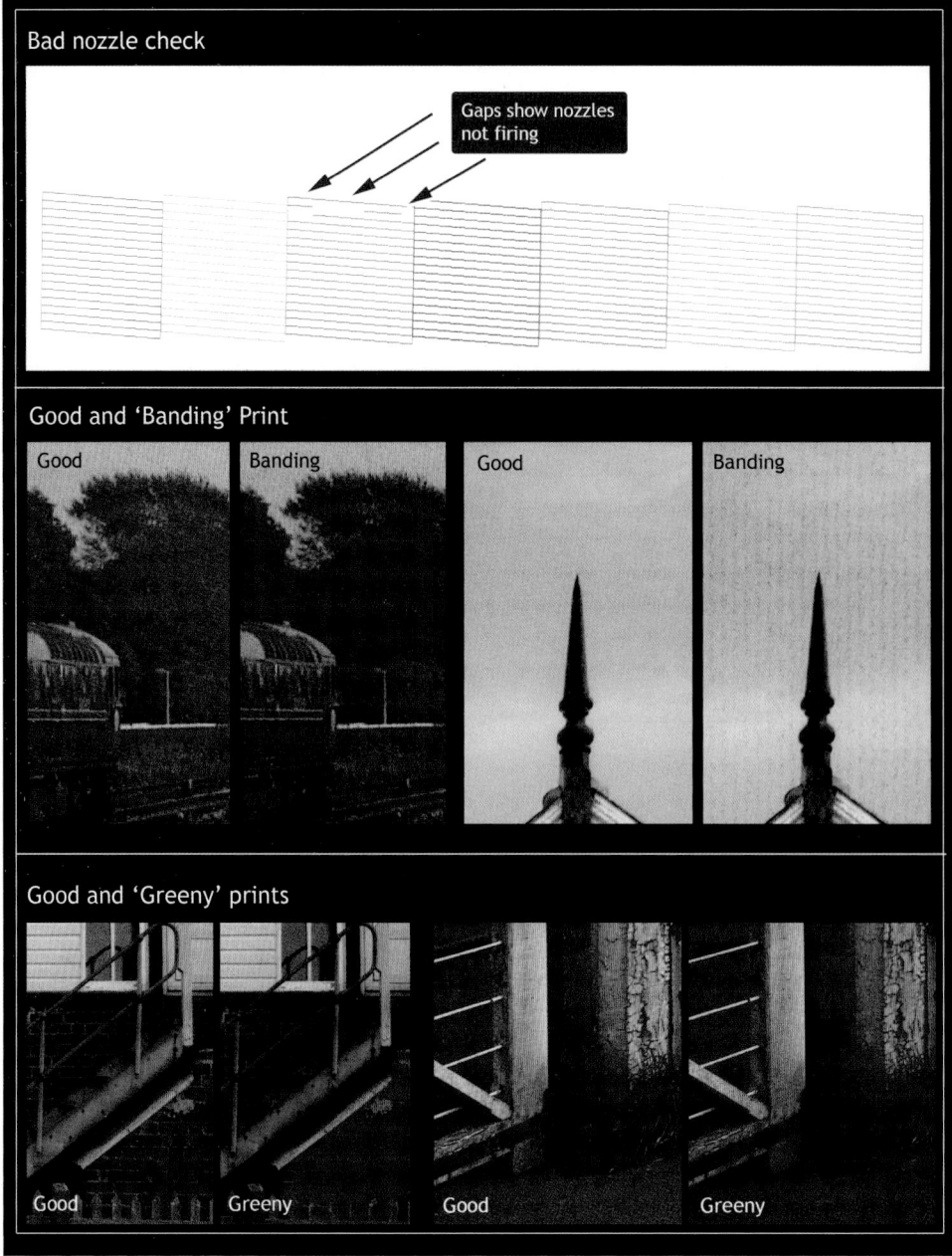

been ruined by poor ink and an image which needs more enhancement.

Choosing the paper

The paper used has a major effect on image sharpness, colour balance and longevity. Standard photocopier paper is not recommended. It is best to start with a good-quality glossy paper that has been recommended by the printer manufacturer so that the printer can give its best results. Once you are familiar with the best results that your printer, paper and images can produce, then you can experiment by substituting paper or ink, or both. Some specialist manufacturers produce papers that give good results, but experimenting with different types will lead to variable results and often causes problems that can be hard to solve. Cheap inks – often referred to as 'compatible' – can produce strange colour casts and – with dye inks especially – premature fading. Some paper manufacturers produce sample packs of their range with different paper weights and surfaces which provide a relatively cheap way of trying their products. Once you have found a combination of ink and paper that meets your requirements you will save time and wastage by sticking with it rather than always trying the next supermarket special offer.

Preparing images for printing

When printing, the highest resolution image should be used. The guideline used by the printing industry is that 300 pixels per inch (ppi) will give excellent detail and an 8 megapixel camera will produce an A4 size print (12in by 8in) at this level of resolution. An older digital camera producing a 6 megapixel image will only deliver a 10in by 7in print (approximately) at 300 ppi. When enlarged to A4 size the resolution drops to around 250 ppi. Fortunately, however, with a good lens and high-quality sensor this should still yield a pleasing result.

When viewing prints the human eye likes to see sharp, contrasty images with a full range of tones from the very brightest white to the darkest black. The first stage of preparing an image for printing is not really any different to producing an image for viewing on a web page. It involves adjusting the levels in an image to achieve a full range of tones, providing that it looks right to the eye of course, and adjusting brightness and colour to suit. The techniques for doing this have been described throughout this book.

A greater degree of sharpening is usually needed for printed images than would be necessary when loading on a web site although the extent is dependent on the subject matter and personal taste. A starting guideline is to display the image on the screen, decrease its scale to half full size, then sharpen it so that it looks right. If viewed at full size on a screen it will look over-sharpened.

Preparing the printer

Inkjet printers work best when used regularly, which in practice means every day or two. However, there is a slight dilemma here because when a typical printer is switched on it normally runs a cleaning cycle which uses up a small amount of ink. The high price of printer ink means that over a long period it can prove quite costly to switch on the printer many times for making just a small number of prints. The most economical way of using a printer is to produce batches of prints in as few sessions as possible. For most hobby photographers their printers will often go a month or more without being used. When starting up an inkjet printer after a period of disuse it will sometimes have nozzles that are not firing correctly. If a print is made with mis-firing nozzles the result will be sub-standard due to a phenomenon known as 'banding'. The visibility and extent of the banding will depend on how many nozzles are not firing and their ink colour. Figure 5.15.1 shows the result when a cyan (light blue) nozzle was not firing properly. It has caused a pattern of different colour vertical bands that are particularly visible in the sky and tree areas.

Whenever beginning a print-making session it is worthwhile running a nozzle check first to ensure that none of the nozzles are blocked as the startup cleaning cycle may not have cleared all the print nozzles.

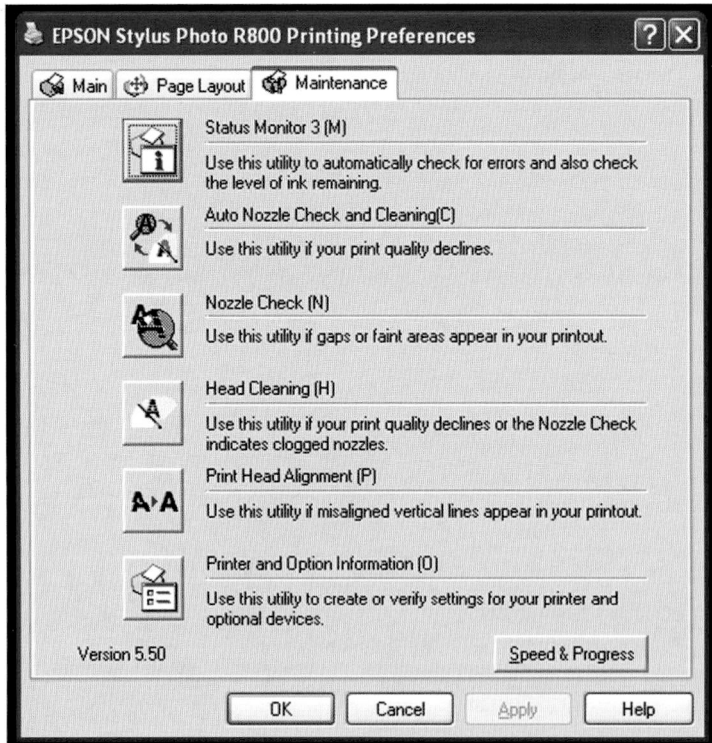

Figure 5.15.2.
Typical printer maintenance options – in this case for an Epson R800.

Preferences'. On an Epson printer the Nozzle Check utility will be available on the Maintenance menu. Ordinary plain paper can be used for the nozzle check rather than expensive photographic paper and is a good opportunity to recycle A4 paper where the back has not been used. A good nozzle check will show a set of coloured bars on the paper with no gaps. If the nozzle check shows gaps as in the example, a cleaning cycle should be run from the set of utility options provided by the manufacturer. A typical set of printer maintenance options is shown in Figure 5.15.2. Options provided will vary according to manufacturer and printer model.

Test prints

To avoid wasting paper and ink it is prudent to make a small test print first. Not only does this show whether the image looks good, it also proves whether the printer is working correctly. The recommended way of doing this is to create a dedicated test sheet in Photoshop, then copy a small area (typically 1in by 3in) from the image to be printed into the test print and print it. A full size sheet of paper is used and each test print is printed in its own small area in the sheet. The test piece

On a PC this will involve the 'Printer and Faxes' option on the Start Menu or alternatively via the Control Panel. Select the printer by name and then a menu option named something like 'Printer → Printing

Figure 5.15.3.
Printer test page as it appears in Photoshop and a photo of a printed page.

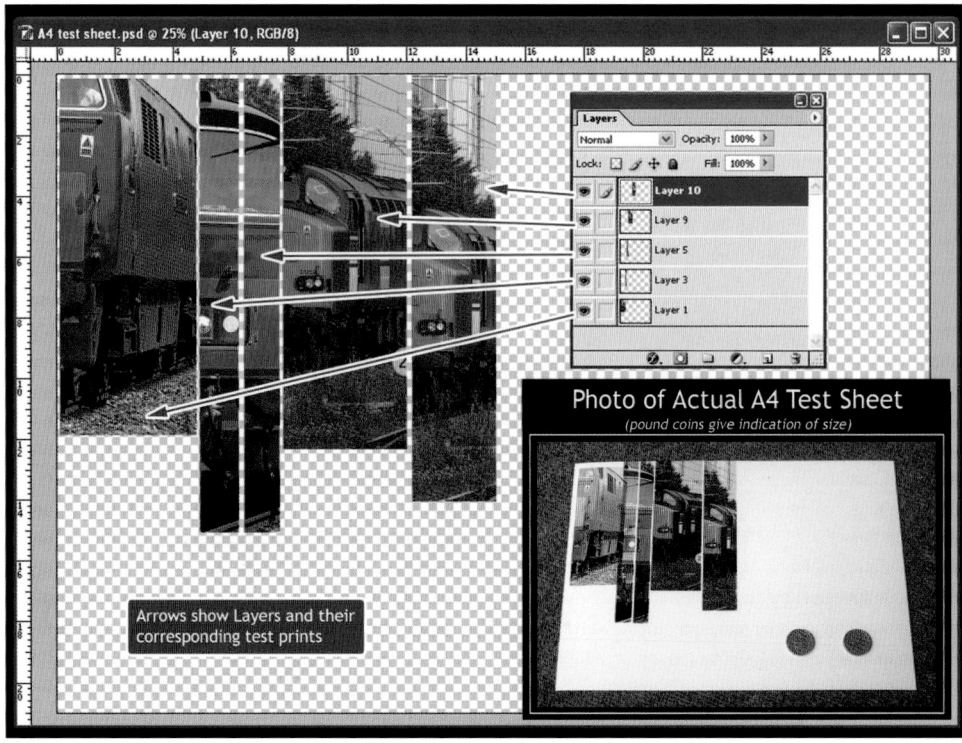

Arrows show Layers and their corresponding test prints

Photo of Actual A4 Test Sheet
(pound coins give indication of size)

should include key light and dark areas or important sections of the subject. Figure 5.15.3 shows an A4-size test print as it appears in Photoshop and also in a photograph.

The key to the technique is to economise by printing a number of test pieces on a single sheet of paper. The same piece of paper is passed through the printer several times and each test piece is printed once without any over-printing. In Photoshop this is accomplished by pasting each test piece into its own separate layer, then only one layer is printed while all other layers are made invisible. This is controlled in the Layers Palette by making the desired layer visible, or not, as appropriate by clicking on the 'eye' symbol for each layer.

If the printed test piece does not look right the original image can be adjusted, a small portion of the revised image is copied into the test print and another test print made. Using small test pieces minimises the amount of paper and ink wasted as well as saving printing time. It will also highlight printer problems due to, for example, banding or the print being too dark. Obviously when the test print is put through the printer only newly-added test pieces should be printed and old test pieces are never overprinted. If it is necessary to reprint a particular test piece it should be copied and the original piece made invisible to avoid overprinting. Note that if the ppi value of the source image is different to the test print, the size of the test piece will change when pasted into the test print.

Tips when making prints

This section gives a number of tips for making top quality prints and looking after the printer.

When running the Print command in Photoshop, check that the Printer Properties are set correctly, such as borderless printing (if desired) and the type of paper being used. It is essential to set the paper type to match the paper being used because this determines how much of each ink the printer applies to the paper and will have a noticeable effect on the colour balance and overall quality of the print.

Both Photoshop and Photoshop Elements have a print preview facility. It is always worth using this to check that the image has been sized correctly for the paper and avoid the common mistake of having a portrait format image on landscape oriented paper or vice versa. Again, this simple check will save time, paper and ink. Beware, though, that in older versions of Photoshop the appearance of the image on the print preview screen will not match the final print.

Ensure that the printer paper is properly supported as it is fed out of the printer and will not hit anything, as this can lead to banding or a smeared print.

When the printing session is finished, always switch off the printer using its own power switch to ensure that the printer heads are parked correctly and prevent the print heads drying out and becoming blocked. Never switch off the printer by cutting the power from the mains socket.

Print Matching

A common problem is that the print colours and brightness don't match what is seen on the screen. The first part of solving this problem is using a monitor calibrator to calibrate your screen so that it shows colours correctly as describe in Chapter 1. Monitor calibrators are available from Jessops and a number of specialist suppliers.

The second part of the solution involves using a colour profile during the printing process. A colour profile is made for a particular combination of printer, ink and paper. If either the paper or brand of ink is changed the profile will no longer be accurate. Creating a profile requires a very expensive piece of equipment known as a spectrophotometer so it is not feasible for most users to create one themselves. There are two types of profile: generic profiles and custom profiles. A generic profile is usually made available by paper and ink manufacturers on their web site and is intended for specific combinations of printer model, paper and ink. This should always be the first option tried when printing and can often give good results.

Figure 5.15.4.
**How to set up
Photoshop Elements
5.0 for a typical printer.**

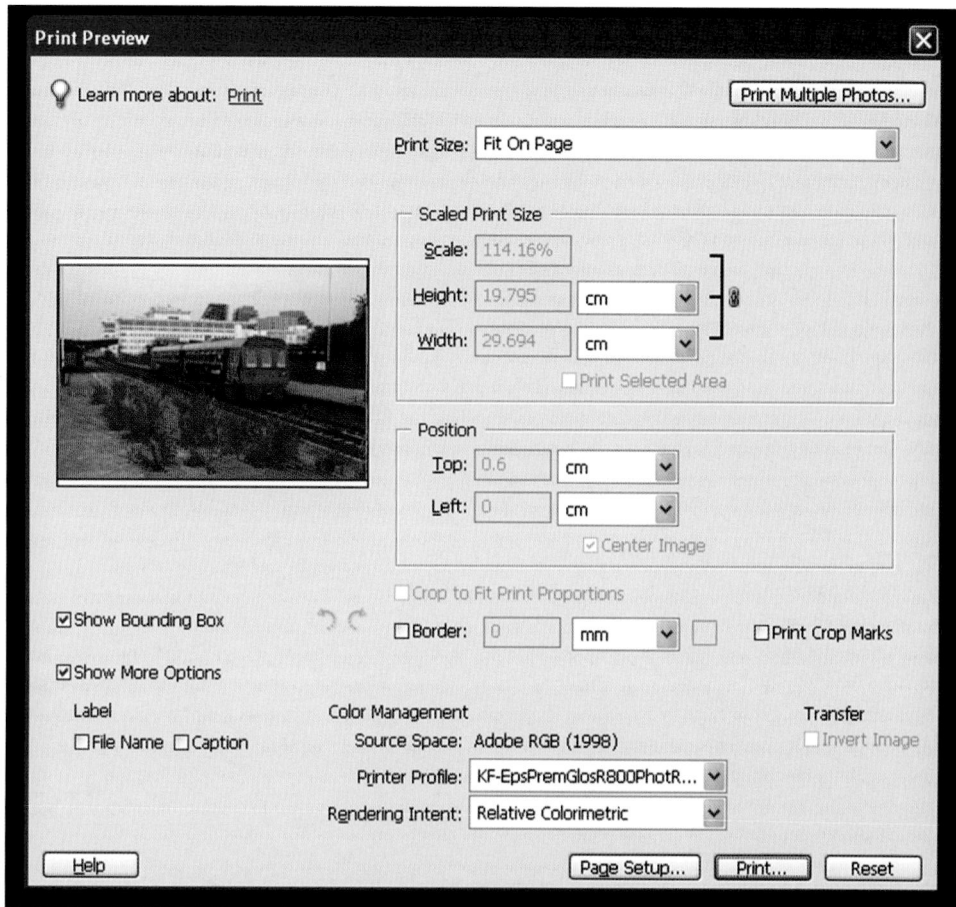

Because printers of the same model vary between individual samples, if a generic profile doesn't give close enough results it may be worth getting a custom profile made for your printer and favourite combination of paper and ink. A different profile is needed for each type of paper that you use. There are various companies that offer a service to create a colour profile at a cost ranging from about £12 upwards. The creation process starts by printing some specialised colour test charts on the printer using the desired ink and paper. The printed charts are then sent to the company to process using a spectrophotometer and profile creation software. The colours on the test charts are read and processed by the software to create the colour profile. The software compares what a particular colour on the test chart should look like with what it actually looks like and the difference is put into the profile. The next time a particular colour is printed, the printer takes note of instructions in the profile to adjust the colour so that on the paper it looks right. Using a printer profile with a calibrated monitor and good quality materials enables the creation of consistently good prints. If you have a custom profile made this is a strong argument in favour of sticking with the same type of paper and ink, otherwise money saved by switching to a cheaper type of paper or ink will be lost by wasting materials while trying to get a good print match.

It is essential that Photoshop is set up correctly to work with your printer. Figures 5.15.4 and 5.15.5 show how to set up Photoshop Elements 5.0 and Photoshop CS3 correctly. A very important setting is the 'Printer Profile' option, which should be set for the printer profile corresponding to your printer/paper/ink combination. Figure 5.15.6 shows the printer driver settings for a typical printer, in this case an Epson R800. It is essential to set the Colour Management controls correctly, which will be to allow Photoshop to control colour with colour control disabled in the printer driver.

Printer problems

The most common printer problem is banding. The most common cause of this is a blocked ink nozzle and can usually be solved by one or more cleaning cycles. A head cleaning cycle carries the penalty of using up ink from all the tanks, not just the nozzle that is misfiring. Running lots of cleaning cycles will use up entire print cartridges surprisingly quickly and may also damage the printer. If two cleaning cycles don't cure the blockage it is a good idea to leave the printer to stand overnight so that any air bubbles can disperse. Sometimes the ink cartridge is the cause of a blocked nozzle especially when near empty and gently shaking the cartridge will sometimes cure the problem, otherwise replacing the cartridge will be necessary. If a blocked nozzle is proving stubborn after several cleaning cycles, cleaning cartridges are available from specialist suppliers. Blocked nozzles show up clearly when running a nozzle check.

Banding can also result from the paper feed being obstructed in some way or the printer being set to the wrong paper thickness.

Another potential cause of banding is the paper feed system. If your printer has an adjustment for different paper thicknesses, check that it is set correctly. If the problem persists check the print head alignment on the chosen paper. The paper may be catching on something as it is fed out of the printer so check that there is nothing in the way. With a large piece of printing paper and a printer where the output slot points slightly upwards the printer may be struggling to push the paper 'uphill'. In this case it can help to tip the printer slightly so that the paper path is completely level or even pointing downwards.

A printer can sometimes create a poor quality print despite producing a perfect

Figure 5.15.5.
How to set up Photoshop CS3 for a typical printer.

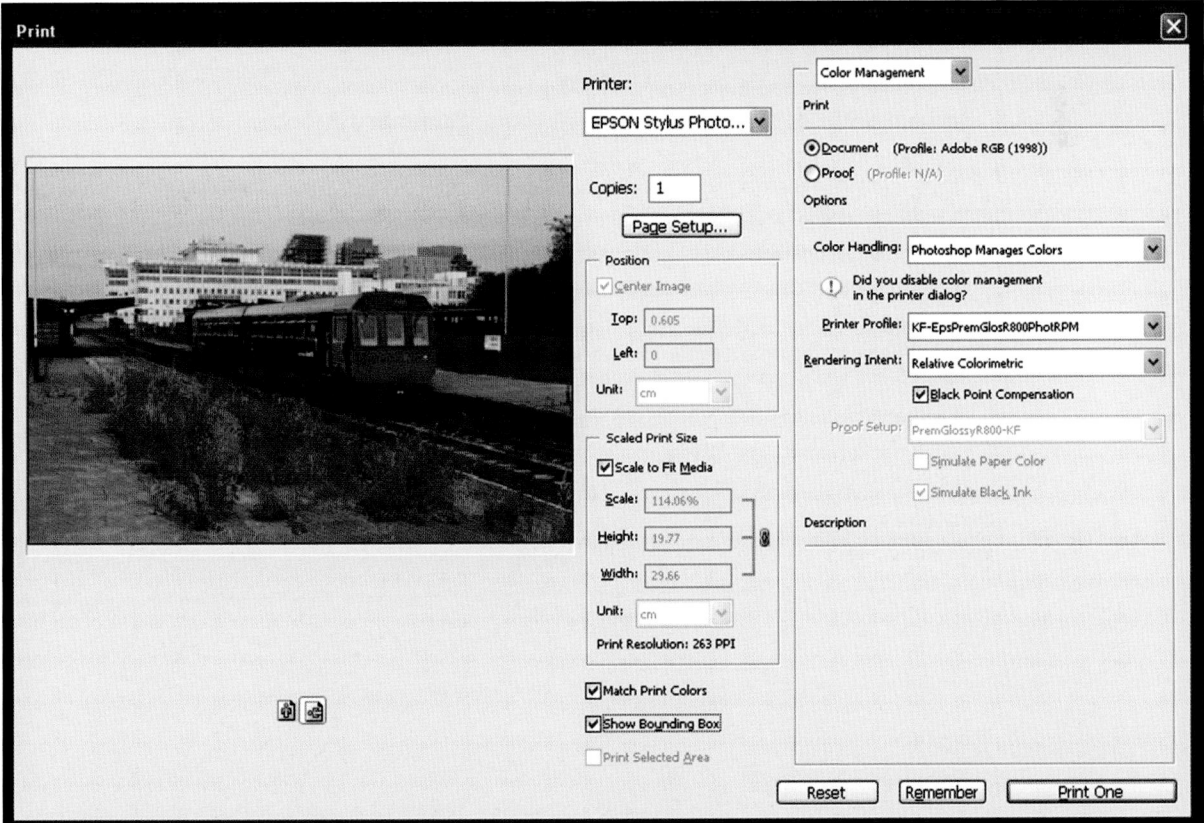

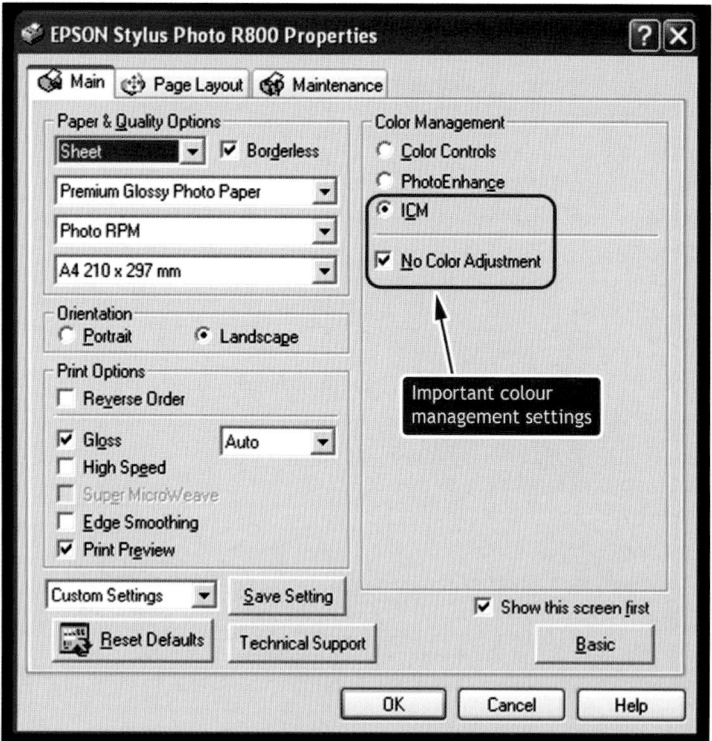

Figure 5.15.6.
How to set up a typical printer in its printer driver – in this case an Epson R800.

nozzle check. An example of this from the author's Epson R800 printer is shown in Figure 5.15.1 and labelled as a 'greeny' print. Some parts of the picture are fine but the colours in certain areas are odd. The greens are particularly bad, taking on a bright green colour with no detail. The signal box brickwork is the wrong colour and there is fine detail missing from several areas. Strangely some areas such as the crossing gates, signal box woodwork and the train look perfect. This problem was cured simply by running a cleaning cycle.

When setting up a printer for the first time prints can turn out especially light or dark. The first area to check is that the Photoshop and printer settings are correct and the values shown in Figures 5.15.4 to 6 should be used as a guide.

Cartridge Replacement

After an ink cartridge is replaced the printer will run a charging cycle to fill the ink lines. This is similar to a cleaning cycle and unfortunately uses up ink from all the cartridges, not just the cartridge that has been replaced. This means that if there are several cartridges approaching the point where they need to be replaced it may be more economic in terms of wasted ink to replace them all at once. As an example, if replacing four cartridges at once there will be ink wasted in one charging cycle and unused ink in some of the cartridges that were removed. The total amount wasted may be less then when replacing each cartridge one-by-one when it is empty and having to run four charging cycles.

When replacing a cartridge shake it gently before inserting into the printer to ensure the contents are properly mixed up. In pigment printers the pigment particles will settle to the bottom over time and gentle shaking will be needed every few months. Any shaking should always be gentle to avoid air bubbles being introduced and causing clogging problems later.

Summary

It is possible to create high quality prints that match their image on the screen without encountering printing problems along the way. If you run into problems and are new to printing, check the settings against the values shown in the diagrams in this section and try working with materials from the printer manufacturer before experimenting with other brands.

This section describes advanced techniques which are best explored by those who are already experienced in photo editing or who have successfully practised the simpler techniques described in previous Chapters. By their nature some of the techniques require more advanced processing software than those described in previous chapters. Most of the techniques have operations that are shared with other techniques so anyone reading through this chapter will notice a certain amount of inevitable repetition.

CHAPTER 6
ADVANCED
TECHNIQUES

● ADVANCED NIGHT PHOTOGRAPHY

IMPROVING THE APPEARANCE OF STATION LIGHTS

Brightness

The use of a digital camera for night photography brings a number of advantages over film but there are some disadvantages too. The most notable disadvantage over film is that bright areas – known as highlights – can easily become too bright and lose detail not just in a bright object but also in the immediate area around it. Film tends to handle overexposure a little more gracefully with less 'leakage' of light. All Raw converters allow the overall brightness of the final image to be set but the difficulty here is how to choose the right level of brightness? If a dark setting is chosen the lights (eg station lamps) will look good but the train will be slightly dark. If a setting is chosen that makes the train look 'right' the lights will be too bright and surrounding detail will be lost. Wouldn't it be nice to be able to combine the lights from the dark setting with the train from the picture with the brighter setting? This can be done manually but is time-consuming and difficult. 'Photomatix Pro' software from HdrSoft (download from www.hdrsoft.com) can do this automatically.

Photomatix

Photomatix is a program intended for a branch of photography known as High Dynamic Range imaging (HDRi) where a particular scene has too high a range of brightness to be captured in a single photograph. HDR has a number of potential areas of use in railway photography and has been used in some Case Studies in Chapter 7. The software has a trial function where the basic features are provided free of charge while use of more advanced features requires purchasing the software. Fortunately, good results can be obtained using basic features with two images. The example shows three sections of the same picture: 1) A dark image where the lamps look good but the train is too dark; 2) A light image where the train and station look good but the lamps are too bright; 3) An image created by Photomatix which has combined the best parts of the light and dark images. When comparing them note how the 'Combined' image has a realistic overall appearance with good detail in the train and the lamp area.

Using Photomatix

To use Photomatix, begin by using Raw conversion software to create two images (light and dark) from the same Raw image. First set the white balance so that the overall colour looks good, then set the brightness for the 'light' image so that the train looks right without worrying about the lights. The brightness control in the Raw converter is often labelled 'Exposure'. Create a TIFF format image using these settings. Then change the brightness so that the overall image is much darker and the lamps have a reasonable amount of detail. Don't touch the white balance. Create a 'dark' TIFF format image using these revised settings. Some Raw converters may require renaming of the first TIFF file to avoid a name clash when creating the second one.

Figure 6.1.1.1.
Compares different versions of the same Raw format image with a version created using HDR techniques.

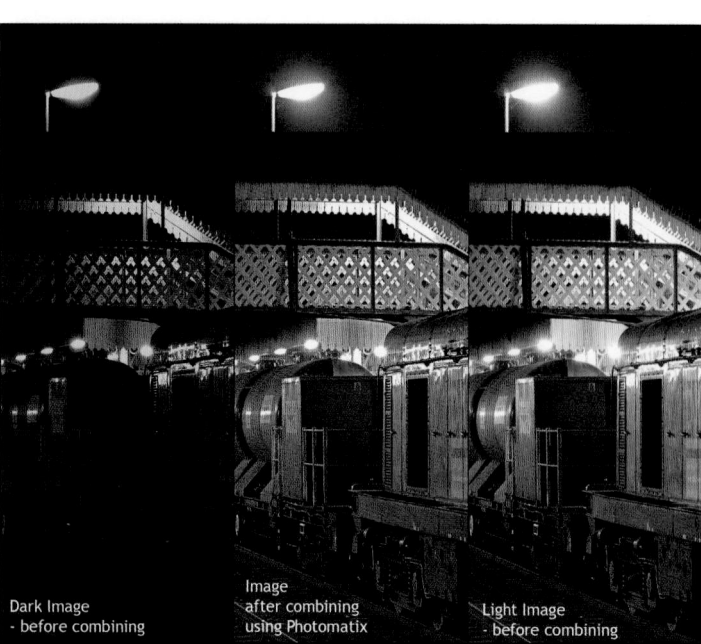

Dark Image
- before combining

Image after combining using Photomatix

Light Image
- before combining

Photomatix Pro is run and the 'Continue Trial' option chosen. The two TIFF images are read into it using the 'File → Open' option. Then from the 'Combine' menu the 'Highlights & Shadows – 2 images' option is chosen. This does what it says – takes the highlights from one image and the shadows from the other, then combines them giving the 'best of both'. The result is saved to a TIFF file, then read into Photoshop or other editing program. Sometimes it may be necessary to perform a Levels adjustment to increase the overall contrast slightly. The Photomatix 'free trial' does a good job on many images but occasionally an advanced option is needed.

Figure 6.1.1.1 shows how the size of the lamps has been reduced so that they look more realistic.

PHOTOGRAPHING MOVING TRAINS

By the early years of the 21st century, photographic equipment and techniques have advanced to the point where it is possible to obtain sharp colourful railway photographs in most conditions. The last barrier has been getting good quality photographs of moving trains at night. With today's digital cameras a station may have bright enough lighting to capture a photograph, particularly in city areas where there will be stray light in the sky as well. Yards and open track are likely to be too dark. Using flash is strongly discouraged and is very dangerous as the flash can temporarily blind a train driver.

Camera Settings
Most modern cameras have automatic settings and some have manual settings as well. Taking pictures at night involves using manual settings because the bright lights and dark areas can confuse the automatic exposure and focusing. To get a good quality result requires an understanding of how each setting affects the final image. The chosen settings should allow the right amount of light to enter the camera and form an image on the film or digital sensor. Too much and the picture will lose detail in the brightest areas; too little and the picture will be dark.

Speed Blur and Shutter Speed
To decide if it is feasible to shoot a moving train at night, several areas need to be considered when choosing the shutter speed. These are how fast the train is likely to be going, its position in the picture and how much speed blur is considered acceptable on the final image. Based on this the lowest possible shutter speed is chosen. Choosing shutter speeds for moving trains was described in Chapter 2.

Lens Aperture
The lens aperture needs to be chosen. For taking shots in low light an important attribute of a lens is the maximum amount of light it will let through to the sensor. The technical term is the maximum aperture of the lens or, put another way, the 'f stop' value when set to its widest opening. Up to the mid 1980s most 35mm SLR film cameras were bought with a 50mm fixed focal length lens which consequently became known as the 'standard' lens. This usually had a maximum aperture of around f1.7 or even f1.4. Since then, zoom lenses have become more popular because of their versatility. Unfortunately the zoom lens comes with the disadvantage of a typical maximum aperture of f4 and in some models this varies with the zoom setting (focal length) so that the widest setting may be as low as f5.6. Although there are zoom lenses available with a maximum aperture as wide as f2.8 they are expensive, bulky and heavy. Generally speaking a fixed focal length lens is capable of letting in more light than a zoom lens and this is a significant advantage for 'moving' night pictures. When choosing the aperture to use, a factor to bear in mind is that no lens gives its best quality when set to its maximum aperture. An f1.4 lens shouldn't be used at f1.4 as the results are likely to be soft. Lenses normally have to be 'stopped down' one or two f stops so that, for example, an f4 zoom will give its best quality when set to f5.6 or f8. A fixed focal length lens with maximum aperture of f1.4 will deliver excellent quality at a much wider aperture value of f2 or f2.8, which gives it a major advantage over any zoom lens for gathering light in dark conditions.

119

JPEG or Raw format?

It is important to use Raw format when taking the picture, not JPEG, for two major reasons. Firstly it allows the 'white balance' to be set when processing on the computer to give a pleasing overall appearance without an unpleasant colour cast. Secondly it allows noise to be controlled based on preference rather than being forced to accept the noise-reduction applied by the camera.

Sensitivity

Digital cameras allow the user to choose the ISO sensitivity for each picture. What setting should be used? The choice is always a trade-off of between speed blur, depth of field and the amount of noise on the final image. On the latest digital SLRs 1600 ISO will give noise levels that are not too intrusive and camera technology is continually improving in this area. Although higher sensitivities may appear to be available it is worth noting that on many digital cameras the very highest ISO settings are only accessible via an 'expansion' function and are actually a cheat. The 3200 ISO setting on some cameras is actually 1600 ISO underexposed by one stop with the histogram shifted to make it look like 3200 ISO had been used. In general it's better to switch off the 'ISO Expansion' so that shots are exposed at the true ISO. Underexposure may often be needed but at least the histogram is real.

Choice of settings

What are the right camera settings? The 'perfect night shot' station would be bright enough to allow a 1/500 sec shutter speed to get rid of speed blur, an aperture of f5.6 to give good sharpness and depth of field with an f4 zoom lens, and 1600 ISO to give good sensitivity without too much noise. Unfortunately this station doesn't exist and the camera will say that compromises are necessary because otherwise the result will be too dark. Dropping the shutter speed to 1/250sec will still give an acceptable result in many circumstances, whereas going as far as 1/125sec will give some speed blur unless the train is going particularly slowly – 30 mph or less. Opening the aperture to wider settings is desirable, maybe to f4.5 on a zoom lens or f2 on a fixed focal length lens. With these values provisionally chosen, they should first be checked by taking a meter reading. If the camera is capable of using different exposure metering patterns, choose 'partial' or 'spot' so that a reading can be taken from a small area without the meter being influenced by very bright or dark patches elsewhere. Take a meter reading from an area of middle brightness such as the platform surface in a brightly lit area. If you're very fortunate these settings will be about right but it's more than likely they are not. Further compromises on the settings will probably be necessary, which in practice means a slower shutter speed and some under-exposure because increasing the ISO sensitivity or opening the aperture further may not be possible.

When the meter indicates the settings look to be acceptable, a test exposure without a train should be taken and the histogram checked as described in Chapter 2. Provided there is minimal clipping at the dark end an acceptable result should be possible. Under-exposure can be addressed by lightening the image when processing on the computer, although with the penalty of extra noise in the darker areas and possibly some mild banding patterns.

Real-world Settings

The author has found that at well-lit stations the following settings will deliver a satisfactory result: 1/180 sec shutter speed, f2 aperture, 1600 ISO sensitivity. Although the results are not as clear and noise-free as a sunny day photograph, acceptable images are nevertheless possible. When underexposure is needed the amount of visible noise increases but small prints look fine, especially when reproduced at A6 size or smaller. Fixed focal length lenses with a wide aperture are the 'king' in this situation. For example a short telephoto lens ('standard' 50mm f1.4 lens on a typical small-sensor digital SLR or 85mm on a full frame SLR) gives a pleasing perspective which reduces the impact of speed blur and is still very sharp at f2. Careful focusing should give adequate depth of field. These 'standard'

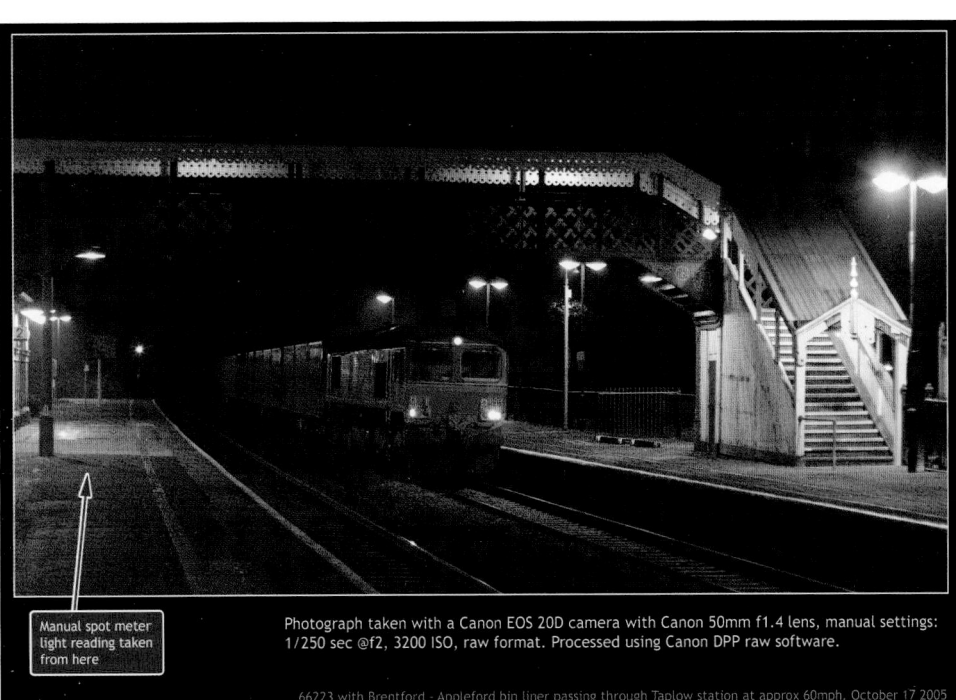

Figure 6.1.2.1.
Night photograph of a train moving at approximately 60mph.

Manual spot meter light reading taken from here

Photograph taken with a Canon EOS 20D camera with Canon 50mm f1.4 lens, manual settings: 1/250 sec @f2, 3200 ISO, raw format. Processed using Canon DPP raw software.

66223 with Brentford - Appleford bin liner passing through Taplow station at approx 60mph. October 17 2005

lenses are unfashionable today and manual focus versions are often available on the secondhand market for a reasonable price.

Figure 6.1.2.1 shows a train moving through the brightly lit station at Taplow at approximately 60 mph. This was taken using settings of 1/250sec @ f2 on a Canon EOS 20D camera 50mm f1.4 lens and 3200 ISO sensitivity. Noting the earlier comment about ISO sensitivity it should be pointed out that this picture was taken before the author had found out that the 3200 ISO setting on the EOS 20D is a cheat.

REDUCING THE EFFECTS OF NOISE

Dark areas of digital photographs often contain a coloured speckled pattern known as noise, particularly at high ISO settings and when the image is under-exposed. The noise performance of digital cameras is continually improving and today's cameras produce excellent low-noise results. However, photography of moving trains at night is still a particularly difficult area for even the lowest-noise cameras and if the results are going to be displayed on a web site of printed some work must be done to remove the worst noise.

Tools

There are numerous specialised software tools available for removing noise with varying degrees of effectiveness. The author uses software called 'Noise Ninja' from www.picturecode.com. Another popular tool is 'Neat Image' (www.neatimage.com). The noise removal process is very effective in some areas but has the major disadvantage that the detail often gets removed from areas of fine detail at the same time as the noise is removed, leaving an unrealistic smooth texture that looks more like a watercolour painting.

A compromise solution to this problem is to alter the controls on the noise removal tool to 50% effectiveness and apply to the whole picture. This leaves more of the fine detail in place but also leaves some of the noise.

A more complex solution is to create the 'best of both'. This involves taking two versions of the same image – with and without noise – and blending them together manually. The blending technique relies on two things: i) noise being less visible in areas with fine detail, for example grass, trees and ballast; ii) noisy areas with smooth tones looking acceptably realistic after the noise has been removed, for example skies and train bodies. The final image is a blend of

121

detailed areas from the noisy picture, smooth areas from the noise-reduced picture and a partial blend from everywhere else.

Figure 6.1.3.1 compares sections of the same image that have been treated differently. They show: i) the original complete with noise; ii) a copy with noise reduced everywhere; iii) a blended combination of the two. Note in the noise-reduced image how there is a noticeable loss of detail in the ballast and to a lesser degree in the locomotive bogie.

Blending Principle

For blending, the principle of the solution in both full Photoshop and Elements is to use two images in separate layers – the original noisy image on top and the noise-reduced image immediately underneath. The noisy image is the starting point and by selectively erasing it the noise-reduced image shows through. Noise is much more visible in plain areas such as the sky and locomotive windscreen, and less noticeable in detailed areas such as the station canopy and ballast. By erasing only those areas where the noise is particularly visible, the appearance is significantly improved. Remembering one of

the key principles of image editing used in this book – that the original image is never changed or deleted – nothing is actually deleted. Instead the Photoshop 'mask' feature is used as described in Chapter 5. The mask is edited, not the image itself. The benefit of this is if a mistake is made, part of the image can be 'unerased' rather than being gone forever.

Preparing for Blending

To prepare for blending the original image is opened in Photoshop. Make sure the Layers Palette is open so that the layers can be seen and manipulated. Use the 'Layer → Duplicate Layer' menu option to create a copy of the layer and change its name from 'Background copy' to something like 'Unchanged Layer'. The bottom layer will be the Background Layer. Select it by clicking on it and convert into a normal layer by using the menu option 'Layer → New → Layer from Background'. At this point there will be two layers, both containing the noisy image. Now select the bottom layer and apply the noise reduction tool to the whole image.

To blend the two images, add a mask to the top 'unchanged' layer. This is easy in full

Figure 6.1.3.1.
Sections of the same original image treated differently for noise removal.

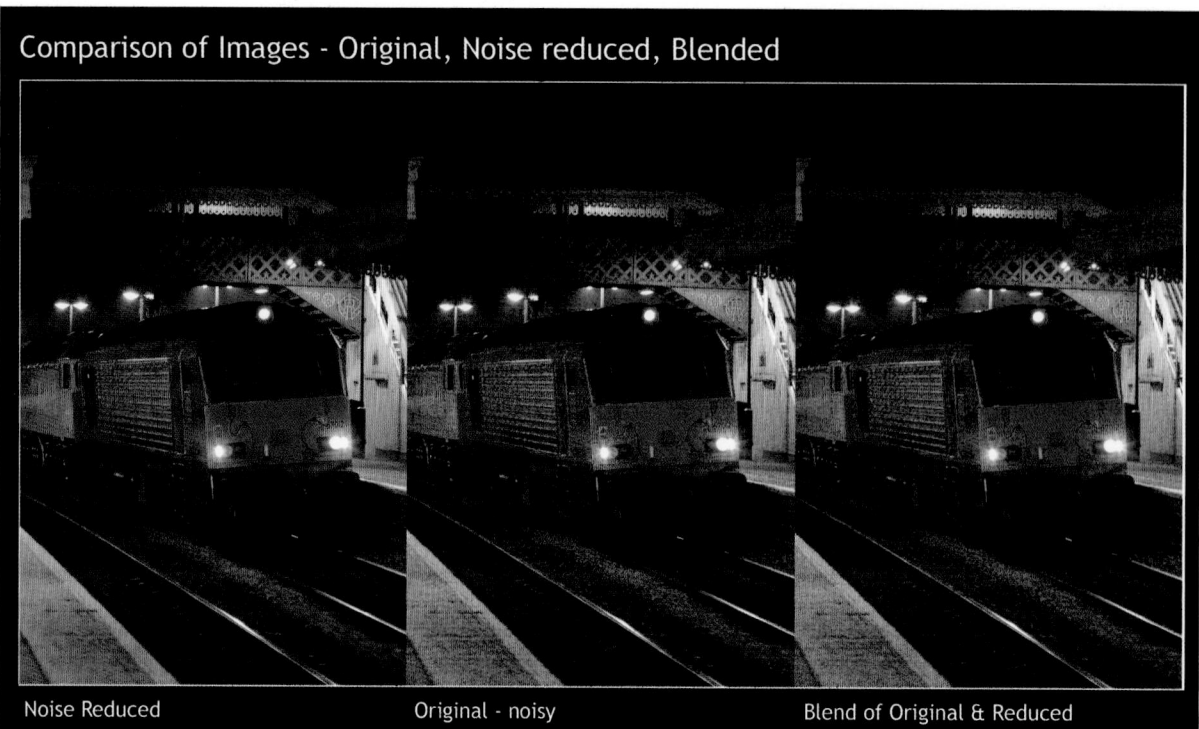

Comparison of Images - Original, Noise reduced, Blended

Noise Reduced · Original - noisy · Blend of Original & Reduced

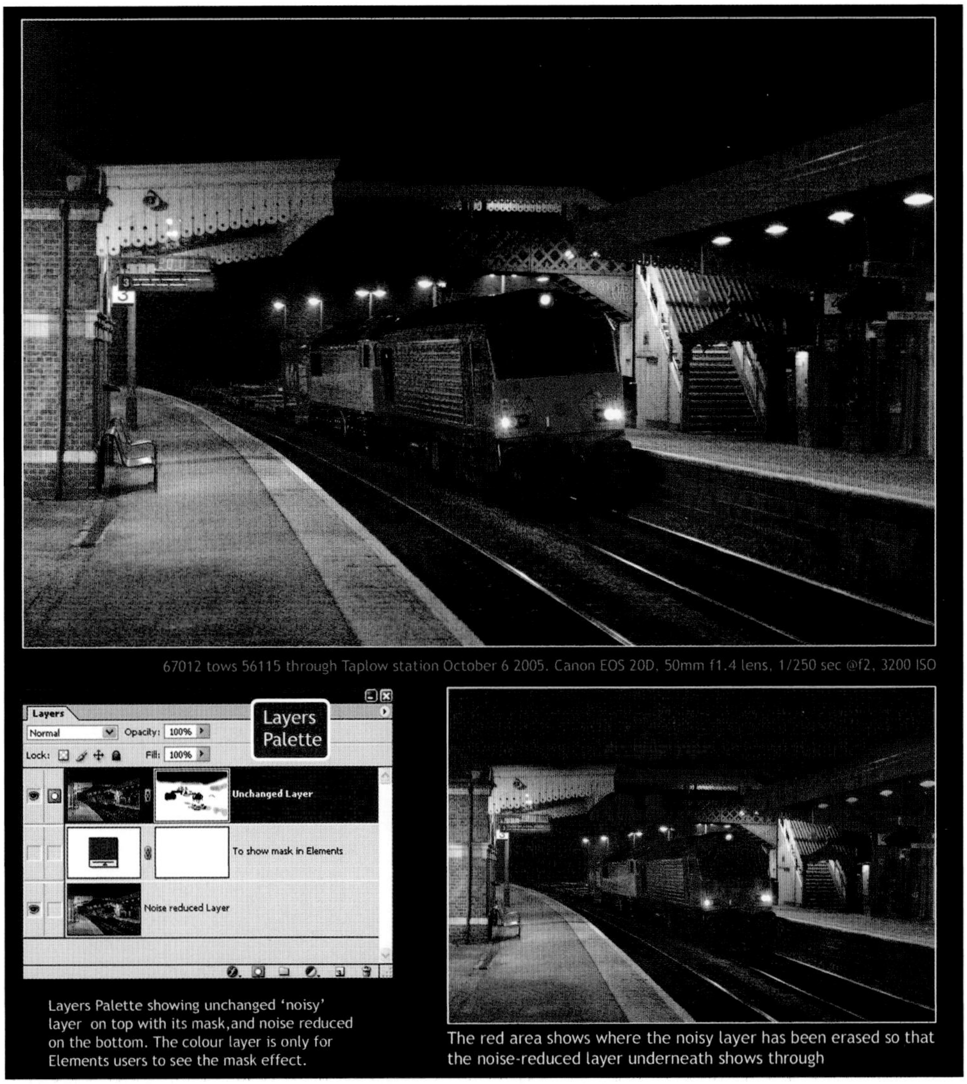

Figure 6.1.3.2.
How to remove noise by the blending technique.

67012 tows 56115 through Taplow station October 6 2005. Canon EOS 20D. 50mm f1.4 lens, 1/250 sec @f2, 3200 ISO

Layers Palette showing unchanged 'noisy' layer on top with its mask, and noise reduced on the bottom. The colour layer is only for Elements users to see the mask effect.

The red area shows where the noisy layer has been erased so that the noise-reduced layer underneath shows through

Photoshop using the 'Layer → Add Layer Mask → Reveal All' menu option. Photoshop Elements does not have a built-in 'Add Mask' function but it is possible to download free software from the web site of the Australian photographer Paul Shipley to perform this function. Web sites often move so the best way of finding this site is to do an Internet search using 'Paul Shipley Photoshop'. Users of Photoshop Elements who prefer not to load this software or wish to avoid using masks can simply use the Delete Tool to delete the original image from the upper layer. In this case it is a good idea to make a backup copy of the original layer and drag it to the bottom of the set of layers so that although invisible it can be copied if there is a need to restore part of the picture that has been deleted.

Blending

The blending involves painting on the mask layer with black 'paint' where the noisy layer is not wanted so that the corresponding area of the noise-reduced layer underneath shows through. A soft brush should be used so that the changes blend smoothly into the surrounding area.

In the example the area where the noise is most visible is the sky. Other areas are the locomotive windscreen, yellow front, buffers and parts of the underframe. It is a good idea to avoid painting on the mask in detailed areas because the noise is less visible here and the detail ought to be kept. If a mistake is made, then either paint on the mask with white 'paint' or use the eraser on the mask with black paint to remove the unwanted black 'paint'. A trick to remove some noise but not eliminate it completely, for example on the platform edge brickwork, is to use a brush set to an opacity value of, for example, 30%. This blends the two images in a way which removes the worst of the noise while still allowing some detail to show through. Compare this with the 'all or nothing' result obtained when the brush opacity is set to 100%. Figure 6.1.3.2 shows the final blend of noisy and noise-reduced images.

Showing the Mask

Sometimes it's useful to be able to see where the mask applies. With full Photoshop it's easy to do this using the Channels Palette. Click on the channel with the name matching the layer in the Layers Palette, then make the channel layer visible / invisible by clicking in the visibility box so that an 'eye' symbol shows (or not).

Photoshop Elements is stripped down and has no mask display function. One way of showing the mask is to create a coloured Fill Layer between the two image layers. This is shown in the Layers Palette in Figure 6.1.3.2 with the coloured layer marked 'To show mask in Elements'. This layer is made visible/invisible by clicking in the visibility box so that an 'eye' symbol shows (or not). This is demonstrated in the small picture lower right where there is a red appearance showing where the noise-reduced layer is visible. The red shows through where the mask has made the upper layer invisible. Note the soft red on the platform edge brickwork and locomotive front to indicate a blend of the noisy and noise-reduced layers.

Final Steps

With the noise reduced, other levels or colour adjustments can be applied as usual. Then the image is saved, flattened, cropped, resized and sharpened as appropriate for viewing on the web or for printing.

● ADVANCED EDITING TECHNIQUES

EDITING IN 16-BIT MODE

Those who are particularly quality conscious or will be doing a lot of editing work on an image should use 16-bit mode. A 16-bit image after editing has smoother colours than the same image in 8-bit mode. Figure 6.2.1 shows an image after repeating the same adjustments in both 8-bit and 16-bit modes. Note how the histogram after editing in 16-bit mode is much smoother than that for 8-bit mode which has the characteristic 'spiky hedgehog' appearance.

Use of 16-bit-mode is strongly recommended when editing in wide gamut colour spaces like ProPhotoRGB or Wide Gamut RGB. This is because a wide gamut colour space has more colours in a particular

Figure 6.2.1.
Comparison of histograms when making the same edits on an image in 8-bit and 16-bit modes.

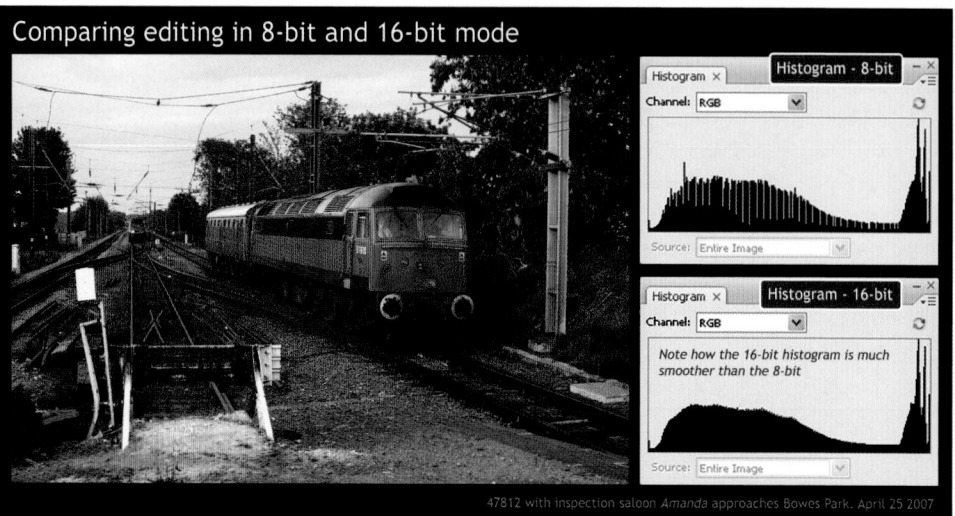

Comparing editing in 8-bit and 16-bit mode

Histogram — 8-bit

Histogram ×
Channel: RGB

Source: Entire Image

Histogram — 16-bit

Histogram ×
Channel: RGB

Note how the 16-bit histogram is much smoother than the 8-bit

Source: Entire Image

47812 with inspection saloon *Amanda* approaches Bowes Park. April 25 2007

range, so if 8-bit mode was used the individual steps (for example from R123 G201 B29 to R123 G201 B30) are smaller. Each step would cover a range of colours that could be noticeable after editing and in the worst case would cause visible colour steps in an image – a phenomenon called 'posterisation'. Use of 16-bit mode allows tiny steps between colours that will never be visible. See Chapter 7 for a case study featuring the use of the ProPhotoRGB colour space.

The downsides of 16-bit mode are using more memory, disk space and processor power as well as restricting the choice of photo editing and manipulation programs. While all editing tools will work with 8-bit, only a few will work with 16-bit. Older versions of Photoshop Elements will not edit 16-bit images, while newer versions have restricted editing options available. Full Photoshop version CS or newer is needed for unrestricted 16-bit editing capability.

CORRECTING LEANING OBJECTS

Railway photography is full of rectangular shapes which can sometimes take on an unexpected 'leaning' appearance. Photographs taken from ground level or on a station platform often contain tall vertical objects such as signals, lamps and electrification posts. When the camera is pointed upwards slightly to avoid cutting off the top of these objects, the result is a 'leaning' appearance in the final image even though the camera was horizontal. Figure 6.2.2.1 shows an Irish Rail '201' class locomotive entering Claremorris station past some superb semaphore signals. The left set of signals in the upper image has a distinct lean inwards towards the train. Why does this happen? The answer is due to geometry. When the camera's film or digital sensor is not parallel to a vertical object it takes on a leaning appearance in the final image even though the effect is not clearly visible through the viewfinder. The leaning effect is more pronounced when the object is towards the edge of the frame. Fortunately leaning objects can be corrected by appropriate processing on the computer.

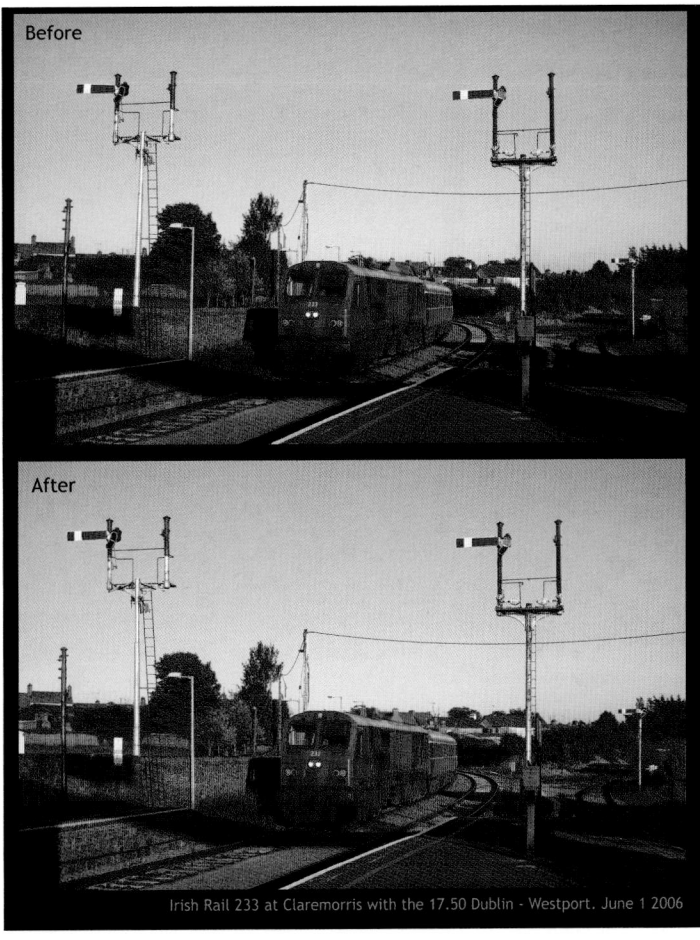

Before

After

Irish Rail 233 at Claremorris with the 17.50 Dublin - Westport. June 1 2006

Avoiding

There are several ways to avoid the problem at the taking stage and removing the need to resort to computer processing. The first is to make sure the sensor in the camera is parallel to the vertical object, that is, horizontal both side-to-side and front-to-back when taking the picture. Unfortunately this is awkward to do in practice and preferably needs a tripod with a spirit level fitted. When levelled correctly the top of tall objects will probably be cut off due to the angle of the camera and, in the case shown here, cutting off the top of the signal would ruin the composition. Using a wide angle lens can include the top of the signal but the downside is that there will then be extra foreground. The second way is to use a specialised lens known as a 'shift' lens. This allows the camera to be kept pointing horizontally while also including all of the tall objects. Most commonly used by

Figure 6.2.2.1.
Two versions of the same image, before and after straightening the leaning signals.

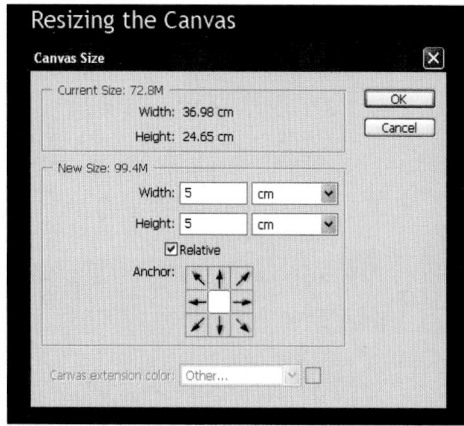

architectural photographers, these lenses are fairly rare, expensive and slow to use, meaning that they are not practical for most railway photographers. Another way is to use a large or medium format camera with 'movements' that permit shifting of the lens in a similar way to use of a shift lens. Again this is a specialised expensive solution and not practical for general use. A more realistic equivalent is to use a medium format camera with a wide angle lens that is mounted perfectly horizontally. This will maintain image quality in the main part of the picture while allowing the 'empty' part of the foreground to be cropped out.

Figure 6.2.2.3.
How to distort the image using 'Skew' to correct the leaning signals.

Principle

The principle for correcting the problem is straightforward and is the same in both Photoshop Elements and full Photoshop. The

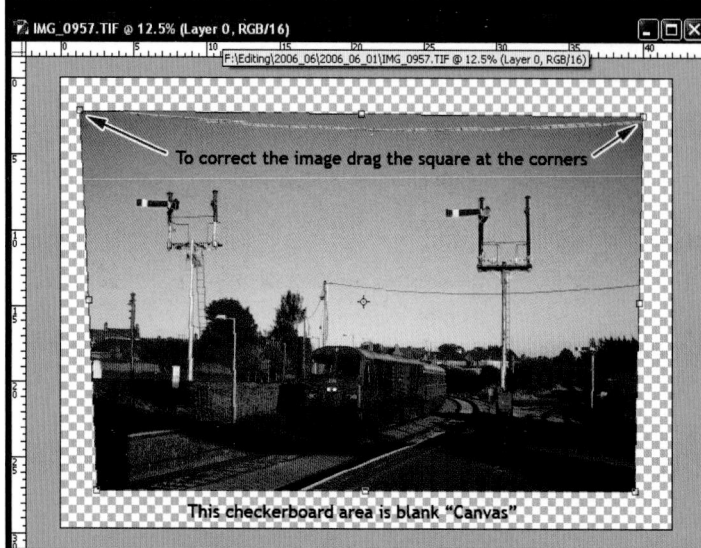

image is distorted using the 'Skew' function to straighten the leaning objects. This process is much easier when using a flat screen display rather than a CRT display with curved glass. After straightening the image is saved, then the usual adjustments are made using Adjustment Layers, followed by saving, cropping and saving again in the desired output format – whether web or printing.

Preparation Steps

There are a few steps necessary to edit the image. First read it into Photoshop. At this stage a Photoshop technicality gets in the way. The image becomes the 'Background' layer but this is locked automatically and can't be distorted. It needs to be changed into a normal layer using the menu option Layer → New → 'Layer from Background...'. Then space needs to be created around the image so that it can be stretched. To do this, enlarge the canvas by an inch or so all round – the screen to do this is shown in Figure 6.2.2.2. Note the use of the 'Relative' option so that the same amount of space is added all round the image. The added space has a white/grey 'checkered' appearance which allows the distortion to be seen more clearly. Now the image can be altered as shown in Figure 6.2.2.3. Choose the 'Image → Transform → Skew' menu option. Square boxes will appear at the corners and sides of the image. Treat each side of the image in turn by clicking on the square at the top left or top right corner with the left mouse button, and dragging it outwards with the mouse button still held down. The image will distort and as the corner is moved outwards the lean will be straightened. When in the correct position the mouse button is released. It is also necessary to move the corners up slightly in order to preserve the proportions of the subject. When happy with the appearance the 'tick' symbol at the top of the screen is clicked, or alternatively the change can be cancelled by clicking on the 'circle' symbol. Sometimes the straightening process is made easier by enabling the Photoshop 'View Grid' feature which overlays fine straight lines on the picture, allowing the modified image to be compared with a 'correct' vertical.

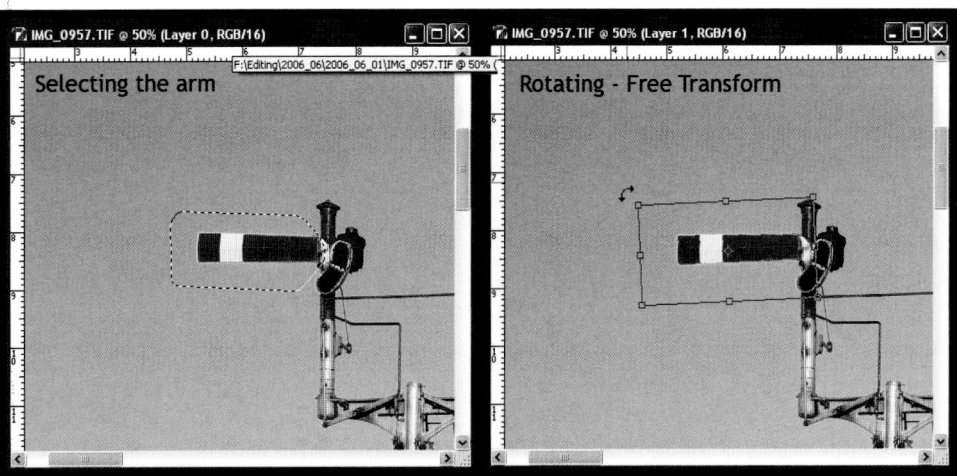

Figure 6.2.2.4.
Rotating the semaphore arm to correct its appearance.

Semaphore

In this picture an unfortunate result of correcting the leaning signal post is that the angle of the semaphore arm now looks wrong. This is easy to correct by rotating the arm slightly. The editing principle is to copy the signal arm and a small area of blue sky around it, cover the old arm by placing the copy on top, then rotating it and aligning with the post.

To make the changes use the Polygonal Lasso Tool with a feather of about five pixels to select the arm and some sky around it. The feather gives a gradual edge. Copy the selected area, then paste. The paste process will put the new arm directly on top of the old one on its own in a new Photoshop layer. By choosing the 'Free Transform' menu option the arm can be rotated slightly using the mouse pointer by clicking on the area near a corner and moving it. The arm can also be moved up/down or left/right using the arrow keys. When happy with the position and angle click the 'tick' option at the top of the screen. Figure 6.2.2.4 shows two stages during the correction of the semaphore – selecting the arm and the rotation using the Free Transform function.

Normal Improvements

With these corrections made, normal improvements can be made such as adjusting the levels to improve the contrast. In this image the shadows have been lightened to make them less obtrusive, the whole image has been lightened slightly and the wires in the sky have been removed by cropping.

Alternative methods

There are alternative methods available for this type of correction including special perspective software. Photoshop Elements 5.0 and newer have a feature called 'Correct Camera Distortion' that will make this type of change.

Panoramic stitching software as used later in this Chapter often has the necessary functions built in. The advantage of panoramic software is that the proportions of the image will be maintained automatically. The disadvantage is added complexity and cost. The drawback of the method described here is that the amount of vertical distortion to maintain proportions has to be estimated and performed manually.

COMBINING IMAGES

Processing digital images on a computer offers new possibilities that are impossible with 'conventional' printing from negatives and slides. One of these involves combining multiple images using special software to produce a single picture where the seams between component images are invisible. The technique has a surprising number of uses for the railway photographer and a range of examples are described. Some people may object to this technique as cheating or unnatural so it is worth pointing out that the human brain combines images from the two eyes into a single overall image, demonstrating that the basic technique predates the invention of the camera.

Principles

The fundamental principle involves taking two or more pictures of the subject from exactly the same point with each picture having a small overlap with the previous one. The camera is rotated carefully between shots, taking care not to move it either side-to-side or up and down. Manual exposure and focus are used to ensure that the camera settings are the same in all the pictures, otherwise getting the individual images to match each other will be more difficult. If the camera is moved in the wrong way, objects will have a different alignment in adjacent pictures, known as a parallax error. Sometimes it is possible to hide these errors in the final image. To avoid unwanted movement, use of a tripod is recommended. Experienced practitioners can often manage without a

tripod providing the main subject is far enough away that any parallax errors are small. A guideline is that major objects in the picture should be at least 16ft away.

The images are joined on a computer using special 'panorama' software. The process of combining multiple images into a single final image is also known as 'stitching'.

With moving trains only one picture can contain the train because it will have moved by the time the later pictures are taken and the seam will usually be obvious.

Panorama Software

Many different panorama software products are available on the market. Basic panorama programs are often supplied with new cameras but have the disadvantage of minimal control over joining the pictures. They are useful as an inexpensive introduction to the subject, allowing photographers to experiment, but rarely work well with railway subjects.

The most suitable panorama software has two key features which make possible the

Figure 6.2.3.1.
Adding more material to the edge of the frame by combining two images.

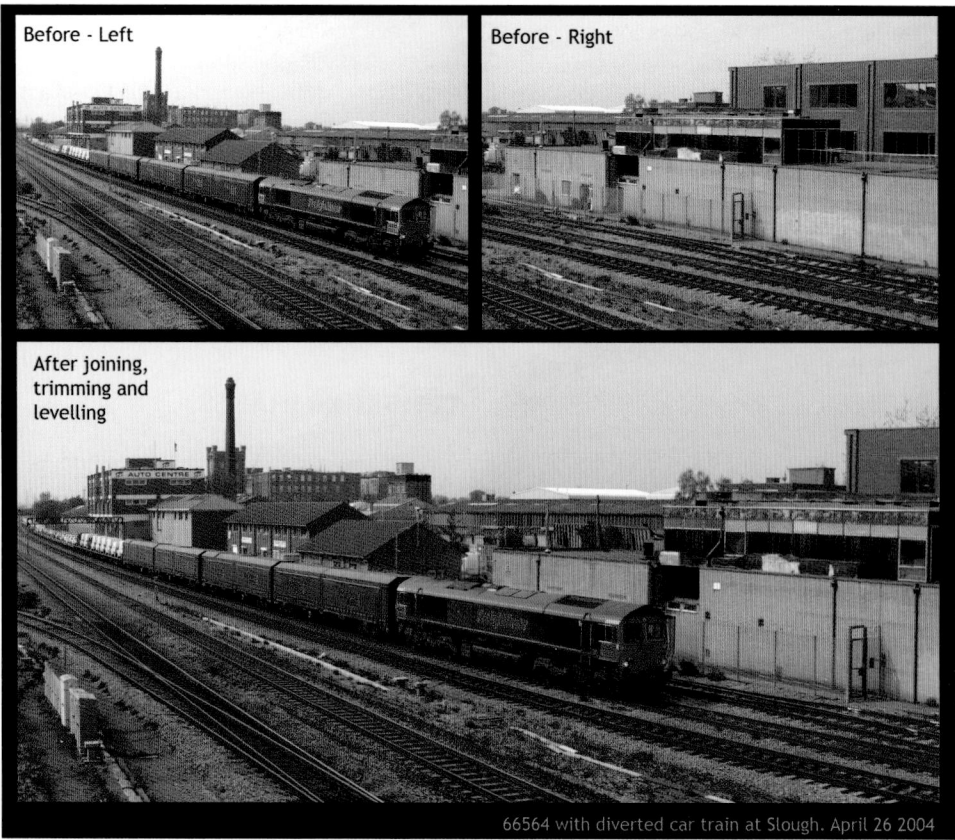

Before - Left

Before - Right

After joining, trimming and levelling

66564 with diverted car train at Slough. April 26 2004

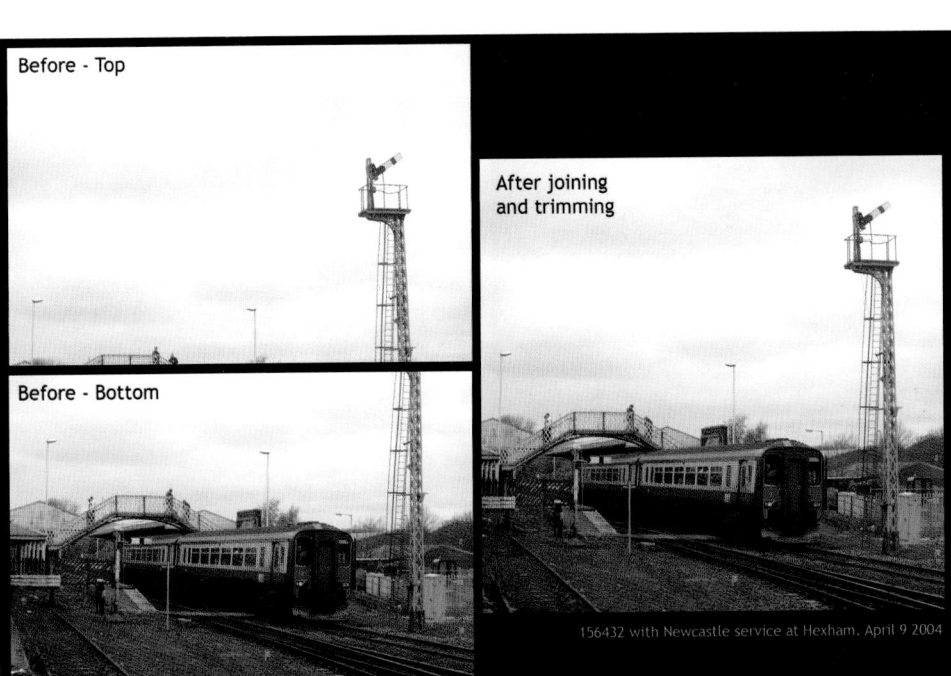

Before - Top

Before - Bottom

After joining
and trimming

156432 with Newcastle service at Hexham. April 9 2004

Figure 6.2.3.2.
**Adding the top of a
signal post that was
too large to fit in a
normal view.**

complete elimination of obvious seams in the final picture. Firstly the user can specify exactly which points on overlapping images should be aligned with each other. Secondly the output allows the photographer to decide exactly where the join between images will be. Typically the output features each image in its own Photoshop layer. An invisible seam is much easier to achieve if it follows sky, grass or ballast than a 'hard' object like a building. Aligning the rails between two different images is a particular challenge that makes convincing panoramic railway pictures harder to achieve than other types of panorama but the best software allows this to be done fairly easily by specifying the alignment points on the rails.

All panorama software creates its output by distorting the input images in a complex way known as 'warping' based on sophisticated maths. By following the right techniques it really is possible to combine several pictures together without any obvious seams.

Examples

Here are a number of situations where combining multiple images is worth considering.

1. Framing Mistake

With moving trains it is easy to make a mistake when framing the shot by aiming the camera wrongly, especially in a 'rushed' situation. Another cause is taking the picture too late. In Figure 6.2.3.1 (Example 1) a fast-moving unit was blocking the front of the freight and pressing the shutter release had to wait until it was out of the way. As a result the locomotive is too close to the right side of the frame. The solution here was to hold the camera still, wait until the freight was out of the way, rotate it and then take a picture of the signalbox. After the two pictures are combined the picture has more space in front of the train and shows more of the signalbox.

2. 'Tight' framing

Hexham station is an example of a location which is awkward for framing the shot with a camera producing a standard oblong image because the ideal framing is 'square' to capture all of the semaphore signal. This is shown in Figure 6.2.3.2 (Example 2). The photographer could move further back or use a wider angle lens but this would make the train small and lose detail in

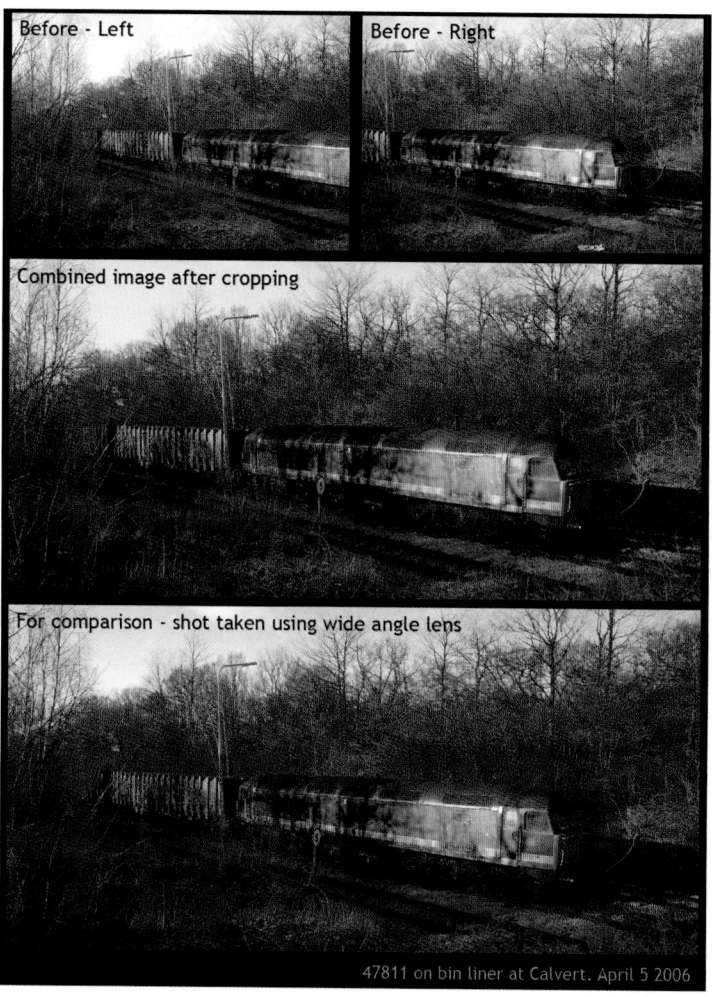

Before - Left

Before - Right

Combined image after cropping

For comparison - shot taken using wide angle lens

47811 on bin liner at Calvert. April 5 2006

Figure 6.2.3.3.
Combining two pictures of a stationary train into a wider angle view.

the area around the train and station. An alternative solution is to take two pictures – one of the moving train and the other of just the sky and top of the signal - and join them. Obviously this technique is only suitable where the moving train appears in one of the pictures.

3. Need a wide angle lens

Some shots need a wider angle lens than the one on the camera. Figure 6.2.3.3 (Example 3) shows No 47811 on a bin liner waiting to leave Calvert. The view from the footpath is restricted and it is not possible to fit both the locomotive and a decent amount of the train into one image when using a slightly wide angle lens (35mm on a full 35mm frame digital camera). By taking two pictures and joining them the effect is comparable to

using a much wider angle lens (such as 24mm on a full 35mm frame digital camera). An extra benefit is that the perspective introduced to the final 'combined' result by the computer processing is more pleasing to the eye than the perspective produced by a typical wide angle lens. For comparison purposes a shot taken using a much wider angle 24mm lens is shown. Although the difference in perspective between the two is visible here it really needs larger pictures for the difference to be clear.

4. Higher resolution images

With a stationary subject it is possible to take several pictures and combine them to create a higher resolution image. For example, if you combine three pictures from a 6 Megapixel camera you can create an image of up to about 14 Megapixels. Note that three 6 Megapixel images cannot create an 18 Megapixel final image, for example, because some pixels are 'lost' due in the overlap between images. For the ambitious it's possible to use a technique known as 'tiling' where the final picture is broken down into, for example, nine images in a three by three grid or 12 images in a four by three grid. Creating the final image is like tiling a wall. This method makes it possible to create a very detailed picture but has the disadvantage of being both time-consuming and very demanding on the computer. There is no example shown as the process is similar to Example 3.

5. Panoramic Photos

There is a long-standing branch of photography dedicated to producing panoramic images. Specialised cameras were needed in the past but today computer processing allows the creation of a panoramic image from several normal images. With moving trains the final image is typically built of one image containing a moving train and up to three others of the scenery around the train.

With stationary trains there is no restriction. This is an area with great potential for those who like large landscape pictures. See Figure 6.2.3.4.

Taking the Picture

Before taking any picture where the result will involve combining several images the decision must be made on how to break up the overall scene into its component images. Two or more pictures of the subject are then taken from exactly the same point by rotating the camera so that each picture has a small overlap with the previous one. It is critical to get the rotation correct otherwise objects will have a different alignment in adjacent pictures, which is known as a parallax error. Technically speaking the camera must be rotated around the lens' nodal point, which is the point inside the lens where the light rays are focused to nearly a point. It corresponds with the mechanical aperture inside the lens. Where a camera has a 'depth of field preview' button the exact position of the aperture can be seen by watching it close down when you press the button. A common mistake when taking a series of pictures is to stand still on the spot and move the

camera in a circular path. Instead, the camera should be held still in the air or braced against, for example, a bridge parapet and the photographer moves around the camera as it is rotated. Better still, a tripod or monopod is used. See Figure 6.2.4.1 for the right and wrong ways to move the camera. Note how, in the 'right' example the camera rotates around the blue grid line and doesn't move, while in the 'wrong' example the whole camera moves. This shows the principles when taking a series of pictures to be joined horizontally. A similar principle applies for rotating the camera about a horizontal axis when taking pictures that will be joined vertically.

If the objects being photographed are close to the camera – typically less than about 16ft (5 metres) away – a tripod is strongly recommended and a specialised panoramic tripod head may be advisable. If the objects are further away as in a typical railway landscape shot it may be possible to manage without a tripod after some practice.

Avoiding obvious seams, especially in the sky, is one of the keys to success. Manual exposure and focus are recommended to ensure that the camera settings are the same in all the images, otherwise it will be more

Figure 6.2.3.4.
An example of a panoramic image created by merging three separate images together.

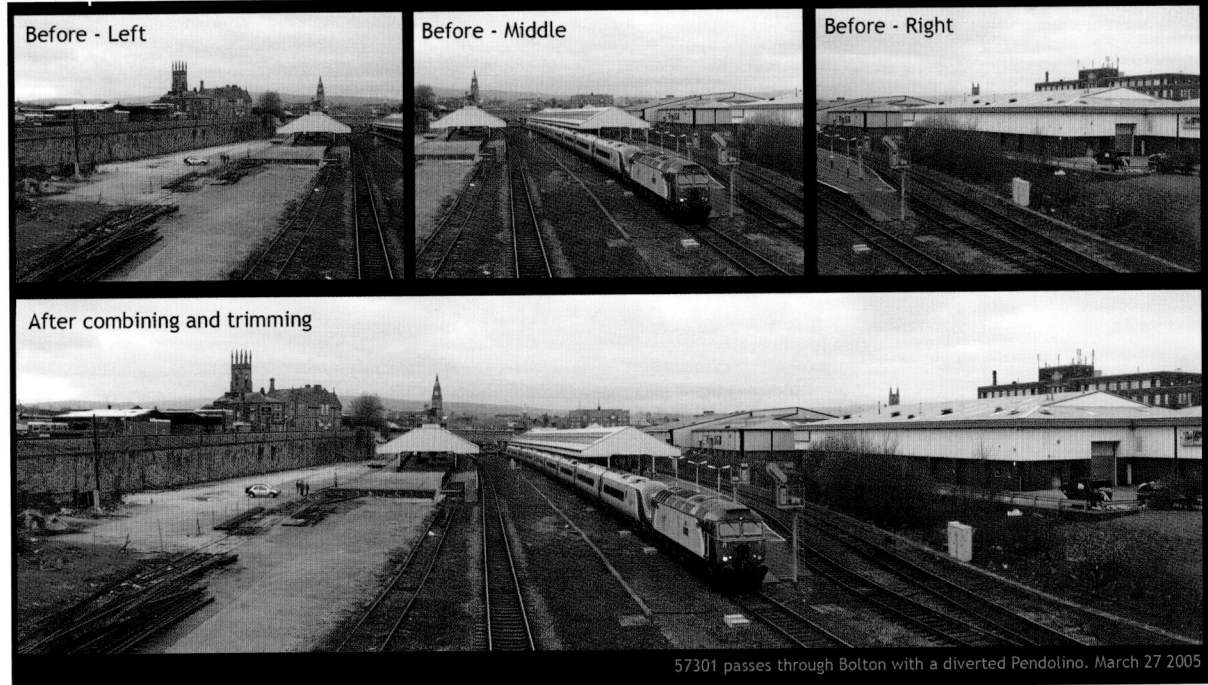

Before - Left

Before - Middle

Before - Right

After combining and trimming

57301 passes through Bolton with a diverted Pendolino. March 27 2005

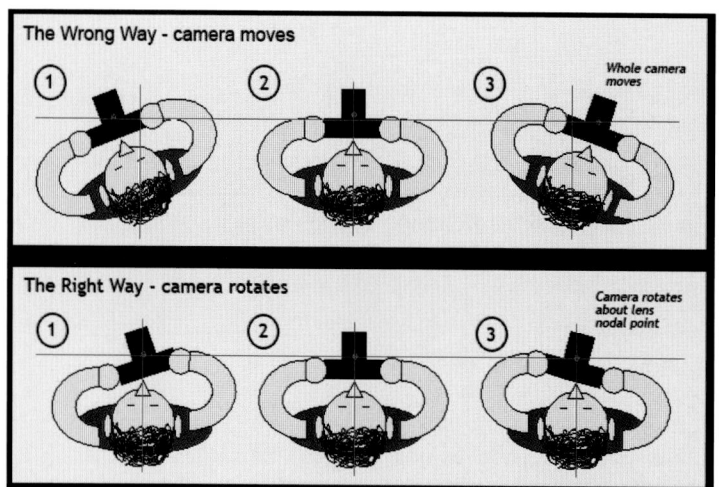

Figure 6.2.4.1.
How to move the camera when taking a series of images to be combined horizontally.

in advance whether to take these pictures before the train arrives or after it has moved out of the way.

Choosing Software
There is a huge range of software available that will combine images, ranging in cost from free to hundreds of pounds. Making panoramas containing railway subjects without visible seams is more difficult than with a typical landscape because of the large number of straight lines that need to be aligned and kept straight. Inevitably the rails will cross the boundary between different images and the seam will be very obvious unless joined carefully. Most stitching software has an 'automatic' mode where it will try to find out itself how to combine the images. Where a set of pictures involves a moving train, typically one image will contain the train while the remainder has just empty tracks. This will often confuse any automatic joining process and the automatically-generated image could have half a train in it. This can be seen in Figure 6.2.4.2. where the rear coaches of the Class 180 unit have been cut off. To deal with this software is needed that offers a manual joining process. There are two main features which are necessary:

difficult to get the individual images to match each other. Raw format is recommended so that there is more flexibility for dealing with any unexpected exposure errors. When processing the Raw images the same settings should be used in the Raw converter for each image, otherwise there will be differences in brightness and colour. All Raw converters have a feature to allow the conversion settings for one image to be copied to others.

When taking a series of images involving a moving train there will be one or more pictures that do not contain the train. Decide

Figure 6.2.4.2.
Comparing different projection types in panoramic images.

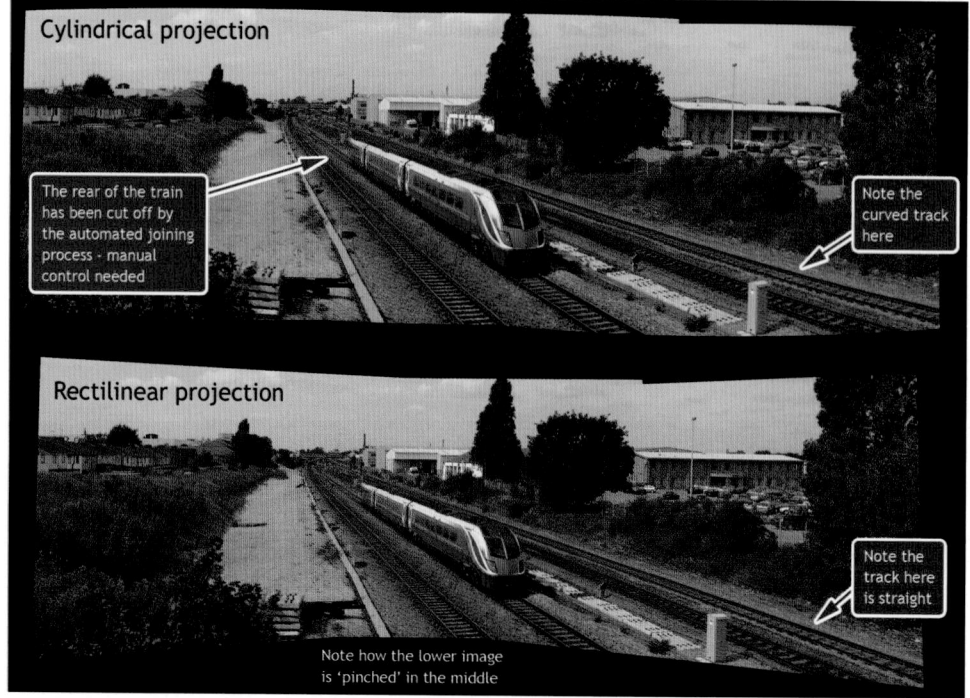

firstly the ability to define a set of control points that must match in each pair of joined images. Secondly the output images need to be capable of being read into separate layers in Photoshop so that the photographer has full control over blending the images together. In the final image the train must take priority over empty track.

Most of the specialised software is available only by downloading from the Internet. Trial versions are usually available, either providing full functionality for a limited trial period such as 14 or 30 days, or having a limitation such as including a watermark in the final panorama until a software licence key is paid for. Some digital cameras are supplied with a suite of software that is capable of creating panoramas while recent versions of Photoshop contain a panorama feature.

Among the free software the best known is a set of programs known as 'Panorama Tools'. These are capable of delivering excellent quality results but with the downside of being difficult to use and slow to run. A number of other software programs such as PTGui and PTAssembler have grown up that use the core of Panorama Tools but are much easier to use. In recent years the Hugin project has created a panorama program which has the advantage of being completely free. When the author tried Hugin it had too many bugs to be recommended for novice users. No doubt it will improve and may be worth considering in future.

Recommendations

There are too many panorama programs available on the market for anyone to have tried them all and the market is constantly evolving. The following selection of PC programs has been used by the author in the mid-2000s with varying degrees of success.

CANON'S PHOTOSTITCH Distributed free with Canon cameras so only feasible for Canon owners; an automatic program with minimal control over the output. The seams are usually visible on high resolution output and there is little control over the blending. It serves as an introduction to the subject and

may be sufficient for low resolution output such as viewing on the web.

PANAVUE A standalone program that offers some control over the stitching process and can create Photoshop layered output. It has a free trial that gives watermarked output. The seams can be visible but often it is possible to work round this in Photoshop. Expensive.

PHOTOSHOP CS, ELEMENTS 2.0 AND NEWER VERSIONS include the 'Photomerge' facility which can give good results on some material but usually produces visible seams. It serves as an inexpensive introduction to the subject.

PTASSEMBLER Inexpensive shareware program that uses Panorama Tools and provides a very high degree of control over the stitching process and the output. Reasonably easy to use after some practice but may be too 'techie' for some.

PTGUI Fully featured program. Originally a 'front end' for Panorama Tools, it has evolved significantly in recent years and now has its own stitching engine. It can operate either automatically or with a manual mode that offers a high degree of control. Major features include producing Photoshop layered output and optional colour blending to improve the matching between images. The automatic modes work surprisingly well although they still get confused when asked to blend a set of images that has a train in one and empty track in the others. Excellent quality output is usually possible with only a small amount of work on the computer. Has a 30-day free trial. Reasonable price considering the flexibility and highly recommended.

For Apple Mac users, PTGui is available and there is also a Mac-only program called PTMac.

Projection

When joining photos, particularly when making a large panorama, there are a number of decisions to make and there are usually some preferences to be set in the stitching software. The best software will allow a choice of the type of projection to be

☑ **More information on panorama programmes**

❑ Canon PhotoStitch: www.canon.co.uk

❑ Hugin: http://hugin.sourceforge.net/

❑ Panavue www.panavue.com

❑ PTAssembler: www.tawbaware.com

❑ PTGui: www.ptgui.com

❑ PTMac: www.ptmac.com

For more information on panoramas generally see:

❑ http://wiki.panotools.org/

used. What does this mean? During stitching, each of the input images needs to be distorted in a controlled way so that they will join together without visible seams. The distorting process is given a special name – warping – and uses sophisticated maths based on a principle known as projection. There are many different types of projection although there are only two that will be of particular interest to railway photographers. The first is known as cylindrical projection and uses only a small amount of distortion. It gives a pleasing perspective but on wide images the rails can look unrealistic due to the amount of curvature towards the edges. The second is known as rectilinear projection. It distorts the images more but straight lines remain relatively straight. The resulting image is long and thin and somewhat 'squashed' in the middle so that the final picture needs to be more heavily cropped. Where stitching software offers the choice, try both settings. Cylindrical projection is usually the best option unless the results appear too curved, in which case rectilinear projection should be tried. Figure 6.2.4.2 shows examples of cylindrical and rectilinear projection in panoramic images created from the same input images.

● BURNOUT

Introduction
Photography on sunny days should be enjoyable and yield successful pictures but every so often reflections from the sun can lead to ugly white areas on a picture – the phenomenon called 'burnout'. What exactly is this, why does it happen and how can it be fixed?

Sensor
A colour digital image on a computer is made up of millions of pixels, each one made up of Red, Green and Blue (RGB) brightness values, as described in Chapter 1. The sensor in a digital camera is made up of millions of tiny light-sensitive individual sensors, each capturing either Red, Green or Blue light. An analogy to the way an individual sensor reacts to light is a cup catching drops of rainwater. When a cup is full it can't hold more water and maximum brightness is recorded. When taking a photograph, the colour of the subject means that a blue locomotive, for example, causes the blue cups in our analogy to fill up faster with raindrops than the others. If too much light enters the camera when taking a picture due to for example, human error, camera fault or a reflection of the sun, there may be many pixels at maximum brightness (full cups of water). Technically this is known as over-exposure and the channels with maximum brightness are 'clipped'. Remembering that a colour image is composed of Red, Green and Blue Channels, there can be clipping in one or more channels. The situation with all three channels clipped is worst because the area shows up as plain white with no detail. This is 'burnout'. Clipping on just one channel may be less visible and some detail will be retained, thanks to the information recorded in the other channels. By shooting in Raw format it will usually be possible to recover some detail from bright areas (highlights) that would be clipped in a JPEG format image. Incidentally, Raw converters differ significantly in the way they handle clipping. Adobe's Raw converter built into Photoshop and Lightroom cover up clipping very well while Canon's own DPP Raw converter is quite poor and displays reduced detail in clipped areas.

The only way of repairing burnout in an image is covering up the white area. The technique described here is called 'patching'.

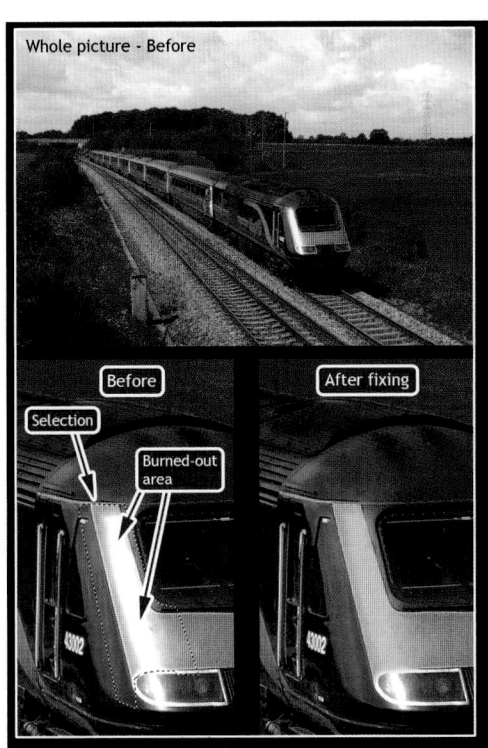

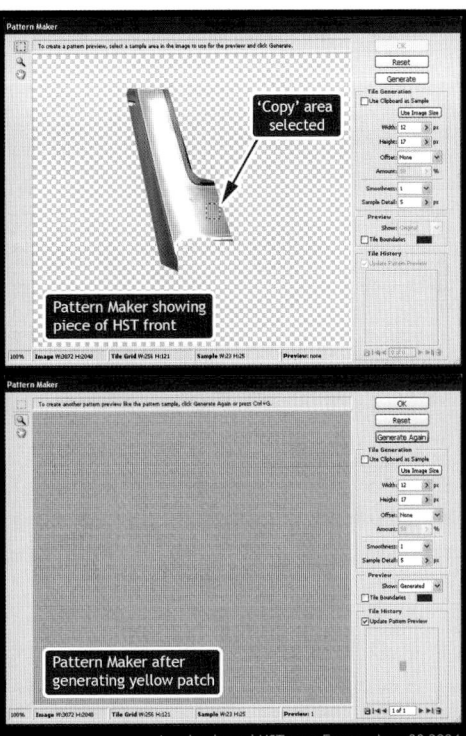

Figure 6.3.1.
Image showing burnout and how to create new material to repair it using the Pattern Maker.

Example

Figure 6.3.1 shows an HST on a sunny day near Frome. The sun has reflected off the yellow curved front edge of the cab and created full 'burnout', as can be seen in the enlarged section. All three channels are clipped and there is an ugly white area that should have been yellow.

Principle

The basic principle used for the repair is to create a separate piece of yellow material to cover up the white area known as a patch. It is positioned over the white area and a feature of Photoshop layers is used so that only the white area is automatically replaced by yellow.

A Photoshop tool known as the 'Pattern Maker' is used to create the patch by taking a small area of the yellow front and uses it as the basis for generating a large yellow pattern in a new layer. The layer settings are then changed in order to blend the patch. An alternative method of repair would be to use the Cloning Tool to repeatedly copy part of the yellow front into a sufficiently large area to cover the burned out area. The cloning tool is fine for small areas but tiresome for larger areas. Use of the Pattern Maker is a little-

known solution which is much quicker and simpler for this type of repair. Because it generates the patch quickly it is easy to see whether the colour matches or contains any repeating patterns. If not suitable, a new one can easily be generated. The clever part of this technique is that by copying a small piece of the existing yellow front it contains the imperfections of a real-world image and avoids the artificial look of a Photoshop-generated colour. In full Photoshop the Pattern Maker is accessible via the 'Filter' menu option. In Photoshop Elements pattern making works in a different way. Those working in 16-bit mode should note that the Pattern Maker only works in 8-bit mode. Anyone working in 16-bit mode should create the patch in 8-bit mode via copy & paste and convert the result to 16-bit before pasting it into the main image.

Creating the patch

Begin by selecting a piece of the HST front which is slightly larger than the white area. This is done so that when the yellow area is generated it will be the right size. It must include some of the yellow front that will be used to generate the yellow patch. The dotted

Figure 6.3.2.
**How to apply the
yellow patch to fix the
burnout problem.**

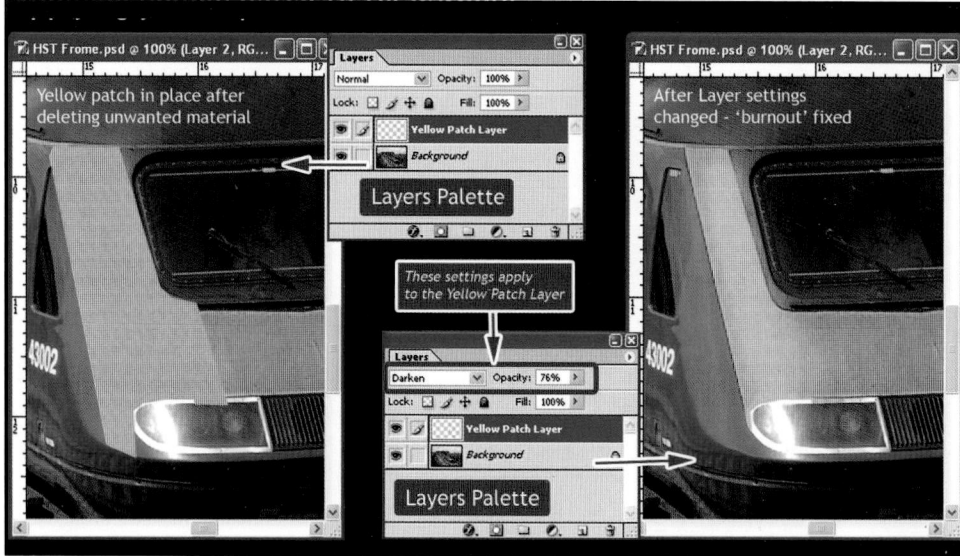

line of the selection is shown in the example in the 'Before' image in Figure 6.3.1. The selection can have either a 'hard' or 'soft' (feathered) edge. The only important thing is that it does not include any areas of the front that are lighter than the desired shade of yellow, so in this case the selection excludes the silver border of the lighting cover. Once the selection is ready, it is important to save it because it will be used again later. Use the 'Select → Save Selection...' to do this. Then do a 'copy' and immediately a 'paste' to create a copy of a piece of the subject – in this case the HST front – on its own in a new layer. To avoid confusion rename the new layer – for example 'Yellow Patch Layer'. Select the Yellow Patch Layer by clicking on it in the Layers Palette so that it turns blue – see the Layers Palette in the example. Start the Pattern Generator and select a yellow rectangular area to be copied. This is shown in the top right of Figure 6.3.1. If your Layers Palette isn't visible, use the Window → Layers menu option to make it appear and there should also be a tick mark next to the word 'Layers' on this menu.

When the 'Generate' button is pressed the Pattern Maker uses the small yellow piece of image from the area just selected to generate a pattern and fill the entire layer with yellow, as shown. Sometimes there will be a problem in the generated pattern – for instance it may contain repeated shapes or have bands of

colour instead of being roughly a single colour. If this happens, 'Undo' the pattern generation, select a slightly different area and try again. After a few tries the yellow patch should have a suitably realistic colour for the next stage.

At this point the entire layer is full of yellow, which is far too much. This is why the original selection was saved – to be used to delete the excess material. The 'Select → Load selection...' menu option is used to load the selection, the 'Inverse' option chosen to select everything except the piece of the HST front. Then the [Delete] key is pressed to delete the unwanted material and leave a yellow patch on the front of the HST. It should now look like the bottom left image of Figure 6.3.1.

Layers

The ingenious part follows now. At the moment an ugly yellow patch is covering the front corner of the HST, obscuring important detail. What is wanted is for the patch to cover only the white area. This is where two features of Photoshop Layers are used, available in the Layers Palette and ringed in red in Figure 6.3.2. The first of these is known as the 'Blending Mode'. This is normally set to 'Normal', which means that the Yellow Patch Layer simply covers the layer underneath. By changing this to 'Darken', the Yellow Patch Layer only covers the parts of layer underneath it where the Yellow layer is darker. Because yellow is darker than white, it covers up the white parts. On the other hand, yellow is lighter than the blue and black surrounds so these areas are unchanged. The last touch is to change the opacity value to about 75% instead of the usual 100%. This causes a small amount of the layer underneath to still be visible, giving the curve of the HST front a slight shine effect and making it look more realistic.

Photoshop Elements

For users of Photoshop Elements the process is similar except when creating the pattern. Then choose the Edit→Define Pattern... menu option. This will create the pattern in the set of preset patterns. Use the Pattern Brush in the Tools Palette to apply the pattern in a new layer to cover the burned out area.

Finishing

Save the picture in Photoshop's .PSD format so that all the layers are saved and it is possible to return to change it in future if required. Those who are fussy may wish to fix other parts of the image like the 'burnt out' part of the lamp cover. The patched-over white area can be viewed as a starting point that gets rid of an obvious fault. Faults in areas containing detail are best fixed by transplanting a piece from another picture, which is a technique described in Chapter 5.

● WINDSCREEN REFLECTIONS

You're ready with your camera, the train is approaching in the distance and the sun is out. What can go wrong? As the train gets closer you can see a reflection from the locomotive windscreen. The reflection gets stronger as the train gets to the 'shoot' position but you press the shutter release anyway. How can the spoiled photograph be rescued by removing a typical reflection?

Assessing the Picture

Figure 6.4.1 shows a Class 37 locomotive on a railtour with reflections on two of the cab windows. Although only a small part of the picture the reflections spoil the overall effect as the windows are the focal point of the locomotive, rather like the eyes in a human portrait. Looking closely at the windows, the reflections are not strong. There is some colour and texture in the window and the frames have all their detail intact so the reflection can be cured fairly easily in Photoshop. If the reflection was very strong to the extent that there is no detail in the window or frames there is no simple cure: the damage can only be repaired by transplanting a new window from a similar picture.

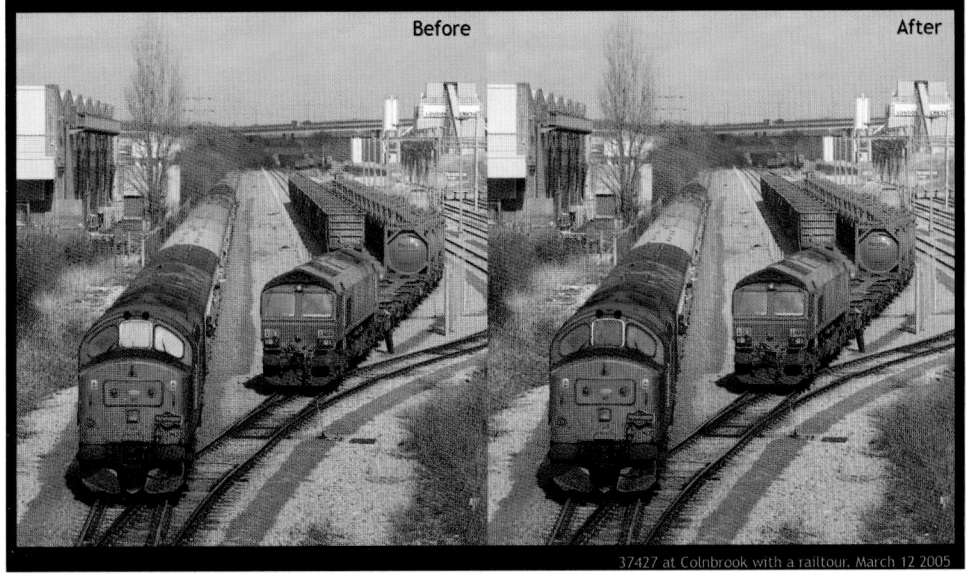

Before   After

37427 at Colnbrook with a railtour, March 12 2005

Figure 6.4.1.
View of locomotive before and after removing reflection from cab windows.

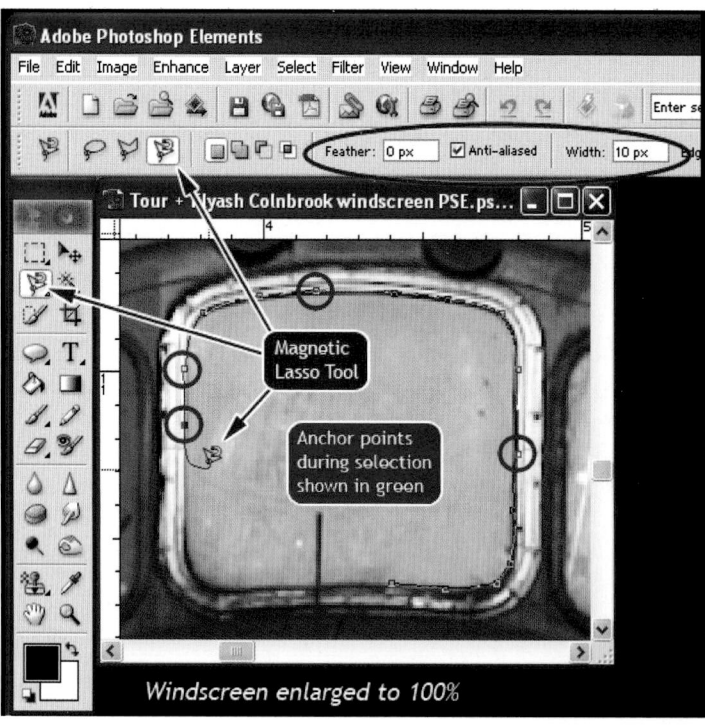

Figure 6.4.2.
Selecting the
windscreen using the
Magnetic Lasso Tool.

colour will be changed slightly on one of them so that it matches the others. As always the original image will not be altered. By using Photoshop's Adjustment Layers the adjustments will be made in a way that means the changes are only applied to the image at the final stage. This approach ensures further changes can be made at a later date without affecting image quality. The whole window will be selected and the adjustments made. The process will then be repeated for the second window.

Selecting the Cab Windows

The windows have clearly defined edges so the simplest way to make the selection is to use the Magnetic Lasso Tool. The 'Magic Wand' may work on some windows but this tool gives inconsistent results and a quick test shows it doesn't work well here. The view of the window is enlarged so it is easier to see the edges. This is shown in Figure 6.4.2. The Magnetic Lasso is clicked on a window edge and moved along the edge. 'Anchor' dots – ringed in green in the example – should appear automatically to fix the selection in position. If any of these are in the wrong place the [Delete] key is pressed to remove the newest point and the tool is moved again.

Principle

To fix the reflection in the two windows each window will be treated individually because their colours and brightness are slightly different. They will be darkened in a controlled way so that the reflection – which is just a patch of brightness – disappears. The

Figure 6.4.3.
Adjusting the
brightness and colour
of the windscreens in
Photoshop Elements
and full Photoshop.

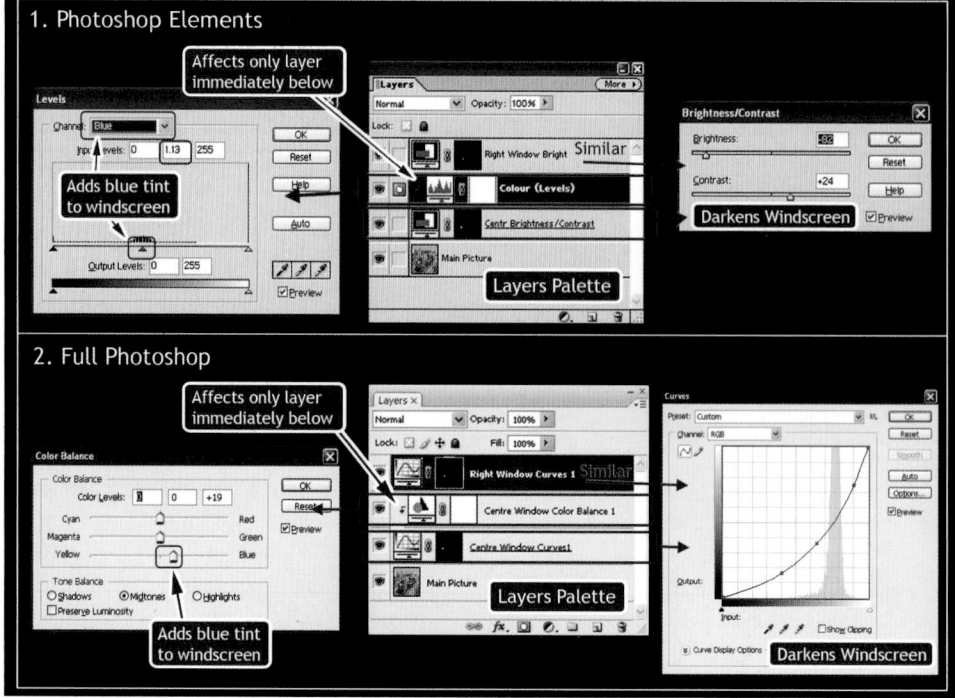

To force creation of an 'anchor' point the left mouse button is clicked when the tool is in the desired position. By gradually working around the window, the end of the selection will soon be close to the beginning. Pressing the [Enter] or [Return] key completes the selection. To get rid of the selection the 'Select → Deselect' menu option can be used.

Darkening

To darken the window when using Photoshop Elements either a 'Brightness/ Contrast' or 'Levels' Adjustment Layer can be used. Those with full Photoshop may prefer a 'Curves Adjustment Layer' as it gives more control over the way the brighter areas are adjusted compared with the mid-tones. Figure 6.4.3 shows equivalents for both full Photoshop and Photoshop Elements. The Photoshop Elements adjustment needed a large decrease in brightness together with a small increase in contrast as shown. Just before creating the Adjustment Layer the Selection created in the previous section should still be active because this ensures that a mask is automatically created to restrict the change to just the selected area. Only the windscreen is darkened, not the whole image.

Colour

When the middle windscreen in this image was darkened the resulting colour wasn't quite right: it needed a slight blue tint to match the others. This is a rather picky point but the improvement is worthwhile. The colour is changed by creating a second Adjustment Layer above the first. The exact method to be used depends on whether you use full Photoshop or Elements.

Full Photoshop users can use a 'Color Balance' Adjustment Layer to change the colour balance. The 'Yellow/Blue' slider is moved towards the blue end to make the windscreen more blue. To ensure that the colour change applies only to the windscreen and not to the whole image the 'Use Previous Layer to Create Clipping Mask' must be chosen when creating the Adjustment Layer. In the Layers Palette this is shown by the Layer being slightly indented to the right. The extent of the colour adjustment is now

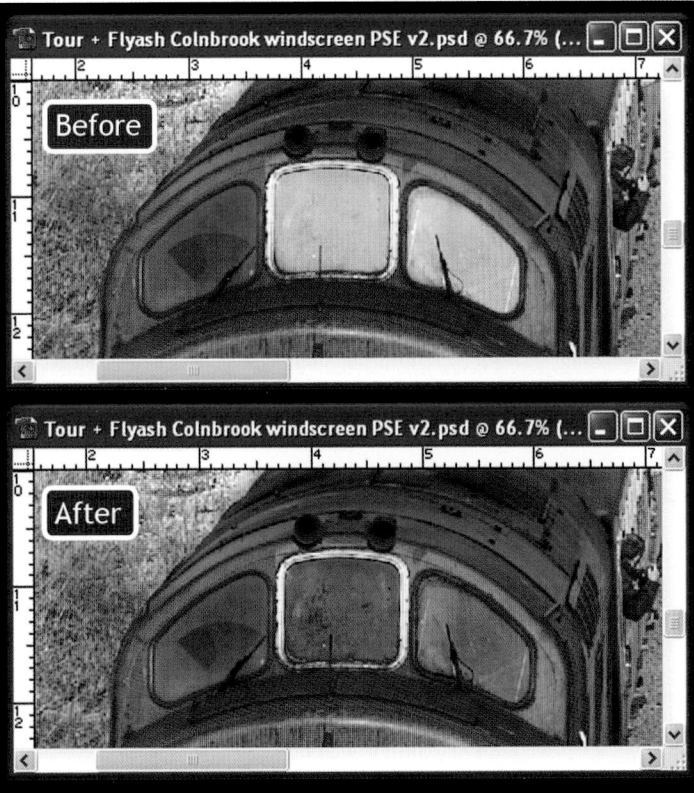

restricted by the mask on the lower layer.

Photoshop Elements has restricted functionality and there is no 'Color Balance' Adjustment Layer. The colour balance is changed by using a Levels Adjustment Layer to alter one or more of the channels (Red, Green or Blue) individually. This has the disadvantage of being difficult to use and is not an obvious technique even to experienced users. To give a blue tint, a Levels Adjustment Layer is created and the Blue Channel selected on the drop-down box: this is ringed in red on the example. Moving the middle triangle (ringed in red) to the left makes the image more blue, or less blue (more yellow) when moved to the right. To ensure that the colour change applies only to the windscreen and not to the whole image the 'Group with Previous Layer' option must be chosen when creating the Adjustment Layer. In the Layers Palette this is shown by the Layer being slightly indented to the right.

Once the result looks good the image should be saved in Photoshop's PSD format in the usual way.

Figure 6.4.4.
Enlargement of the windscreens before and after adjustment.

● BLACK & WHITE

For many years black & white film was the most popular way of photographing railways. By the 1990s, use of colour film – both slide and negative – had overtaken black & white thanks to much lower prices in real terms and excellent quality results. The advent of digital photography may be seen by some as a 'nail in the coffin' for black & white but the reality is that digital cameras and computer processing make the creation of black & white images easier than with film.

Taking Black & White Pictures

With film the camera must be loaded with different films to be able to take both colour and black & white pictures. Digital changes this. A special digital camera is not needed to take black & white. Any colour image can be converted to black & white on a computer. Some digital cameras have a special 'black & white' option for taking pictures. In these cameras a normal colour picture is converted to black & white internally, saved to the memory card and the colour image thrown away. These options are not recommended because the colour information is lost. Taking a colour picture and converting it to black & white later is much more flexible because there is always the option of using the colour picture or black & white or both. Raw format should be used to take the picture, not JPEG, as this gives maximum flexibility for later computer processing.

Introduction to Conversion

In the past colour film pictures converted to black & white often looked unrealistic. Colour films were often grainy and the grain showed up particularly badly after black & white conversion. More seriously the tones often looked wrong. Colour images from digital SLRs are, generally speaking, very clean with minimal 'grain' or 'noise'. In recent years the conversion techniques have been perfected and a good quality colour image is capable of producing a clear, sharp black & white equivalent.

It would be easy to think that converting a colour picture to black & white involves a simple button press in Photoshop. In reality there are many techniques for doing the conversion, enough to fill a book, varying from simple to complex and based on different principles. After explaining the background the most common conversion methods will be described.

Shades of Grey

In any photograph the light needed to create the image is reflected from objects in the picture and is made up of different colours. Black and white and colour films respond to the different colours of light in different ways. Should a dark blue be rendered as a dark grey or mid-grey? Should yellow be mid-grey or light grey? There is no 'correct' answer and different black & white films will react differently.

Black and white film and printing papers have been around for more than 150 years and the system has been fine-tuned to give pleasing pictures. Most of the tones in a typical print are light and mid-grey without too many dark greys which would give a muddy appearance. There should also be plenty of small areas of white and black to provide a full range of tones. Software on a computer that converts colour to black & white must make a decision about the shade of grey used to render each colour and various options are provided. Ultimately the photographer makes the final decision by selecting the conversion method used and its accompanying settings.

Conversion Options

Colour images are usually of a type called RGB (Red, Green, and Blue). (Photoshop supports other types of colour image such as Lab Color but these are rarely used). After conversion to black & white an image may still be an RGB colour image even though it contains no visible colours. Alternatively it could be of type 'Greyscale'. There are three major options built into full Photoshop for converting an RGB colour image to black & white while Photoshop Elements has two:

i 'Convert to Greyscale'. The colour information is removed and each pixel is converted to a simple brightness value to give a Greyscale image. This is the 'Image → Mode → Greyscale' menu option and is based on conversion settings built into Photoshop that cannot be changed.

ii 'Desaturate'. A saturation adjustment is used with the saturation control set to minimum. The colour information is removed, leaving an RGB image with no colour.

iii 'Channel Mixer'. This allows an image to be converted to black & white in a way that gives the user control of the proportions of the red, green and blue channels making up the final image. The colour information is removed, leaving an RGB image with no colour. The Channel Mixer is not available in Photoshop Elements but can be added as a plug-in.

It is also possible to do the conversion using extra-cost optional software. There are many Photoshop plug-ins available to do the conversion which offer varying degrees of control: some are literally 'push button' while others have a huge number of controls. Most of them work on the basis of copying the response to colours of various popular black & white films so that, for example, a 'Tri-X' or 'Pan F' appearance can be chosen. The plug-ins usually have an option to simulate putting a coloured filter (for example red or yellow) on the camera lens to enhance certain colours.

The author's findings are that the Greyscale conversion is fine for small images and general purposes. The 'Desaturate' option is not recommended as it creates strange looking results, particularly yellow fronts on locomotives and units which are too dark. Some photographers favour the Channel Mixer but the author has never had any success with it. While adjusting the different channels to get a reasonable level of contrast some areas always seem to burn out and lose detail. The author's preferred method is the plug-in which is quick and easy. The lens filters work quite well, particularly the yellow which is recommended for most conversions although there appears to be little difference between the various film settings.

Conversion Comparison

Figure 6.5.1 shows a set of four versions of the same image of a Class 47 locomotive hauling a passenger train: the original colour image and three different black & white

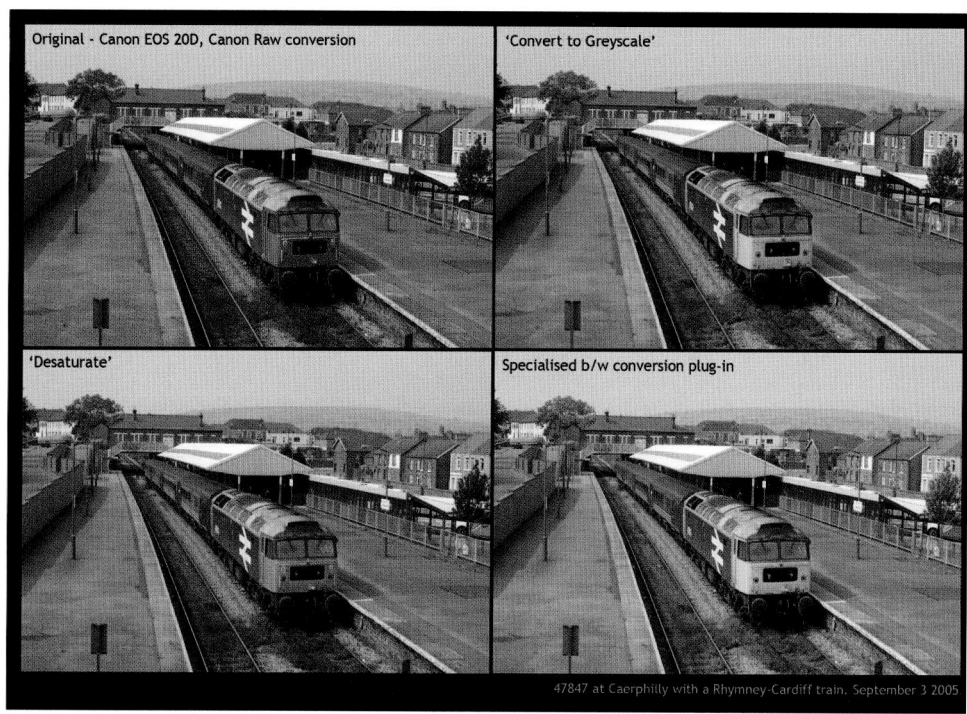

Original - Canon EOS 20D, Canon Raw conversion

'Convert to Greyscale'

'Desaturate'

Specialised b/w conversion plug-in

47847 at Caerphilly with a Rhymney-Cardiff train. September 3 2005

Figure 6.5.1.
Shows the results from different methods of converting a colour image to black & white.

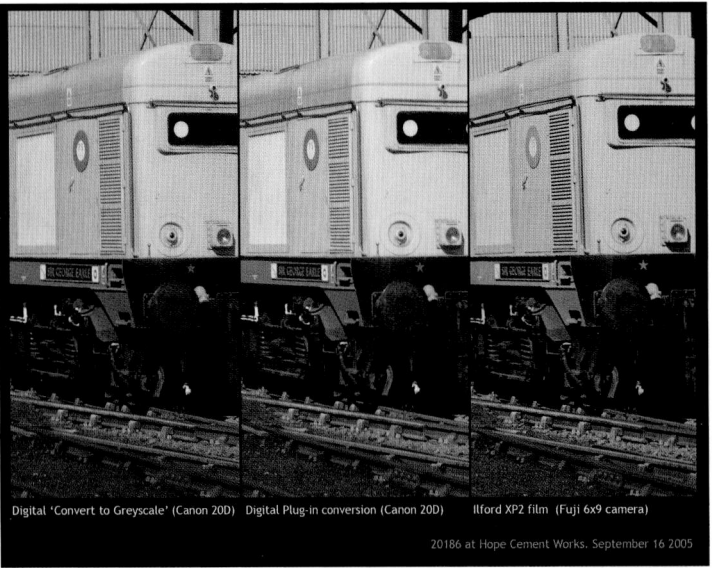

Digital 'Convert to Greyscale' (Canon 20D) Digital Plug-in conversion (Canon 20D) Ilford XP2 film (Fuji 6x9 camera)

20186 at Hope Cement Works. September 16 2005

Figure 6.5.2.
**Comparing a black &
white conversion from
a digital colour image
with an image from
black & white film.**

conversions. Note particularly how the grey equivalent of the yellow and blue parts of the locomotive vary between the conversions. The differences are particularly noticeable on large prints. The author's favourite conversion is from the 'Power Retouche Black & White Studio' plug-in using its 'Pan F film' setting with a yellow filter.

In Figure 6.5.2 a set of three image sections of a Class 20 at Hope Cement Works compares greyscale and plug-in conversion from a Canon EOS 20D digital image with a medium format image on Ilford XP2 black & white film. Note how close the tonal rendition of the plug-in is to the film. The greyscale conversion produces different results in some areas, particularly the blue chassis side which is darker than that produced by the film. The key message demonstrated here is that a small sensor digital camera can produce a black & white image which, when converted from colour using a suitable method is surprisingly close in tonal quality to an image from medium format film. Areas of detail such as the grilles and lamps are comparable although to be fair, medium format produces better fine detail in some areas such as the foreground ballast. The plug-in has again produced a realistic conversion from colour.

Raw Conversion

Some Raw converters such as newer

versions of Canon's Digital Photo Professional software are able to produce a black & white result directly without having to produce a colour image first. This is an excellent option as it is fast, convenient and produces good quality results.

Colour Settings

It may seem strange to describe colour settings when discussing black & white images. A standard colour image uses RGB format (RGB = Red, Green and Blue). When taking all the colour out of it by using, for example the Desaturate option, it may be a black & white image to look at but technically it is still RGB and therefore colour. When using the 'Convert to Greyscale' option an RGB colour image is changed to Greyscale format.

For web display it makes a small difference which of these formats you use – RGB or Greyscale. When saving an image in JPEG format, Photoshop will give you the option of saving an ICC profile with it. With a colour image it is essential to include an sRGB profile otherwise the colour will appear weaker than it should. With a greyscale image whatever type of ICC profile is saved with it (or even if none is saved) the appearance of a black & white image varies between images and web browsers but overall tends towards making an image slightly darker overall than it appears inside Photoshop. Recommended practice is to save black & white web JPEG images in RGB format with a sRGB colour profile. This may involve converting a greyscale image to RGB.

Appearance

Black & white images create the best viewing impression when they have a wide range of contrast. Unfortunately, a black & white image viewed on the computer screen or in a print straight after conversion from colour often appears bland even though all the tones look right and despite increasing contrast in the usual way by making various Levels adjustments. The image needs to have good contrast even in small areas and a way of achieving this uses a process known as 'Local Contrast Enhancement' (LCE).

Local Contrast Enhancement

A simple and very effective way of enhancing local contrast uses the same 'Unsharp Mask' tool (USM) that most photographers use for sharpening. Unsharp Mask doesn't actually increase sharpness, it simply makes an image seem sharper to the human eye by increasing the contrast at the boundary between areas of different brightness. By using appropriate settings, USM can enhance the local contrast without the destructive effect seen with sharpening. It works by comparing the brightness of adjacent pixels and adjusting their brightness accordingly. As with many powerful tools USM needs to be applied with care, otherwise it can create a result which appears too harsh.

Two successful ways of applying LCE with Unsharp Mask are:

i   Light touch to the whole image using the settings: Amount 20%, Radius 50 and Threshold 0. This is simple to do and should be sufficient for many images.

ii Stronger application to selective parts of the image using the settings: Amount 60%, Radius 50 and Threshold 0.

Selective application takes more effort but gives good results on flatter images.

Giving a strong enhancement to the whole image is something that should only be done to certain images. This is because areas close to black become full black while those that are close to white become fully white. Detail is lost and the image takes on a harsh overall appearance.

Although the example used here shows a black & white image the same technique can also be used to enhance the contrast in a colour image.

Selective Application

The principle used in selective application is to create two versions of the image, each in their own Photoshop Layer. The original image is on top and an image with a strong enhancement is underneath. The upper image is then selectively deleted so that the increased contrast shows through in the layer underneath. There are two ways of doing the deletion: i) using a mask; ii) by actually deleting the contents of a layer. Option i) is recommended for users with full Photoshop, whereas with Photoshop

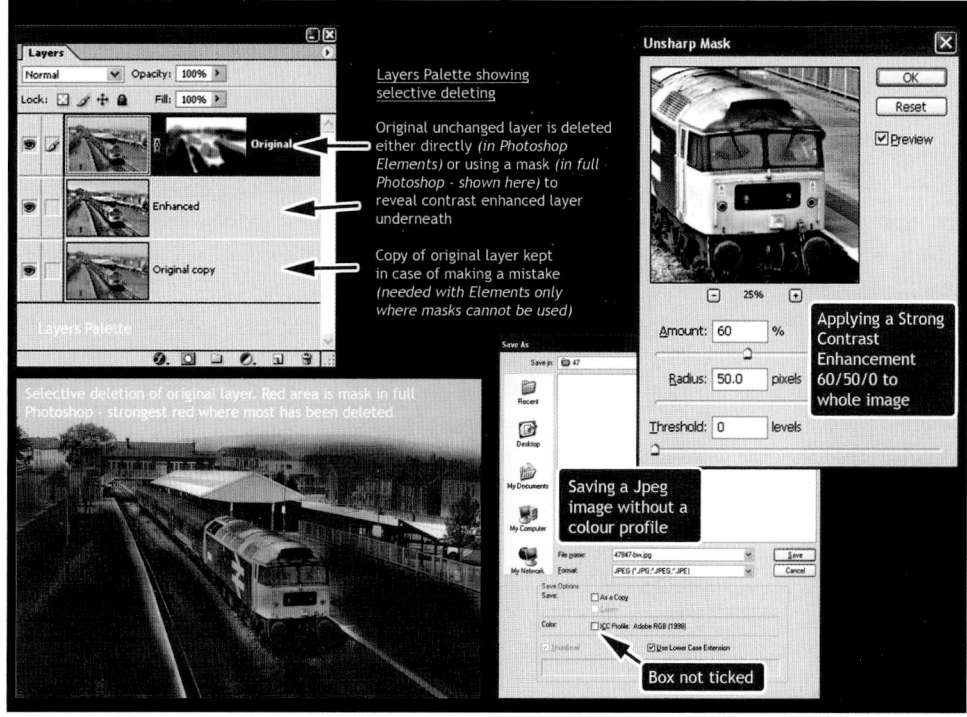

Figure 6.5.3.
How to apply local contrast enhancement to an image.

Figure 6.5.4.
Comparing different amounts of contrast enhancement applied to the same image.

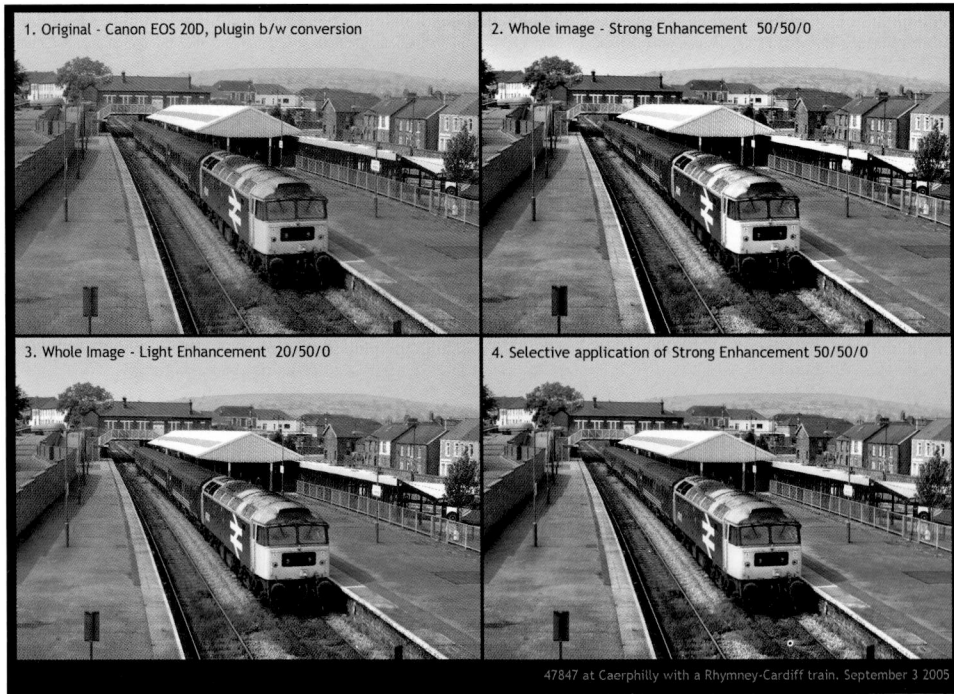

1. Original - Canon EOS 20D, plugin b/w conversion

2. Whole image - Strong Enhancement 50/50/0

3. Whole Image - Light Enhancement 20/50/0

4. Selective application of Strong Enhancement 50/50/0

47847 at Caerphilly with a Rhymney-Cardiff train. September 3 2005

Elements the features for manipulation of masks are limited and Option ii) will be easier.

In both cases the starting point is to take the original image and duplicate it. If using Option ii) above – deletion – it is a good idea to make an extra copy in another layer as a backup against making a mistake by deleting too much. Then apply the strong enhancement to the lower layer. In the example in Figure 6.5.3, this layer is labelled as 'Enhanced'. The top layer is the unchanged layer. In full Photoshop, the process consists of adding a mask to the top layer and 'deleting' the image by painting black 'paint' on the mask. With Photoshop Elements the Eraser Tool with black paint is used to delete the top layer. As this is done the enhanced layer underneath shows through and the contrast in that area increases. It is best to concentrate on areas such as the platforms and track while avoiding light and dark areas like the sky, station canopy and train underframe. To get a partial effect a brush with opacity value in the 30% to 60% range is used. Use of a soft-edged brush ensures that the changes blend neatly into the surrounding area.

Figure 6.5.3 shows an image covered in red to demonstrate selective deletion. 100% red means all material has been deleted, while as the red gets weaker more material underneath shows through. Note how the red is strongest in the area around the platforms, track and background houses, showing that the strong enhancement shows through in place of the original image.

Comparisons

In Figure 6.5.4 the same image of No 47847 on a passenger train from the earlier example is used to compare different types of contrast enhancement. The individual images are as follows:

1 The unchanged original.

2 Strong enhancement to the whole image. This has plenty of visual 'snap' but is harsh overall. Some areas such as the station canopy and locomotive underframe are too light or dark and have lost detail.

3 Light contrast enhancement to the whole image. It has better visual 'snap' than the original. Some areas such as the track would benefit from additional enhancement.

4 Strong enhancement applied to selective areas of the image. This combines the best of the light and strong enhancements.

● WEB IMAGE COPYRIGHTING

Watermarking

Displaying photographs on Internet web pages is very popular and there are large numbers of railway-related sites to browse. Unfortunately there have been numerous examples of copyright theft where images were taken from the photographer's site and displayed elsewhere without permission or acknowledgement. One way to tackle this is to add a photographer's copyright label to each image in a process sometimes called watermarking. A copyright label can be as simple as adding something like '© Photograph by Kim Fullbrook' to the bottom of an image. Some photographers also add a distinctive logo or graphic. There are many ways in which this can be done and there are no right or wrong techniques for creating them.

Obtrusiveness

The photographer has to choose how large and obtrusive they want their labels to be as there is a trade-off to make. A small label does not distract attention from the photograph, but on the other hand a copyright thief can easily crop it off or cover it with cloned material. A larger label that intrudes into the picture area will be harder to remove and more effective at discouraging theft but may be obtrusive to viewers. One way of reducing the visual impact of a larger label is to make it a see-through overlay on the picture.

Simple Label

What is the best way to create a label or graphic? One option is to use Photoshop since it was originally designed as a general purpose graphics package and has many useful built-in features. Photoshop Elements is similar, although reduced in scope.

A simple label is made up of two parts – text and a background. A coloured strip across the bottom of the photograph is easily created by using the Rectangle Shape Tool. To do this, choose the tool in the Tool Palette, then click the left mouse button, drag the cursor across the photo and release the button. This is shown in Figure 6.6.1. The colour is selected on the menu bar where shown and is known as the fill colour although the label only says 'color'. The

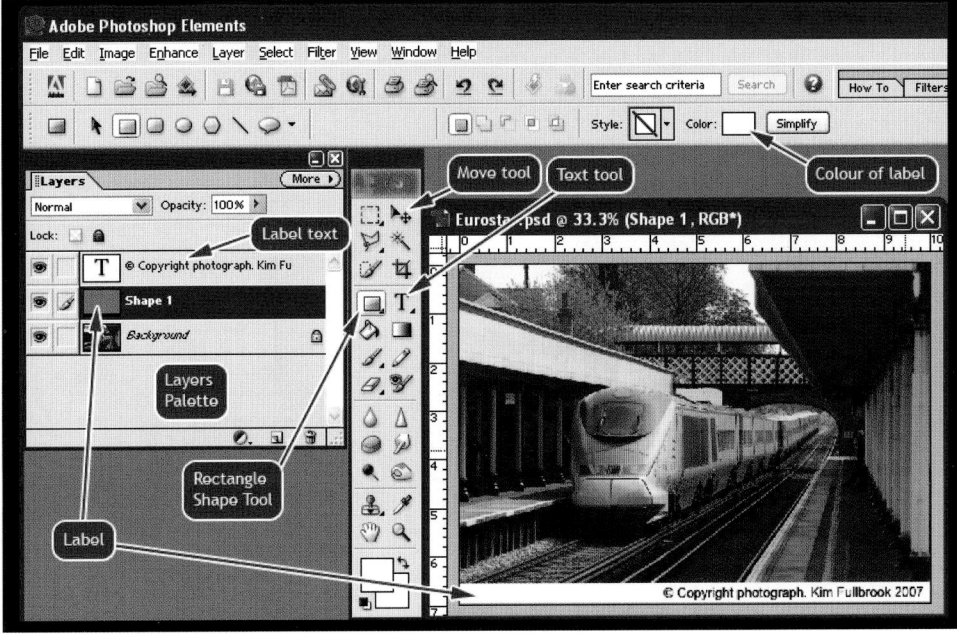

Figure 6.6.1.
Adding a label to the lower side of an image using Photoshop Elements.

Figure 6.6.2.
Increasing the size of
the image to add
material to its lower
edge.

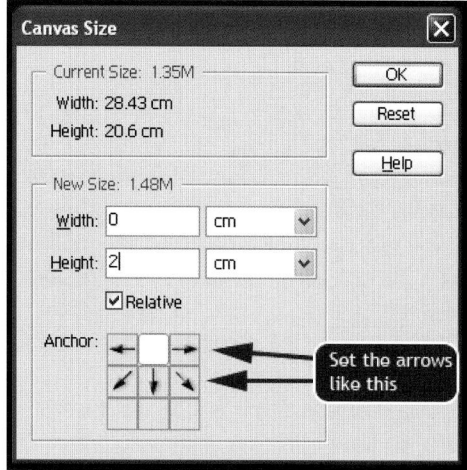

shape is automatically created in its own layer – in this case called 'Shape 1'. To alter the shape to fit the image, the method differs depending on the type of Photoshop. In Elements click the Move Tool first, while in full Photoshop choose the 'Free Transform' option on the Edit menu. Then in either program click the left mouse button on one of the edge or corner 'handles' and drag across the screen while holding the mouse button down. To finalise the change, click the 'tick' symbol at the middle of the screen near the top, otherwise click the cross to abandon it.

To avoid covering up any of the photo with the label and text it's necessary to increase the size of the picture. This is done by adding extra material to the bottom edge of the image using the 'Canvas Size...' option found on the 'Image' menu option or on one of its sub-

options. In the example shown in Figure 6.6.2, two centimetres are being added to the bottom edge of the image. The arrows in the 'Anchor' boxes are used to indicate the direction in which the canvas size will be increased.

To add the text, select the Text Tool and type in the text. For text containing specialised characters like the Copyright symbol © it is easiest to create this in a word processing package like Microsoft Word or OpenOffice Writer and then copy & paste it instead of typing it in directly. In Word, specialist characters are added using the 'Insert → Symbol...' menu option.

To create the final image collapse all the layers together using the 'Layer → Flatten Image' menu option, then save in the desired output file format such as TIFF or JPEG.

Simple Graphic

Adding a small railway-related graphic to your images makes them more distinctive and consistent. They can be created in any graphics package, saved to disk and then imported into Photoshop for adding to images.

To create one from a photograph, take a suitable photograph and isolate an item of interest. In this example in Figure 6.6.3, a head-on photograph of a Class 37 locomotive was used. To select just the area of interest, in this case the locomotive, the Polygonal Selection tool was used with a feather of a couple of pixels to give a soft edge. Having

Figure 6.6.3.
Creating a graphic
from a photographic
image.

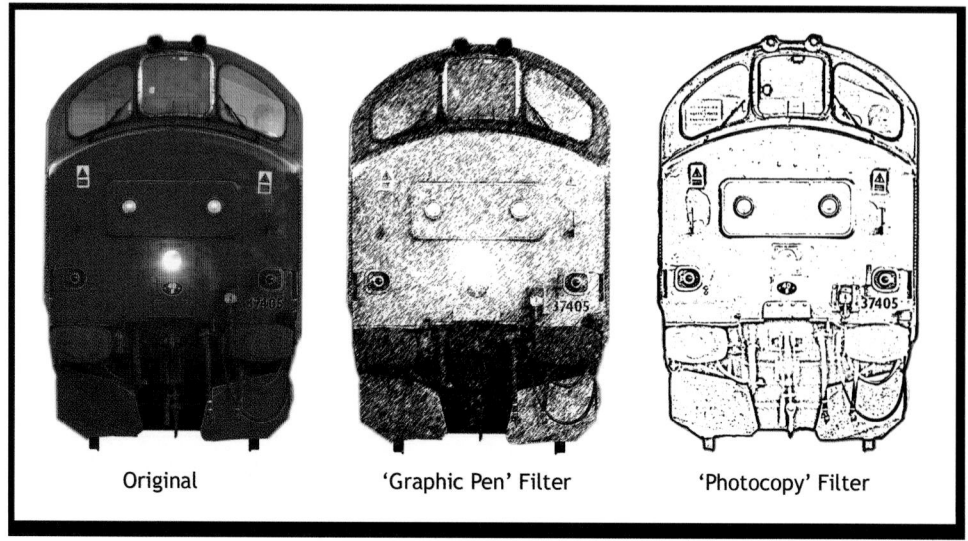

Original   'Graphic Pen' Filter   'Photocopy' Filter

selected the locomotive, the rest of the picture was deleted. This was done by selecting the 'opposite' of the current selection using the 'Select → Inverse' menu option and then pressing the [Delete] key. Lastly the image was cropped to leave just the small picture. Those with full Photoshop may prefer to delete the unwanted material by applying a mask and drawing on the mask with black paint in those areas because this allows material to be easily 'undeleted' after making a mistake.

Converting the photograph into an arty graphic is an opportunity to try out some of Photoshop's built in 'filter' effects. One of them may well produce a suitable result.

Figure 6.6.3 shows a couple of conversions of the original photograph on the left. The author's favourite was using the 'Photocopy' filter, then inverting it to swap over the black and white. Adjusting the brightness and contrast appropriately gives an effect that looks like an ink drawing.

One potential problem area is getting the size of the graphics right when added to the final picture. The key setting here is the resolution. Web images are normally set to a resolution of 72 pixels per inch (ppi) and the graphics should match this. The Image Resize option is used to set the right width and height for the graphic while at the same time fixing the resolution to 72 ppi. A width somewhere

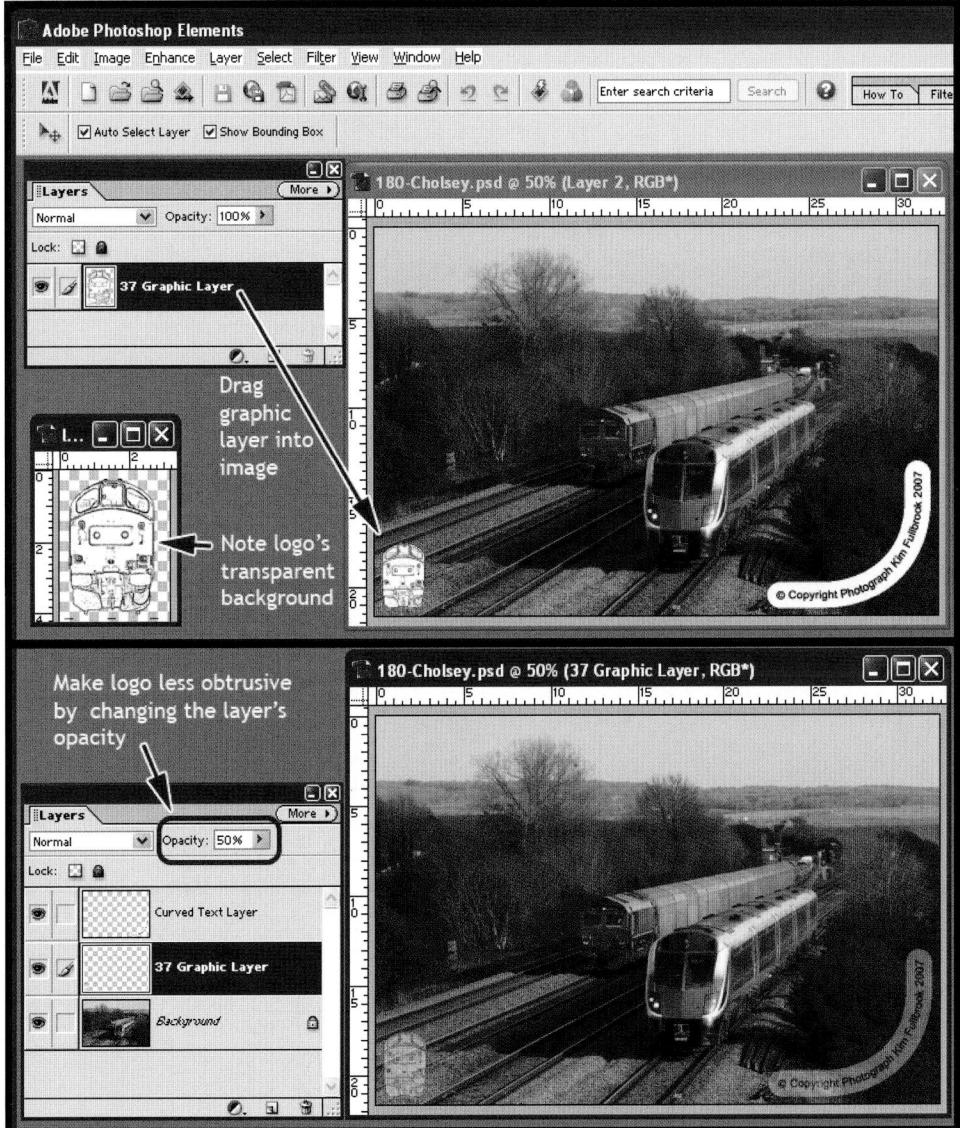

Figure 6.6.4.
Applying a logo using the 'Drag and Drop' technique.

around 3/4in (2cm) is usually suitable – experiment to see what looks right. It should be added that it's not essential to set web images to 72 ppi because web browsers ignore this setting. On the other hand, setting all web images to a single value such as 72 ppi provides consistency and allows a graphic to be added at the right size as in this example.

The graphic needs to be saved and choosing the format to use is an area that may cause trouble. If the logo or graphic has any areas of transparency a format must be used that allows this – the main ones being Gif, PNG and Photoshop's own PSD. Transparency means that part of the graphic allows the original image underneath to be seen through it. The Class 37 graphic example has transparent areas – see this in Figure 6.6.4 where Photoshop's 'checkerboard' pattern shows through. Using JPEG format to save a graphic causes the transparent areas to be filled in with colour, which may not be wanted.

Add to the image

To add a graphic to the desired image, ensure both are opened in Photoshop and resized to 72 ppi for consistency. There are then two simple alternative options for adding the graphic. The first of these is to select the whole graphic, copy, paste into the desired image, then use the Move Tool to move it where desired. The second option is to use 'drag and drop', which will now be described. With the graphic selected by clicking on the Layers Palette, click and hold the left mouse button on the layer containing the graphic in the Layers Palette, then drag the cursor to any point within the image. Release the mouse button and the graphic will be copied. Then use the Move Tool to move it where it looks good – typically in one of the lower corners. The drag operation is shown in Figure 6.6.4. Repeat for any second graphic.

At this point the picture will look like the upper example and the graphics will be quite intrusive. To reduce the visual impact the layer settings are changed to make them partially transparent. This is done by selecting the layer – click on it in the Layers Palette – then using the drop-down box to change the

Opacity setting from its normal 100% value to somewhere around 40-50%. The lower image in the example has both graphics at around 45% opacity. Note how the label is visible but much less annoying to the eye.

Finishing the Picture

To finish, flatten the image to merge all the layers into one and crop if necessary. Lastly save in JPEG format ready to load on to your web site, being sure to include an RGB colour profile (see Chapter 4).

● SHADOW SIDE PHOTOGRAPHY

There are times when a photographer has to take a picture on the shadow side of the train. In these circumstances there are a number of different recommendations and available techniques, both when taking the picture and when processing the results on a computer. In all cases shooting in Raw format is recommended as this gives the most flexibility.

Recommendations

The first recommendation is to shoot in Raw format instead of JPEG as this gives much more flexibility when setting the picture brightness. The second recommendation is to follow one of the following options:

Option 1 Take the picture using normal sunny settings on the camera and brighten the shadowed area on the computer so that the detail becomes visible.

Option 2 Take the picture using shadow settings on the camera so that dark areas are recorded well and accept that the sky is going to burn out and produce a plain white area. A second picture is taken containing just the sky using camera settings that produce a pleasing blue result. The images are processed later on a computer to replace the blank sky with the blue sky from the separate picture.

Option 3 Use a graduated grey filter in front of the lens together with shadow settings on the camera. These filters are most commonly used by landscape photographers when the ground is dark and the sky quite bright. The filter is positioned on the lens so that it darkens the sky without darkening the train. In some circumstances this can work but lining up the filter can be awkward. When looking towards the sun there is the likelihood of getting unwanted flare, especially when the sun is very bright, due to the lack of anti-reflection coatings on the filters. Dirt and greasy smears on the filter increase the risk of flare.

Option 4 With a stationary train there is an additional option – the use of High Dynamic Range (HDR) techniques. A set of pictures is taken using different camera exposure settings so that bright, mid-tone and shadow areas are all captured correctly. Special HDR software is then used to automatically combine the best parts of each image into a single result.

Options 1, 2 and 4 will now be explained in more detail. The examples feature the same Class 66 locomotive at Rugby that was used to illustrate sun angles in Chapter 2.

OPTION 1 – SUNNY SETTINGS

Camera settings are chosen so that the sunny areas of the picture are captured without burnout. On some occasions when the light is soft, due to thin cloud for example, camera settings that are a compromise between 'sunny settings' and 'shadow settings' can be used – effectively Option 1½. In this case the photographer must be careful to ensure that no parts of the picture 'burn out' otherwise the result is a picture where nothing looks completely right.

The main advantage of Option 1 is that it is the simplest, both when taking the picture and when processing on a computer. The disadvantage is that although it generally works well when the shadow is mild, the results are less realistic after processing when the shadows are deep. Any noise in the shadow areas of the image will be made more visible and the colours can take on a harsh, grainy nature.

When taking the picture, manual exposure control is a good choice. Simply take a meter reading from a sunny area of the picture and use the same settings for taking the picture of the shadowed area. Alternatively, on a camera with automatic exposure settings use the 'exposure lock' feature (where fitted) by pointing the camera at a sunny area, locking the exposure settings, then pointing the camera at the shadowed area and pressing the shutter release. The downside of using exposure lock is that it is awkward to use with a moving train.

Raw Processing

Having taken the shot in Raw format, it needs to be processed in Raw conversion software. Raw conversion was described in detail in Chapter 5. For the shadowed shot the simplest method is to process the image in the same way as if it was a completely sunny shot and ignore the shadowed areas. Brightness, colour and contrast settings are used so that the sunny areas took good. Some Raw conversion software allows the contrast setting to be decreased. This can be helpful for making the shadows less strong but the potential downside is that other areas of the picture are spoiled due to losing the deep blacks that are essential for pleasing appearance. A slight contrast decrease is recommended as a starting point. If the processed Raw image has to be saved, use TIFF format, not JPEG, to avoid losing quality.

If Raw format was not used when taking the shot, a JPEG format image from the camera will have to be used but will probably give a less realistic final appearance.

Principle

The editing principle involves first selecting the shadowed areas using a selection with a soft edge (known as a feathered edge) so that the changes gradually blend into the surrounding area. Then the selected areas are lightened with a Levels Adjustment Layer. The important point here is that the change to the shadow area involves increasing the contrast as well as making it lighter.

Figure 6.7.1.1.
Lightening the
shadowed side of the
locomotive.

Figure 6.7.1.2.
Softening other
shadowed areas near
the side of the
locomotive.

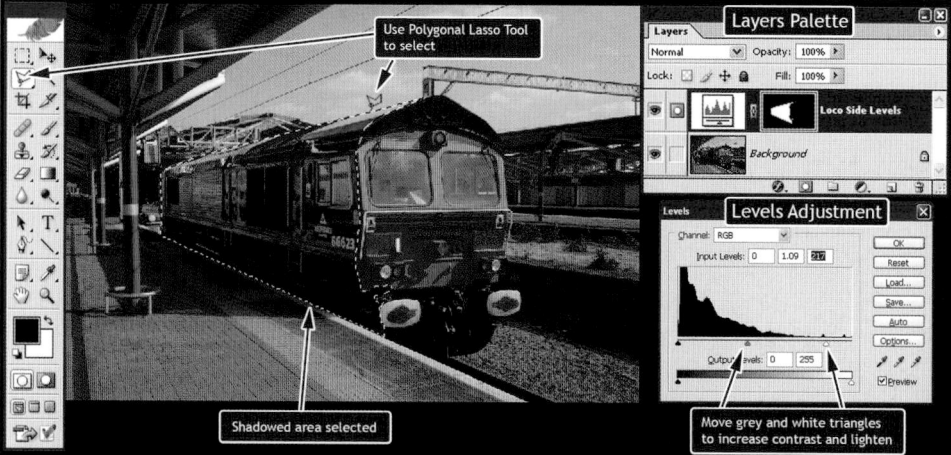

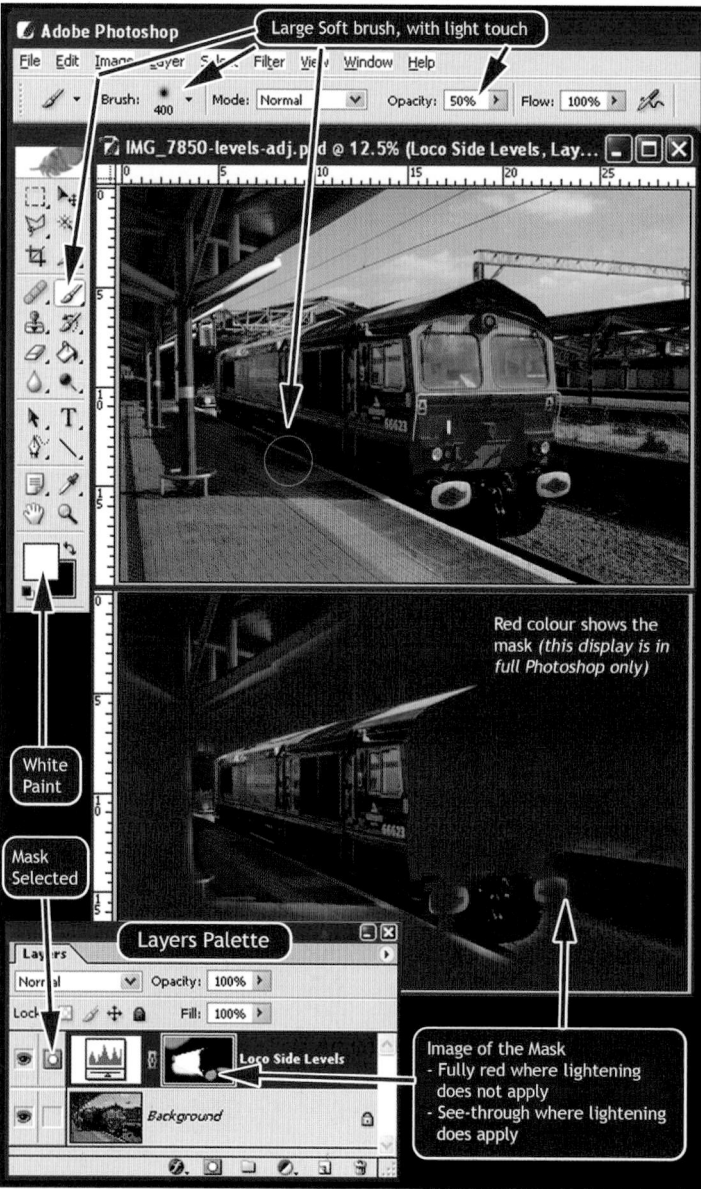

Lightening on its own would look unrealistic to the eye.

If the shadow was mild initially the end result may be close to a normal sunny picture. Deeper shadows in pictures will have their strength reduced so that they are less intrusive visually.

Mild Shadow

In Figure 6.7.1.1 the end of the locomotive is in sun while the side is in shadow. Although the strength of the shadow is fairly mild, detail is not as good as it should be, especially in the buffer beam area. The detail can be made more visible by slight lightening.

The image is read into Photoshop and the shadowed area is selected using a selection with a feathered edge – typically a small feather of three pixels is about right. The Polygonal Lasso Tool works well. Zoom in so that the area is fairly large on the screen. Then select the desired area, working around the area, creating the selection point by point. To add a point to 'fix' the selection, click the left mouse key. To get rid of the most recently added point press the [Delete] key. To complete the selection, double click the mouse button or press the [Enter] key.

With the selection created, the brightness is changed using a Levels Adjustment Layer, which is created using the 'Layer → New Adjustment Layer...' menu option. A graph-like display appears with three tiny triangles underneath. First, the white triangle on the right side is moved inwards to increase the contrast until it looks okay to the eye. If the

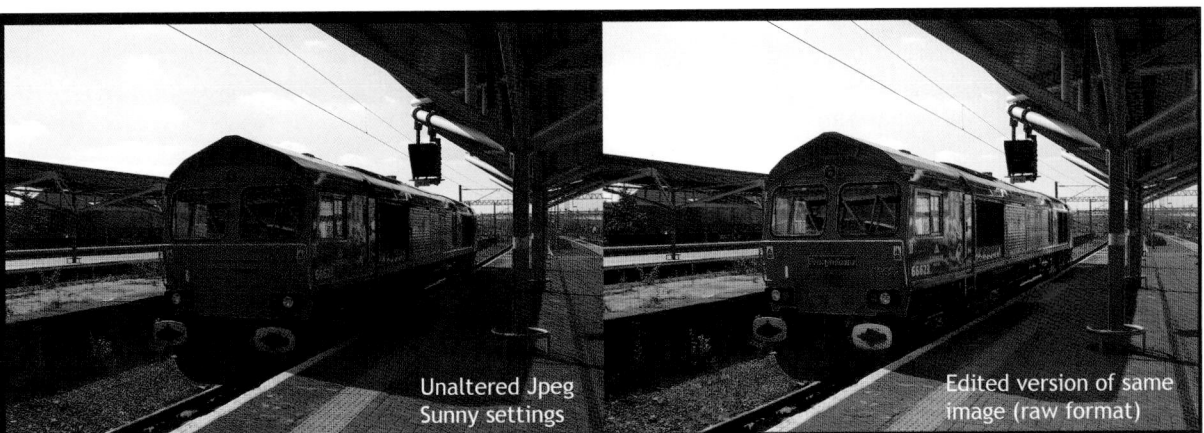

Unaltered Jpeg
Sunny settings

Edited version of same
image (raw format)

result is too contrasty, the triangle should be moved back to the right. Next, move the middle triangle left or right to adjust the overall brightness. When the result looks realistic, press the 'OK' button to create the Adjustment Layer.

To lighten other areas slightly, draw on the mask using the Brush Tool with a low opacity value and white paint as shown in Figure 6.7.1.2. This applies the Levels adjustment to areas outside the original selection. The mask must first be selected by clicking on the mask in the Layers Palette and the indicator will show a small white circle in a grey square. Deleting the mask by using the Brush Tool with white paint is functionally the same as using the Eraser Tool (with black paint). For Photoshop Elements users the Brush Tool has more settings and is more flexible than the Eraser Tool.

Lastly, other adjustments are made as desired. On this picture the yellow front of the locomotive was darkened slightly by applying a Levels Adjustment. (This was done by selecting just the front and moving the middle triangle on the Adjustment screen to darken

the area). The result is saved in Photoshop's own .PSD format so that it is possible to return to the image in future to make more changes. The editing process is completed by flattening to remove the layers, cropping, resizing, sharpening, and finally saving in the desired output format such as JPEG for a web site or TIFF for printing.

Deep Shadow

In Figure 6.7.1.3 the locomotive end is in light shadow while the side is in deep shadow. The simple option is to treat both shadows in the same way by lightening them both with the same adjustment. The approach delivering the best quality result but requiring more work is to treat them separately because the strength of shadow on the side is different to that on the end. When treating them separately, the end is given the same adjustment as in the previous example. Be sure that where the side joins the end there is no overlap in adjustments or areas that have been missed. 'Before' and 'After' pictures are shown. If there is, the mask will have to be adjusted. The details of the edits have not been shown but in general the

Figure 6.7.1.3.
Comparing original and edited pictures where both the side and end are in shadow.

Figure 6.7.1.4.
Comparing original and edited pictures where just the side is in shadow.

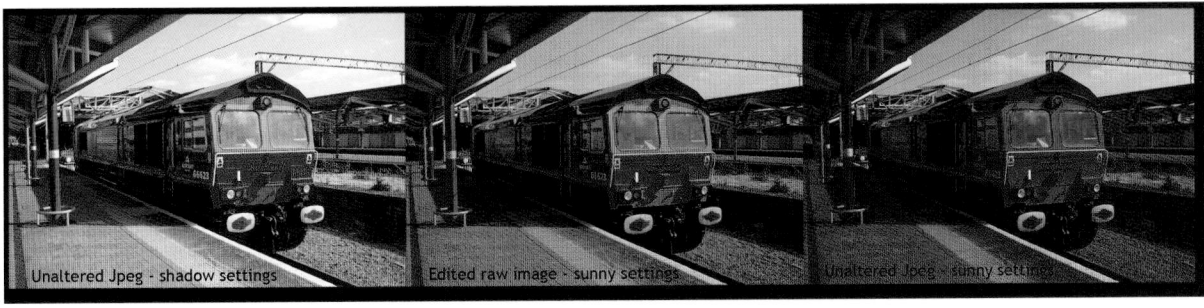

Unaltered Jpeg - shadow settings

Edited raw image - sunny settings

Unaltered Jpeg - sunny settings

editing principles are the same as for the previous picture.

Comparison

Figure 6.7.1.4 compares three images showing an unaltered JPEG image taken with 'shadow settings', an unaltered JPEG image taken with 'sunny settings' and a Raw image taken with 'sunny settings' that was processed using the techniques described here. The processed image is a good compromise featuring the best parts of the other two images. It is worth noting that the JPEG image has a strongly blue coloured sky. This is typical JPEG processing where the camera has boosted the colour to a point where it is probably unrealistic. Raw format allows the photographer to choose the colours they want – natural appearance was chosen here.

Summary

When photographs need to be taken on the shadow side of the train, extra work has to be done to make the result attractive. With light shadows 'sunny' camera settings can be used and the shadow areas lightened on the computer to give a reasonable result. With deep shadows the technique delivers results that are not as good and more complex techniques have to be used to get the best result.

OPTION 2 –REPLACING THE SKY

If a picture has a white sky but a blue one is wanted the sky needs to be replaced. An example picture with a white sky is shown in Figure 6.7.2.1. For the best result the new sky should have the same 'character' as the rest of the picture, which means that the time of day and time of year should be comparable between the two pictures. Also important is that the angle between the camera and the sun is similar in the two pictures. A simple practice is to take the picture of the sky on the same occasion as the main picture. When taking the picture of the sky, aim the camera carefully to avoid unwanted objects in the sky, particularly poles, wires and trees. Although these can be removed using cloning or patching techniques, it's better to avoid them in the first place. Unfortunately a picture of the sky is likely to show up any dust spots on the camera's sensor. These need to be removed using the techniques described in Chapter 3. To avoid any 'burn out' in the new sky different camera settings should be used compared with those chosen when photographing a normal scene because the sky is always much brighter than the ground. Good practice is to take the picture and then check the histogram on the back of the camera. The edge of the histogram plot, particularly the right side, should be well away from the right edge as shown in the accompanying example. Figure 6.7.2.2 shows two skies that could be used for replacing a blank sky on another picture. Although at first sight both look suitable, the one on the left is too bright – note how the plot in the histogram crosses the right edge. The plot in

Figure 6.7.2.1.
The same Rugby example, shown before and after replacing a sky which is too light.

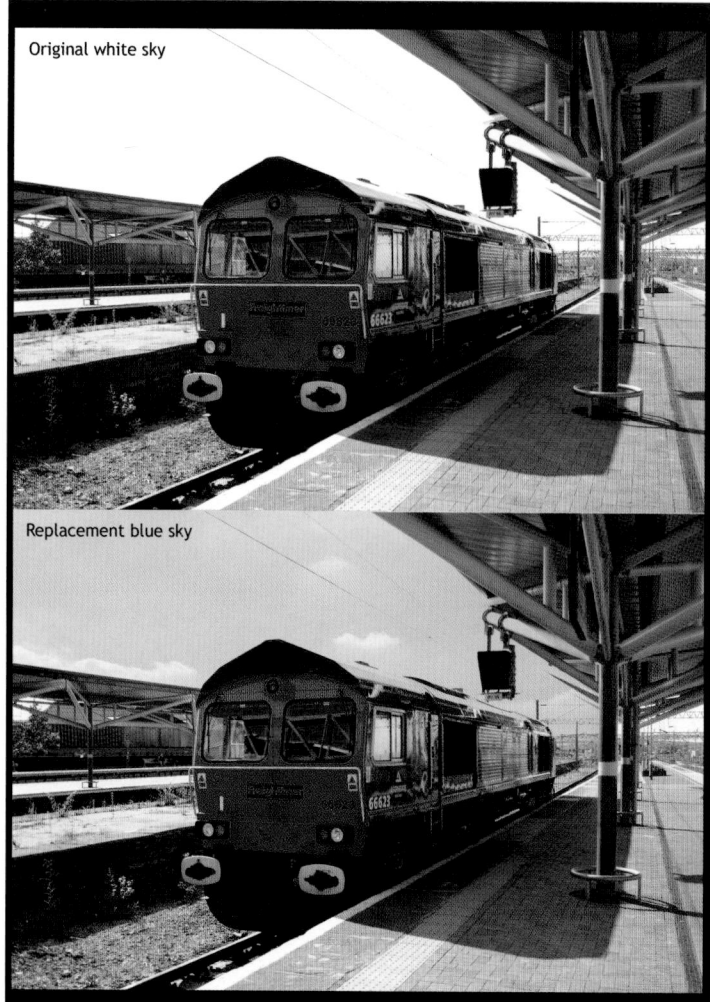

Original white sky

Replacement blue sky

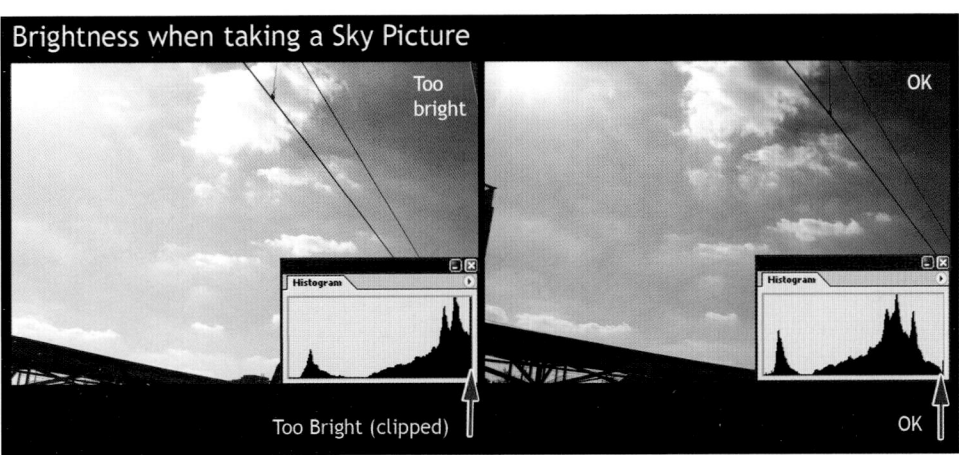

Figure 6.7.2.2.
Taking a photograph of
the sky to replace a sky
which is too light.

the histogram for the sky on the right is much better as it crosses the base and although the top left is a little too bright and there are some wires, the rest of the sky is acceptable.

Principles

The principles used for replacing the sky using full Photoshop or Photoshop Elements are as follows. First find a picture with a sky that is suitable for the original picture. Combine the two pictures by putting them in different Photoshop layers in the same image so that they can be manipulated separately. The new sky is then moved and, if necessary, stretched to cover the old sky. Unwanted parts of the new sky are deleted. A layer-related feature of Photoshop is used so that the new sky replaces the old one but leaves other areas untouched. Some tidying up may be needed around the join between new and old sky. Then the new picture can be saved and further improvements made in the usual way. Sky replacement is now described in more detail.

Preparation

If Raw format has been used when taking the pictures, the Raw images should be processed and opened in Photoshop. A recommended optional first step is to create some 'elbow room' around the main picture by increasing the Canvas Size as shown in Figure 6.7.2.3. The extra material can be cropped off later.

Next the sky picture is combined with the original picture by reading it into its own layer. There are several ways to do this. The quick

way is by 'dragging': place the pointer over the sky layer in the Layers Palette, press and hold the left mouse button, then drag the pointer to any point in the main picture and release the mouse button.

Another way is by using copy and paste. Go to the sky picture and select all of it by using the 'Select → All' menu option or pressing the [Ctrl] and [A] keys together. Copy the sky by using the 'Edit → Copy' menu option or pressing the [Ctrl] and [C] keys together. Then go to the main picture and paste the sky using the 'Edit → Paste' menu option or pressing the [Ctrl] and [V] keys together. The sky will be copied into its own layer.

Positioning

The replacement sky image needs to be positioned so that it completely covers the old sky. This is shown in Figure 6.7.2.4. Often the new sky is too narrow and a simple way to deal with this is to stretch it using the Free Transform Tool. Select the

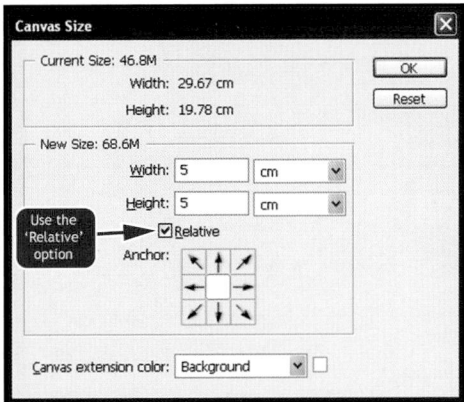

Figure 6.7.2.3.
Making the picture
bigger to allow space
for adding the new sky.

sky layer in the Layers Palette by clicking on it, then choose the 'Edit → Free Transform...' menu option (the menu for this option may vary with different versions of Photoshop). A box will appear surrounding the sky and by clicking on a box at the edge and dragging it, the sky can be stretched. By clicking in the middle of the box the sky can be moved or alternatively it can be moved a tiny amount at a time by pressing one of the arrow keys. The replacement sky will probably cover up other parts of the picture and it is worth deleting some of the overlap to avoid problems later. To see what is underneath, decrease the opacity setting in the Layers Palette to a value such as 50%. When using full Photoshop, use of a mask is recommended for deleting the unwanted parts of the sky so that it can be 'undeleted' later if necessary.

Layer Feature

At this point the new sky will overlap the old one. What is wanted in the final result is for the new sky to replace the old one but not to cover up any of the rest of the picture. How can this be done easily? A feature of Photoshop layers is used, known as the Blending Mode. The setting of the Blending Mode decides how a particular layer interacts with the layer beneath it. Normally a particular layer simply covers up the layer below it and the Blending Mode is 'Normal'. The Blending Mode 'Darken' setting works by comparing the brightness of each pixel in the upper layer with that of the layer below it. Where the upper pixel is darker, it is used in the result, otherwise the lower pixel is used. The sky to be replaced is white and is very bright, whereas the replacement sky in the layer above has more colour in it and is darker. The use of 'Darken' makes the new sky take the place of the white sky but leaves everywhere else as it is – providing that other parts of the picture are not so light that the sky replaces them. This is exactly what is wanted. If the sky does replace a lighter area and this is unwanted, the sky is deleted from that area in the Sky Layer.

Wires and Trees

The method just described works very well but there can sometimes be a problem with wires and trees in the sky. The edge of wires and trees can be lighter than might be expected, and 'Darken' causes the sky to replace them. This can cause wires to disappear or the leaves of trees to look strange. Figure 6.7.2.5 shows how the overhead wires behind the Class 66 have partly disappeared. The simplest way of dealing with this is to decrease the opacity setting of the new sky layer so that the dark areas of the wires underneath show through from the old sky. Change these settings on the Layers Palette as shown in the example. This change also has the side effect of making the colour of the new sky less intense and more realistic. The example compares a sky with the standard 100% opacity (so it completely covers the layer below it) with a setting of 40% opacity. The overhead wires and masts show through in the 40% and look reasonably realistic. To make wires and trees more visible there are more complex techniques that can be used. One of these is to use a Curves Adjustment Layer to darken

Figure 6.7.2.4.
How to position the new sky in the right place.

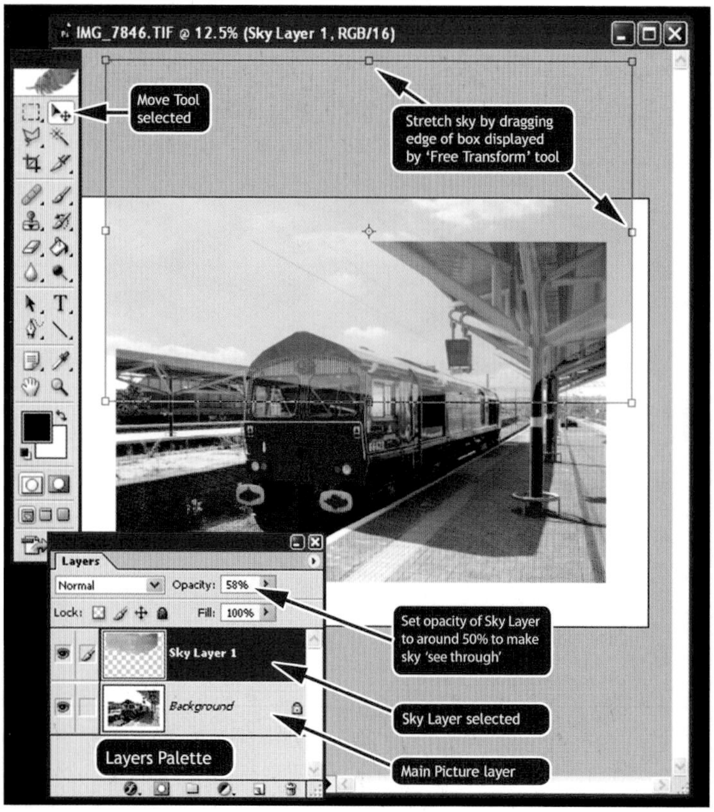

just the wires or leaves while leaving other areas untouched, a technique which is not described here.

Bright Areas

A possible side-effect is that other bright areas might acquire sky colour and look slightly strange. In this example the high parts of the Class 66 roof had reflections and were so bright that the sky colour was darker and has replaced them. These areas could be returned to a more appropriate colour using the patching technique described earlier in this Chapter for dealing with Burnout.

Summary

A white sky in a photo can be replaced fairly easily. The new sky is stretched and trimmed to fit the space, then the layer settings in Photoshop are changed so that the new sky covers up the old one with no overlap or gaps while ensuring that wires and similar objects look right. This method works quite well and is quick and simple. Where there are wires and trees the results are good but sometimes may not give a totally convincing result without further work.

OPTION 4 – HDR

Background

Any camera, whether digital or film-based, can only capture a particular range of brightness values in a single picture. This range is determined by the characteristics of the sensor or film. Another way of describing this is that a single picture can only capture a certain amount of contrast. If an object in a picture is brighter, for example a lamp or a bright sky, the object will appear white and lack any detail. If the object is darker, for example a shadowed area around a locomotive underframe, the object will turn black and lack detail. A view of the 'shadow side' of a train on a sunny day is an example where the range of contrast is too high to be recorded in a single picture. Another example is taking a picture inside a building on a sunny day where the view contains a window. It's not possible to take a single picture and get a result where both the room and window look

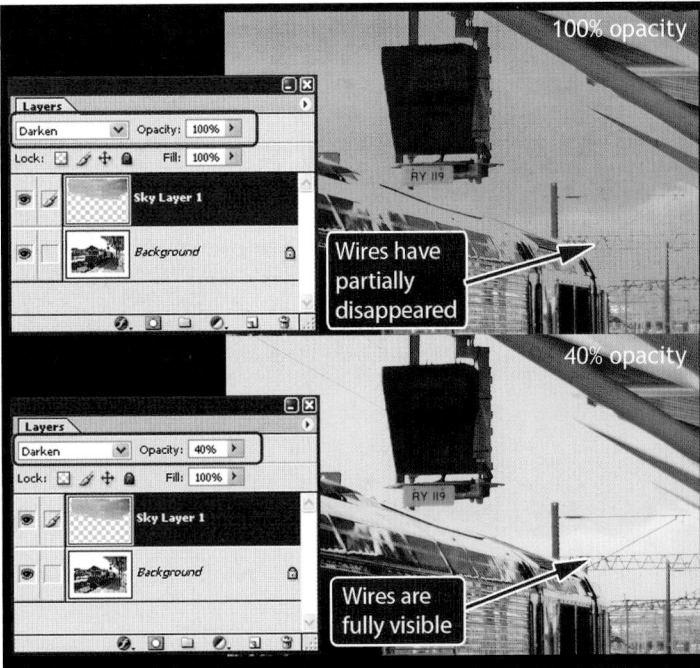

realistic. If the camera is set to get good detail in the room, the window will be too bright, whereas if set so that the view out of the window looks good the room will be too dark and lack detail. The ideal result would combine the best parts from several pictures. With computer-based processing it is possible to combine separate images in this way and a new branch of photography has grown up called High Dynamic Range imaging, usually abbreviated to HDR.

HDR

HDR involves taking a series of pictures of a particular scene using different camera settings. Special software is used later to combine these pictures into a single HDR image. An HDR image cannot be viewed on a screen or printed because the range of brightness involved is too great. It needs to be processed using a process called Tone Mapping to create an image that can be displayed or printed.

Recent versions of full Photoshop – CS2 and CS3 – have an HDR capability included but this does not work as well as dedicated HDR software, the best known being a product called Photomatix.

When taking a photo of the shadow side of the train the camera is facing, broadly

Figure 6.7.2.5.
How to deal with wires in the sky that partially disappeared when the new sky was added.

speaking, towards the sun. This means that the sky is very bright and the amount of contrast is high. A single image cannot capture both the dark shadow areas of the train and the bright sky. By taking several pictures with different camera settings and combining them using HDR software a more pleasing result can be achieved.

Movement

Because HDR involves a series of pictures of the same subject, it is not feasible to capture moving subjects because different pictures in the sequence will have the same objects in slightly different places, leading to a 'ghosting' effect. HDR can work well for pictures of static subjects such as a locomotive in a depot. The individual pictures need to be taken carefully to ensure the camera is not moved. For many railway locations, especially on a busy station, it's not practical to use a tripod and handholding a camera is usual practice. The author has found that with hand holding there will be a small amount of camera movement between shots, no matter how carefully the photographer tries to hold the camera still. HDR software usually has an optional feature to align the images before processing them but it can't work miracles and there may still

be a small amount of movement visible. Use of a sturdy tripod produces better results. Although there may be camera movement between shots when using a tripod, the amount of movement will usually be small and the pictures can be accurately aligned to eliminate ghosting. Aligning the images manually before opening them in the HDR software usually gives better results than the automatic alignment feature. Misaligned pictures typically look fine on a web image or small print but will show slight fuzziness when viewing as an A4-size print.

Exposure

When taking pictures to use in HDR photography the normal practice is to take a sequence of three or five pictures at different exposure settings. What exposure settings should be used? Each picture in the sequence should have the same spacing such as, for example, one stop different to the previous picture. The term 'stop' is explained in a separate panel.

For typical railway pictures the author recommends a sequence of three pictures either one stop or 1½ stops apart. One image will be slightly dark, one will have mid-range settings and look a good average to the eye while one will be slightly too light.

Figure 6.7.3.1.
Comparing the different images as taken with the result generated using HDR software.

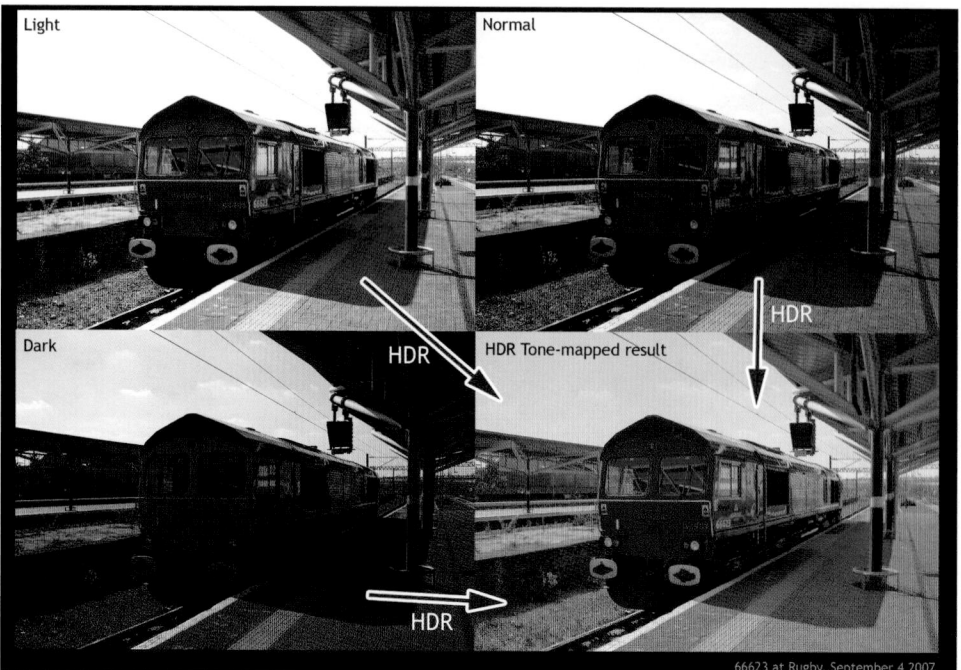

In this example a spacing of one stop was used. Experimenting with a different spacing is recommended, such as two stops apart, to see which gives the best result. In a scene with very high contrast a sequence of five pictures may be worth trying but the author has found a three-picture sequence to be sufficient. Exposure on a digital camera is set using three different controls: sensor sensitivity (ISO), shutter speed and aperture. The ISO should be kept to a low value (eg up to 200 ISO) to minimise noise because this interferes with the HDR process. Although the ISO could be changed between pictures in a sequence the author prefers to leave it fixed because the controls for making the changes are so fiddly that unwanted camera movement is inevitable. Best results are obtained by leaving the aperture fixed and varying only the shutter speed because this gives the same depth of field in all the shots. The use of manual exposure settings is recommended to ensure that the right settings are used. The alternative is to use automatic exposure and vary the 'exposure compensation' setting between, for example, -1, 0 and +1, but this may not deliver an accurate result if the automatic control suddenly changes a setting unexpectedly.

The pictures can be taken in any sequence. When the results are assembled the middle one should have settings that are a compromise between the dark and light. In a series of three the first picture will have areas that are too light while the dark areas of the picture have good detail. The last picture in the series will have areas that are too dark while the light areas have good detail.

Example
Figure 6.7.3.1 shows views of No 66623 at Rugby that are similar to those used in previous examples. Three pictures were taken handheld from the same viewpoint with a Canon EOS 20D camera and 18-55mm standard lens using manual exposure and Raw format. A sequence of three shots was taken one stop apart at 200 ISO with the same shutter speed and varying only the lens aperture. The following settings were used:

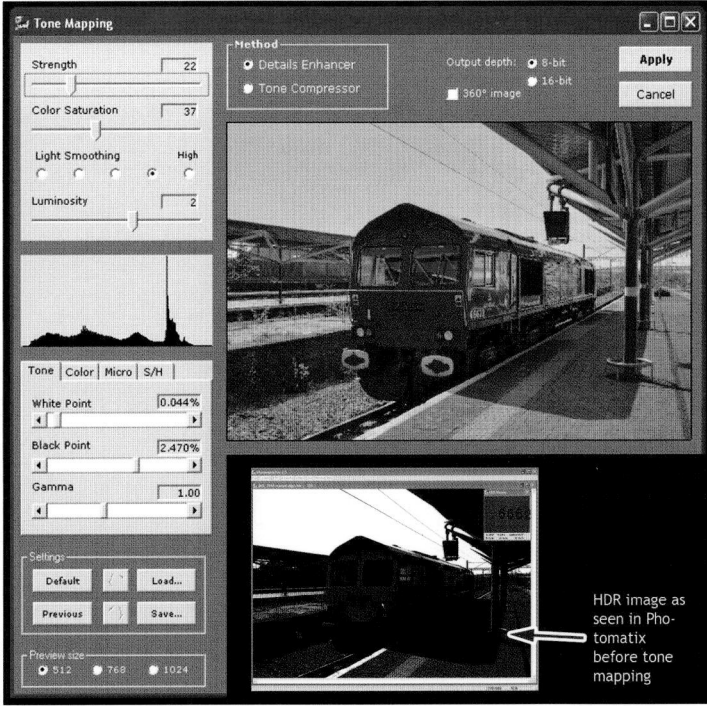

1/500 f4-5.6, 1/500 f5.6-8, 1/500 f8-11. Each was processed in Raw conversion software using 'as taken' settings without any adjustments to create TIFF format images.

Manual Alignment
The converted Raw images were aligned manually in Photoshop using the 'Free transform' menu option to rotate and move the images. Explaining this in more detail, each image was opened in Photoshop, then combined into the same image using copy and paste so that each Raw conversion was in its own layer. One layer was chosen as the master and then the other two layers were aligned to the master layer, one at a time, using the 'Free transform' menu option. By moving the image slightly with the arrow keys and rotating as necessary, a reasonable alignment was achieved, although not perfect. The combined image was then cropped so that each layer had exactly the same borders. Each layer was then saved to a separate TIFF format file using copy and paste.

HDR Creation
The three TIFF images were then opened in Photomatix software and an HDR image

Figure 6.7.3.2.
The tonemapping process inside Photomatix HDR software.

HDR image as seen in Photomatix before tone mapping

Exposure settings for HDR

Shutter speeds on a camera typically have the option of fixed manual settings such as 1sec, 1/2, 1/4, 1/8, 1/15, 1/30, 1/60, 1/125, 1/250, 1/500, 1/1000. This is the time in seconds that the shutter of the camera opens so that light can pass through the lens to the imaging sensor. The spacing between these settings is known as a stop, which is short for 'f stop'. Some cameras have intermediate shutter speeds at intervals of half or third of a stop.

The lens aperture will normally have fixed settings such as f2.8, f4, f5.6, f8, f11 and f16. The spacing between these is also known as a stop, or f stop. There are usually intermediate settings at intervals of half or third of a stop. For example between f2.8 and f4 the half stop value is f3.5.

When taking a sequence of pictures for HDR photography, each picture in the sequence should have the same spacing from its neighbour, such as one stop apart. The exposure in a sequence can be varied by fixing the aperture and varying the shutter speed, fixing the shutter speed and changing the aperture, or changing both. The following are all valid settings for sequences of three pictures:

A 1/500sec f4-5.6, 1/500sec f5.6-8, 1/500sec f8-11 (1 stop apart)

B 1/250sec f5.6, 1/500sec f5.6, 1/1000sec f5.6 (1 stop apart)

C 1/250sec f5.6, 1/500sec f5.6-8, 1/1000sec f8 (1½ stops apart)

For those making large prints it is best to leave the aperture fixed so that the amount of the picture in focus stays constant and only the shutter speed is changed.

generated without choosing the 'automatic alignment' option. Lastly a viewable image was created using tone mapping. There are many settings to adjust during the tone mapping process and it can be fiddly trying to get the best result. Photomatix is available for download from the Internet and has a 'free trial' mode where the tone mapping can be run but creates an image containing 'watermarks'. After purchasing a license code an image without the watermarks can be created.

Figure 6.7.3.2 shows the Photomatix screen for the tonemapping process and how the tone mapped image looks before adjusting any of the controls. Note how the

HDR process has combined the best parts of the individual component images. There is good detail in both the sky and the shadowed side of the locomotive. The downside is that some viewers feel that images created using the HDR process look unnatural. Some images created by HDR software benefit from further work such as increasing the contrast and lightening or darkening using a Levels Adjustment. Figure 6.7.3.1 compares the three component images with the result generated by HDR software.

Summary

HDR is one of a number of different options for capturing a scene with a high level of contrast, such as when shooting the shadow side of the train on a sunny day, but it is only applicable to static subjects. Special HDR software is needed to process the images. Some viewers believe that the HDR process creates a result which combines the best parts of the input images while others consider the result to look unnatural. Photographers should try the technique and make up their own mind.

● SUBMITTING PHOTOGRAPHS FOR PUBLICATION

The widespread take-up of digital photography has led to more photographers submitting their photographs for publication. Digital technology allows a copy of an image to be made almost instantly and sent across the Internet in seconds. No longer are there delays while film is processed and prints are made. Concern at potentially losing an irreplaceable colour slide in the post can now be completely forgotten.

What's the best way of submitting photographs? Of course different publications and different editors will have slightly their own preferences but a few points can be generalised.

Less is more. Don't submit a huge batch of pictures. Send your best efforts, pictures of unusual workings or specific trains/

locomotives depending on what the editor has asked for.

If you're sending pictures that haven't been specifically requested some editors prefer to receive a small selection of low resolution pictures from which they will select the ones they want and then ask for high resolution pictures to be sent.

Low resolution pictures are prepared as simple web images as described in Chapter 4 with size no more than 1024 pixels wide, JPEG format and containing a sRGB colour profile. They are then attached to an email containing the captions and a brief covering note including the photographer's contact details.

Sending Options

Publication quality photographs take up several Megabytes of space each and are uncomfortably large for sending more than a couple at a time by email. There are three suitable methods for sending the publication-quality images:

1 Attachments in an email
2 CD or DVD sent by post
3 Web space and links

Looking at these three options in more detail:

1 Email is suitable for a small number of images that are needed in a hurry and in these circumstances JPEG format is essential for reducing the file size. Resizing down to perhaps 10in wide with a resolution of 300 ppi (pixels per inch) may be beneficial with a 12 MP or higher camera because otherwise the file size will be too big to send by email. Many Internet Service Providers impose limits on the size of emails and 10 Mbytes is a typical limit. This is even more restrictive than it may appear at first because the size of an image is increased by ~25% when it is attached to an email (technically this is due to the encoding process). In practice this means that two 4 Mbyte images will fill an email when there is a 10 MByte limit.

2 A CD or DVD offers a huge amount of storage space but with the risk of potential delays, damage or loss in the post. The space allows the use of TIFF file format which provides better quality than JPEG.

3 A less common option which is useful for working around limits on the size of emails is to use web space and links. Many broadband and dialup Internet packages include web space which is intended for storing a personal web site but it can also be used for transferring images. A certain level of familiarity with web site building is useful here. The images are uploaded into the web space in the same way as you might upload a web site. Then a link to the images is sent in an email to the editor which also contains a covering note and the captions. By clicking on the link the editor can download the images when he or she wishes. JPEG or TIFF format image can be used in theory but for size reasons JPEG is the only feasible option in practice.

Publication Image Options

This section describes options and settings for images being prepared for publication.

JPEG or TIFF format?

JPEG provides sufficient quality for pictures up to A5 size. For A4 and larger compressed TIFF is recommended for better quality as it doesn't involve throwing away any detail. Whether the quality difference can be seen in magazines with a fairly coarse dot pattern and regular quality paper is a point for discussion. For books where an image will be enlarged to A4 size or even a double-spread A3 format and printed on good quality paper, TIFF is almost essential. Compressed TIFF images are much larger than JPEG format so CD or DVD submission is necessary for TIFF.

Publishers insist on a resolution of 300 ppi, whereas low resolution preview images sent by email are typically resized to about

1000 pixels wide and a resolution of 72 ppi. Any 16-bit images should always be converted to 8-bit.

Images should always contain an embedded colour profile otherwise the colour reproduction will suffer by losing saturation. The industry doesn't have any common guidelines here. The author's practice is to use sRGB colour profile with JPEGs and AdobeRGB with TIFFs on the basis that for small images where JPEG format is appropriate the limited colour range of sRGB will not be noticeable. For images that may be reproduced larger it's important to have a wide range of colour which is more accurate so AdobeRGB is used.

Avoid making large colour corrections to your pictures as the need to make such corrections is often a sign that your equipment is not set up properly. Calibrate your monitor as described in Chapter 1 and then you can make small colour corrections with confidence.

The publishing world tends to use Macintosh computers whereas PCs are more widely used among home users and this has led to problems when transferring images between the different types of computer. Some editors insist that TIFF format images have no compression so that any compatibility problems can be avoided. Because uncompressed TIFF images are very large, CD or DVD has to be used for submitting the images.

Sharpening was described in Chapter 5 as a two- or three-stage process. The first stage of sharpening is applied when the image is created, either in the camera as a JPEG format image or when converting a Raw format image on a computer. Any specific problems with sharpness should be corrected but otherwise no further sharpening should be applied. This is because the amount of final sharpening needed depends on several factors – the size of the image on the page, the amount of resizing from the submitted version and the printing process. The production team will apply the necessary amount of final sharpening. Applying too many sharpening stages will affect the appearance of the image.

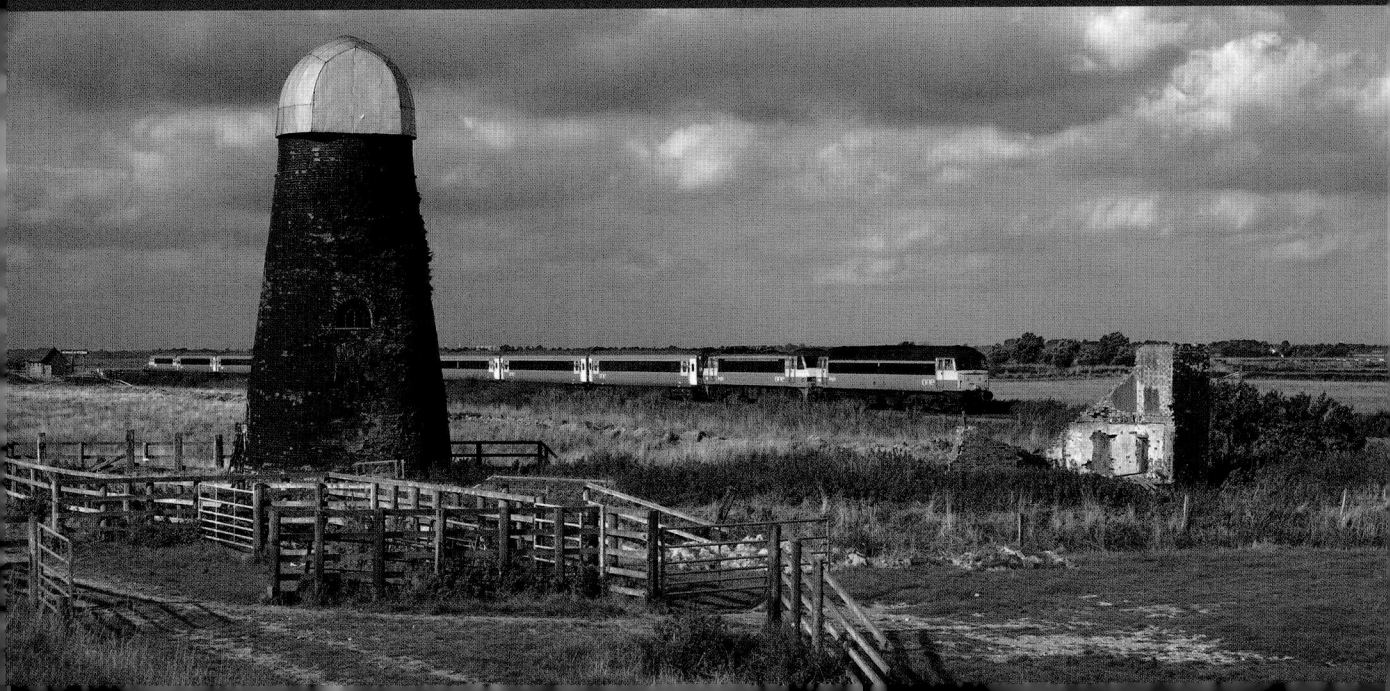

CHAPTER 7
CASE
STUDIES

● RAW CONVERSION AND BRIGHT OBJECTS

Most pictures benefit from a contrast increase, even those taken on a sunny day. Care needs to be taken when the contrast is increased in a picture containing bright objects because unless preventative measures are taken they can turn white and lose detail – also known as highlight clipping or 'burnout'. Many railway scenes contain bright objects and consequently 'burnout' is a very common fault which can often be seen when browsing photos on the Internet and in magazines.

Figure 7.1.1 shows a Chiltern Class 168 unit passing through the station at Denham Golf Club on a bright sunny spring morning. A Canon EOS 20D camera was used with a 35mm lens. The exposure of 1/1500 sec @f4 on 100 ISO with Raw format was chosen to give slight under-exposure to allow for the brightness of the white livery and prevent 'burnout'. Photoshop Elements 5.0 was chosen for the Raw conversion and editing for its excellent handling of clipping. When first loading the image into the Raw converter the Highlight Clipping indicator was switched on using the tick box at the top of the screen and immediately highlight clipping in red could be seen on the unit front, hut on the right and station sign as shown in Figure 7.1.2. To remove the

clipping the Exposure setting was decreased until the red disappeared. This left the image looking slightly dark so the Brightness setting was increased until the image looked pleasing to the eye, being sure to back off the control if any clipping appeared. The Shadows setting was decreased to give a little more detail in the dark areas. Typically nothing else needs changing at this point and the Raw conversion can be run. Any changes to colour saturation are left until later.

The contrast increase was made in Photoshop Elements with a Levels Adjustment Layer in the usual way and the histogram showed that the white triangle on the right side should be moved inwards to increase the contrast. This tends to lighten the image and if the brightness looks wrong the middle triangle can be moved to compensate until the preview looks right to the eye. There was no need to move the black triangle on the left side in this image. Potentially the contrast increase can cause highlight clipping and the best way to show it is by using the clipping display built into the Levels Adjustment. The clipping display is fiddly to use: by putting the mouse pointer on the right triangle and pressing the left mouse button and [Alt] key at the same time, the display appears. This is shown in Figure 7.1.3. Where there is no clipping the screen is black. Any other colour indicates which channel is clipped. White causes greatest concern because it means that all three channels (Red, Green, Blue) are clipped.

Figure 7.1.1.
The effect of highlight clipping on light coloured detail.

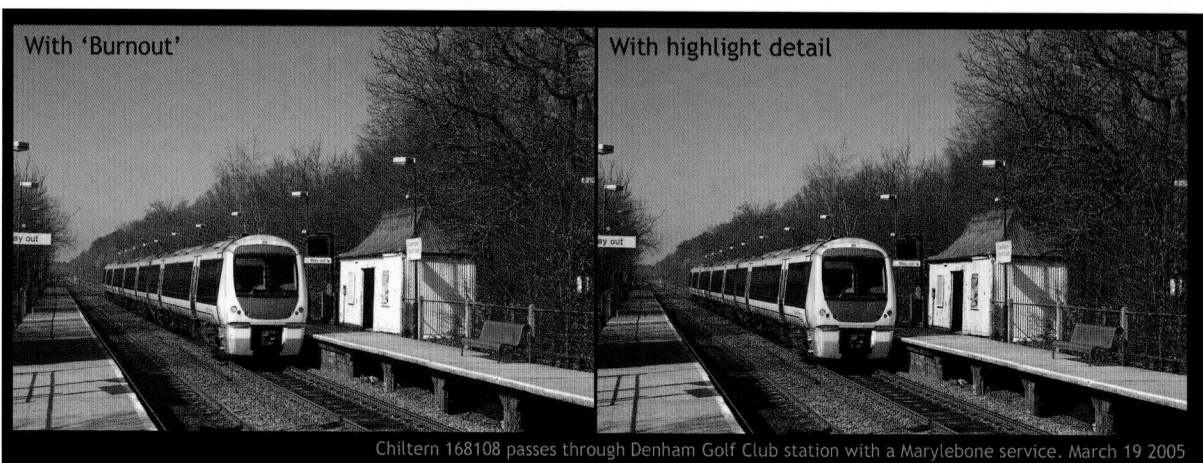

With 'Burnout'   With highlight detail

ay out

Chiltern 168108 passes through Denham Golf Club station with a Marylebone service. March 19 2005

In this image the indicator showed clipping on the side of the unit cab and the front face of the platform hut. This wasn't a surprise as it was easy to see that they were bright. It was a surprise that the red patch on the yellow panel of the unit showed that the red channel was clipped in that area. All the clipping was dealt with by applying black paint to the mask to cancel the adjustment in that spot. Images can clip in the shadows when the black triangle on the left side of the Levels Adjustment Screen is moved, in which case similar masking would be used but was not needed in this image.

There were four clipped areas to be tackled: the hut front, the white parts of the unit front, part of the unit's yellow panel, the station nameboard by the hut. To deal with the hut, the white areas were selected using the Polygonal Lasso Tool with a feather of 2px, then the area inside the selection was filled with black paint using the Paint Bucket tool. The selection was saved using the 'Selection $\rightarrow$ Save Selection...' menu option so that it could be used again later. A similar technique was used on the station nameboard. The white area of the unit cab was selected using the Magnetic Lasso Tool and filled with black paint using a soft brush (0% hardness) and 100% opacity. The mask only needed to go half way along the white panel above the coupler so a soft brush was used to give a smooth transition. At the same time the flat part of the front valence was treated. As soon as the black paint was applied the texture in these areas reappeared. The next area to treat was the red channel clipping in the yellow panel which caused the shade of yellow to look wrong. The whole yellow panel was selected using the Magnetic Lasso Tool. Then a thin layer of black paint was applied to the left side of the yellow panel (as viewed – for the driver it's the right side). By setting the opacity to about 25% and using a soft brush around 200 px diameter a thin layer could be applied in several strokes until the panel looked right to the eye. This was enough to restore a realistic yellow by stopping the clipping while keeping a slight lightening effect. The

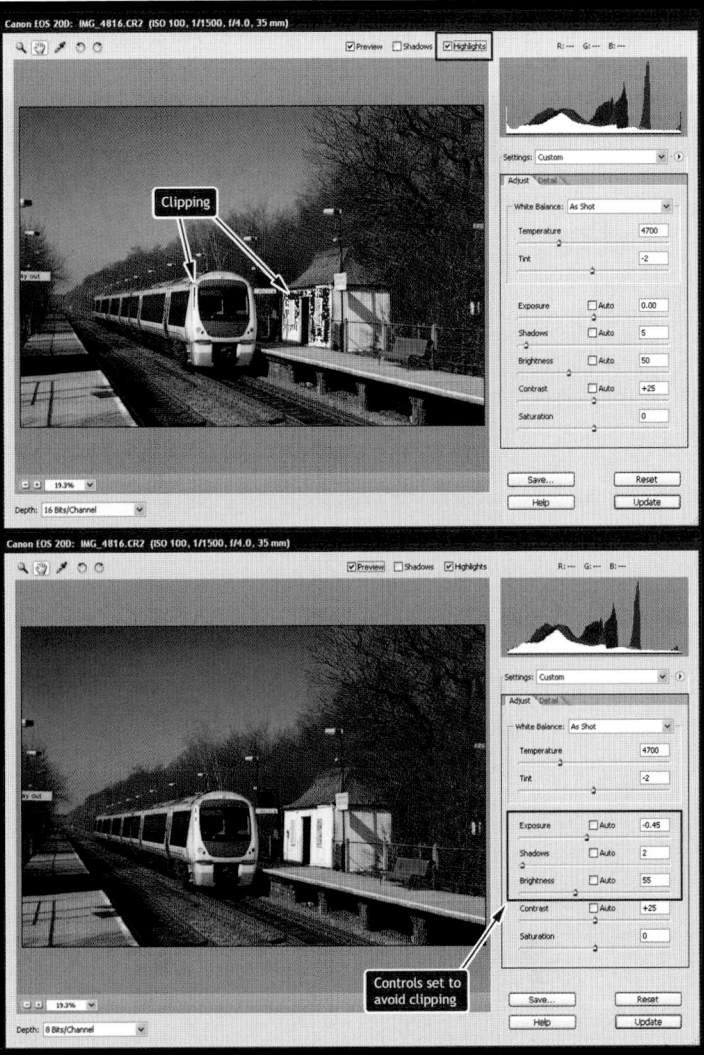

example shows the Levels Adjustment with the masked area in bright red: the thickness of the red covering corresponds to the thickness of the mask so a pale red means a mask with less than 100% opacity.

The final touch is to darken the hut slightly while also increasing the contrast using a Levels Adjustment. This makes the textures stand out more clearly. The selection of the bright areas of the hut that was saved earlier is now loaded using the 'Selection $\rightarrow$ Load Selection...' menu option. A new Levels Adjustment Layer is created and because the selection of the hut is active a mask is created to restrict the adjustment to the selected area. The contrast is increased by moving the left triangle to the right and the hut front is

Figure 7.1.2.
Raw Conversion and avoiding clipping.

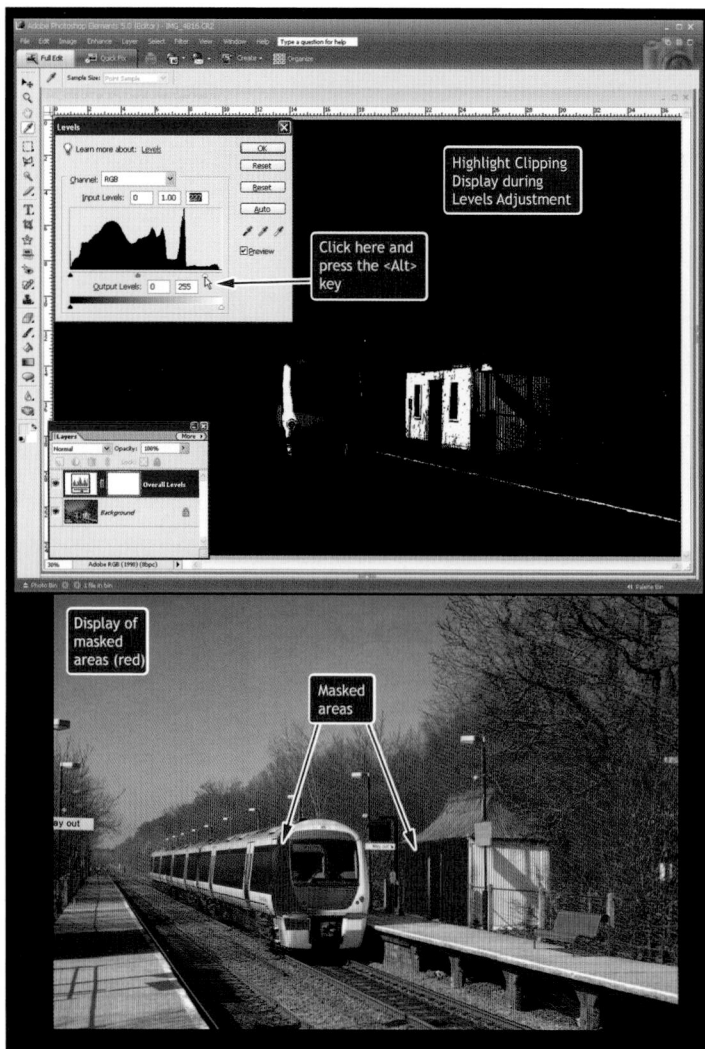

Figure 7.1.3.
How to display highlight clipping during a Levels Adjustment.

Figure 7.1.4.
Darkening the hut.

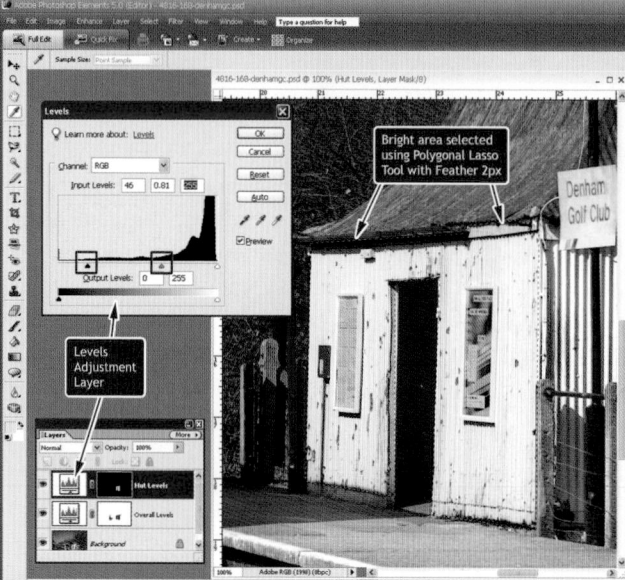

darkened by moving the centre triangle to the right until the image looks good to the eye. This is shown in Figure 7.1.4.

Some observers may say that making these adjustments is being slightly too fussy and there is no need to make any changes to these areas because they are small. The author argues that these bright areas will distract attention from the main subject if left untreated and they only need a fairly small amount of work to look realistic. Viewers can judge for themselves in Figure 7.1.1 which compares two versions of the image. The image on the left has burnt out highlights while the one on the right has all the highlight detail due to masking the bright areas and the slight darkening described. In all other respects both images are the same. This technique – a Levels Adjustment with small areas excluded by masking – is simple and quick and is applicable to many images.

CASE 2

● RAW CONVERSION AND CLIPPING

Shooting in Raw format gives maximum flexibility when processing an image. During the Raw conversion process one of the main intentions is to provide sufficient contrast to give a pleasing appearance while at the same time avoiding clipping. This case study shows two different types of clipping and explains how to avoid them.

Figure 7.2.1 shows a GBRF-liveried Class 73 electro-diesel locomotive on an engineers train on a sunny afternoon with beautiful puffy clouds in the sky. Maintaining the appearance of the clouds during the editing process is essential for creating an attractive result. Because clouds have very bright areas in practice this means avoiding highlight clipping as far as possible, otherwise the clouds will 'burn out' to give

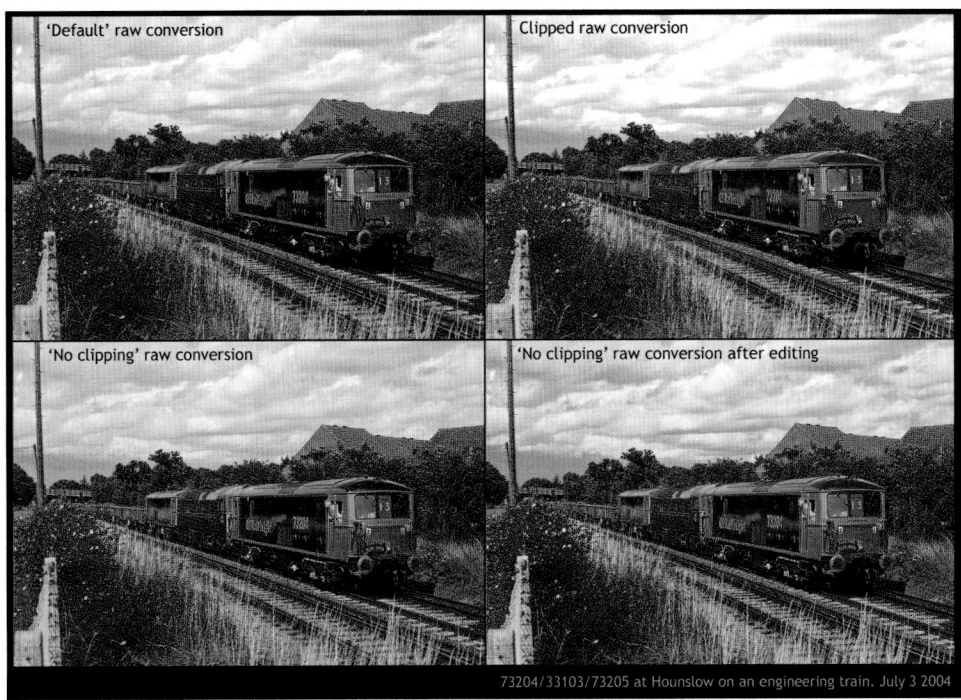

Figure 7.2.1.
Comparing images with different amounts of clipping before and after editing.

unpleasant white patches. The original Raw image was taken using a manual exposure of 1/350sec @f5.6-8 at 100 ISO on a Canon EOS 10D camera with 35mm lens. The time of day was around 1630 so the exposure setting was right for 'full sun' conditions. Editing and Raw conversion were done using Photoshop CS3. The intention was to print the image so normal practice is to use the AdobeRGB colour space and 16-bit editing mode.

When the Raw image is loaded into Photoshop the Camera Raw screen

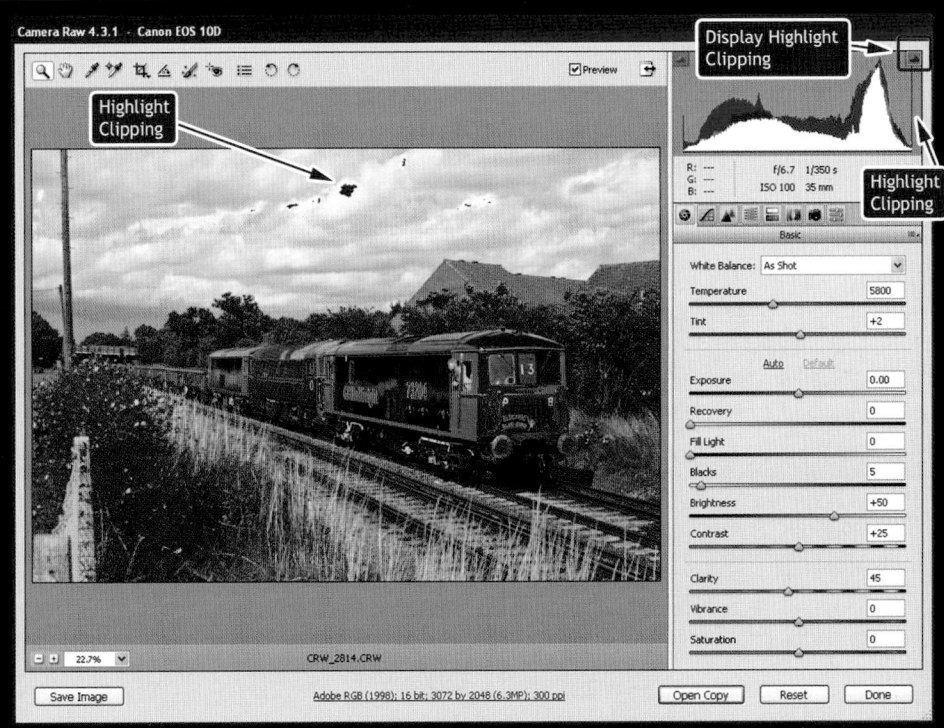

Figure 7.2.2.
Raw conversion and clipping after first opening the image.

Figure 7.2.3.
Raw conversion
settings after
eliminating highlight
clipping.

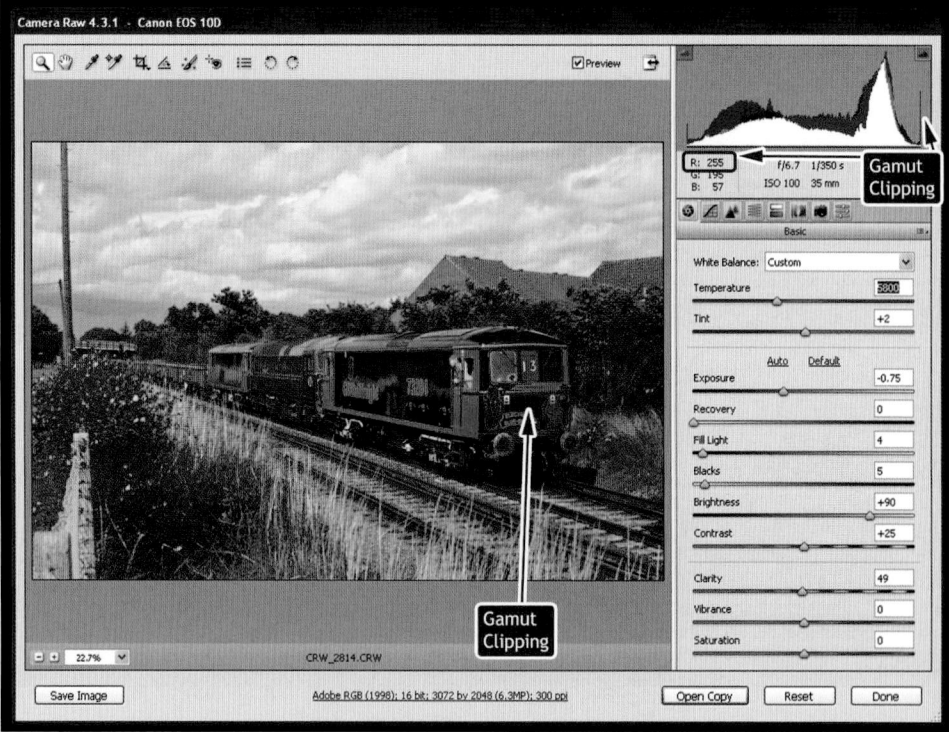

appears with 'default' conversion settings. To display highlight clipping the tiny red arrow beside the histogram is clicked as shown in the example. In Photoshop Elements there is a separate tick box for this. A red blob appears in some of the clouds to show clipping as shown in Figure 7.2.2. There is also a red line at the right side of the histogram showing that there is a lot of clipping in the red channel – more

Figure 7.2.4.
How an image looks if
highlight clipping is
ignored when adjusting
contrast.

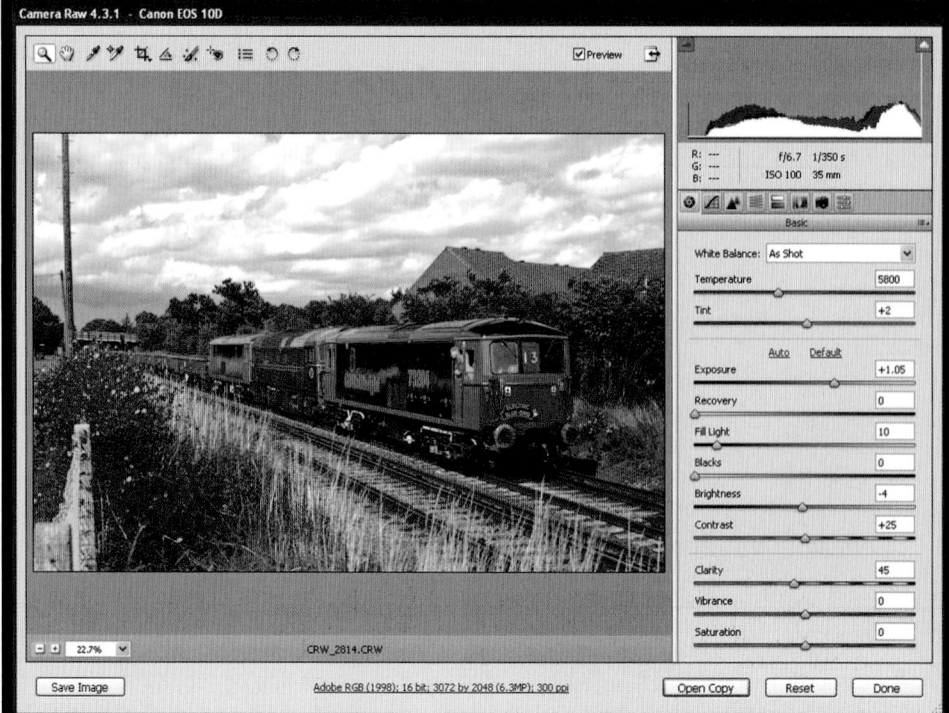

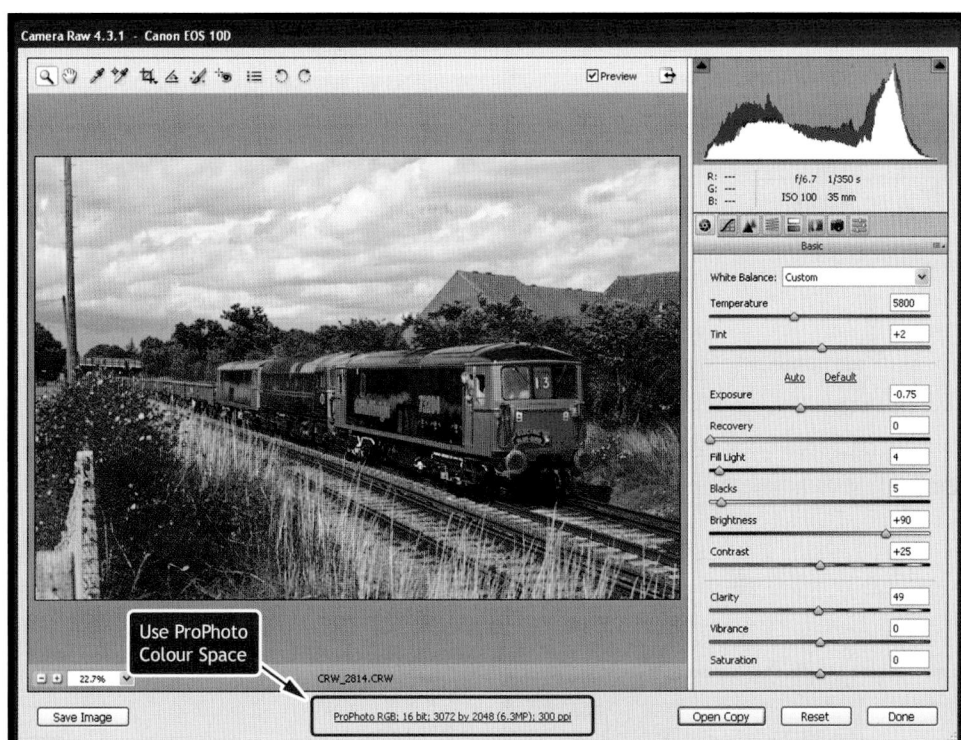

Figure 7.2.5.
Demonstrates how the gamut clipping disappears when the colour space is changed to ProPhotoRGB.

about this later. To get rid of the clipping in the clouds the 'Exposure' setting is reduced. Because this darkens the image the 'Brightness' control is increased until the brightness of the image looks right to the eye. If any clipping re-appears the 'Exposure' setting should be decreased slightly and the 'Brightness' increased again. See Figure 7.2.3 for the Raw conversion settings and the preview image. Some photographers take no notice of highlight clipping and Figure 7.2.4 shows how the image would look if clipping was allowed. Notice the large ugly white patches in the clouds and compare to the surrounding pictures where all the detail in the clouds is shown. Highlight clipping in clouds is a very common sight in Internet photo galleries.

Keen-eyed readers will have noted the red colour of the clipping indicator appearing on the yellow front of the Class 73 in Figure 7.2.3. Decreasing the 'Exposure' setting makes little difference. What is this clipping and why does it happen? Looking at the Raw conversion screen in more detail, there is a red line at the right side of the histogram, which

indicates clipping in the red channel. Just below the histogram are some rows of figures marked R, G and B which indicate the values of the Red, Green and Blue channels at the current mouse pointer position (the locomotive front) when the screenshot was taken.. The R value is 255 which is the maximum possible value and is confirmation that there is clipping in the red channel. Why has this clipping occurred? The answer involves the choice of colour space and understanding the reason requires some general discussion about colour spaces. The AdobeRGB colour space was chosen for editing this image, as usual. Note that any colour space can only display a certain range of colours. The AdobeRGB colour space is fine for general photography but railway subjects include certain colours that it cannot display and the yellow front of the Class 73 is one of these colours. The GBRF livery is more awkward than most because the orange colour around the cab windows also shows clipping in AdobeRGB. The only solution is to use a colour space with a wider range – technically speaking, a colour space with a wider gamut – such as ProPhotoRGB.

Figure 7.2.6.
The Curve used to adjust the sky.

Figure 7.3.1.1.
Compares different JPEG and Raw versions of the whole image with a version merged from two different Raw conversions.

When a colour won't fit into a particular colour space the term is 'gamut clipping'. In this case study, when the colour space was changed to ProPhotoRGB the clipping

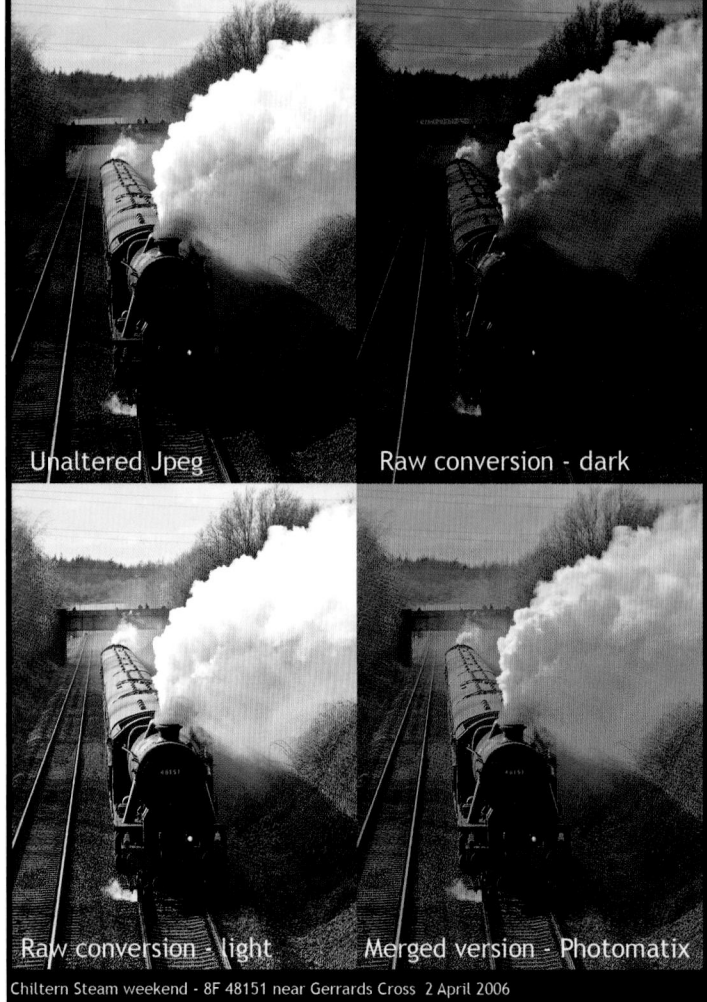

Chiltern Steam weekend - 8F 48151 near Gerrards Cross 2 April 2006

disappeared as shown in Figure 7.2.5. The Raw conversion could then be started.

To complete the edit, the contrast in the sky area was increased by using a Curves Adjustment Layer. By selecting just the sky and a little of the background, the curve slightly lightened the lightest parts of the sky, darkened the darker parts of the sky and left the background unchanged because the curve did not change the darkest areas. This curve is shown in Figure 7.2.6. Lastly, a Levels Adjustment Layer was applied to increase the contrast slightly in the foreground only.

The edited image was then printed. Some of the colours could not be fully reproduced by the printer, which had to select the nearest equivalent. For web display the image would need to be converted to the sRGB colour space which has an even narrower range of colours, meaning that the GBRF livery cannot be displayed accurately on a screen.

For those using Photoshop Elements this image is one where the limitations of Elements make themselves felt. It would be necessary to work throughout in the AdobeRGB colour space and accept the gamut clipping as it is not possible to use a wider colour space. Whether the gamut clipping is noticeable when printing depends on the capability of your printer and how fussy you are. The sky editing would need to use a Levels Adjustment Layer because Elements does not have curves built in. Alternatively additional software is available which provides a very basic Curves Adjustment layer.

CASE 3

● STEAM ENGINES

Although almost 40 years have passed since the demise of regular main line steam workings in Britain, photography of steam engines is still a popular leisure pursuit. What are the important photographic techniques for the steam photographer using a digital camera?

Most of the digital photography techniques applicable to diesel and electric

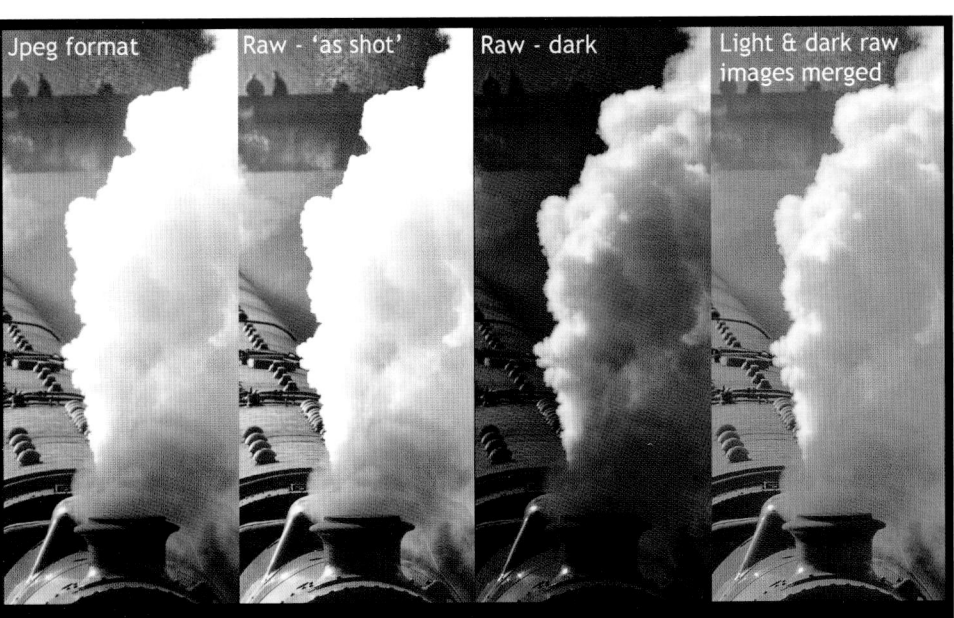

Jpeg format | Raw - 'as shot' | Raw - dark | Light & dark raw images merged

Figure 7.3.1.2.
Section of the locomotive exhaust comparing different JPEG and Raw versions.

traction are relevant to steam engines as well. The unique aspects of a steam engine are its exhaust and escaping steam. Capturing these well is vital to the success of any steam photograph. Also worthy of note is that the majority of steam engines are painted in a dark livery at the front around the smokebox.

Exposure

The biggest drawback with today's digital cameras is their lack of tolerance to over-exposure. This is the technical term describing the situation when too much light reaches the digital sensor or film. As the amount of light reaching the sensor inside a digital camera increases, the image becomes lighter and the brightest areas turn white. The transition to whiteness and the point of losing detail is sudden so it is important to get the camera settings right. In comparison, film, particularly print film, has a more gradual response although detail will still be lost as the amount of over-exposure increases. There can be a large difference between the brightness of the exhaust and the dark smokebox area, especially on bright sunny days, and special attention is necessary to avoid losing detail. The first case study looks at the problems posed by a bright exhaust.

BRIGHT EXHAUST

Figure 7.3.1.1 shows a particularly difficult situation for choosing the exposure. A black steam engine with the sun behind it approaches the photographer. The smokebox area is in shadow and very dark while the exhaust is lit by the sun and is very bright. If the exposure is chosen to give good detail in the exhaust the smokebox area will be particularly dark and it is likely that noise will become visible in the dark areas when the picture is lightened during later processing. Noise is visible as coloured speckles and a grainy black colour instead of a smooth shiny black. This is a particular concern around the smokebox because the front of the engine attracts the attention of viewers. On the other hand, if the exposure is chosen to give sufficient brightness in the smokebox area, the exhaust will be too bright and detail will be lost. What's the best choice?

Overall the appearance of the exhaust takes priority over the black front end because any burned-out areas of the exhaust are difficult to fix whereas the noise can be dealt with. The camera exposure settings are chosen to be suitable for recording the bright areas of the picture. The photographer can choose whether to use manual or automatic exposure control. Manual control is preferable because in automatic mode the camera might be influenced too much by shadowed areas and deliver an image which is too bright. In the example the author used a Canon EOS 5D camera with standard 'sunny day' manual exposure settings: shutter speed 1/1000sec, aperture f5.6 and sensitivity 200 ISO. A setting of 1/1000sec at f5.6-8 would have been better for recording more detail in the exhaust, but the black areas would have been even darker with more noise appearing.

Raw Format

For shots of this type Raw format should always be used because it is the best choice for capturing scenes with a wide range of brightness. If JPEG format is used it is probable that detail will be lost from the

brightest areas and a realistic result can only be achieved by repairing the damage with time-consuming transplant work. This is because when a JPEG format image is created inside the camera, much of the information recorded on the sensor is thrown away. Raw format keeps all the information that was recorded, allowing the Raw conversion process on the computer to make use of it if needed. This is illustrated in Figure 7.3.1.2 showing a section of the exhaust. Note how much of the JPEG format image is completely white and shows no detail. Another way of saying this is that the highlights are burnt out. Good quality Raw conversion software can often restore detail from burnt-out highlights in a process known as highlight recovery. The Raw conversion software known as Adobe Camera Raw (or ACR) built into versions of full Photoshop (CS2 onwards) and Photoshop Elements (version 5.0 onwards) is the best on the market for highlight recovery and is much better than, for example, Canon's own software in this regard. The lost detail is recovered by reducing the 'Exposure' setting and creating a dark version of the image. Note how all the textures in the exhaust can be seen. For comparison a version of the exhaust using created using ACR with 'as shot' settings is also shown. This has no more detail than the JPEG, demonstrating that it is important to make appropriate adjustments during the conversion process to get the best out of Raw format.

Principle

The principle to be used to create the final image is to create two versions – light and dark – of the original Raw format image using ACR then combine the best parts of both using Photomatix software. This has the advantage of being quick to do and straightforward.

Raw Conversion

A screenshot in Figure 7.3.1.3 shows the creation of the dark image in ACR in Photoshop Elements 5.0. The settings in Photoshop CS2 and CS3 are broadly similar.

Figure 7.3.1.3.
Screenshot showing how to prepare the Raw conversion.

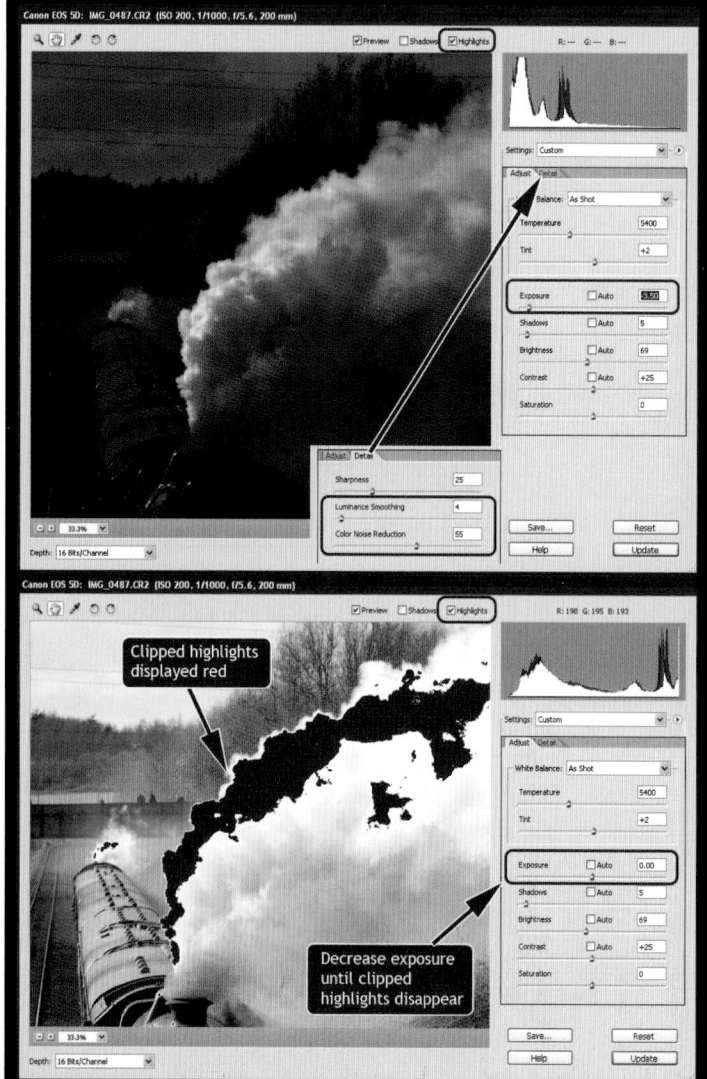

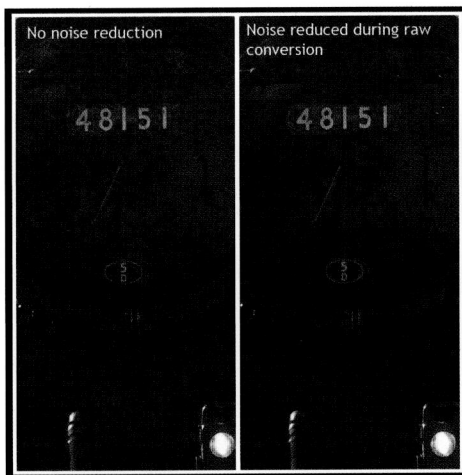

No noise reduction | Noise reduced during raw conversion

48151 | 48151

There are some control settings to note for this image. Firstly the 'Highlights' option at the top of the screen is ticked so that any burnt-out areas are clearly shown in red. Then the exposure is chosen by moving the slider until the clipped highlights have either disappeared or are very small and all the textures in the exhaust are visible. The final exposure value is very low (-3.5) so the image is dark in the preview window. If making an A4 size print or larger it's important to reduce the noise in the dark areas. To do this, two controls on the Detail tab are used: Colour Noise Reduction, sometimes called Chrominance Noise refers to the tiny coloured speckled pattern and is set to a high value (55). Luminance Smoothing, sometimes called Luminance Noise is set to a small value (4) because higher values will cause fine detail to be lost. Noise is less visible when creating a low resolution image for a web page but use of these settings is still recommended.

The Exposure setting for the light image is chosen so that the brightness of the front of the engine looks 'right' to the eye and the over-bright exhaust is ignored. Other settings are left unchanged. Figure 7.3.1.4 shows noise in the brightened locomotive front and the improvement obtained by using noise reduction.

Photomatix

Photomatix Pro software (www.hdrsoft.com) is used to combine the best parts from the light & dark Raw conversions. It can be downloaded from the Internet and purchasing a registration key costs approximately £50. There is limited functionality available to combine the two images without registering the software, such as the 'Highlight & Shadow – 2 images' option which gives a good result. The 'Highlight & Shadow – Adjust' option as used in the example gives a slightly better result with more contrast but requires a registration key.

When comparing the different images in the Figure 7.3.1.1, note how the Photomatix image contains the best parts of its two 'ingredient' images – all the detail in the exhaust and locomotive front are revealed while the train and background have realistic brightness. Sometimes images created using Photomatix can be improved further by increasing the contrast slightly using a small Levels Adjustment, although care must be taken to avoid blowing out the highlights or clogging the shadows.

DARK EXHAUST

The second example shows how to improve the appearance of a steam locomotive exhaust in a bland sky. The same technique can be used for emphasising the exhaust on a diesel locomotive and also for darkening the sky in any landscape picture.

Example

Figure 7.3.2.1 shows GWR 2-6-2 Prairie Tank No 4566 in dull weather at

Figure 7.3.1.4.
Demonstrates the improvement.

Figure 7.3.2.1.
Compares images before and after editing.

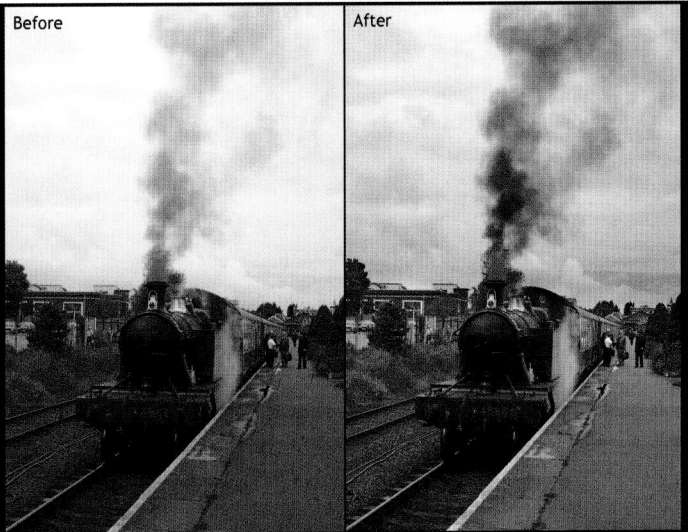

Before | After

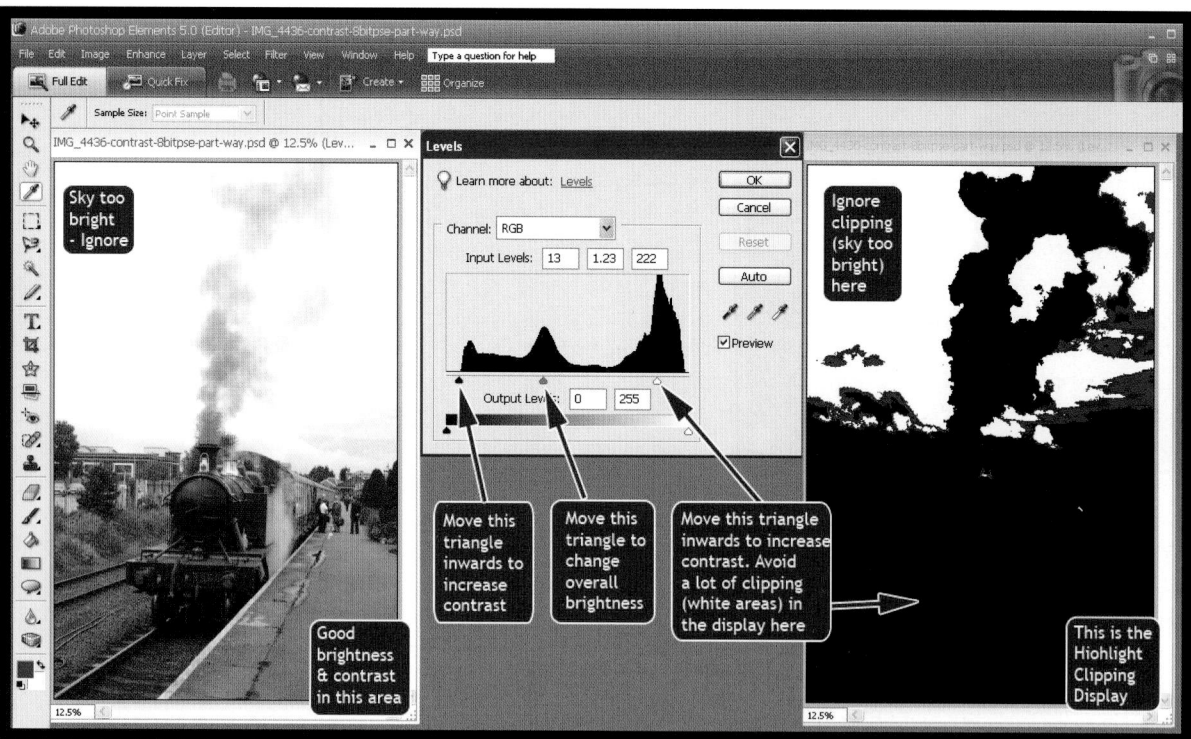

Within the image (Photoshop Elements screenshot labels):

- Sky too bright - Ignore
- Learn more about: Levels
- Channel: RGB
- Input Levels: 13 1.23 222
- OK / Cancel / Reset / Auto
- ☑Preview
- Output Levels: 0 255
- Ignore clipping (sky too bright) here
- Good brightness & contrast in this area
- Move this triangle inwards to increase contrast
- Move this triangle to change overall brightness
- Move this triangle inwards to increase contrast. Avoid a lot of clipping (white areas) in the display here
- This is the Hiohlight Clipping Display
- 12.5%

Figure 7.3.2.2.
Adjusting the levels for the lower half of the image.

Kidderminster on the Severn Valley Railway. The foreground is dark and flat while the exhaust doesn't stand out strongly enough against the bright sky. The picture broadly has two parts: the upper half with the sky and exhaust, and the lower half with everything else. To improve the picture requires two main sets of changes. Firstly the sky needs to be darkened, together with a slight increase in contrast to emphasise the exhaust. Secondly the lower half of the picture needs to be lightened slightly and the contrast increased so that the picture has more visual 'snap'. The difficult part of the process is making the change in one half of the picture without interfering with the changes in the other half while also avoiding an obvious dividing line. It's not possible to apply a 'one size fits all' set of adjustments to the whole picture and still get a good result because the settings needed for the upper half are different to those needed for the lower half.

Principle

Photoshop Elements 5.0 will be used for making the adjustments. The principles involve applying two different Levels

Adjustments to the image – one to the sky and the other to the remainder. To restrict each change to its corresponding half of the image a mask will be used together with a Gradient to achieve a smooth edge between the two halves. Where the join shows, fine-tuning the mask with a soft brush will be done by hand.

Raw vs JPEG Format

In steam pictures it is important that bright skies and exhausts are captured correctly, so it is even more important than usual to use Raw format instead of JPEG. Raw is much better than JPEG for capturing scenes with a wide range of brightness.

Contrast

The Raw image is processed using Raw conversion software, being sure to avoid creating any clipped areas (an area of maximum brightness) in the sky. Next it is opened in Photoshop Elements. The first editing step is to adjust the contrast for the lower half of the image as shown in Figure 7.3.2.2. To do this a Levels Adjustment Layer is created using the 'Layer → New Adjustment Layer → Levels...' menu option. The contrast and brightness are adjusted by moving the triangles beneath the graph-like display. First the black triangle on the left is dragged inwards to meet the edge of the graph. Dragging involves placing the mouse pointer on the triangle, pressing the left mouse button, then moving the mouse with the button still held down. The button is released when in the right position. The white triangle on the right is then dragged inwards so that the area around the train becomes lighter and more contrasty. This will also cause the sky to become too bright but can be ignored as it will be fixed later. A potential problem that needs to be checked is clipping, which is when a light area becomes too bright and loses detail. This can be seen using the 'Clipping Display' feature. Press the [Alt] key at the same time as clicking the left mouse button while the mouse pointer is positioned on the white triangle. The image will turn black except where there is clipping, when it will change colour. White indicates clipping in all channels (Red, Blue, Green) while a different colour indicates clipping in one or two channels. Clipping in all channels should be eliminated except in small areas or tiny points of detail. The triangle is moved outwards until the unwanted clipping has disappeared, then the layer saved by clicking on the 'OK' button. In the example there is clipping around the brass cap causing the golden colour to become too light. This will be fixed later. Lastly the brightness is adjusted by dragging the middle triangle until the image looks 'right' to the eye.

Mask

At this point the train has improved contrast and the right brightness but the sky is too bright. The sky brightness will be changed by using a mask to cancel the Levels Adjustment. A mask can be black, white, or any shade of grey in the middle. Where the mask is black the adjustment – in this case a Levels Adjustment – has no effect. Where the mask is white the adjustment has maximum effect. Where the mask is grey the effect

varies – it becomes stronger as the shade of grey becomes lighter. By applying black to the sky the Levels Adjustment is cancelled. On the skyline the mask effect needs to be gradually applied without showing an obvious join. This is achieved using a gradient which joins black and white areas with a smoothly increasing (or decreasing) strength of grey.

Gradient Tool

A Gradient is created on the mask using the Gradient Tool as shown in Figure 7.3.2.3. It is a fiddly tool to use and usually several attempts are needed to create a gradient that has the intended effect. Fortunately it is easy to remove a newly-added gradient using Undo and to try again. It is selected in the Tools Palette as shown and an options bar appears across the top of the screen. A Gradient is just one solution and the mask could be created using the Brush Tool. There are different types of gradient available and the chosen type appears in a drop-down box which is ringed in red in the example. The gradient type 'foreground to background' should be selected. The Foreground & Background colours are shown in the pair of squares at the bottom of the Tools Palette. The front square indicates the Foreground colour and should be white while the square behind it indicates the background colour and should be black. If one or both of the colours are wrong, the mouse pointer should be clicked on the tiny black & white squares at the lower left. If they are the wrong way round, the mouse pointer should be clicked on the tiny black curved double arrows at the upper right to swap them. Clicking on the Levels Adjustment Layer in the Layers Palette makes it the current layer and it will turn blue. To create the gradient the mouse pointer is placed where the start of the gradient is wanted, and the left mouse button is pressed. The mouse is then moved in the direction of the gradient and the mouse button released. The gradient should be automatically created on the mask with the white part at the start of the mouse movement and the black part at the end. The gradient on the mask should cause the bright sky to change back to its original state. In the screenshot note how the line created by the Gradient Tool is at an angle to the vertical. The gradient always runs at right angles to the direction that the mouse was moved and the line created by the Gradient Tool. In the 'After' copy of the Layers Palette there is a miniature image of the mask showing the gradient at an angle. If the gradient is wrong in some way, undo it, then check the settings are as described above and try again.

Darken the Sky

At this point the area around the train has good contrast and brightness while the sky is too bright. The sky will be darkened in a similar way by using a mask that is the 'opposite' of the one already in place. The Photoshop term for this is the 'inverse'. A selection will be used to create the 'opposite'. First a selection is created which is the same as the mask by placing the mouse pointer over the miniature image of the mask in the Layers Palette, then pressing the left mouse button at the same time as holding down the [CTRL] key. The 'Select → Inverse' menu option is then used to create the 'opposite' of the first selection. Then a new Levels Adjustment Layer is created using the 'Layer → New Adjustment Layer → Levels...' menu option. A small graph-like screen appears, similar to before but with a slight difference. Because a selection was already active when the layer was created, a mask will be included on the Adjustment Layer. The

Figure 7.3.2.3.
Darkening part of the mask using the Gradient Tool.

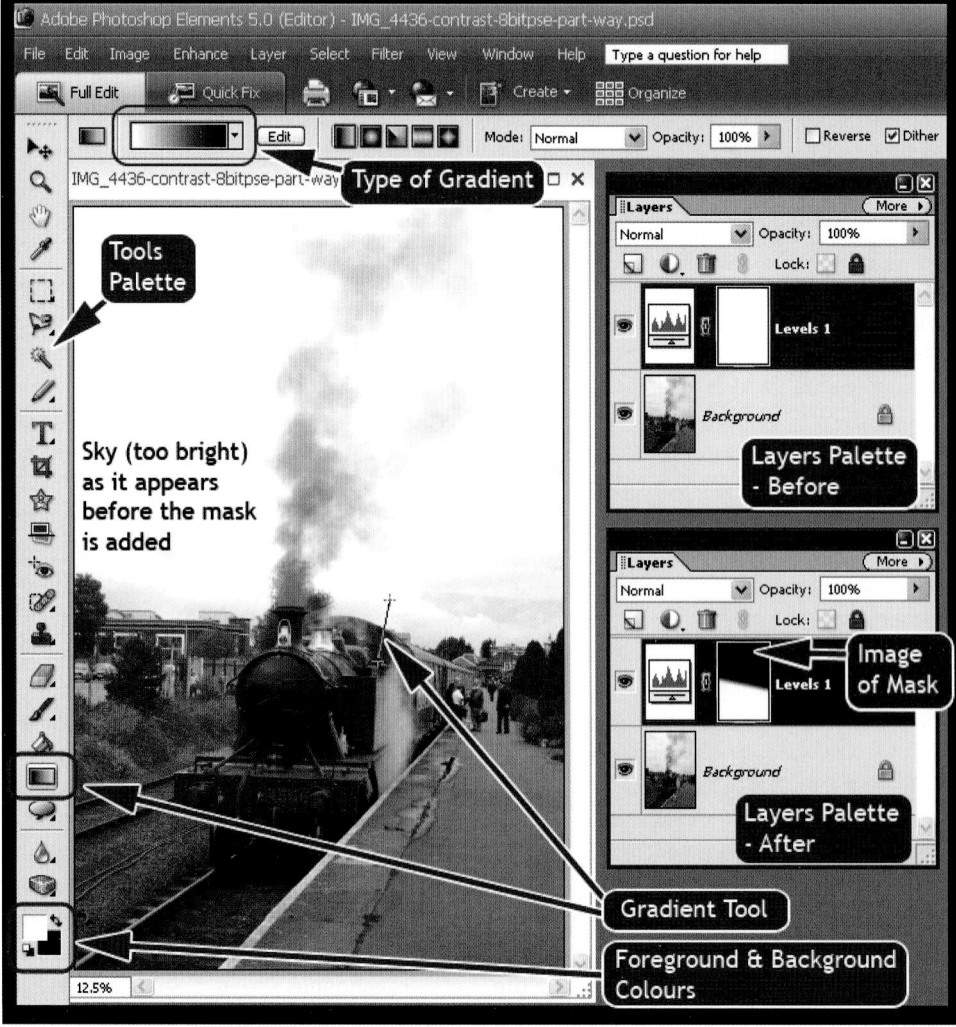

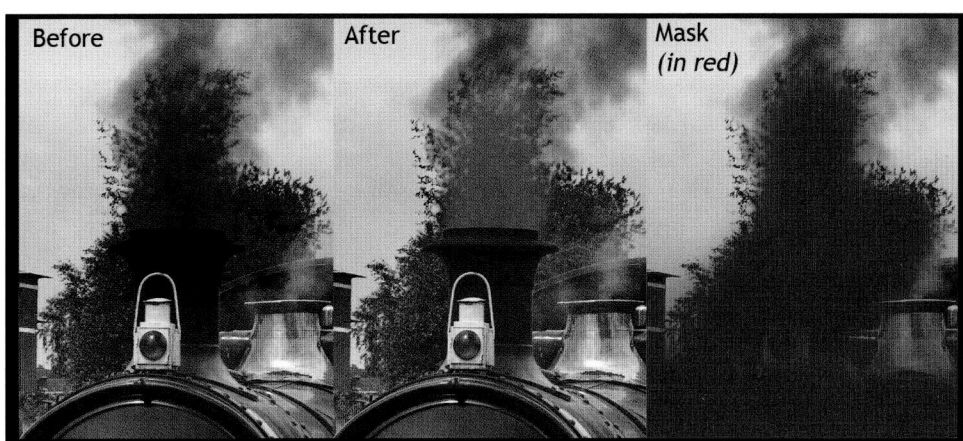

Before   After   Mask
(in red)

Figure 7.3.2.4.
Extending the mask to fix an area that is too dark.

contrast is increased by moving the black triangle on the left to the right while the sky area is darkened by moving the middle triangle. The layer is then saved by clicking on the 'OK' button.

Tidy Up

The join between the two areas of the picture may be obvious in some places. In this example the trees and locomotive chimney have visible dark patches caused by the Levels Adjustment and the mask following a straight line. This can be changed by applying black to the mask on top of the dark patches. On a mask, black means that the effect of the Adjustment Layer does not apply. By using the Brush Tool with a small soft brush about 50 to 100 pixels in size to apply the black paint, the join can be hidden. The clipped brass dome is fixed by applying black paint to the corresponding area of the mask. Figure 7.3.2.4 shows 'before' and 'after' hiding the join as well as the mask – in bright red – overlaid on to the picture. Mistakes can be changed by using the Eraser Tool with black paint or applying white paint with the Brush Tool.

CASE 4

● LOW SUN (1)

When processing a digital image on a computer there are usually many alternative techniques for achieving the same result. There is rarely a 'correct'

technique where other techniques are 'wrong'. Usually the greatest difference between techniques is in the amount of time taken or manual effort required. Sometimes additional software can yield a better result with less effort than simply using Photoshop on its own. This example shows how to improve a winter afternoon picture using the same Photomatix software featured in the earlier case study on steam engines.

Low Sun

The hour before sunset and the first hour after sunrise when the sun is low can potentially yield spectacular photographs due to the strong sky colours. Because the sky remains fairly bright while the ground is dark the 'as shot' image usually needs some improvement work. The example shows a DRS Rail Head Treatment Train passing Tring during late afternoon. The sky behind the train has beautiful clouds and colours so the exposure settings were chosen carefully to avoid 'burning out' the brightest areas of sky. The side-effect of these settings has been to create a dark foreground because the sun had almost disappeared behind a nearby hill and was only shining softly on the ground and train. A Canon EOS 5D full-frame digital camera was used for the shot and a 50mm f1.8 lens chosen to give a pleasing perspective. As the locomotive was fairly close to the photographer and moving across the frame at a reasonable speed a shutter speed of 1/1000sec was chosen to avoid speed blur.

ISO settings of 400, 800 or 1600 could potentially be used with an aperture to suit the brightness of the scene. A test image taken before the train arrived showed that 400 ISO with aperture f2.5 would be an appropriate exposure. Equivalent combinations are: 800 ISO with aperture f3.5 or 1600 ISO with aperture f4.5. The f 2.5 aperture setting was rejected due to the slim depth of field that would result while the 1600 ISO setting was rejected due to the relatively high noise delivered at that sensitivity. This left the combination of f3.5 aperture and 800 ISO as the best compromise giving high sensitivity, reasonably low noise and sufficient depth of field providing that focusing is done accurately. In this case the lens was pre-focused before the train came on the track on a point where the cab door would be.

Figure 7.4.1.
Different versions of the same image.

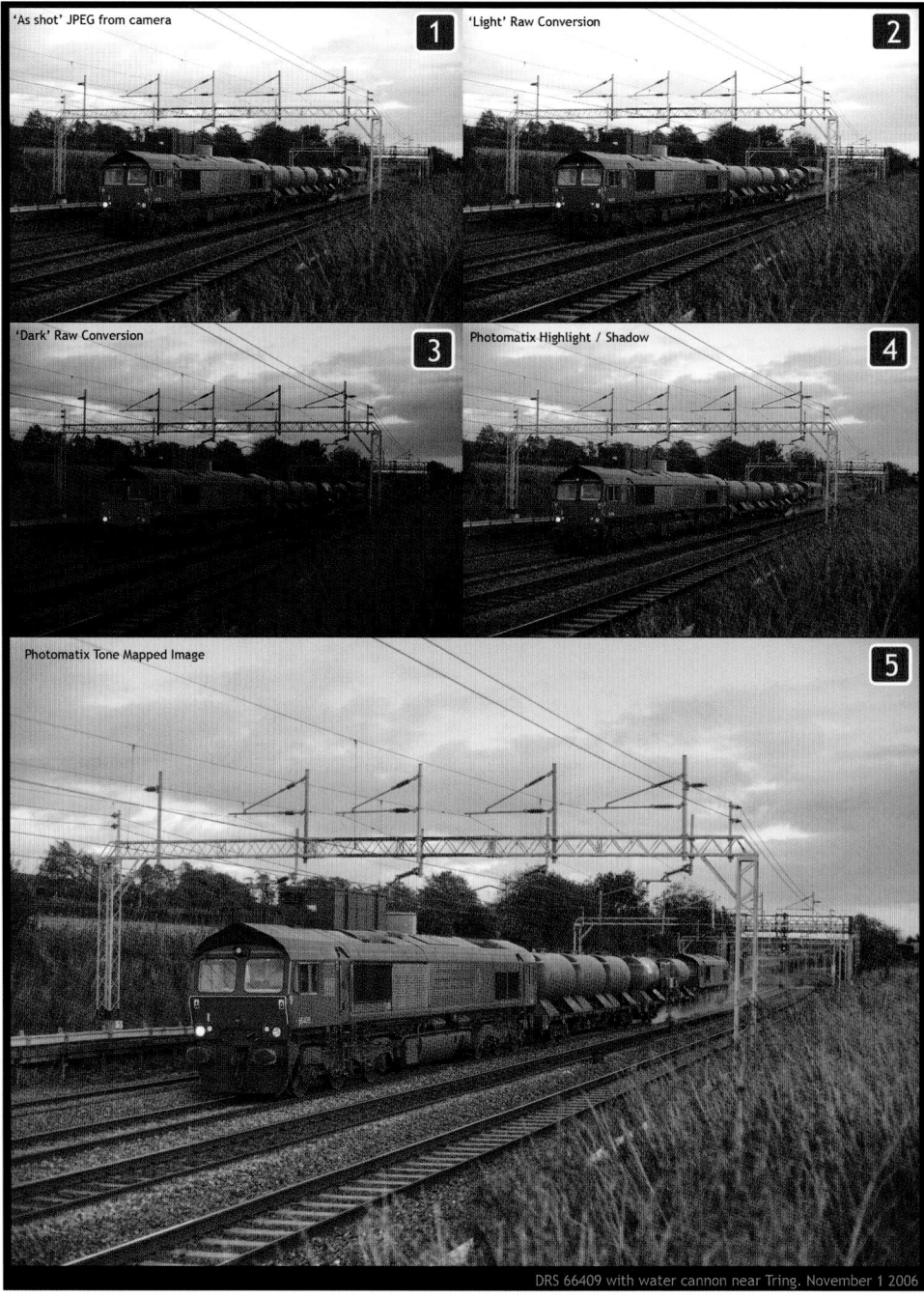

'As shot' JPEG from camera 1

'Light' Raw Conversion 2

'Dark' Raw Conversion 3

Photomatix Highlight / Shadow 4

Photomatix Tone Mapped Image 5

DRS 66409 with water cannon near Tring. November 1 2006

As usual manual exposure and Raw format were used to take the shot.

Improvements Needed

The 'as shot' image has a bright sky with washed-out colours and the clouds don't stand out as well as they should. The train and track area is dark and fairly flat. The whole foreground area needs to be slightly lighter and the contrast increased. What is the best way of doing this? The overhead masts and wires create extra difficulty for the improvement process because they cross the sky. Changes to the sky will inevitably affect the wires and masts, creating an obvious 'join' between different areas of manipulation. Although in theory it is possible to select just the sky area while excluding the masts and wires, creating such a selection would be difficult and take a lot of manual work.

Raw Benefit

One of the major benefits of shooting in Raw format is that when processing the Raw image on a computer in Raw conversion software, any brightness and colour balance can be chosen. With an image like this one the decision on which settings to choose is not easy because of the imbalance between sky and foreground. Settings can be chosen to make the sky look good but the train will then be too dark. On the other hand if settings are chosen to make the train look good the sky will be too light with the brightest areas burned-out. Compromise settings will make the whole picture look acceptable but not great and further work will be required to produce a pleasing picture. Different versions of the same original image are shown in Figure 7.4.1.

A Raw image contains much more information than a JPEG. In Figure 7.4.1 image 1 is a JPEG produced by the camera whereas all the others are produced on a computer from the Raw image. Notice how the darker Raw image (3) has detail in the sky that has been lost from the JPEG (1).

Combination

The 'best' picture would be created by combining the two versions described previously – the good sky from the darker picture (3) and the good train from the lighter picture (2). To do this manually and avoid obvious joins would take a large amount of work. Fortunately there is specialised software available which does this automatically and the final result looks fairly natural. The software is 'Photomatix Pro' from HdrSoft (download from www.hdrsoft.com) which was used in an earlier case study.

Photomatix and HDR

Photomatix Pro is a program intended for a branch of photography known as High Dynamic Range imaging (HDR) where the range of brightness in a scene is too great to be properly recorded using a normal camera. Typically several pictures of the same scene are taken using different camera exposure settings and then combined into a single HDR image. For example three pictures of an outdoor scene are taken, the first being rather dark so there is good colour in the sky, the second is bright to get good detail in shadowed areas while the third is a compromise between the previous two. HDR software takes the best parts of each picture and combines them into a single final image. Because of the need for multiple images of the same subject, HDR imaging is not suitable for moving subjects. Another difficulty is that it's not possible to view an HDR image on a computer screen or to print it because of the wide range of brightness. To view or print an HDR image it first needs to be converted to a conventional image using a technique known as tone-mapping. An important part of this process is contrast enhancement where the contrast in certain areas of the image is enhanced. Without this the finished image would look flat and dull.

In this case study the use of Photomatix Pro is not true HDR imaging because different versions of the same original Raw image are being used. Nevertheless it delivers a pleasing result thanks to the contrast enhancement part of the tone mapping process. The major benefit of using Photomatix here is that creating the final image is much quicker and simpler than using Photoshop with manual methods.

Creation

Photomatix Pro has a trial function where basic features are provided free of charge while use of more advanced features requires purchasing a license key for the software. Fortunately fairly good results can be obtained using the 'free' features with two images. It is possible to get slightly better results using the 'tone mapping' feature of the paid-for software.

Different Versions

Figure 7.4.1 shows five different versions of the same image, numbered 1 to 5. Compare the brightness of the sky, the clarity and colour of the clouds, the brightness of the train & track area, and the detail in the locomotive between all five.

Image 1 is an unaltered JPEG image produced by the camera at the same time as the Raw image. The sky has good colour but the train and foreground are dark and flat.

Image 2 has been created in the Raw conversion software with the train & track having realistic brightness while the sky is deliberately too bright

Image 3 has also been created in the Raw conversion software but with different settings to those used for Image 2. The sky has superb rich colour and detail while the train and track are deliberately too dark.

Image 4 has been created in Photomatix from Images 2 and 3 using the free trial 'Highlight & Shadow' option. The sky is superb and the train is pretty good. Nevertheless, the locomotive is slightly dark and would benefit from more contrast.

Image 5 has been created in Photomatix from Images 2 and 3 using the full HDR and tone mapping process, then lightened slightly in Photoshop. The sky is very good while the locomotive

and train have excellent brightness and detail. The contrast has been enhanced nicely and the effects of the weak sunlight are now visible where they had been lost in the other images. The image could be further improved with a small Levels Adjustment to increase the contrast.

Overall Image 5 gives the most pleasing result and has been possible in a short time with only a small amount of effort using Raw format, multiple Raw conversions and Photomatix software. It would be possible to create a comparable image using just the Raw conversion software and manual methods in Photoshop without extra-cost software but with the penalty of requiring more time and effort.

CASE 5

● LOW SUN (2)

Most photographers dream of an attractive working arriving in dramatic light which is what happened for this photo. The author was waiting near Tring on the afternoon of 3 December 2007. The sun had been behind cloud for more than an hour but a clear patch of sky was approaching and just as the sun was nearing the horizon it burst into the clear patch and bathed the foreground in beautiful winter sunlight. The light softened slightly when the train approached but it was still a dramatic sight. This case study has similar circumstances to Case 4 but the lighting is stronger and a different editing technique has been used.

Judging the exposure is tricky in circumstances like this. The clouds had a beautiful range of colours and it was absolutely essential to retain all their tones from dark to full brightness so that the final image would capture the character of that moment. This meant setting the exposure to avoid burning out the bright area of the clouds while hoping that any burnout of the glint on the side of the train could be avoided. At the same time, clipping at the dark end had to be avoided as well. A Canon

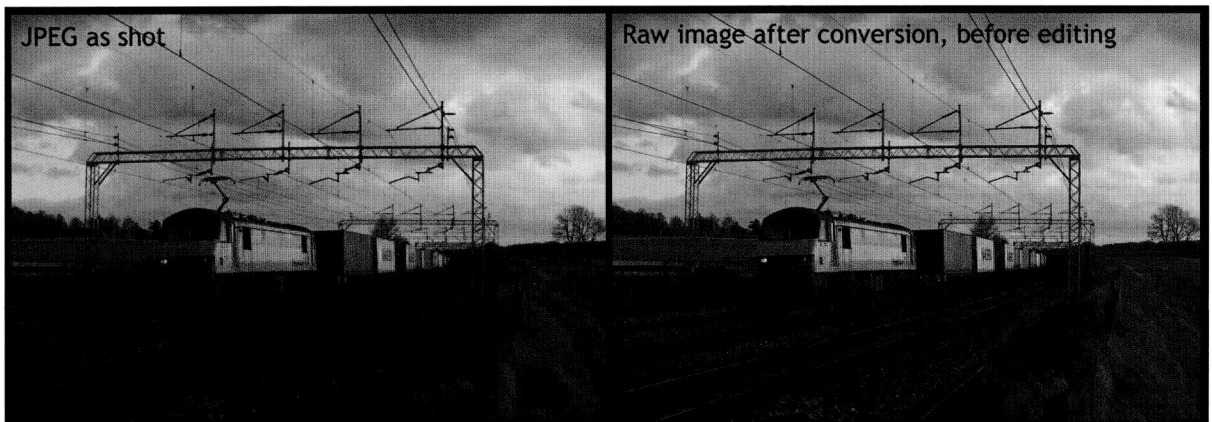

JPEG as shot

Raw image after conversion, before editing

EOS 5D camera with a 50mm f1.8 lens was used with a manual exposure of 1/750sec @ f4 on 400 ISO and a check of the histogram from a test shot showed that these settings were fine with no clipping in the sky or shadows. A setting of 400 ISO ensured low noise in the dark areas of the picture, which is important given that much of the foreground was slightly dark and any under-exposure would emphasise noise. A shutter speed of 1/750sec for a train at

about 50mph going across the frame was just enough to freeze the action without getting any speed blur. Raw format was used of course.

Much of the work needed to improve this image involved increasing the contrast. Given the different levels of brightness & contrast in the picture the contrast changes would have to be localised, so the 'Zone Approach' from Chapter 5 was necessary. By dividing the image into different zones each zone

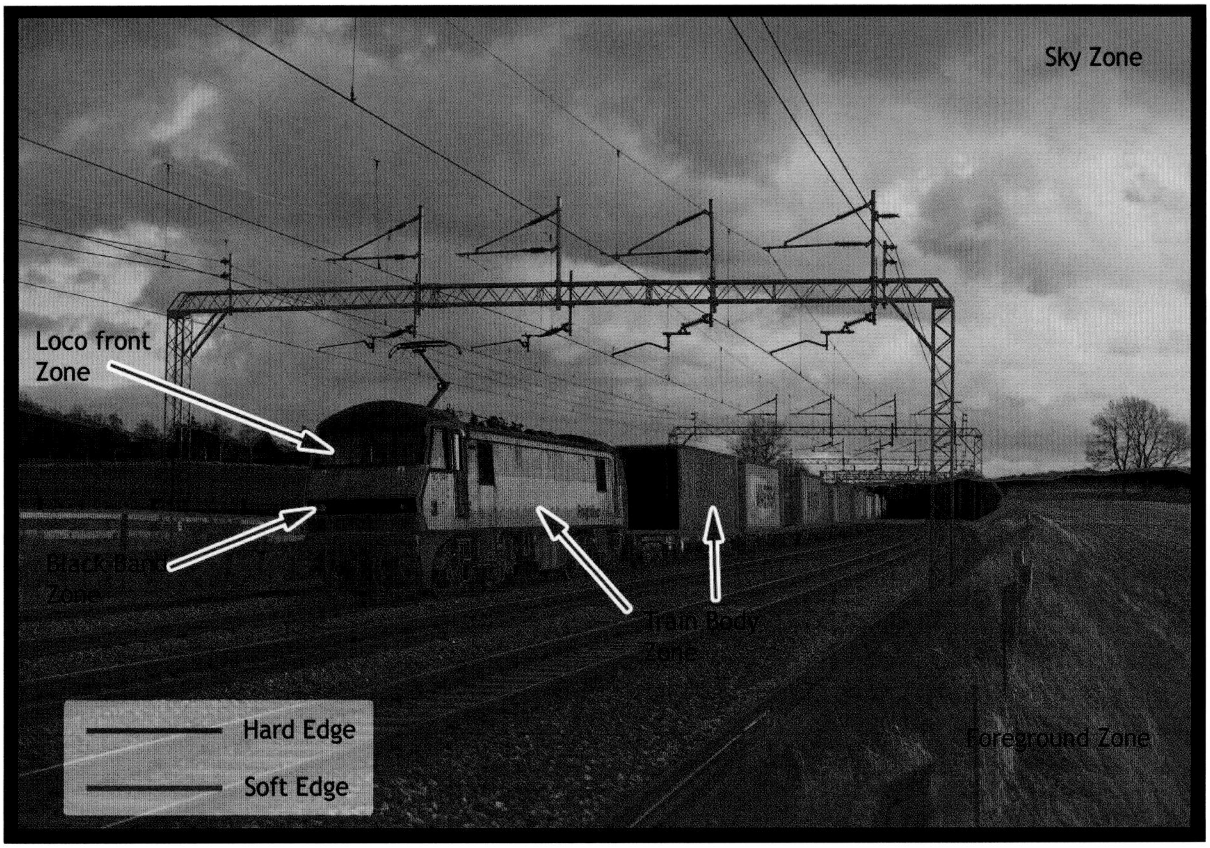

Figure 7.5.1.
Comparison of an 'as-shot' JPEG format image with a Raw format image before editing.

Figure 7.5.2.
The different zones for editing are shown in different colours, together with their boundaries.

Sky Zone

Loco front Zone

Black Band Zone

Train Body Zone

Foreground Zone

——— Hard Edge
——— Soft Edge

179

Figure 7.5.3.
Curve used to adjust the brightness of the sky.

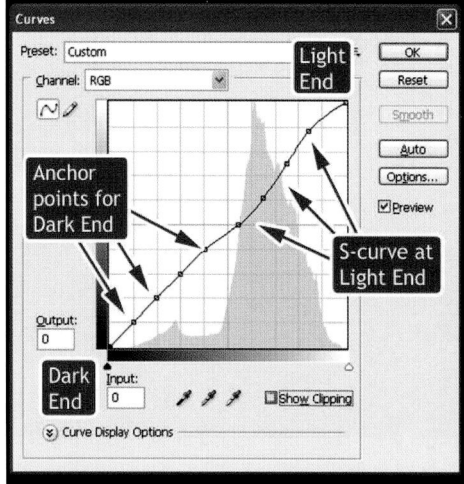

Figure 7.5.4.
Compares Raw image before editing with the same image after editing.

could be given its own adjustment but where should the zones be? Viewing the image, the sky is bright in places with a dramatic cloud formation and superb colour and tones. The light on the side of the locomotive and containers is fairly bright with no awkward reflections or burnout. Although it has a good glint a slight contrast increase will improve it. The foreground and fields are on the dark side, however, and the lower half of the picture generally has a dull 'feel'. It certainly looks duller than it appeared to the eye at the time of shooting, which is inevitable given that the exposure for the image was chosen to keep all the detail in the sky causing everywhere else to be slightly dark. The overall colour of the image has some of the warm orange tint expected at sunset, but could be stronger.

The starting point for any image like this is the Raw conversion. The sky is very

important to the composition and the Raw conversion must keep all the bright areas and detail in the clouds by avoiding burnout in the bright areas. When opening the image in the Raw converter there was slight clipping in the clouds so Photoshop's Raw converter was chosen for its ability to recover the highlights. The 'Exposure' setting was decreased and the 'Brightness' increased. It's important to understand that when converting a Raw image for further editing its appearance may not be ideal because the emphasis is on providing a suitable base for editing rather than looking authentic. Figure 7.5.1 compares a JPEG version of the image straight out the camera with a Raw image after conversion. Note how the Raw image has a less 'heavy' appearance because the blacks are less deep and the colours are less saturated.

The Zones were chosen as shown in Figure 7.5.2: sky, locomotive side plus bright areas of the containers, locomotive front, track and fields. At a late stage in the editing process it was discovered that the black band on the locomotive front looked much better with an increase in contrast so this was chosen as another zone. Although a small area, it acts as part of the 'face' of the locomotive so even a small adjustment makes an improvement. Figure 7.5.2 shows all the zones with a red line indicating a hard edge and a green line for a soft edge. To demonstrate the lines more clearly the zones have been tinted with a colour. Most zones meet other zones without gaps but

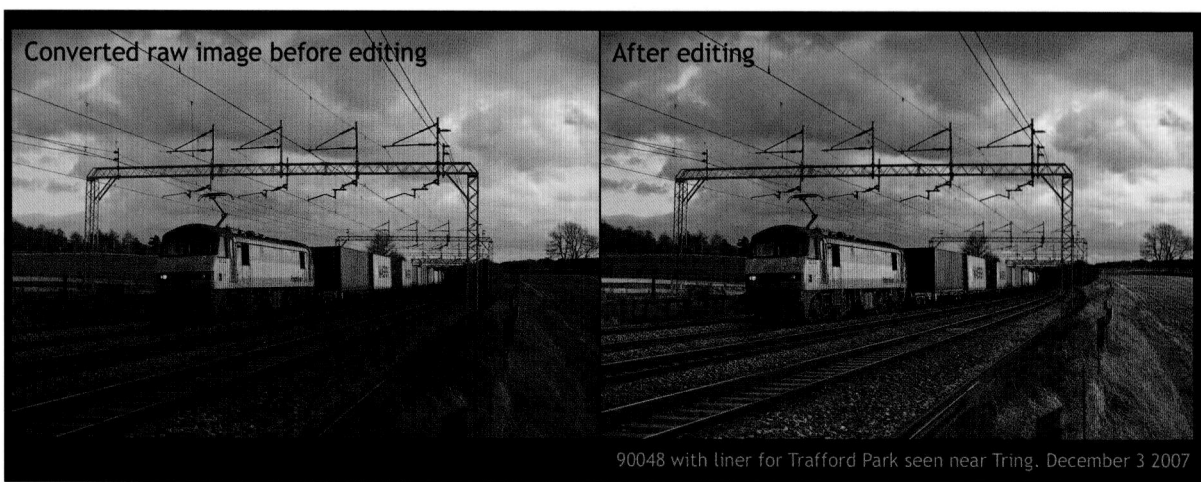

Converted raw image before editing · After editing

90048 with liner for Trafford Park seen near Tring. December 3 2007 there are a few small areas of the image that aren't adjusted.

The first zone to adjust was the sky. A Levels Adjustment was tried and found to be unsuitable because there was already a wide range of tones in the area and darkening the clouds also darkened the overhead power equipment, causing an unrealistic appearance. The solution chosen was to use a Curves Adjustment Layer. The overhead power equipment is quite dark and the sky is noticeably brighter so by using an 'S-curve' the contrast in the sky can be increased while leaving the brightness of the overhead power equipment unchanged. The adjustment curve used is shown in Figure 7.5.3. The lower end of the curve has been fixed with numerous anchor points so that the brightness is not changed. Going up the curve it has an 'S-shape' to increase the contrast. The mid tones are darkened slightly while the lightest areas are lightened. A curve that didn't change the brightness at all would be straight from lower left corner to upper right. The edge of the sky zone reaches down into the fields with a soft edge while following a hard edge along the top of the train. The join with the fields was created initially with the Polygonal Lasso Tool and was then adjusted further using a soft brush and black or white paint on the mask where appropriate.

All the other zones were adjusted using Levels Adjustments, with both an increase in contrast and a change in brightness.

Where the Foreground Zone met the lower part of the electrification mast there was initially a small problem because the mast was lightened by the Levels Adjustment and didn't match the colour of the upper part. It has to be excluded from the Levels Adjustment by creating a selection along its edges and painting with black paint on the mask. This demonstrates the power of using adjustment layers with the masks because changes can easily be made at any time.

Figure 7.5.4 compares the Raw image before editing with the same image after editing and demonstrates how several small changes combine to produce a dramatic difference. All changes were made with small Levels and Curves Adjustments.

● CLOUDY DAY

Railway photography often involves capturing unusual workings in dull weather. Unfortunately the weather causes images to look fairly dull. How can they be improved? Chapter 5 explained the 'Zone Approach' for use when comprehensive improvements are needed but the amount of work involved in the full process is too much for many circumstances. In this case study something quick and fairly simple was wanted. The improvement consists of a small number of areas being chosen and given their own adjustments – effectively a simplified version of the 'Zone Approach'. The various steps are now described as well as some of the problems arising during the editing process.

Figure 7.6.1 shows a Colas Class 47 locomotive hauling a track machine through Slough station on a very dull day. In the image the locomotive and train are the most important parts of the composition and must look good. A Canon EOS 5D camera with 50mm f1.8 lens was used and a manual exposure of 1/750sec @f3.5 on 400 ISO to capture both Raw and JPEG formats, the JPEG being used for demonstration purposes only. The shutter speed was just sufficient to stop the locomotive crossing the frame without noticeable speed blur, while 400 ISO ensured low noise. An aperture of f3.5 gave the right exposure and adequate depth of field provided the focusing was accurate.

After loading the Raw image into the Photoshop CS3 Raw converter a few points were noticeable:

● The lens has caused slight vignetting – darkening in the corners, which the Photoshop Converter can fix easily. Unfortunately this feature is not available in Photoshop Elements.

Figure 7.6.1.
Shows an unaltered
JPEG format image
and the final edited
Raw format image.

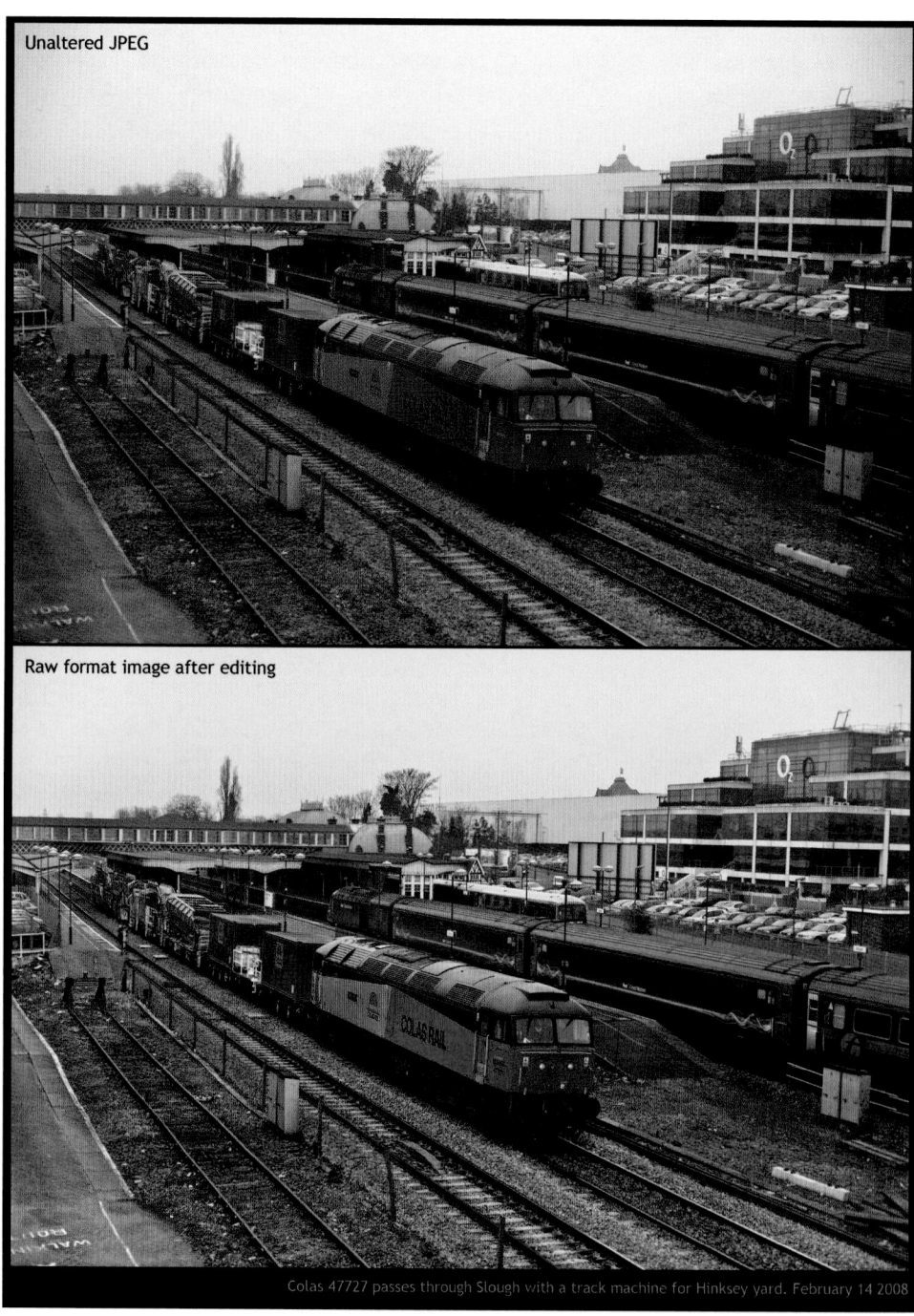

Unaltered JPEG

Raw format image after editing

Colas 47727 passes through Slough with a track machine for Hinksey yard. February 14 2008

- The sky had little texture and to capture its atmosphere would need to be kept fairly dark. Increasing the 'Exposure' control would make the sky too bright.
- The locomotive is the focal point of the photograph and it is important to get its colour right. Good contrast is needed in the body to give a pleasing overall appearance.

- The shutter release was pressed a shade too early and cropping will be needed to get rid of the excess track in front of the train.
- Comparing the Raw image with the JPEG, the JPEG has excessive colour saturation: the locomotive yellow front is too dark and the boxes on the first wagon are almost red where they

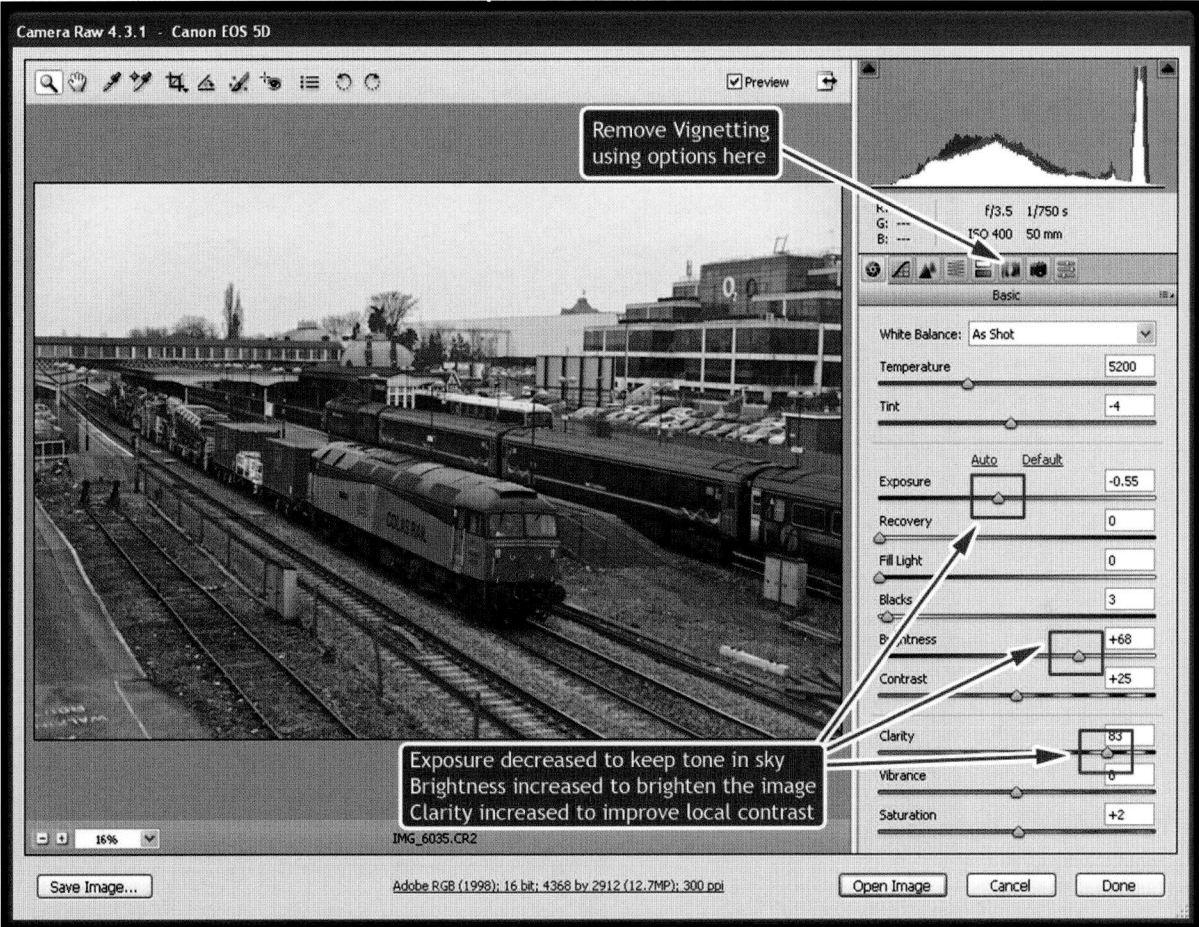

Camera Raw 4.3.1 - Canon EOS 5D

Remove Vignetting using options here

Exposure decreased to keep tone in sky
Brightness increased to brighten the image
Clarity increased to improve local contrast

Figure 7.6.2.
A screenshot of the Photoshop CS3's Raw converter.

should be orange.

- Overall sharpness is excellent and the focusing was accurate.
- Much of the picture is quite dull and needs a contrast increase. The Raw converter couldn't deliver enough contrast so a further increase would be needed in Photoshop by using a Levels Adjustment.
- A few items in the background are quite bright and will need masking during the Levels Adjustment to avoid them burning out.

In the Raw converter the vignetting was addressed first to remove the darkening in the corners using controls that appear on the 'lens' tab. The 'Exposure' control was decreased so that the sky could be kept dark. The 'Brightness' control was then increased to restore the brightness lost in the previous step. The 'Clarity' slider –

which is also only available in full Photoshop – was moved to increase the local contrast which is particularly needed in the ballast area. The colour saturation was kept unchanged as it is easier to add later in a realistic way than to remove after adding too much. These adjustments are shown in a screenshot of the Raw converter in Figure 7.6.2.

Once the Raw conversion had been done and the image opened in Photoshop a Levels Adjustment was made to the whole image with the intention of cancelling this adjustment in some parts of the picture. Specifically, a soft-edged brush was used to apply black paint to the mask to cancel the adjustment in the sky with a small overlap on to the background. Similarly, black paint was applied to the mask corresponding to the white unit roof in the background and a few cars in the car park that were too bright.

Figure 7.6.3.
An enlargement of the locomotive front showing the posterisation caused by gamut clipping.

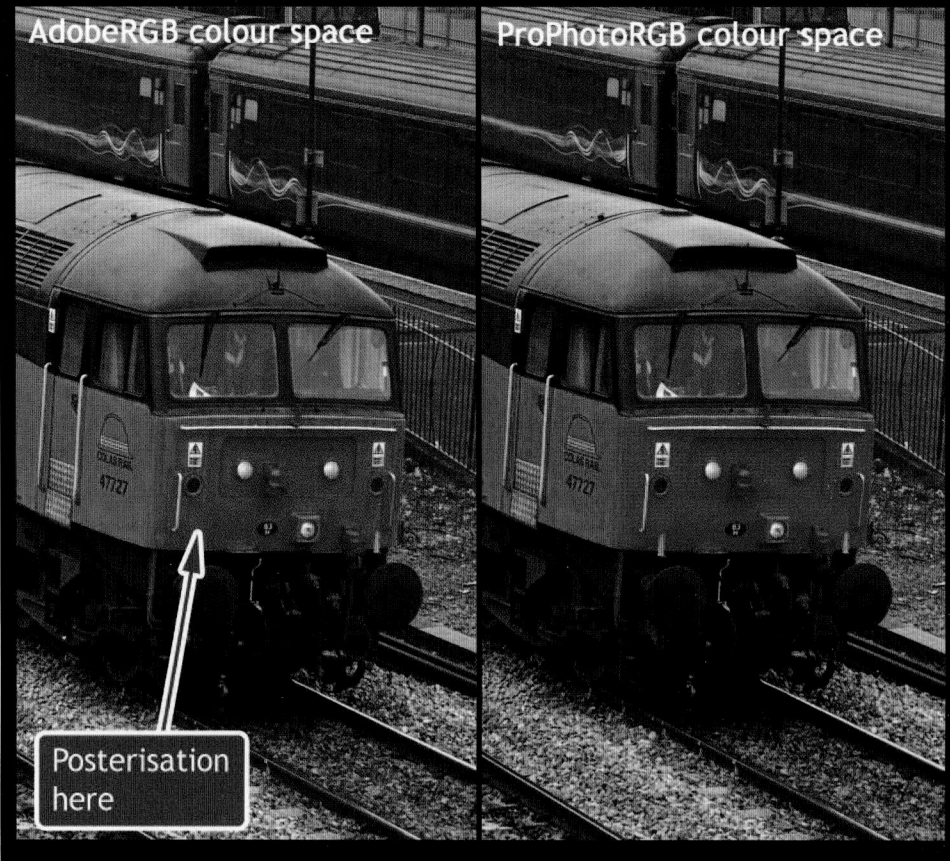

Figure 7.6.4.
The Layers Palette summarises the adjustments made to the image.

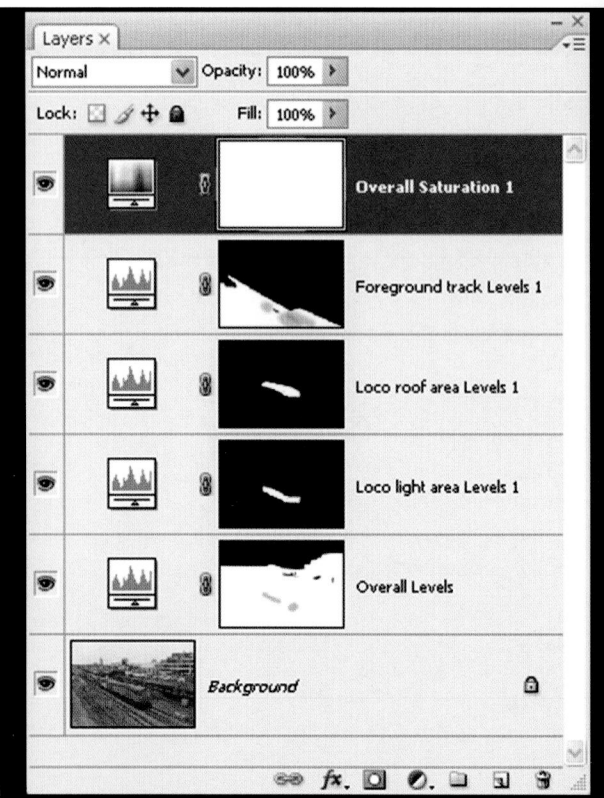

Next the locomotive body needed a small contrast increase and it was decided to treat it in two parts – the light colours and the black. The yellow front and yellow and orange paintwork on the side were selected using the Magnetic Lasso tool with a 1px feather to soften the edge slightly. A Levels Adjustment layer was then created and the contrast increased for this area as well as lightening slightly. The black upper half of the locomotive looked dull so this was selected using the Polygonal Lasso Tool with a 2px feather, then the yellow/orange area mask was subtracted from this selection to avoid any unwanted overlap between adjusted areas. This was done by right-clicking on the mask for the yellow/orange adjustment layer in the Layers Palette and choosing the 'Subtract from Selection' menu option. With the black area selected a Levels Adjustment layer was created and the contrast increased for this area, then darkened slightly to deepen the shade of black.

The foreground track area still looked slightly flat so this was selected and given its own small contrast increase. Lastly the whole image was viewed with a critical eye and the colours felt to be slightly weak so a Hue/Saturation Adjustment Layer was created to apply to the whole image and boost the saturation. At this point a rare but serious problem was seen. As the saturation was increased the yellow front of the locomotive developed a speckled appearance commonly called 'posterisation' which was due to gamut clipping. In simple terms the boosting of the yellow colour created colours which the AdobeRGB colour space could not contain. The nearest substitute for the colour was used by Photoshop, resulting in the speckled pattern. The solution was to change the colour space for the image to ProPhotoRGB which is much wider than AdobeRGB and capable of holding saturated yellows. This eliminated the posterisation and gave a realistic colour appearance. Figure 7.6.3 shows an enlargement of the locomotive in the different colour spaces with and without posterisation. Note that 'consumer oriented' photo editing programs such as Photoshop Elements are unable to work in the ProPhotoRGB colour space.

A warning though: the ProPhotoRGB colour space is so wide that it can hold colours which can't be displayed on a normal screen. These colours can often be printable even though they are not displayable. Occasionally this can lead to a colourful surprise when printing with certain tones having a more saturated appearance than expected from their appearance on the screen.

The Layers Palette in Figure 7.6.4 shows the Adjustment Layers. The miniature view of the mask on each layer shows the area where the adjustment is effective.

In summary, this case study has shown how to improve a cloudy day picture quickly and easily while tackling lens vignetting and the difficulty caused by certain saturated colours. Finding colours that don't fit into the AdobeRGB colour space is much more common in railway photography than in general landscape photography.

CASE 7

● CLOUDY PATCH ON A SUNNY DAY

One of the most stressful aspects of railway photography on a sunny day is watching the train approaching from one direction with clouds approaching from another direction and worrying about the picture being ruined by unwanted shadows. The example in Figure 7.7.2 shows a Class 47 diesel 'dragging' a Class 90 electric and coaches across the marshes near Great Yarmouth. Clouds are streaming in from the sea and as the train approaches in sun one of the clouds covers the foreground in shadow. The effect of the shadow on the appearance of the image is dramatic and it appears to be ruined. Certainly if taken on slide film it would be unusable for projection or conventional reproduction.

The dark foreground is quite easy to treat: the sun was still shining on it through the cloud but it is slightly dark and the depth of shadows is less than if the sun was fully

Figure 7.7.1.
Layers Palette showing the adjustments.

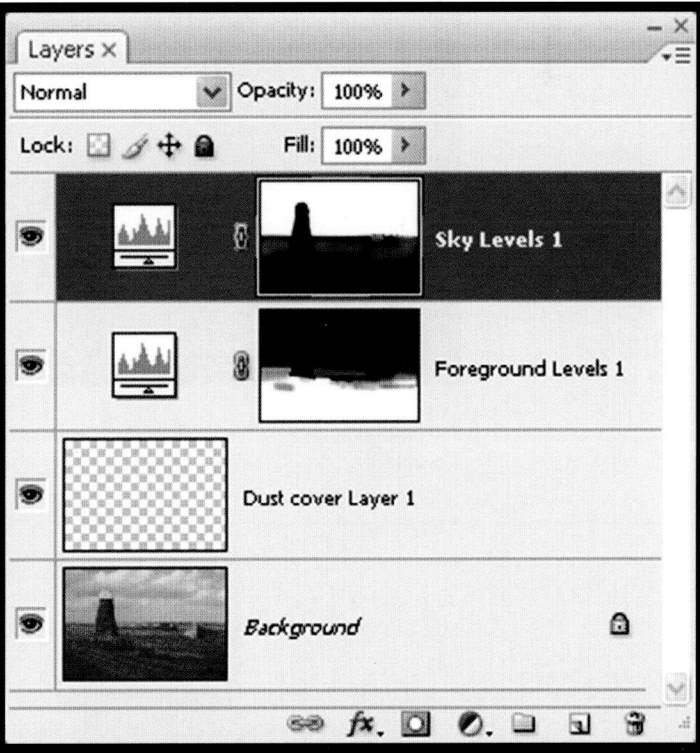

Figure 7.7.2.
Image before and after adjustment.

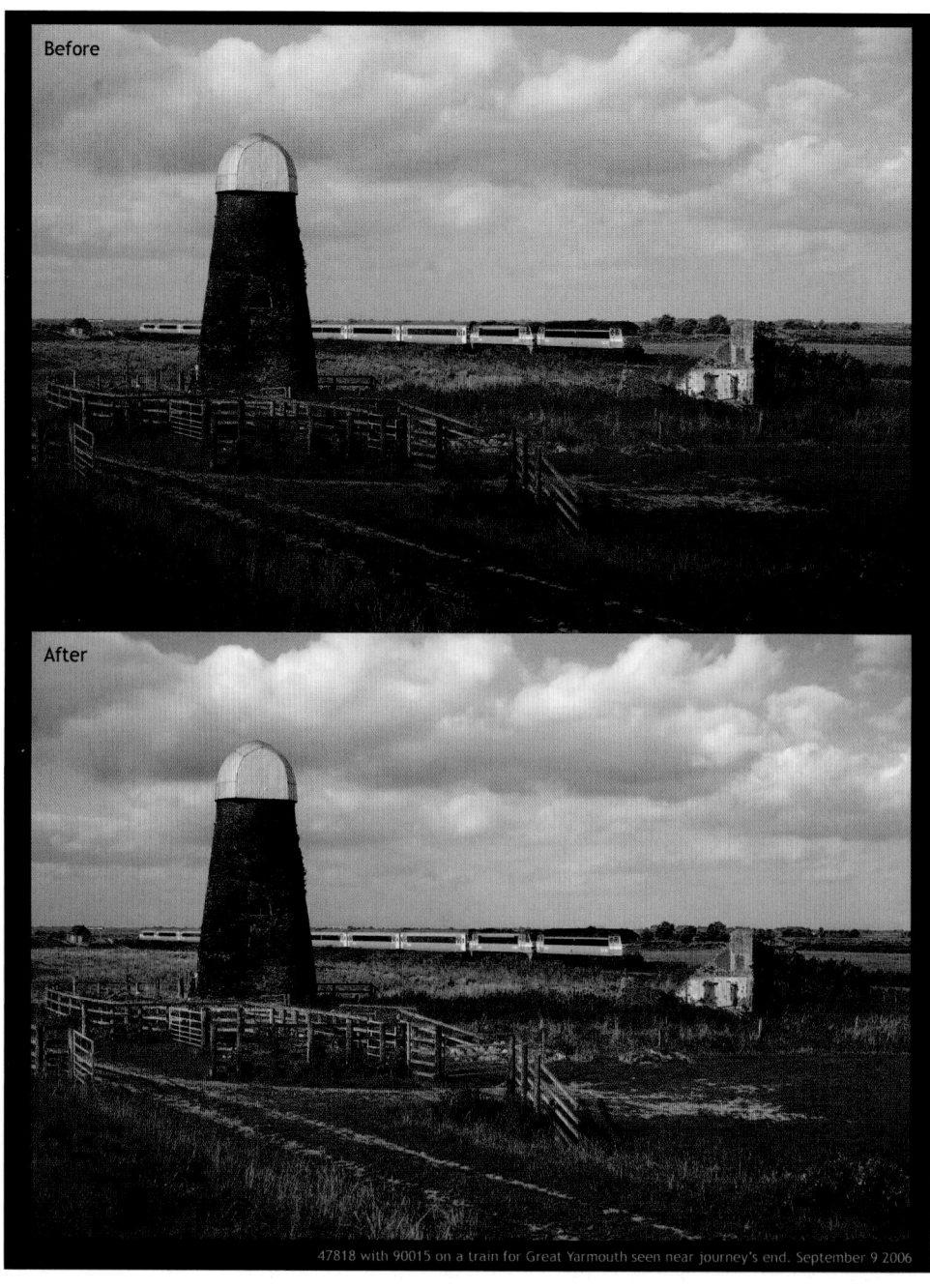

Before

After

47818 with 90015 on a train for Great Yarmouth seen near journey's end. September 9 2006

out. As usual it will be treated with a Levels Adjustment to increase the contrast and lighten it slightly. The sky was given a Levels Adjustment to increase the contrast and darken it to accentuate the beautiful clouds. There was a dust spot affecting one of the clouds, which was easily fixed with a small piece of cloning. The layer containing the cloned sky to cover the dust spot must be below the Adjustment Layers otherwise the colour of the dust spot cover will not match

the surrounding clouds. The Layers Palette in Figure 7.7.1 reveals the work done.

The Sky Levels adjustment has needed careful work to hide the join of masked area (brick tower) and unmasked area (sky). The adjustment is wanted in the sky but not on the tower. This required enlarging the view of the tower and careful work with selections and Brush Tool.

Once the work with Adjustment Layers was complete the file was saved in

Photoshop's PSD format, then flattened and printed.

● COMBINING IMAGES

Every photographer has at some time made the mistake of pressing the shutter release slightly too late when a moving train is approaching. Figure 7.8.1 shows an Irish Rail '201'class-hauled express approaching Lisburn in Northern Ireland where the locomotive is too close to the edge of the frame to create a balanced picture. The author was hundreds of miles from home and with no similar trains due the shot could not be repeated. The only option for getting a reasonable result was to 'repair' the deficient image in some way. By taking a picture of empty track and joining it to the picture with the train using a stitching program, then simulating the 'missing' shadow it has been possible to create an entirely satisfactory result.

Empty Track

A check of the image on the camera immediately after taking the picture demonstrated the problem. Fortunately a tripod was used for the first shot and the camera was still in position. The author rotated the camera downwards – taking care not to move it in any other direction – and took a picture of the empty track using the same manual exposure settings.

Figure 7.8.1.
How to blend images together using PTGui and masks in Photoshop.

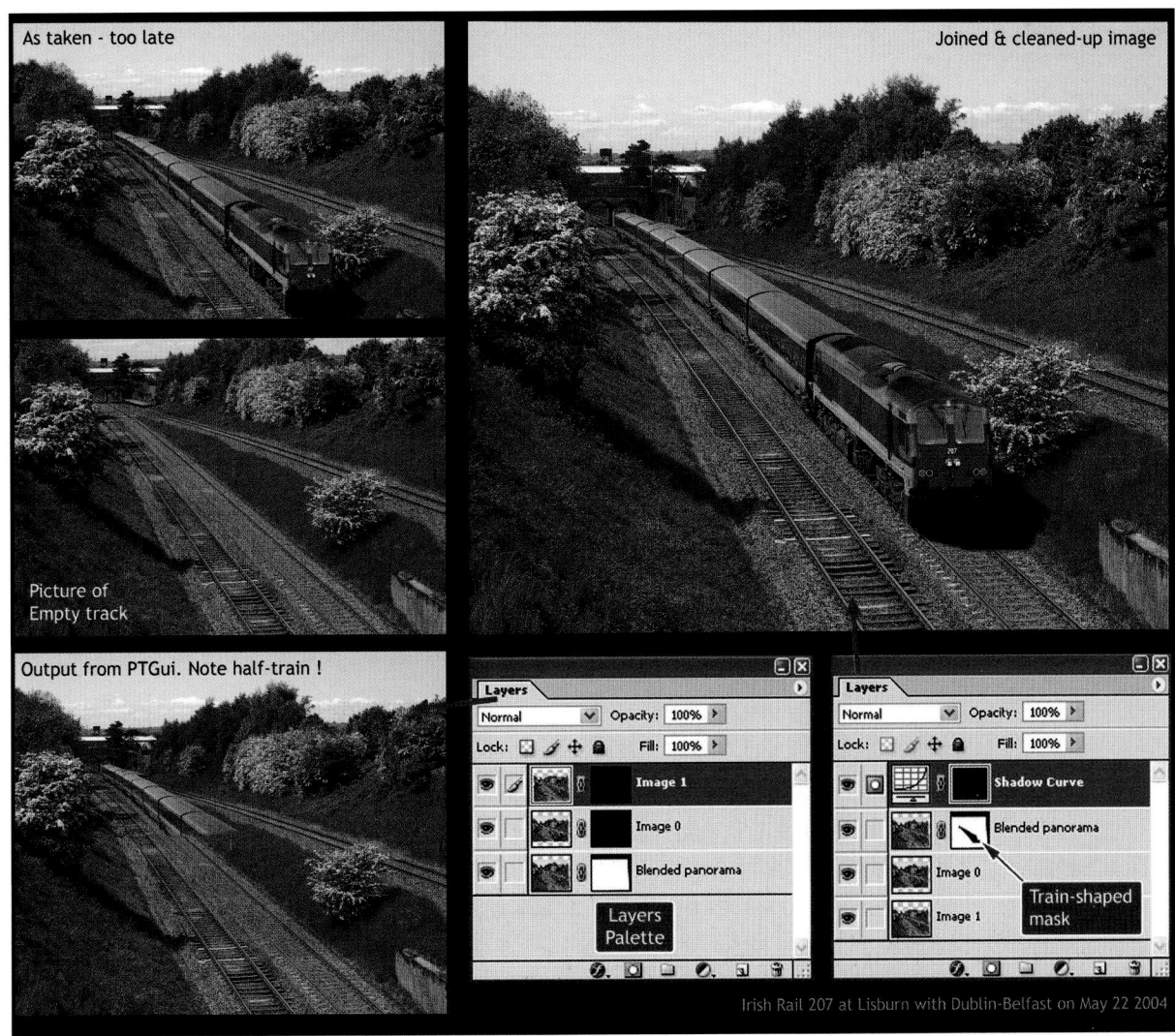

As taken - too late

Joined & cleaned-up image

Picture of Empty track

Output from PTGui. Note half-train !

Layers
Normal | Opacity: 100%
Lock: | Fill: 100%
Image 1
Image 0
Blended panorama
Layers Palette

Layers
Normal | Opacity: 100%
Lock: | Fill: 100%
Shadow Curve
Blended panorama
Image 0
Image 1
Train-shaped mask

Irish Rail 207 at Lisburn with Dublin-Belfast on May 22 2004

187

Stitching Software

There are many different stitching software programs available. To be suitable for railway photography the software has to offer full manual control over the merging process because the built-in 'automatic' features can make mistakes as demonstrated in this case study. The author has used PTGui stitching software on railway images with great success. It offers a convenient combination of automatic and manual features at a reasonable price. See www.ptgui.com for more information. This case study describes how PTGui and Photoshop were used to create the final image on a PC. The principles

Figure 7.8.2. **Using PTGui, showing the main windows in the program.**

will be the same with the Mac versions of these two programs.

Using PTGui

PTGui can be controlled with minimal manual control from the 'Project Assistant' tab. The first step is to prepare all the images for reading into the program. When starting from Raw format images they should be converted from Raw to TIFF format because the alternative of using JPEG format would mean losing data. The same Raw converter settings must be used for every image so that each one has matching brightness and colour. Images are opened in PTGui using the 'File $\rightarrow$

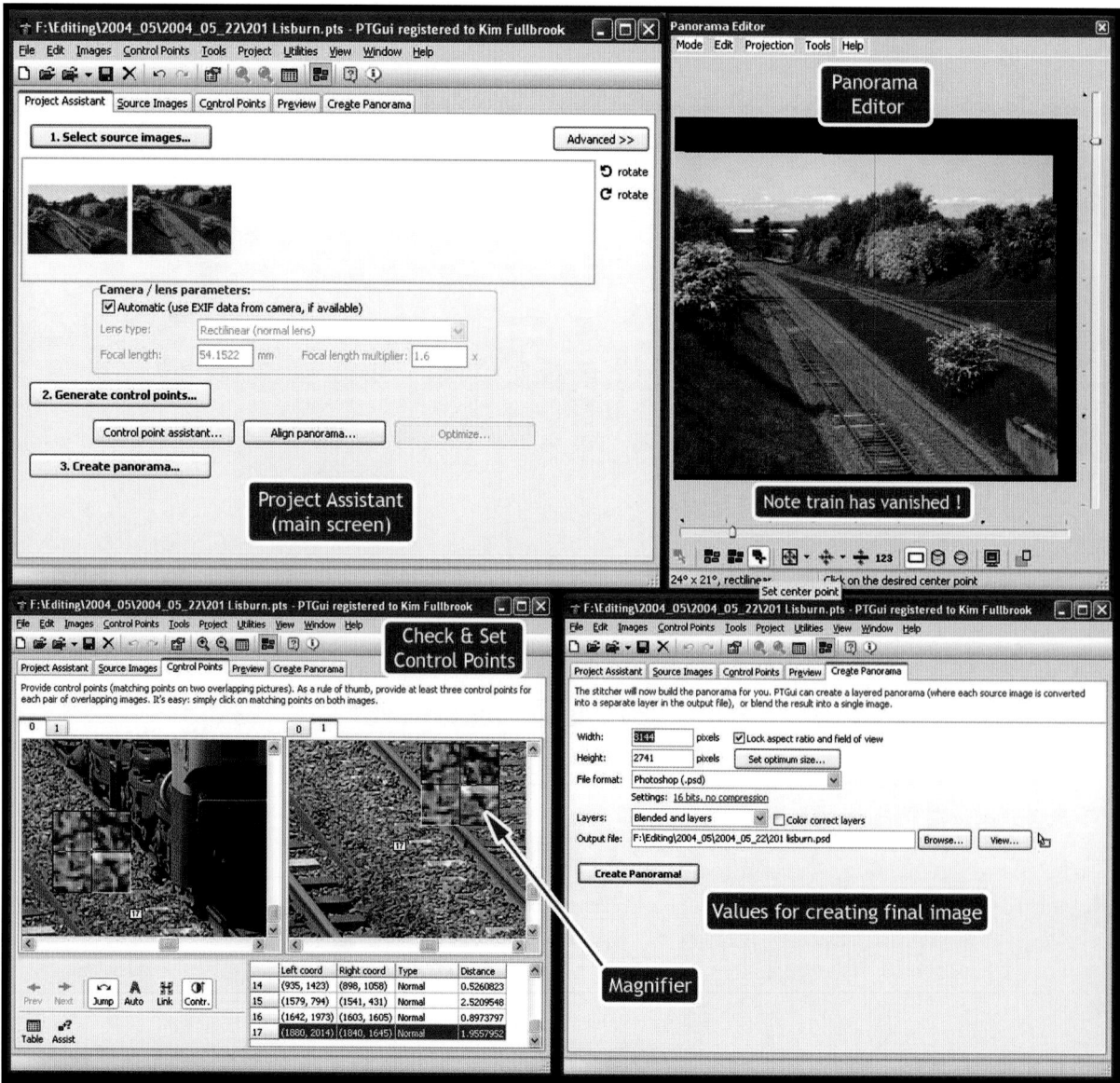

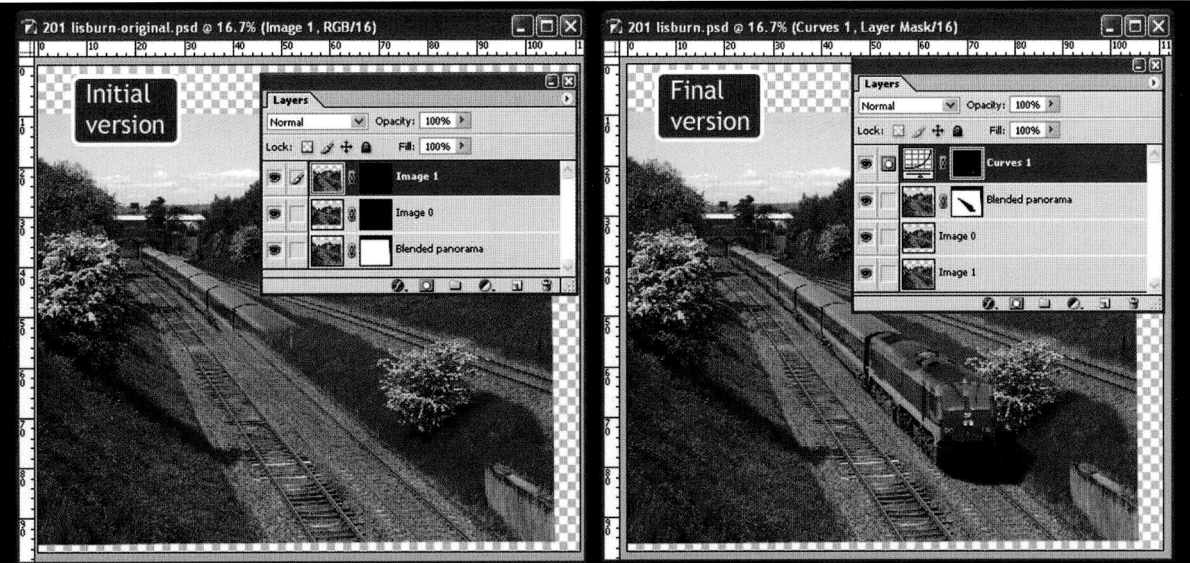

Figure 7.8.3. **Using Photoshop layers and masks to blend the images.**

Open...' menu option. A quicker option is to 'drag' the files from Windows Explorer to the main PTGui window.

Control Points

Once all the images are open the next step is to create the Control Points. A Control Point is a point in two separate images that represents the same point in the final image. The stitching software will attempt to make sure all Control Point pairs are aligned in the final image. For example, the corner of a chair supporting the rail or a rail fastening clip can be defined as control points. A quick way to start is for PTGui to create Control Points automatically by pressing the 'Generate Control Points...' button. Those who seek the best quality results should use the 'Control Point' tab to check by eye that all the automatically created control points are visually correct. It is also a good idea to manually create some pairs of Control Points throughout the track area to ensure that the rails are correctly aligned. Figure 7.8.2 shows the creation of Control Point number 17. The two windows contain the train and track-only images respectively and the control point is the corner of the same concrete sleeper. Small magnifiers make the checking job easier. A tip here is to use the keyboard for moving the pointer small distances rather than the mouse. Holding the [Alt] key while also pressing an arrow key moves the pointer.

Holding [Alt] while pressing the [Enter] key creates the Control Point.

Settings

To begin the next stage select the 'Create Panorama' option tab or press the 'Create Panorama...' button on the Project Assistant page. There are important options here to be selected. Firstly set the size of the final image by pressing the 'Set optimum size...' button and choose the 'Maximum size' option. The output from the stitching process is going to need some work in Photoshop so choose 'Photoshop.psd' file format. The images must be in individual Photoshop layers as well as having a blended final image so choose the 'Blended and layers' option. PTGui will do some colour blending on the final image but you don't want the individual layers to be changed so ensure the 'Color correct layers' option is not ticked. PTGui contains a powerful 'Panorama Editor' function which displays a simulated version of the final stitched image and updates as settings are changed. This screen is used to set the centre point of the final image and eliminate distortion such as curved lines that should be straight. The centre point is set by pressing a small button at the bottom of the window (selected in the example and labelled as 'Set center point') and then clicking on the desired position. Note that in this case study the Panorama Editor disconcertingly shows no

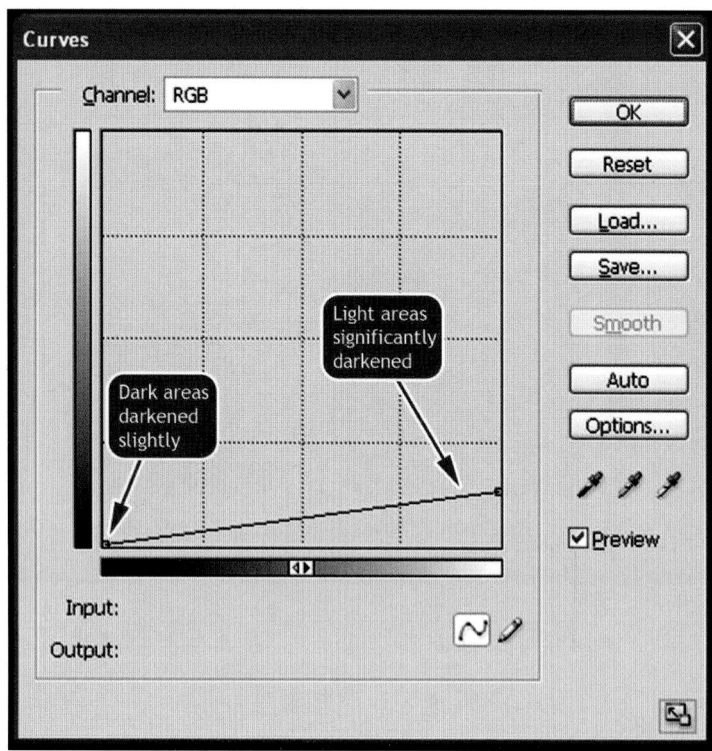

Figure 7.8.4.
Adjustment curve used to darken the track to create the appearance of a shadow.

Shadow

The last stage involves creating the missing shadow in front of the locomotive. This is done by darkening the track appropriately. A Curves Adjustment Layer is used to apply the darkening while a mask on the Layer limits the darkening to the desired area. The curve used is shown in Figure 7.8.4. Unfortunately the Curves Adjustment Layer feature is not available in standard Photoshop Elements.

The initial mask is created by selecting the shadow area roughly before creating the Adjustment Layer and can be refined. On the Layers Palette in the Figure 7.8.3 note how the mask on the Curves layer is mostly black with just a small white area where the shadow is.

When the mask is modified the appearance of the shadow changes. To make the shadow darker the mask must be less black in that area. To do this, the mask is first selected by clicking on it in the Layers Palette. The layer will go blue and the small box to the right of the 'eye' symbol will go grey with a white circle in it – as shown in the Layers Palette on the right side in Figure 7.8.3. The mask is changed by drawing on it using the Brush Tool or Eraser Tool. Using a 'soft' brush creates edges that cause the painting effect to be gradual. This allows the shadow to be merged gently with what is already there. To apply less paint, the opacity value of the Brush Tool is set to much less than 100%. For example using 8% will alter the shadow very slightly. By altering the edges and 'strength' of the mask a realistic shadow can be created.

Conclusion

PTGui has merged the two images easily and quickly, allowing the rescue of an image that would otherwise have been unusable. Completing the work by creating a 'fake' shadow is straightforward. Using Photoshop on its own instead of PTGui and distorting the images manually would have been time consuming due to the difficulty in aligning the images and matching the colours between them.

train and illustrates the limitation of totally automatic control. Manual intervention will be needed later. Lastly, on the main tab, choose the name of the output file and then press the 'Create Panorama' button. The software will take several minutes to generate the panorama.

Finishing the image

In the panorama created by PTGui the train has almost disappeared because the image with empty track has been given priority over the one containing the train. To make the train visible requires re-ordering the layers so that the blended result is at the top and removing the all-black masks from the other layers. Figure 7.8.3 shows how this was done using the Layers Palettes in the initial and final versions. Then the area where the train should be has been made to disappear by painting black paint on the corresponding area of the mask to reveal the train underneath. Note how the 'Blended Panorama' has a train-shaped black area on its mask. The benefit of using the mask rather than actually deleting the image is that if you make a mistake you can make the image reappear by simply painting white paint on the mask.

● Index